A Student Commentary on Pausanias Book 2

MICHIGAN CLASSICAL COMMENTARIES

Patrick Paul Hogan
A Student Commentary on Pausanius Book 1

Celia E. Schultz
A Commentary on Cicero, *De Divinatione I*

Erin K. Moodie
Plautus' *Poenulus*: A Student Commentary

Donka D. Markus
Reading Medieval Latin with the Legend of Barlaam and Josaphat

Patrick Paul Hogan
A Student Commentary on Pausanius Book 2

A Student Commentary on Pausanias Book 2

Patrick Paul Hogan

University of Michigan Press
Ann Arbor

Published in the United States of America by the
University of Michigan Press
Manufactured in the United States of America
Printed on acid-free paper

A CIP catalog record for this book is available from the British Library.

Library of Congress Cataloging-in-Publication Data

Names: Hogan, Patrick Paul, author. | Pausanias, active approximately 150–175. Attica. Book 2. English. 2018.
Title: A student commentary on Pausanias book 2 / Patrick Paul Hogan.
Other titles: Michigan classical commentaries.
Description: Ann Arbor : University of Michigan Press, 2018. | Series: Michigan classical commentaries | Text in Greek and English with commentary in English.
Identifiers: LCCN 2018008575 | ISBN 9780472053988 (pbk. : alk. paper) | ISBN 9780472073986 (hardcover : alk. paper)
Subjects: LCSH: Pausanias, active approximately 150–175. Attica. | Pausanias, active approximately 150–175—Political and social views. | Attikåe (Greece)—Description and travel—Early works to 1800. | Athens (Greece)—Description and travel—Early works to 1800. | Attikåe (Greece)—Antiquities. | Athens (Greece)—Antiquities. | Greece—Civilization—Roman influences. | Hellenism. | Greek language—Texts.
Classification: LCC PA4264 .A314 2018 | DDC 913.804/9—dc23
LC record available at https://lccn.loc.gov/2018008575

Contents

Preface

Pausanias has proven to be an amiable companion to me for several years now, and I wrote this student commentary on book 2 of his *Periegesis* with as much pleasure as I did the first. And if the gods give me the strength and the fates permit me the years, I would be willing to tackle the next eight in due course! At any rate, here I would like to thank Ellen Bauerle for suggesting a sequel to my earlier volume and both her and Susan Cronin for guiding me this time as the last; the staff of the ASCSA and Corinth excavations for the use of the maps included in this book; Mary Hashman for her thorough and knowledgeable proofreading of my shaggy manuscript; and the anonymous readers and referees whose comments and suggestions improved my manuscript greatly and saved me from many mistakes. Finally, I would also like to thank LaDonna Boeckman, *mea domina*, for accompanying me to Greece in the fall of 2016 to explore old Corinth, for taking the photographs contained in this book, and for being the best companion *in rure urbeque.*

Introduction

The Author and His Milieu

PAUSANIAS

Pausanias' enthusiasm for and focus on the stories and sights of ancient Greece is not so great that it completely effaces the man himself in his *Periegesis*: the reader will soon notice that the work is only impersonal on its face and that the mind behind the stylus shows itself not only in frequent first-person remarks but also through several guiding principles (discussed later in this introduction). What we know about Pausanias comes almost entirely from occasional remarks in his work. He probably came from a wealthy family of Magnesia-on-Sipylos, a city mentioned much more frequently than one would expect for a place so far removed from the geographical limits of Pausanias' Greece. He lived around the 120s–170s CE and clearly spent a long time—according to some estimates, twenty years—traveling extensively throughout mainland Greece. Although he was not a citizen of Old Greece, so to speak, he shows a deep knowledge of the land and its people, and as he makes clear from occasional comments, he regularly listened to and questioned local guides (*exegetai*) when he visited sites. He was, in short, a learned tourist, much like a classicist visiting Greece today.

Pausanias has only recently been rehabilitated as a mindful author and as a veracious reporter of archaeological sites. In the nineteenth century, "the liar school of Pausanias" cast doubt on whether he had actually traveled around Greece; Wilamowitz in particular envisioned him as a lazy writer who stitched together his work from the writings of other *periegetai* (writers of guides to sites) before him. The growing awareness of Pausanias' value as a guide to archaeological sites and monuments in the late nineteenth and early twentieth centuries led many scholars to think of him as an honest drudge or "dependable dullard" who merely recorded what lay before him, without any higher artistic or scholarly aims. In the last few decades, however, classicists have begun to see him as a self-consciously literary author and to rehabilitate him as a true member of the Second Sophistic (see below). Monographs by Habicht

(1998) and Hutton (2005) have especially championed this new evaluation of Pausanias.

THE SECOND SOPHISTIC

The second century CE was the heyday of the movement labeled the "Second Sophistic" by the Greek author Philostratus of the third century CE. Hellenism and, on the Roman side, philhellenism experienced a strong renewal throughout the Roman Empire. Emperor Hadrian (r. 117–38 CE) epitomized many aspects of the age, through his widespread travels; his benefactions to Greek cities (especially in Old Greece), which Pausanias notes occasionally; and his deep appreciation for Greek literature and his generous patronage of Greek writers and orators. Greek sophists, such as Favorinus and Polemo, achieved prominence not only as public speakers and litterateurs but also as representatives from their poleis to Roman governors and emperors: in that era, cultural power translated, to a certain degree, into political power.[1]

Political and cultural power in that age stemmed from the system of Greek education that developed in the Hellenistic age—the tripartite system of *grammatistes* (teacher of letters), *grammatikos* (grammarian), and *rhetor* (rhetorical teacher). Education was a major factor in the cultural revival and shared in its popularity. *Pepaideumenoi* (literally, "educated men") were the products and proponents of Greek learning. The major authors of the classical past constituted the syllabus of the *pepaideumenoi*'s curriculum as students and inform their literary work. As I will explain below, Herodotus was Pausanias' model, although in terms more of historical outlook than of style.

The Work

ITS EXTENT

The *Periegesis* of Pausanias, which appears to have survived intact from antiquity, spans ten books and covers most of mainland Greece: (1) Attica and Megaris, (2) "Corinthiaca" (it is so labeled in the mss. but this book actually encompasses Corinthia, Argolis, Sicyonia, Epidauria, and several other subregions of the Peloponnesus), (3) Laconia, (4) Messenia, (5–6) Elis and Olympia, (7) Achaea, (8) Arcadia, (9) Boeotia, and (10) Phocis along with Ozolian Locris. Pausanias keeps his discussion almost entirely to the mainland, covering only a few islands; he entirely omits mention of the island of Euboea, despite its importance throughout Greek history.

1. For examples of this, see the two-issue article series "Writing Imperial Politics in Greek" in *Classical World* 110.1–2 (2016–17).

In the absence of a proper preface—whether Pausanias intentionally omitted one or chance has disposed of it has long been the subject of discussion among scholars—Pausanias' intent in writing his work must be gleaned from occasional comments. After a long digression in book 1, Pausanias mentions, in passing, that he must get back on his course of "describing all Greek affairs alike" (1.24.4; πάντα ὁμοίως ἐπεξιόντα τὰ Ἑλληνικά). That he uses this phrasing rather than saying "all of Greece" (πᾶσαν τὴν Ἑλλάδα), for example, is very interesting and may explain why his work includes not only antiquities and topography but also mythological and historical digressions (see below).

ITS NATURE

Pausanias' first-time readers expecting a travel diary of ancient Greece or the ancient version of a Baedeker guide will be disappointed, and despite Pausanias' religious interests, the *Periegesis* is not a pilgrimage diary. Pausanias gives no details regarding his schedule of travel, and his narrative only occasionally admits any information about accommodations, transportation, and local cuisine. He can be specific when he states the distances (usually in stadia) between places (e.g., at 2.5.4). But the reader cannot easily make his or her way around these regions on the basis of this written guide alone, as Wilamowitz learned, to his chagrin, in his attempt to use Pausanias as a guide in showing a small group of friends around Olympia. Pausanias evidently intended his work to supplement the information one could gather on-site from local *exegetai*—even though he does not hesitate to contradict such men or counter local accounts. He makes it clear that he does not swallow every story he hears, and he is quite aware of the Greek tendency to boast about local myths and antiquities (cf. his comments on this characteristic of the Troezenians at 2.30.5).

ITS GUIDING PRINCIPLES

One of Pausanias' clearest statements about his writing principles occurs at the end of his account of Athens in book 1: "Such are in my opinion the most famous stories and sights among the Athenians, and my account has from the start selected from many possibilities what was appropriate for my writing" (1.39.3; Τοσαῦτα κατὰ γνώμην τὴν ἐμὴν Ἀθηναίοις γνωριμώτατα ἦν ἔν τε λόγοις καὶ θεωρήμασιν, ἀπέκρινε δὲ ἀπὸ τῶν πολλῶν ἐξ ἀρχῆς ὁ λόγος μοι τὰ ἐς συγγραφὴν ἀνήκοντα). Indeed, broadly speaking, Pausanias' main aim in his description of Greece is to record significant stories (λόγοι) and sights (θεωρήματα) for his reader. His selectivity in this regard is guided primarily by his piety. Readers will notice immediately how Pausanias is very careful to note shrines, temples, sacred precincts, altars, statues of the gods, and so forth, taking pains to explain any unusual epithets of deities that he encounters (e.g., Hera Bunaia at 2.4.7). Obscure and unusual religious rites do not fail to gain his attention (e.g., the festival of Demeter Chthonia at Hermione at 2.35.4–8). Occasionally, Pausanias feels a strong compulsion to rein in his speech, lest he disclose religious mysteries that must not be divulged to the uninitiated (e.g., those revealed in the rites of the Great Mother at 2.3.4). Indeed, it could be argued, with some justice, that Pausanias is as important to religious historians as he is to modern archaeologists, for mythology and ritual appear at almost every turn in his book, and every sort of monument, even a stone or the mere name that a place acquired over time, may have a story attached to it. Furthermore, he is generally uninterested in secular buildings, although some may conjure up memories of historical episodes that he thinks it profitable to relate.

Paintings, statues, and all manner of artwork—the older the better—catch Pausanias' eye at every turn. As a result, he becomes for modern readers a valuable witness to long-vanished works of art (e.g., the elaborate offering of Herodes Atticus at the temple of Poseidon in the Isthmian sanctuary at 2.1.7–8). He takes pains to verify the identity of the artists behind the works, and although he focuses chiefly on their subject matter, he occasionally remarks on their technique. Unusual pieces of any kind, such as archaic *xoana* (wooden images) and aniconic figures, attract his notice. Pausanias positions himself as a connoisseur of art as much as of mythical traditions, cataloging, sorting, and sometimes discarding variant traditions of myths and attributions of artists.

Although Pausanias is a denizen of the Roman Empire at its height, his focus is on the grand past of Greece. Romans figure neither as enemies nor as allies in his work and are mentioned only occasionally, usually when they intrude in a material fashion into the landscape. In book 2, the most salient case is the city of Corinth, which suffered capture and destruction at the hands of the Romans during the Achaean War in 146 BCE, a fact that Pausanias occasionally mentions (e.g., 2.1.2). Roman emperors likewise figure in the work rarely, sometimes in ambiguous contexts; for example, at 2.8.1, Pausanias notes that a precinct in Sicyon now dedicated to the Roman emperors was once the house of the tyrant Cleon. The only emperor who appears with any regularity is Hadrian—admittedly an unusual case, because of Hadrian's passion for Greek culture and letters. Often, Pausanias silently passes by large Roman-era buildings that archaeologists know were there when Pausanias was: for example, the Corinthian agora was full of Roman buildings in Pausanias' time, but he names only two, including the local temple of Jupiter Capitolinus, which he helpfully translates into Greek terms for his audience (2.4.5).

Another surprise that awaits the reader is the amount of space Pausanias devotes to long narratives. In book 1, his accounts of the Hellenistic kings who succeeded Alexander the Great and of prominent Greek figures of the Hellenistic period occupy nearly a fifth of the space. In his extended *logoi,* Pausanias generally passes over the most well-known events in Greek history, such as the Persian Wars and the Peloponnesian Wars, topics with which he assumes his learned audience is familiar, as they are endlessly referred to in the speeches of the sophists of his age. Seminal figures like Pericles, Themistocles, and Miltiades are mentioned where appropriate, but Pausanias' *logoi* are intended to fill out the historical gaps in the minds of educated readers who already know their Herodotus and Thucydides very well. In book 2, a sizable digression (2.8.1–2.9.5) is devoted to Aratus of Sicyon (271–231 BCE), a famous Greek politician and general who succeeded not only in freeing his own city from tyranny but also in uniting the whole region in a league of poleis to oppose the power of both Macedonia and a resurgent Sparta. In fact, instances of the Greeks uniting against barbarians are of special concern to Pausanias: accounts of the defense of Greece against a Celtic invasion in the early third century BCE bookend his entire *Periegesis* (1.4.1–4 and 10.19.5–10.23.14).

The reader will also note that mythological narratives take up much space in the *Periegesis*. Each time Pausanias enters a new region, he describes the mythological origins of its major polis (e.g., Sicyon at 2.5.6–2.7.1). These digressions often involve extended genealogical backgrounds for the heroic figures involved.

ITS GENRE

In antiquity, especially in major cities and sanctuaries, a class of guides, variously called *exegetai* and *periegetai*, gradually developed to explain (ἐξηγεῖσθαι) local monuments to visitors and to lead guests around (περιηγεῖσθαι) the sites. In the period of the Second Sophistic, these individuals were often members of the educated local elite, who fulfilled an important social function through welcoming visitors and acting as representatives of their homeland. They were able to display knowledge and learning that could be appreciated by their learned visitors. One reason for Pausanias' omission of inns and accommodations was probably that he relied on networks of *xenoi* and stayed as a guest in the homes of local aristocrats. In this way, cities that once rivaled each other in the martial arena accommodated their *philotimia* (desire for honor and distinction) to a more peaceful age by boasting of their antique and Hellenic character.

Starting in the Hellenistic period, a new genre of literature developed as a complement to such human actors. Periegetic literature is imperfectly understood because of the fragmentary nature of the early sources, but Hutton (2005, 255) well sums up the main characteristics of the genre: (1) an interest in ancient monuments and the stories related to them; (2) an interest in the inscriptions, artists, and so on related to these monuments; (3) an interest in religion and mythology; (4) a tendency to deal with monuments in specific localities; (5) a tendency to deal with artworks on an objective and informational level, without subjective aesthetic response; and (6) an appetite for unusual stories. Judging from the oeuvre of the prolific periegetic writer Polemo of Ilion, many authors of this genre focused on very narrow locales or on discrete classes of objects, such as inscriptions or votive offerings.

Although he is the only major surviving author of this genre, it is clear that Pausanias stood apart from his predecessors in many ways. Most prominently, although the manuscripts give the title of Pausanias' work as *Hellados Periegesis*, Pausanias never uses the term *periegesis* to refer to his own text, instead revealing his greater ambitions for it by employing the terms συγγραφή (treatise) and λόγος (discourse). His work has a vastly greater scope than the more focused treatises of his predecessors, and his blend of narrative and monuments is more reminiscent of Herodotus and Thucydides. Pausanias also treats monuments individually, not topically; for him, the landscape is paramount, and his descriptions of sites give the reader a vicarious experience of visiting them. Lastly, Pausanias' moral tone and his emphasis on the perils of power and the need for wisdom and moderation in rulers are not found in the fragments of earlier *periegeses* but are certainly appropriate for the other literary genre that he was using, history. Indeed, the first Western readers of Pausanias in the Renaissance regarded him as a historian and his work history.

IMITATION OF HERODOTUS

Writers of the Second Sophistic routinely adopted classical predecessors as models, in order to display their own learning and fit themselves into the centuries-long tradition of Greek *paideia*. Pausanias adopts Herodotus as his model in many respects, but not in the same way as his contemporaries. Arrian (ca. 88–160 CE) adopted Herodotus' Ionic dialect for his *Indica*, and Lucian (ca. 125–180 CE) did the same for his *De dea Syria*. Pausanias avoids specifically Ionic forms, but he does ape Herodotus in his ethnographic, historical, and geographic outlook. Sharing Herodotus' interest in unusual customs and natural curiosities, Pausanias displays a traditional moral and religious outlook that generally denies the direct intervention of gods in human affairs (in contrast with Homer and the epic tradition) but accepts the effect of divine forces in the world. He also employs lengthy digressions and makes references to his own travel in his work. Although he does not have a specific overarching historical narrative, as did Herodotus in tracing the origins and events of the Persian Wars, some scholars have drawn parallels between the prominence of the Celtic invasion of Greece and Asia Minor in Pausanias' *Periegesis* and the Persian invasions of Darius and Xerxes in Herodotus' *Histories*. Pausanias also alludes to passages from Herodotus and assumes that his reader has direct knowledge of Herodotus' work. Pausanias also reports various versions of *logoi*, acquired both through texts and through direct questioning of locals; sometimes he refrains from judgment, and sometimes he places his finger on one end of the scales.

OVERVIEW OF BOOK 2

Unlike book 1, which focuses on a region closely associated with one polis (i.e., Attica and Athens), book 2 has several focal points (as I noted above). At the beginning of book 2, Pausanias begins directly from the last polis he covered in book 1, Megara, and heads across the Isthmus of Corinth to the cities of Corinth and Tenea (2.1.1–2.5.5). He then goes to Sicyon (2.5.6–2.12.2); Phlius (2.12.3–2.14.4); Cleonae, Nemea, Mycenae, and the Heraion of Argos (2.15.1–2.17.7); and Argos proper (2.18.1–2.24.4). The other large sites he describes are Epidaurus (2.26.1–2.30.4), Troezen (2.30.5–2.34.3), and Hermione (2.34.4–2.36.3).

In making his way through these areas, Pausanias usually follows what Frazer terms the "radial plan": he first narrates the mythology and history of the district in outline; he then goes from the frontier to the capital, where he follows radiating streets; after describing the area around the capital, he follows the chief roads out of the capital, returning to the capital at the end of each jaunt; finally, he moves into the next district. Hutton generally agrees with this assessment but adds that Pausanias recognizes primary and secondary "hubs" that serve as jumping-off points for side trips. I highly recommend that the reader read beforehand and reference Hutton's lucid and insightful description of Pausanias' movements in book 2, which Hutton selected for his case study of Pausanias' method (2005, 97–118); Hutton's account will make the peregrinations of the *periegete* more intelligible.

NATURE OF THIS COMMENTARY

The commentary in this book focuses, above all, on the syntax, vocabulary, and prose style of Pausanias' second book, adding selected historical, mythical, archaeological, and literary notes to elucidate his many references. My qualifications as a classical philologist and the dedicated scope of this book and the commentary series to which it belongs do not allow me to include more than a little of the vast array and evolving analysis of archaeological discoveries for the many cities and sites Pausanias mentions. I leave it to readers and classroom instructors to use my commentary as a base camp—or "hub," if you will—from which to explore the topography of those lands.

NOTE TO THE READER

The Greek text in this volume and the references to it in the lemmas of my commentary follow Rocha-Pereira's second edition (1989–90). For the sake of consistency, I have followed the *Oxford Classical Dictionary* (4th ed.) in the spelling of Greek and Roman names.

Abbreviations

acc. = accusative
act. = active
adj. = adjective
adv. = adverb
aor. = aorist
D = Denniston, J. D. 1996. ed. J. K. Dover. *The Greek Particles*. 2nd ed. Indianapolis: Hackett Publishing.
dat. = dative
dir. = direct
fem. = feminine
Frazer = Frazer, J. G. (trans. and comm.), 1897–1913. *Pausanias's Description of Greece*. 6 vols. London: Macmillan.
G = Goodwin, W. W. 1992. *Syntax of the Moods and Tenses of the Greek Verb*. Philadelphia: William H. Allen.
gen. = genitive
H. = Herodotus
imperf. = imperfect
inf. = infinitive
Loeb = Loeb Classical Library series. Harvard University Press.
LSJ = Liddell, H. G., and R. Scott. 1968. *A Greek-English Lexicon*. Revised by Sir Henry Stuart Jones with the assistance of Roderick McKenzie, with a supplement. Oxford: Clarendon.
masc. = masculine
MT = Musti, Domenico, ed., trans., and comm., and Mario Torelli, comm. 1986. *Pausania, Guida della Grecia, libro II: La Corinzia e l'Argolide*. Rome: Fondazione Lorenzo Valla.
neut. = neuter
NH = *Naturalis historia*, by Pliny the Elder
nom. = nominative
P. = Pausanias

perf. = perfect
pl. = plural
pluperf. = pluperfect
prep. = preposition
ps.-Apollod. = Apollodorus. 1921. *Apollodorus' "The Library."* Trans. J. G. Frazer. 2 vols. Cambridge, MA: Harvard University Press.
Roux = Roux, Georges, ed., trans., and comm. 1958. *Pausanias en Corinthie (livre II, 1 à 5): Texte, traduction, commentaire archéologie et topographique.* Paris: Les Belles Lettres.
RPC = *Roman Provincial Coinage Online.* http://rpc.ashmus.ox.ac.uk/project/.
S = Smyth, Herbert Weir. 1972. *Greek Grammar*. Revised by Gordon Messing. Cambridge, MA: Harvard University Press.
sg. = singular
v. = vide

Brief Observations on Grammar and Style

The most salient aspect of Pausanias' style is his steadfast avoidance of parallelism, even when this risks obscurity or leads to unusual and perhaps unnatural phrases. He most definitely aimed for a distinctive style for his work, something to set him apart from his peers. Attempts to tie Pausanias to the florid Asiatic style—the validity of which is itself a topic of scholarly debate—have been undercut by Ove Strid in her research. The reader will notice foremost Pausanias' habit of using "quasi-impersonal generic participles" (nearly thirty in book 2 alone) to indicate movement around the cities and territories he explores. He also employs prepositions and adverbs vaguely to set monuments in relation with each other, and he deliberately chooses the order of his words for stylistic effect more than topographical clarity. More detailed analysis of Pausanias' style can be found in Strid 1976, from which I derived the following summary.

WORD PLACEMENT

1. Pausanias especially favors the word order of noun, article, and adjective or modifying phrase, sometimes with the latter two parts postponed: for example, πολιτείαν . . . τὴν ἐφ' ἡμῶν (2.1.2) and νόμοις τοῖς καθεστηκόσιν (2.9.1). He uses this type of placement even more frequently than classical authors, but students of his text will also recognize the much more common types of word order: article, adjective, noun; and article, noun, article, adjective. Strid (1976, 80) asserts that opting for the first of these three arrangements gives Pausanias' style an air of lightness and illusory improvisation.
2. Pausanias uses the neuter article in the accusative with a prepositional phrase to create an adverbial expression: for example, τὸ ἐξ ἀρχῆς (2.21.10) instead of simply ἐξ ἀρχῆς.

3. In his striving for *variatio*, Pausanias often chooses periphrastic constructions:
   (a) the verbs συμπίπτειν and συμβαίνειν with dative/accusative with infinitive: for example, Δημοσθένει δὲ φυγῆς τε συνέπεσεν ἐν γήρᾳ λαβεῖν πεῖραν (2.33.3; and it befell Demosthenes to experience exile in old age);
   (b) verbs like ποιεῖσθαι, ἔχειν, λαμβάνειν, and χρῆσθαι with an object instead of a more specific verb: for example, οὐκ ἐποιήσατο . . . μνήμην (2.25.5; he [Homer] made no mention of . . .) instead of ἐμνήσατο;
   (c) ἔχειν with an adverb (S 1438): for example, καὶ ὁ λόγος ἐς αὐτὴν <οὐ> διαφόρως τῷ Βοιωτῶν ἔχει (2.31.9; the account [of the Troezenians] about it [the fountain] does not differ from that of the Boeotians) instead of οὐ διαφέρει.

SENTENCE CONSTRUCTION

Epanalepsis. This construction is the resumption of substantives or clauses already expressed by use of demonstrative pronouns or anaphoric (repeated) pronouns. Pausanias often uses οὗτος, the oblique cases of αὐτός, and the forms σφᾶς, σφῖσι, and οἱ: for example, τὸν δὲ ἐν οὐρανῷ καλούμενον ἡνίοχον, τοῦτον εἶναι νομίζουσιν ἐκεῖνον Ἱππόλυτον τιμὴν παρὰ θεῶν ταύτην ἔχοντα (2.32.1; the so-called Charioteer in the heavens—they think that this one is the famous hero Hippolytus, who has this honor from the gods).

Anakyklesis. This construction is the repetition of a finite verb (usually with the aorist participle): for example, κρατοῦσιν οἱ τοῦ δήμου, κρατήσαντες δὲ οὐδένα ὑπὸ τοῦ θυμοῦ τῶν ἐναντίων ἔλιπον (2.20.2; the popular party won, and in their victory they out of anger left none of their opponents alive).

Appositio partitiva, or σχῆμα καθ᾽ ὅλον καὶ μέρος. This construction is a substantive expressing the idea of a group by means of substantive modifiers in apposition that show the parts of the whole: for example, ὁμολογεῖ δέ σφισι καὶ Ἄσιος, ἐπεὶ Ἡσίοδός γε καὶ Ἴβυκος, ὁ μὲν ἐποίησεν ὡς Ἐρεχθέως εἴη Σικυών, Ἴβυκος δὲ εἶναι Πέλοπός φησιν αὐτόν (2.6.5; There is agreement between them and Asius, since Hesiod and Ibycus—the former writes in his poetry that Erechtheus was a Sicyonian, but Ibycus says that he is the son of Pelops).

Sentence parenthesis. Pausanias occasionally interrupts a sentence in order to insert an entire and sometimes lengthy second sentence to explain a term or concept: for example, ἀνιοῦσι δὲ ἐς τὸν Ἀκροκόρινθον—ἡ δέ ἐστιν ὄρους ὑπὲρ τὴν πόλιν κορυφή, Βριάρεω μὲν Ἡλίῳ δόντος αὐτὴν ὅτε ἐδίκαζεν, Ἡλίου δὲ ὡς οἱ Κορίνθιοί φασιν Ἀφροδίτῃ παρέντος—ἐς δὴ τὸν Ἀκροκόρινθον (2.4.6; When you go up into the Acrocorinth—and it is the peak of the mountain over the city that Briareos once gave Helios when he settled the dispute [over guardianship of the land] and which Helios gave Aphrodite, as the Corinthians say—into Acrocorinth then). Epanalepsis is often employed to "reboot" the main sentence, as in the preceding example.

Asyndeton. This term designates the absence of conjunctions either between sentences or between nouns in a long series (S 3016): for example, ἐσίασι μὲν δὴ ἐς αὐτὸ γυνή τε νεωκόρος, ᾗ μηκέτι θέμις παρ' ἄνδρα φοιτῆσαι, καὶ παρθένος ἱερωσύνην ἐπέτειον ἔχουσα· λουτροφόρον τὴν παρθένον ὀνομάζουσι (2.10.4; The female custodian, for whom it is forbidden to lie with a man, and a maiden who holds a year-long term as priestess enter this [sanctuary]; they call the maiden a basin-bearer).

RHETORICAL FIGURES

Anaphora. This figure involves the placement of a word in the same or a similar form from one clause or sentence at the beginning of the next clause or sentence (S 3010): for example, ἀρχαῖος μὲν οὖν . . . ἀρχαῖος δὲ . . . (2.31.6).

Chiasmus. This figure is the abba arrangement of two contrasted pairs (S 3020). Pausanias uses it with τε . . . καί or μὲν . . . δέ: for example, τὰ μὲν ἐσθίουσιν ὡς ἀπὸ ἱερείου, τὰ δὲ ὡς ἥρωι τῶν κρεῶν ἐναγίζουσι (2.10.1; some of the meat they eat, as it is from a sacrifice to a god, but the rest they dedicate to him [Heracles] as a hero).

Parallelismus Antitheticus. Pausanias often employs parallel phrases that he distorts through *variatio*: for example, he writes ἅτε τοῦ θανάτου βιαίου καὶ οὐ σὺν τῷ δικαίῳ γενομένου (2.3.7; Inasmuch as their death was violent and not done within the strictures of justice) where he could have simply written ἀδίκου.

Litotes. This figure is affirmation expressed by the negative of the contrary (S 3032). Pausanias especially enjoys using the οὐχ ἥκιστα: for example, οὐ χαλεπῶς (2.8.3; easily) and οὐκ ἀπιθάνους (2.9.4; trustworthy).

Common Terms

The following list is based on Jones 1959–61, 1:xxvi ("A Few Synonyms"), but I have also taken up the insights of Vinciane Pirenne-Delforge in her article "Le lexique des lieux de culte dans la *Periegese* de Pausanias," *Archiv für Religionsgeschichte* 10 (2008): 143–78.

ἄγαλμα (v. LSJ 3): statue of a god or hero; a cult statue.
ἀνδριάς (v. LSJ): statue of a human figure, whether mortal, heroic, or divine.
βωμός (v. LSJ 2): altar.
γραφή (v. LSJ I.2): drawing, painting.
εἰκών (v. LSJ I.1): portrait statue, likeness, or image.
ἡρῷον (v. LSJ 1): shrine of a hero.
ἱερόν (v. LSJ ἱερός A.III.3): sanctuary; the holy space belonging to a god or (sometimes) a hero and generally containing a temple; Pausanias also uses the term for the temple itself.
μνῆμα (v. LSJ I.2): mound or building in honor of the dead; monument, tomb, memorial.
ναός (v. LSJ A.I): temple, the actual building.
ξόανον (v. LSJ I): image carved out of wood; generally, image, statue, especially of a god.
οἰκία, οἶκος, οἰκοδόμημα, οἴκημα: house, building.
περίβολος (v. LSJ II.2): a sacred precinct or enclosure.
τάφος (v. LSJ II.1): grave, tomb.
τέμενος (v. LSJ II): piece of land marked off from common uses and dedicated to a god or hero; sacred precinct.

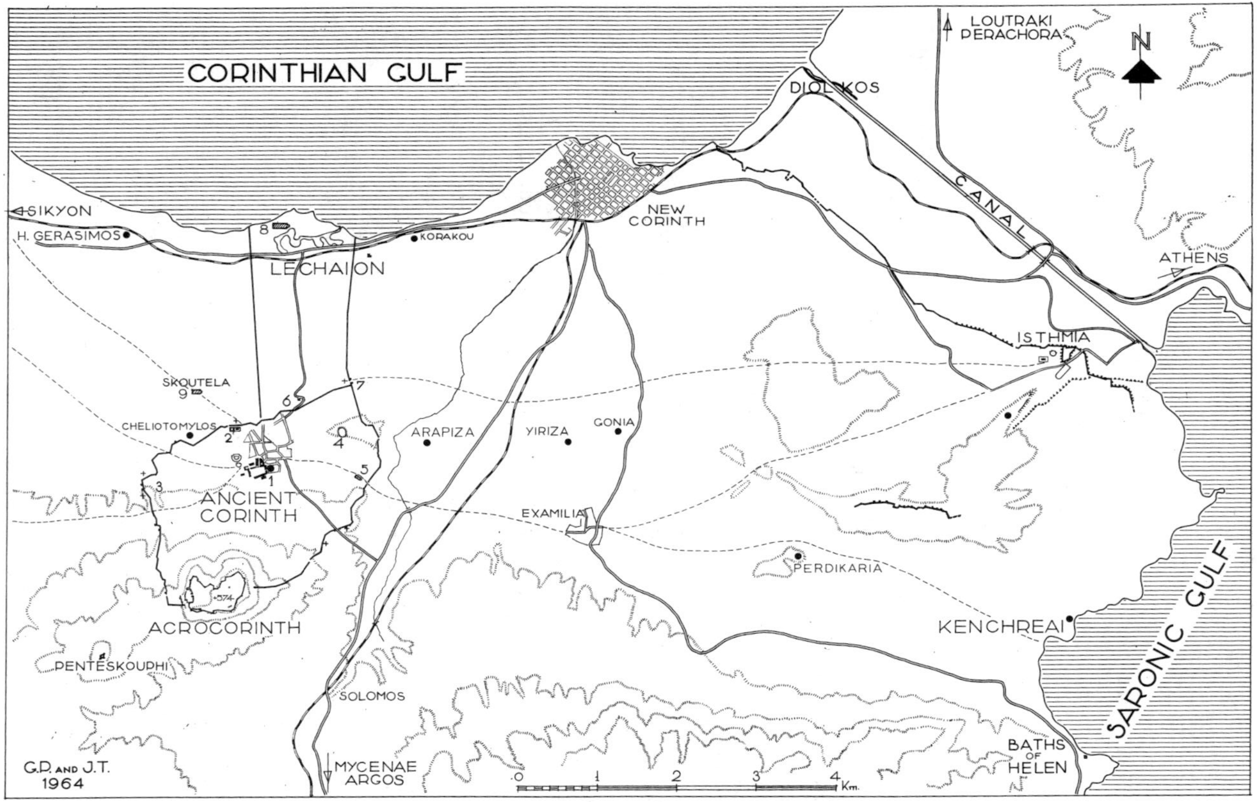

Map 1. Map of ancient Corinthia. *Corinth: A Guide to the Excavations*, 1972, plan I. Photo: Ino Ioannidou and Lenio Bartzioti or Petros Dellatolas. American School of Classical Studies at Athens, Corinth Excavations.

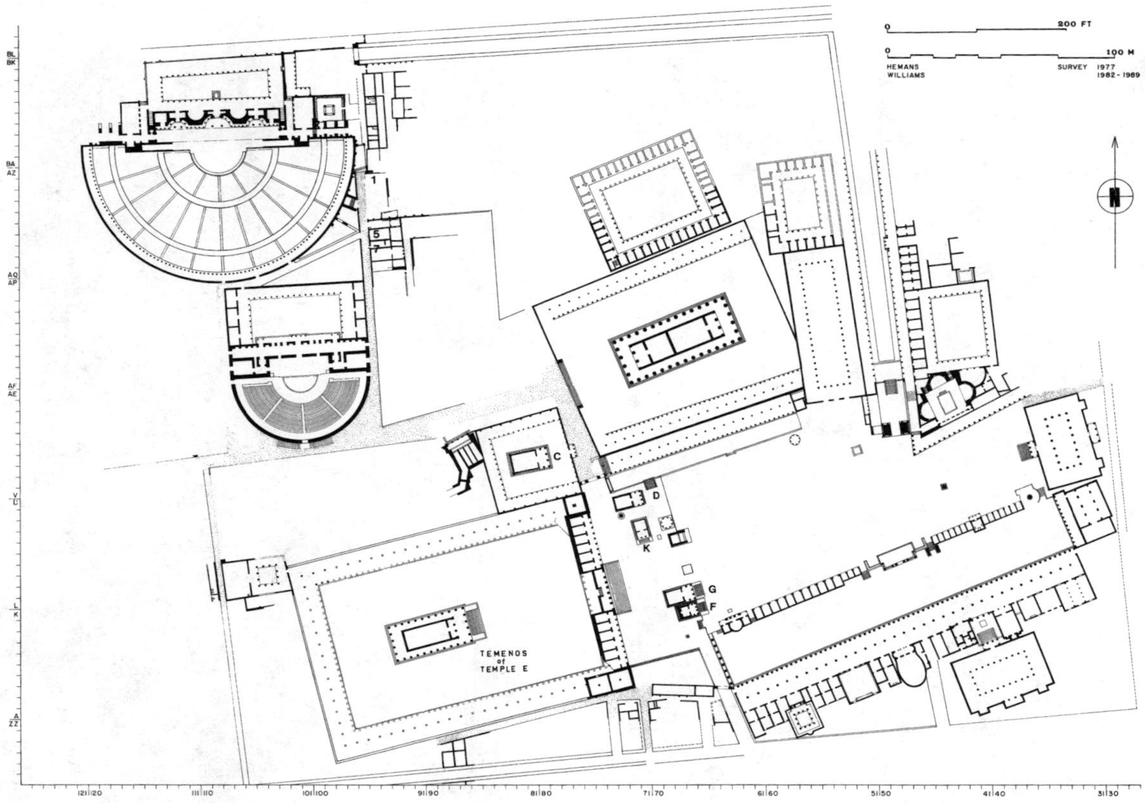

Map 2. Drawing of the central area and theater district of Corinth, early Roman period. *Corinth: A Guide to the Excavations*, 1972, plan II. Photo: Ino Ioannidou and Lenio Bartzioti or Petros Dellatolas. American School of Classical Studies at Athens, Corinth Excavations.

Fig. 1. The entrance to the Acrocorinth. Photograph taken by LaDonna Boeckman in November 2016.

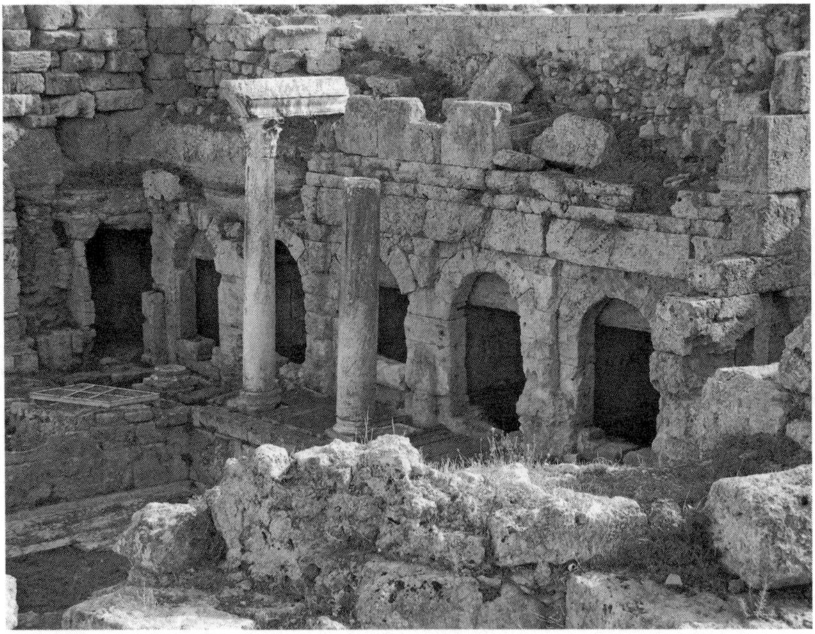

Fig. 2. The Peirene Fountainhouse in the Forum of Corinth. Photograph taken by LaDonna Boeckman in November 2016.

Fig. 3. The Temple of Apollo at Corinth. Photograph taken by LaDonna Boeckman in November 2016.

Text

Book 2
Corinthiaca

2.1.1 ἡ δὲ Κορινθία χώρα μοῖρα οὖσα τῆς Ἀργείας ἀπὸ Κορίνθου τὸ ὄνομα ἔσχηκε. Διὸς δὲ εἶναι Κόρινθον οὐδένα οἶδα εἰπόντα πω σπουδῇ πλὴν Κορινθίων τῶν πολλῶν· Εὔμηλός γε ὁ Ἀμφιλύτου τῶν Βακχιδῶν καλουμένων, ὃς καὶ τὰ ἔπη λέγεται ποιῆσαι, φησὶν ἐν τῇ Κορινθίᾳ συγγραφῇ—εἰ δὴ Εὐμήλου γε ἡ συγγραφή—Ἐφύραν Ὠκεανοῦ θυγατέρα οἰκῆσαι πρῶτον ἐν τῇ γῇ ταύτῃ, Μαραθῶνα δὲ ὕστερον τὸν Ἐπωπέως τοῦ Ἀλωέως τοῦ Ἡλίου φεύγοντα ἀνομίαν καὶ ὕβριν τοῦ πατρὸς ἐς τὰ παραθαλάσσια μετοικῆσαι τῆς Ἀττικῆς, ἀποθανόντος δὲ Ἐπωπέως ἀφικόμενον ἐς Πελοπόννησον καὶ τὴν ἀρχὴν διανείμαντα τοῖς παισὶν αὐτὸν ἐς τὴν Ἀττικὴν αὖθις ἀναχωρῆσαι, καὶ ἀπὸ μὲν Σικυῶνος τὴν Ἀσωπίαν, ἀπὸ δὲ Κορίνθου τὴν Ἐφυραίαν μετονομασθῆναι.

2.1.2 Κόρινθον δὲ οἰκοῦσι Κορινθίων μὲν οὐδεὶς ἔτι τῶν ἀρχαίων, ἔποικοι δὲ ἀποσταλέντες ὑπὸ Ῥωμαίων. αἴτιον δὲ τὸ συνέδριον τὸ Ἀχαιῶν· συντελοῦντες γὰρ ἐς αὐτὸ καὶ οἱ Κορίνθιοι μετέσχον τοῦ πολέμου τοῦ πρὸς Ῥωμαίους, ὃν Κριτόλαος στρατηγεῖν Ἀχαιῶν ἀποδειχθεὶς παρεσκεύασε γενέσθαι τούς τε Ἀχαιοὺς ἀναπείσας ἀποστῆναι καὶ τῶν ἔξω Πελοποννήσου τοὺς πολλούς. Ῥωμαῖοι δὲ ὡς ἐκράτησαν τῷ πολέμῳ, παρείλοντο μὲν καὶ τῶν ἄλλων Ἑλλήνων τὰ ὅπλα καὶ τείχη περιεῖλον ὅσαι τετειχισμέναι πόλεις ἦσαν· Κόρινθον δὲ ἀνάστατον Μομμίου ποιήσαντος τοῦ τότε ἡγουμένου τῶν ἐπὶ στρατοπέδου Ῥωμαίων, ὕστερον λέγουσιν ἀνοικίσαι Καίσαρα, ὃς πολιτείαν ἐν Ῥώμῃ πρῶτος τὴν ἐφ᾽ ἡμῶν κατεστήσατο· ἀνοικίσαι δὲ καὶ Καρχηδόνα ἐπὶ τῆς ἀρχῆς τῆς αὐτοῦ.

2.1.3 τῆς δὲ Κορινθίας ἐστὶ γῆς καὶ ὁ καλούμενος Κρομυὼν ἀπὸ τοῦ Κρόμου τοῦ Ποσειδῶνος. ἐνταῦθα τραφῆναί φασι <Φαιάν>, καὶ τῶν λεγομένων Θησέως καὶ τὸ ἐς τὴν ὗν ταύτην ἐστὶν ἔργον. προϊοῦσι δὲ ἡ πίτυς ἄχρι γε ἐμοῦ πεφύκει παρὰ τὸν αἰγιαλὸν καὶ Μελικέρτου βωμὸς ἦν. ἐς τοῦτον τὸν τόπον ἐκκομισθῆναι τὸν παῖδα ὑπὸ δελφῖνος λέγουσι· κειμένῳ δὲ ἐπιτυχόντα Σίσυφον θάψαι τε ἐν τῷ ἰσθμῷ καὶ τὸν ἀγῶνα ἐπ᾽ αὐτῷ ποιῆσαι τῶν Ἰσθμίων.

2.1.4 ἔστι δὲ ἐπὶ τοῦ ἰσθμοῦ τῆς ἀρχῆς, ἔνθα ὁ λῃστὴς Σίνις λαμβανόμενος πιτύων ἦγεν ἐς τὸ κάτω σφᾶς· ὁπόσων δὲ μάχῃ κρατήσειεν, ἀπ᾽ αὐτῶν δήσας ἀφῆκεν ἂν τὰ δένδρα ἄνω φέρεσθαι· ἐνταῦθα ἑκατέρα τῶν πιτύων τὸν δεθέντα ἐφ᾽ αὐτὴν εἷλκε, καὶ τοῦ δεσμοῦ μηδετέρωσε εἴκοντος ἀλλ᾽ ἀμφοτέρωθεν ἐπ᾽ ἴσης βιαζομένου διεσπᾶτο ὁ δεδεμένος. τοιούτῳ διεφθάρη τρόπῳ καὶ αὐτὸς ὑπὸ Θησέως ὁ Σίνις· ἐκάθηρε γὰρ Θησεὺς τῶν κακούργων τὴν ὁδὸν τὴν ἐς Ἀθήνας ἐκ Τροιζῆνος, οὕς τε πρότερον κατηρίθμησα ἀνελὼν καὶ ἐν Ἐπιδαύρῳ τῇ ἱερᾷ Περιφήτην Ἡφαίστου νομιζόμενον, κορύνῃ χαλκῇ χρώμενον ἐς τὰς μάχας.

2.1.5 καθήκει δὲ ὁ τῶν Κορινθίων ἰσθμὸς τῇ μὲν ἐς τὴν ἐπὶ Κεγχρέαις, τῇ δὲ ἐς τὴν ἐπὶ Λεχαίῳ θάλασσαν· τοῦτο γὰρ ἤπειρον ποιεῖ τὴν ἐντὸς χώραν. ὃς δὲ ἐπεχείρησε Πελοπόννησον ἐργάσασθαι νῆσον, προαπέλιπε διορύσσων ἰσθμόν· καὶ ὅθεν μὲν διορύσσειν ἤρξαντο δῆλόν ἐστιν, ἐς δὲ τὸ πετρῶδες οὐ προεχώρησαν ἀρχήν· μένει δὲ ὡς πεφύκει καὶ νῦν ἤπειρος ὤν. Ἀλεξάνδρῳ τε τῷ Φιλίππου διασκάψαι Μίμαντα ἐθελήσαντι μόνον τοῦτο οὐ προεχώρησε ἔργων· Κνιδίους δὲ ἡ Πυθία τὸν ἰσθμὸν ὀρύσσοντας ἔπαυσεν. οὕτω χαλεπὸν ἀνθρώπῳ τὰ θεῖα βιάσασθαι.

2.1.6 τὸ δὲ οὐ Κορινθίοις μόνον περὶ τῆς χώρας ἐστὶν εἰρημένον, ἀλλὰ ἐμοὶ δοκεῖν Ἀθηναῖοι πρῶτοι περὶ τῆς Ἀττικῆς ἐσεμνολόγησαν· λέγουσι δὲ καὶ οἱ Κορίνθιοι Ποσειδῶνα ἐλθεῖν Ἡλίῳ περὶ τῆς γῆς ἐς ἀμφισβήτησιν, Βριάρεων δὲ διαλλακτὴν γενέσθαι σφίσιν, ἰσθμὸν μὲν καὶ ὅσα ταύτῃ δικάσαντα εἶναι Ποσειδῶνος, τὴν δὲ ἄκραν Ἡλίῳ δόντα τὴν ὑπὲρ τῆς πόλεως· ἀπὸ μὲν τούτου λέγουσιν εἶναι τὸν ἰσθμὸν Ποσειδῶνος·

2.1.7 θέας δὲ αὐτόθι ἄξια ἔστι μὲν θέατρον, ἔστι δὲ στάδιον λίθου λευκοῦ. ἐλθόντι δὲ ἐς τοῦ θεοῦ τὸ ἱερὸν τοῦτο μὲν ἀθλητῶν νικησάντων τὰ Ἴσθμια ἑστήκασιν εἰκόνες, τοῦτο δὲ πιτύων δένδρα ἐστὶ πεφυτευμένα ἐπὶ στοίχου, τὰ πολλὰ ἐς εὐθὺ αὐτῶν ἀνήκοντα. τῷ ναῷ δὲ ὄντι μέγεθος οὐ μείζονι ἐφεστήκασι Τρίτωνες χαλκοῖ. καὶ ἀγάλματά ἐστιν ἐν τῷ προνάῳ δύο μὲν Ποσειδῶνος, τρίτον δὲ Ἀμφιτρίτης, καὶ Θάλασσα καὶ αὕτη χαλκῆ. τὰ δὲ ἔνδον ἐφ᾽ ἡμῶν ἀνέθηκεν Ἡρώδης Ἀθηναῖος, ἵππους τέσσαρας ἐπιχρύσους πλὴν τῶν ὁπλῶν· ὁπλαὶ δέ σφισίν εἰσιν ἐλέφαντος.

2.1.8 καὶ Τρίτωνες δύο παρὰ τοὺς ἵππους εἰσὶ χρυσοῖ, τὰ μετ᾽ ἰξὺν ἐλέφαντος καὶ οὗτοι· τῷ δὲ ἅρματι Ἀμφιτρίτη καὶ Ποσειδῶν ἐφεστήκασι, καὶ παῖς ὀρθός ἐστιν ἐπὶ δελφῖνος ὁ Παλαίμων· ἐλέφαντος δὲ καὶ χρυσοῦ καὶ οὗτοι πεποίηνται. τῷ βάθρῳ δὲ ἐφ᾽ οὗ τὸ ἅρμα μέση μὲν ἐπείργασται Θάλασσα ἀνέχουσα Ἀφροδίτην παῖδα, ἑκατέρωθεν δέ εἰσιν αἱ Νηρηίδες καλούμεναι. ταύταις καὶ ἑτέρωθι τῆς Ἑλλάδος βωμοὺς οἶδα ὄντας, τοὺς δὲ καὶ τεμένη σφίσιν ἀναθέντας πρὸς ἠιόσιν, ἔνθα καὶ Ἀχιλλεῖ τιμαί· Δωτοῦς δὲ ἐν Γαβάλοις ἱερόν ἐστιν ἅγιον, ἔνθα πέπλος ἔτι ἐλείπετο, ὃν Ἕλληνες Ἐριφύλην λέγουσιν ἐπὶ τῷ παιδὶ λαβεῖν Ἀλκμαίωνι.

2.1.9 τοῦ Ποσειδῶνος δέ εἰσιν ἐπειργασμένοι τῷ βάθρῳ καὶ οἱ Τυνδάρεω παῖδες, ὅτι δὴ σωτῆρες καὶ οὗτοι νεῶν καὶ ἀνθρώπων εἰσὶ ναυτιλλομένων. τὰ δὲ ἄλλα ἀνάκειται Γαλήνης ἄγαλμα καὶ Θαλάσσης καὶ ἵππος εἰκασμένος κήτει τὰ μετὰ τὸ στέρνον, Ἰνώ τε καὶ Βελλεροφόντης καὶ ὁ ἵππος ὁ Πήγασος.

2.2.1 τοῦ περιβόλου δέ ἐστιν ἐντὸς Παλαίμονος ἐν ἀριστερᾷ ναός, ἀγάλματα δὲ ἐν αὐτῷ Ποσειδῶν καὶ Λευκοθέα καὶ αὐτὸς ὁ Παλαίμων. ἔστι δὲ καὶ ἄλλο Ἄδυτον καλούμενον, κάθοδος δὲ ἐς αὐτὸ ὑπόγεως, ἔνθα δὴ τὸν Παλαίμονα κεκρύφθαι φασίν· ὃς δ᾽ ἂν ἐνταῦθα ἢ Κορινθίων ἢ ξένος ἐπίορκα ὀμόσῃ, οὐδεμία ἐστίν οἱ μηχανὴ διαφυγεῖν τοῦ ὅρκου. καὶ δὴ ἱερόν ἐστιν ἀρχαῖον Κυκλώπων καλούμενος βωμός, καὶ θύουσιν ἐπ᾽ αὐτῷ Κύκλωψι.

2.2.2 <τάφους δὲ> Σισύφου καὶ Νηλέως—καὶ γὰρ Νηλέα ἀφικόμενον ἐς Κόρινθον νόσῳ τελευτῆσαί φασι καὶ περὶ τὸν ἰσθμὸν ταφῆναι—οὐκ ἂν οἶδ᾽ εἰ ζητοίη τις ἐπιλεξάμενος τὰ Εὐμήλου·· Νηλέως μὲν γὰρ οὐδὲ Νέστορι ἐπιδειχθῆναι τὸ μνῆμα ὑπὸ τοῦ Σισύφου φησί, χρῆναι γὰρ ἄγνωστον τοῖς πᾶσιν ὁμοίως εἶναι, Σίσυφον δὲ ταφῆναι μὲν ἐν τῷ ἰσθμῷ, τὸν δέ οἱ τάφον καὶ τῶν ἐφ᾽ αὑτοῦ Κορινθίων ὀλίγους εἶναι τοὺς εἰδότας. ὁ δὲ Ἰσθμικὸς ἀγὼν οὐδὲ ἀναστάντων ὑπὸ Μομμίου Κορινθίων ἐξέλιπεν, ἀλλ᾽ ὅσον μὲν χρόνον ἠρήμωτο ἡ πόλις, Σικυωνίοις ἄγειν ἐπετέτραπτο τὰ Ἴσθμια, οἰκισθείσης δὲ αὖθις ἐς τοὺς νῦν οἰκήτορας περιῆλθεν ἡ τιμή.

2.2.3 Κορινθίοις δὲ τοῖς ἐπινείοις τὰ ὀνόματα Λέχης καὶ Κεγχρίας ἔδοσαν, Ποσειδῶνος εἶναι καὶ Πειρήνης τῆς Ἀχελῴου λεγόμενοι· πεποίηται δὲ ἐν Ἠοίαις μεγάλαις Οἰβάλου θυγατέρα εἶναι Πειρήνην. ἔστι δὲ ἐν Λεχαίῳ μὲν Ποσειδῶνος ἱερὸν καὶ ἄγαλμα χαλκοῦν, τὴν δὲ ἐς Κεγχρέας ἰόντων ἐξ ἰσθμοῦ ναὸς Ἀρτέμιδος καὶ ξόανον ἀρχαῖον. ἐν δὲ Κεγχρέαις Ἀφροδίτης τέ ἐστι ναὸς καὶ ἄγαλμα λίθου, μετὰ δὲ αὐτὸν ἐπὶ τῷ ἐρύματι τῷ διὰ τῆς θαλάσσης Ποσειδῶνος χαλκοῦν, κατὰ δὲ τὸ ἕτερον πέρας τοῦ λιμένος Ἀσκληπιοῦ καὶ Ἴσιδος ἱερά. Κεγχρεῶν δὲ ἀπαντικρὺ τὸ Ἑλένης ἐστὶ λουτρόν· ὕδωρ ἐς θάλασσαν ἐκ πέτρας ῥεῖ πολὺ καὶ ἁλμυρὸν ὕδατι ὅμοιον ἀρχομένῳ θερμαίνεσθαι.

2.2.4 ἀνιοῦσι δὲ ἐς Κόρινθον καὶ ἄλλα ἐστὶ κατὰ τὴν ὁδὸν μνήματα καὶ πρὸς τῇ πύλῃ Διογένης τέθαπται ὁ Σινωπεύς, ὃν κύνα ἐπίκλησιν καλοῦσιν Ἕλληνες. πρὸ δὲ τῆς πόλεως κυπαρίσσων ἐστὶν ἄλσος ὀνομαζόμενον Κράνειον. ἐνταῦθα Βελλεροφόντου τέ ἐστι τέμενος καὶ Ἀφροδίτης ναὸς

Μελαινίδος καὶ τάφος Λαΐδος, ᾧ δὴ λέαινα ἐπίθημά ἐστι κριὸν ἔχουσα ἐν τοῖς προτέροις ποσίν.

2.2.5 ἔστι δὲ καὶ ἄλλο ἐν Θεσσαλίᾳ Λαΐδος φάμενον μνῆμα εἶναι· παρεγένετο γὰρ καὶ ἐς Θεσσαλίαν ἐρασθεῖσα Ἱπποστράτου. τὸ δὲ ἐξ ἀρχῆς ἐξ Ὑκάρων αὐτὴν τῶν ἐν Σικελίᾳ λέγεται παῖδα οὖσαν ὑπὸ Νικίου καὶ Ἀθηναίων ἁλῶναι, πραθεῖσαν δὲ ἐς Κόρινθον ὑπερβαλέσθαι κάλλει τὰς τότε ἑταίρας, θαυμασθῆναί τε· οὕτω παρὰ Κορινθίοις ὡς ἀμφισβητεῖν σφᾶς καὶ νῦν ἔτι Λαΐδος.

2.2.6 λόγου δὲ ἄξια ἐν τῇ πόλει τὰ μὲν λειπόμενα ἔτι τῶν ἀρχαίων ἐστίν, τὰ δὲ πολλὰ αὐτῶν ἐπὶ τῆς ἀκμῆς ἐποιήθη τῆς ὕστερον. ἔστιν οὖν ἐπὶ τῆς ἀγορᾶς—ἐνταῦθα γὰρ πλεῖστά ἐστι τῶν ἱερῶν—Ἄρτεμίς τε ἐπίκλησιν Ἐφεσία καὶ Διονύσου ξόανα ἐπίχρυσα πλὴν τῶν προσώπων: τὰ δὲ πρόσωπα ἀλοιφῇ σφισιν ἐρυθρᾷ κεκόσμηται· Λύσιον δέ, τὸν δὲ Βάκχειον ὀνομάζουσι.

2.2.7 τὰ δὲ λεγόμενα ἐς τὰ ξόανα καὶ ἐγὼ γράφω. Πενθέα ὑβρίζοντα ἐς Διόνυσον καὶ ἄλλα τολμᾶν λέγουσι καὶ τέλος ἐς τὸν Κιθαιρῶνα ἐλθεῖν ἐπὶ κατασκοπῇ τῶν γυναικῶν, ἀναβάντα δὲ ἐς δένδρον θεάσασθαι τὰ ποιούμενα· τὰς δέ, ὡς ἐφώρασαν, καθελκύσαι τε αὐτίκα Πενθέα καὶ ζῶντος ἀποσπᾶν ἄλλο ἄλλην τοῦ σώματος. ὕστερον δέ, ὡς Κορίνθιοι λέγουσιν, ἡ Πυθία χρᾷ σφισιν ἀνευρόντας τὸ δένδρον ἐκεῖνο ἴσα τῷ θεῷ σέβειν· καὶ ἀπ᾽ αὐτοῦ διὰ τόδε τὰς εἰκόνας πεποίηνται ταύτας.

2.2.8 ἔστι δὲ καὶ Τύχης ναός· ἄγαλμα ὀρθὸν Παρίου λίθου· παρὰ δὲ αὐτὸν θεοῖς πᾶσίν ἐστιν ἱερόν· πλησίον δὲ ᾠκοδόμηται κρήνη, καὶ Ποσειδῶν ἐπ᾽ αὐτῇ χαλκοῦς καὶ δελφὶς ὑπὸ τοῖς ποσίν ἐστι τοῦ Ποσειδῶνος ἀφιεὶς ὕδωρ. καὶ Ἀπόλλων ἐπίκλησιν Κλάριος χαλκοῦς ἐστι καὶ ἄγαλμα Ἀφροδίτης Ἑρμογένους Κυθηρίου ποιήσαντος. Ἑρμοῦ τέ ἐστιν ἀγάλματα χαλκοῦ μὲν καὶ ὀρθὰ ἀμφότερα, τῷ δὲ ἑτέρῳ καὶ ναὸς πεποίηται. τὰ δὲ τοῦ Διός, καὶ ταῦτα ὄντα ἐν ὑπαίθρῳ, τὸ μὲν ἐπίκλησιν οὐκ εἶχε, τὸν δὲ αὐτῶν Χθόνιον καὶ τὸν τρίτον καλοῦσιν Ὕψιστον.

2.3.1 ἐν μέσῳ δὲ τῆς ἀγορᾶς ἐστιν Ἀθηνᾶ χαλκῆ· τῷ βάθρῳ δὲ αὐτῆς ἐστι Μουσῶν ἀγάλματα ἐπειργασμένα. ὑπὲρ δὲ τὴν ἀγοράν ἐστιν Ὀκταβίας ναὸς ἀδελφῆς Αὐγούστου βασιλεύσαντος Ῥωμαίων μετὰ Καίσαρα τὸν οἰκιστὴν Κορίνθου τῆς νῦν.

2.3.2 ἐκ δὲ τῆς ἀγορᾶς ἐξιόντων τὴν ἐπὶ Λεχαίου προπύλαιά ἐστι καὶ ἐπ᾽ αὐτῶν ἅρματα ἐπίχρυσα, τὸ μὲν Φαέθοντα Ἡλίου παῖδα, τὸ δὲ Ἥλιον αὐτὸν φέρον. ὀλίγον δὲ ἀπωτέρω τῶν προπυλαίων ἐξιοῦσιν ἐν δεξιᾷ ἐστιν Ἡρακλῆς χαλκοῦς. μετὰ δὲ αὐτὸν ἔσοδός ἐστι τῆς Πειρήνης ἐς τὸ ὕδωρ. ἐπὶ δὲ αὐτῇ λέγουσιν ὡς ἥ Πειρήνη γένοιτο ὑπὸ δακρύων ἐξ ἀνθρώπου πηγή, τὸν παῖδα ὀδυρομένη Κεγχρίαν ὑπὸ Ἀρτέμιδος ἀκούσης ἀποθανόντα.

2.3.3 κεκόσμηται δὲ ἡ πηγὴ λίθῳ λευκῷ, καὶ πεποιημένα ἐστὶν οἰκήματα σπηλαίοις κατὰ ταὐτά, ἐξ ὧν τὸ ὕδωρ ἐς κρήνην ὕπαιθρον ῥεῖ πιεῖν τε ἡδὺ καὶ τὸν Κορίνθιον χαλκὸν διάπυρον καὶ θερμὸν ὄντα ὑπὸ ὕδατος τούτου βάπτεσθαι λέγουσιν, ἐπεὶ χαλκός γε οὐκ ἔστι Κορινθίοις. ἔτι γε δὴ καὶ Ἀπόλλωνος ἄγαλμα πρὸς τῇ Πειρήνῃ καὶ περίβολός ἐστιν, ἐν δὲ αὐτῷ γραφὴ τὸ Ὀδυσσέως ἐς τοὺς μνηστῆρας ἔχουσα τόλμημα.

2.3.4 αὖθις δ' ἰοῦσιν ἐπὶ Λεχαίου τὴν εὐθεῖαν χαλκοῦς καθήμενός ἐστιν Ἑρμῆς, παρέστηκε δέ οἱ κριός, ὅτι Ἑρμῆς μάλιστα δοκεῖ θεῶν ἐφορᾶν καὶ αὔξειν ποίμνας, καθὰ δὴ καὶ Ὅμηρος ἐν Ἰλιάδι ἐποίησεν·

> υἱὸν Φόρβαντος πολυμήλου, τόν ῥα μάλιστα
> Ἑρμείας Τρώων ἐφίλει καὶ κτῆσιν ὄπασσε·

τὸν δὲ ἐν τελετῇ Μητρὸς ἐπὶ Ἑρμῇ λεγόμενον καὶ τῷ κριῷ λόγον ἐπιστάμενος οὐ λέγω. μετὰ δὲ τὸ ἄγαλμα τοῦ Ἑρμοῦ Ποσειδῶν καὶ Λευκοθέα καὶ ἐπὶ δελφῖνός ἐστιν ὁ Παλαίμων.

2.3.5 λουτρὰ δὲ ἔστι μὲν πολλαχοῦ Κορινθίοις καὶ ἄλλα, τὰ μὲν ἀπὸ τοῦ κοινοῦ, τὸ δὲ βασιλέως Ἀδριανοῦ κατασκευάσαντος· τὸ δὲ ὀνομαστότατον αὐτῶν πλησίον τοῦ Ποσειδῶνος. τοῦτο δὲ Εὐρυκλῆς ἐποίησεν ἀνὴρ Σπαρτιάτης λίθοις κοσμήσας καὶ ἄλλοις καὶ ὃν ἐν Κροκεαῖς χώρας τῆς Λακωνικῆς ὀρύσσουσιν. ἐν ἀριστερᾷ δὲ τῆς ἐσόδου Ποσειδῶν καὶ μετ' αὐτὸν Ἄρτεμις θηρεύουσα ἕστηκε. κρῆναι δὲ πολλαὶ μὲν ἀνὰ τὴν πόλιν πεποίηνται πᾶσαν ἅτε ἀφθόνου ῥέοντός σφισιν ὕδατος καὶ ὃ δὴ βασιλεὺς Ἀδριανὸς ἐσήγαγεν ἐκ Στυμφήλου, θέας δὲ μάλιστα ἀξία <ἡ> παρὰ τὸ ἄγαλμα τὸ τῆς Ἀρτέμιδος· καί οἱ Βελλεροφόντης ἔπεστι καὶ τὸ ὕδωρ {ὁ} δι' ὁπλῆς ἵππου ῥεῖ τοῦ Πηγάσου.

2.3.6 ἑτέραν δὲ ἐκ τῆς ἀγορᾶς τὴν ἐπὶ Σικυῶνα ἐρχομένοις ἔστιν ἰδεῖν ἐν δεξιᾷ τῆς ὁδοῦ ναὸς καὶ ἄγαλμα χαλκοῦν Ἀπόλλωνος καὶ ὀλίγον ἀπωτέρω κρήνη καλουμένη Γλαύκης· ἐς γὰρ ταύτην ἔρριψεν αὑτήν, ὡς λέγουσι, τῶν Μηδείας ἔσεσθαι φαρμάκων τὸ ὕδωρ νομίζουσα ἴαμα. ὑπὲρ ταύτην πεποίηται τὴν κρήνην καὶ τὸ καλούμενον Ὠιδεῖον, παρὰ δὲ αὐτὸ μνῆμά ἐστι τοῖς Μηδείας παισίν· {ὧν} ὀνόματα μέν σφισι Μέρμερος καὶ Φέρης, καταλιθωθῆναι δὲ ὑπὸ Κορινθίων λέγονται τῶν δώρων ἕνεκα ὧν τῇ Γλαύκῃ κομίσαι φασὶν αὐτούς·

2.3.7 ἅτε δὲ τοῦ θανάτου βιαίου καὶ οὐ σὺν τῷ δικαίῳ γενομένου, τὰ τέκνα Κορινθίων τὰ νήπια ὑπ᾽ αὐτῶν ἐφθείρετο, πρὶν ἢ χρήσαντος τοῦ θεοῦ θυσίαι τε αὐτοῖς ἐπέτειοι κατέστησαν καὶ Δεῖμα ἐπεστάθη. τοῦτο μὲν δὴ καὶ ἐς ἡμᾶς ἔτι λείπεται, γυναικὸς ἐς τὸ φοβερώτερον εἰκὼν πεποιημένη· Κορίνθου δὲ ἀναστάτου γενομένης ὑπὸ Ῥωμαίων καὶ Κορινθίων τῶν ἀρχαίων ἀπολομένων, οὐκέτι ἐκεῖναι καθεστήκασιν αὐτοῖς αἱ θυσίαι παρὰ τῶν ἐποίκων οὐδὲ ἀποκείρονταί σφισιν οἱ παῖδες οὐδὲ μέλαιναν φοροῦσιν ἐσθῆτα.

2.3.8 Μήδεια δὲ τότε μὲν ἐλθοῦσα ἐς Ἀθήνας συνῴκησεν Αἰγεῖ, χρόνῳ δὲ ὕστερον φωραθεῖσα ἐπιβουλεύειν Θησεῖ καὶ ἐξ Ἀθηνῶν ἔφυγε, παραγενομένη δὲ ἐς τὴν λεγομένην τότε Ἀρίαν τοῖς ἀνθρώποις ἔδωκε τὸ ὄνομα καλεῖσθαι Μήδους ἀπ᾽ αὐτῆς. τὸν δὲ παῖδα, ὃν ἐπήγετο φεύγουσα ἐς τοὺς Ἀρίους, γενέσθαι λέγουσιν ἐξ Αἰγέως, ὄνομα δέ οἱ Μῆδον εἶναι· Ἑλλάνικος δὲ αὐτὸν Πολύξενον καλεῖ καὶ πατρὸς Ἰάσονός φησιν εἶναι.

2.3.9 ἔπη δὲ ἔστιν ἐν Ἕλλησι Ναυπάκτια ὀνομαζόμενα· πεποίηται δὲ ἐν αὐτοῖς Ἰάσονα ἐξ Ἰωλκοῦ μετὰ τὸν Πελίου θάνατον ἐς Κόρκυραν μετοικῆσαι καί οἱ Μέρμερον μὲν τὸν πρεσβύτερον τῶν παίδων ὑπὸ λεαίνης διαφθαρῆναι θηρεύοντα ἐν τῇ πέραν ἠπείρῳ· Φέρητι δὲ οὐδέν ἐστιν ἐς μνήμην προσκείμενον. Κιναίθων δὲ ὁ Λακεδαιμόνιος—ἐγενεαλόγησε γὰρ καὶ οὗτος ἔπεσι—Μήδειον καὶ θυγατέρα Ἐριῶπιν Ἰάσονι εἶπεν ἐκ Μηδείας γενέσθαι· πέρα δὲ ἐς τοὺς παῖδας οὐδὲ τούτῳ πεποιημένα ἐστίν.

2.3.10 Εὔμηλος δὲ Ἥλιον ἔφη δοῦναι τὴν χώραν Ἀλωεῖ μὲν τὴν Ἀσωπίαν, Αἰήτῃ δὲ τὴν Ἐφυραίαν· καὶ Αἰήτην ἀπιόντα ἐς Κόλχους παρακαταθέσθαι Βούνῳ τὴν γῆν, Βοῦνον δὲ Ἑρμοῦ καὶ Ἀλκιδαμείας εἶναι, καὶ ἐπεὶ Βοῦνος ἐτελεύτησεν, οὕτως Ἐπωπέα τὸν Ἀλωέως καὶ τὴν Ἐφυραίων σχεῖν ἀρχήν· Κορίνθου δὲ ὕστερον τοῦ Μαραθῶνος οὐδένα ὑπολειπομένου παῖδα, τοὺς Κορινθίους Μήδειαν μεταπεμψαμένους ἐξ Ἰωλκοῦ παραδοῦναί οἱ τὴν ἀρχήν.

2.3.11 βασιλεύειν μὲν δὴ δι᾽ αὐτὴν Ἰάσονα ἐν Κορίνθῳ, Μηδείᾳ δὲ παῖδας μὲν γίνεσθαι, τὸ δὲ ἀεὶ τικτόμενον κατακρύπτειν αὐτὸ ἐς τὸ ἱερὸν φέρουσαν τῆς Ἥρας, κατακρύπτειν δὲ ἀθανάτους ἔσεσθαι νομίζουσαν· τέλος δὲ αὐτήν τε μαθεῖν ὡς ἡμαρτήκοι τῆς ἐλπίδος καὶ ἅμα ὑπὸ τοῦ Ἰάσονος φωραθεῖσαν—οὐ γὰρ αὐτὸν ἔχειν δεομένῃ συγγνώμην, ἀποπλέοντα <δὲ> ἐς Ἰωλκὸν οἴχεσθαι—, τούτων δὲ ἕνεκα ἀπελθεῖν καὶ Μήδειαν παραδοῦσαν Σισύφῳ τὴν ἀρχήν.

2.4.1 τάδε μὲν οὕτως ἔχοντα ἐπελεξάμην· τοῦ μνήματος δέ ἐστιν οὐ πόρρω Χαλινίτιδος Ἀθηνᾶς ἱερόν· Ἀθηνᾶν γὰρ θεῶν μάλιστα συγκατεργάσασθαι τά τε ἄλλα Βελλεροφόντῃ φασὶ καὶ ὡς τὸν Πήγασόν οἱ παραδοίη χειρωσαμένη τε καὶ ἐνθεῖσα αὐτὴ τῷ ἵππῳ χαλινόν. τὸ δὲ ἄγαλμα τοῦτο ξόανόν ἐστι, πρόσωπον δὲ καὶ χεῖρες καὶ ἀκρόποδες εἰσὶ λευκοῦ λίθου.

2.4.2 Βελλεροφόντην δὲ οὐκ αὐτοκράτορα ὄντα βασιλεύειν, εἶναι δὲ ἐπὶ Προίτῳ καὶ Ἀργείοις ἐγώ τε πείθομαι καὶ ὅστις τὰ Ὁμήρου μὴ πάρεργον ἐπελέξατο. φαίνονται δὲ καὶ Βελλεροφόντου μετοικήσαντος ἐς Λυκίαν οὐδὲν ἧσσον οἱ Κορίνθιοι τῶν ἐν Ἄργει δυναστῶν ἢ Μυκήναις ὑπακούοντες· ἰδίᾳ τε οὐδένα παρέσχοντο ἄρχοντα τῆς ἐπὶ Τροίαν στρατιᾶς, συντεταγμένοι δὲ Μυκηναίοις καὶ ὅσων ἄλλων Ἀγαμέμνων ἡγεῖτο μετέσχον τοῦ στόλου.

2.4.3 Σισύφῳ δὲ οὔτι Γλαῦκος μόνον ὁ Βελλεροφόντου πατὴρ ἀλλὰ καὶ ἕτερος υἱὸς ἐγένετο Ὀρνυτίων, ἐπὶ δὲ αὐτῷ Θέρσανδρός τε καὶ Ἅλμος. Ὀρνυτίωνος δὲ ἦν Φῶκος, Ποσειδῶνος δὲ ἐπίκλησιν. καὶ ὁ μὲν ἀπῴκησεν ἐς Τιθορέαν τῆς νῦν καλουμένης Φωκίδος, Θόας δὲ Ὀρνυτίωνος υἱὸς νεώτερος κατέμεινεν ἐν τῇ Κορίνθῳ. Θόαντος δὲ Δαμοφῶν, Δαμοφῶντος δὲ ἦν Προπόδας, Προπόδα δὲ Δωρίδας καὶ Ὑανθίδας. τούτων βασιλευόντων Δωριεῖς στρατεύουσιν ἐπὶ Κόρινθον· ἡγεῖτο δὲ Ἀλήτης Ἱππότου <τοῦ> Φύλαντος τοῦ Ἀντιόχου τοῦ Ἡρακλέους. Δωρίδας μὲν οὖν καὶ Ὑανθίδας παραδόντες τὴν βασιλείαν Ἀλήτῃ καταμένουσιν αὐτοῦ, τῶν δὲ Κορινθίων ὁ δῆμος ἐξέπεσεν ὑπὸ Δωριέων κρατηθεὶς μάχῃ.

2.4.4 Ἀλήτης δὲ αὐτός τε καὶ οἱ ἀπόγονοι βασιλεύουσιν ἐς μὲν Βάκχιν τὸν Προύμνιδος ἐπὶ γενεὰς πέντε, ἀπὸ τού<του> δὲ οἱ Βακχίδαι καλούμενοι πέντε ἄλλας γενεὰς ἐς Τελέστην τὸν Ἀριστοδήμου. καὶ Τελέστην μὲν κατὰ ἔχθος Ἀριεὺς καὶ Περάντας κτείνουσι, βασιλεὺς δὲ οὐδεὶς ἔτι ἐγένετο, πρυτάνεις δὲ ἐκ Βακχιδῶν ἐνιαυτὸν ἄρχοντες, ἐς ὃ Κύψελος τυραννήσας ὁ Ἠετίωνος ἐξέβαλε τοὺς Βακχίδας· ἀπόγονος δὲ ἦν ὁ Κύψελος Μέλανος τοῦ Ἀντάσου. Μέλανα δὲ ἐκ Γονούσσης τῆς ὑπὲρ Σικυῶνος στρατεύοντα σὺν Δωριεῦσιν ἐπὶ Κόρινθον Ἀλήτης τὸ μὲν παραυτίκα ἀπειπόντος τοῦ θεοῦ παρ᾽ ἄλλους τῶν Ἑλλήνων ἐκέλευσεν ἀποχωρεῖν, ὕστερον δὲ ἁμαρτὼν τοῦ χρησμοῦ δέχεται σύνοικον. τοιαῦτα μὲν ἐς τοὺς Κορινθίων βασιλέας συμβάντα εὕρισκον.

2.4.5 τὸ δὲ ἱερὸν τῆς Ἀθηνᾶς τῆς Χαλινίτιδος πρὸς τῷ θεάτρῳ σφίσιν ἐστὶν καὶ πλησίον ξόανον γυμνὸν Ἡρακλέους, Δαιδάλου δὲ αὐτό φασιν εἶναι τέχνην. Δαίδαλος δὲ ὁπόσα εἰργάσατο, ἀτοπώτερα μέν ἐστιν ἐς τὴν ὄψιν, ἐπιπρέπει δὲ ὅμως τι καὶ ἔνθεον τούτοις. ὑπὲρ δὲ τὸ θεατρόν ἐστιν ἱερὸν Διὸς Καπετωλίου φωνῇ τῇ Ῥωμαίων· κατὰ Ἑλλάδα δὲ γλῶσσαν Κορυφαῖος ὀνομάζοιτο ἄν. τοῦ θεάτρου δέ ἐστι τοῦδε <οὐ> πόρρω γυμνάσιον τὸ ἀρχαῖον καὶ πηγὴ καλουμένη Λέρνα· κίονες δὲ ἑστήκασι περὶ αὐτὴν καὶ καθέδραι πεποίηνται τοὺς ἐσελθόντας ἀναψύχειν ὥρᾳ θέρους. πρὸς τούτῳ τῷ γυμνασίῳ ναοὶ θεῶν εἰσιν ὁ μὲν Διός, ὁ δὲ Ἀσκληπιοῦ· τὰ δὲ ἀγάλματα Ἀσκληπιὸς μὲν καὶ Ὑγεία λευκοῦ λίθου, τὸ δὲ τοῦ Διὸς χαλκοῦν ἐστιν.

2.4.6 ἀνιοῦσι δὲ ἐς τὸν Ἀκροκόρινθον—ἡ δέ ἐστιν ὄρους ὑπὲρ τὴν πόλιν κορυφή, Βριάρεω μὲν Ἡλίῳ δόντος αὐτὴν ὅτε ἐδίκαζεν, Ἡλίου δὲ ὡς οἱ Κορίνθιοί φασιν Ἀφροδίτῃ παρέντος—ἐς δὴ τὸν Ἀκροκόρινθον τοῦτον ἀνιοῦσίν ἐστιν Ἴσιδος τεμένη, ὧν τὴν μὲν Πελαγίαν, τὴν δὲ Αἰγυπτίαν αὐτῶν ἐπονομάζουσιν, καὶ δύο Σαράπιδος, ἐν Κανώβῳ καλουμένου τὸ ἕτερον. μετὰ δὲ αὐτὰ Ἡλίῳ πεποίηνται βωμοί, καὶ Ἀνάγκης καὶ Βίας ἐστὶν ἱερόν· ἐσιέναι δὲ ἐς αὐτὸ οὐ νομίζουσιν.

2.4.7 ὑπὲρ τοῦτο Μητρὸς θεῶν ναός ἐστι καὶ στήλη καὶ θρόνος· λίθων καὶ αὐτὴ καὶ ὁ θρόνος. ὁ δὲ τῶν Μοιρῶν καὶ <ὁ> Δήμητρος καὶ Κόρης οὐ φανερὰ ἔχουσι τὰ ἀγάλματα. ταύτῃ καὶ τὸ τῆς Βουναίας ἐστὶν Ἥρας ἱερὸν ἱδρυσαμένου Βούνου τοῦ Ἑρμοῦ· καὶ δι᾽ αὐτὸ ἡ θεὸς καλεῖται Βουναία.

2.5.1 ἀνελθοῦσι δὲ ἐς τὸν Ἀκροκόρινθον ναός ἐστιν Ἀφροδίτης· ἀγάλματα δὲ αὐτή τε ὡπλισμένη καὶ Ἥλιος καὶ Ἔρως ἔχων τόξον. τὴν δὲ πηγήν, ἥ ἐστιν ὄπισθεν τοῦ ναοῦ, δῶρον μὲν Ἀσωποῦ λέγουσιν εἶναι, δοθῆναι δὲ Σισύφῳ· τοῦτον γὰρ εἰδότα, ὡς εἴη Ζεὺς ἡρπακὼς Αἴγιναν θυγατέρα Ἀσωποῦ, μὴ πρότερον φάναι ζητοῦντι μηνύσειν πρὶν ἤ οἱ καὶ ἐν Ἀκροκορίνθῳ γένοιτο ὕδωρ· δόντος δὲ Ἀσωποῦ μηνύει τε οὕτως καὶ ἀντὶ τοῦ μηνύματος δίκην—ὅτῳ πιστὰ—ἐν Ἅιδου δίδωσιν. ἤκουσα δὲ ἤδη τὴν Πειρήνην φαμένων εἶναι ταύτην καὶ τὸ ὕδωρ αὐτόθεν ὑπορρεῖν τὸ ἐν τῇ πόλει.

2.5.2 ὁ δὲ Ἀσωπὸς οὗτος ἄρχεται μὲν ἐκ τῆς Φλιασίας, ῥέων δὲ καὶ διὰ τῆς Σικυωνίας ἐκδίδωσιν ἐς τὴν ταύτῃ θάλασσαν. θυγατέρας δὲ αὐτοῦ γενέσθαι Φλιάσιοί φασι Κόρκυραν καὶ Αἴγιναν καὶ Θήβην· ἀπὸ μὲν δὴ Κορκύρας καὶ Αἰγίνης τὰς νήσους Σχερίαν καὶ Οἰνώνην καλουμένας μετονομασθῆναι, ἀπὸ δὲ Θήβης τὴν ὑπὸ τῇ Καδμείᾳ κληθῆναι. Θηβαῖοι δὲ οὐχ ὁμολογοῦσι, φάμενοι τοῦ Βοιωτίου τὴν Θήβην Ἀσωποῦ καὶ οὐ τοῦ {παρὰ} Φλιασίου εἶναι.

2.5.3 τὰ δὲ ἄλλα ἐς τὸν ποταμὸν Φλιάσιοι καὶ Σικυώνιοι λέγουσι, τὸ ὕδωρ ἔπηλυ καὶ οὐκ ἐγχώριον εἶναί οἱ· Μαίανδρον γὰρ κατιόντα ἐκ Κελαινῶν διὰ Φρυγίας καὶ Καρίας καὶ ἐκδιδόντα ἐς τὴν πρὸς Μιλήτῳ θάλασσαν ἐς Πελοπόννησον ἔρχεσθαι καὶ ποιεῖν τὸν Ἀσωπόν. οἶδα δὲ καὶ Δηλίων τοιοῦτο ἀκούσας ἕτερον, ὕδωρ ὃ καλοῦσιν Ἰνωπὸν εἶναί σφισιν ἐκ τοῦ Νείλου· καὶ δὴ καὶ αὐτὸν ἔχει τὸν Νεῖλον λόγος Εὐφράτην ὄντα ἐς ἕλος ἀφανίζεσθαι καὶ αὖθις ἀνιόντα ὑπὲρ Αἰθιοπίας Νεῖλον γίνεσθαι. Ἀσωποῦ μὲν πέρι τοιαῦτα ἤκουσα.

2.5.4 ἐκ δὲ τοῦ Ἀκροκορίνθου τραπεῖσι τὴν ὀρεινὴν πύλη τέ ἐστιν ἡ Τενεατικὴ καὶ Εἰληθυίας ἱερόν· ἑξήκοντα δὲ ἀπέχει μάλιστα στάδια ἡ καλουμένη Τενέα. οἱ δὲ ἄνθρωποί φασιν οἱ ταύτῃ Τρῶες εἶναι, αἰχμάλωτοι δὲ ὑπὸ Ἑλλήνων ἐκ Τενέδου γενόμενοι ἐνταῦθα Ἀγαμέμνονος δόντος οἰκῆσαι· καὶ διὰ τοῦτο θεῶν μάλιστα Ἀπόλλωνα τιμῶσιν.

2.5.5 ἐκ Κορίνθου δὲ οὐκ ἐς μεσόγαιαν ἀλλὰ τὴν ἐπὶ Σικυῶνα ἰοῦσι ναὸς ἐμπεπρησμένος ἐστὶν οὐ πόρρω τῆς πόλεως, ἐν ἀριστερᾷ δὲ τῆς ὁδοῦ. γεγόνασι μὲν δὴ καὶ ἄλλοι πόλεμοι περὶ τὴν Κορινθίαν καὶ πῦρ ἐπέλαβεν ὡς τὸ εἰκὸς καὶ οἰκίας καὶ ἱερὰ τὰ ἔξω τείχους· ἀλλὰ τοῦτόν γε τὸν ναὸν Ἀπόλλωνος εἶναι λέγουσι καὶ ὅτι Πύρρος κατακαύσειεν ὁ Ἀχιλλέως αὐτόν. χρόνῳ δὲ ὕστερον ἤκουσα καὶ ἄλλο τοιόνδε, ὡς οἱ Κορίνθιοι Διὶ ποιήσαιντο Ὀλυμπίῳ τὸν ναὸν καὶ ὡς ἐξαίφνης πῦρ ποθὲν ἐμπεσὸν διαφθείρειεν αὐτόν.

2.5.6 Σικυώνιοι δὲ—οὗτοι γὰρ ταύτῃ Κορινθίοις εἰσὶν ὅμοροι—περὶ τῆς χώρας τῆς σφετέρας λέγουσιν ὡς Αἰγιαλεὺς αὐτόχθων πρῶτος ἐν αὐτῇ γένοιτο, καὶ Πελοποννήσου δὲ ὅσον ἔτι καλεῖται καὶ νῦν Αἰγιαλὸς ἀπ᾽ ἐκείνου βασιλεύοντος ὀνομασθῆναι, καὶ Αἰγιάλειαν αὐτὸν οἰκίσαι πρῶτον ἐν τῷ πεδίῳ πόλιν· οὗ δέ ἐστι νῦν σφισι τὸ ἱερὸν τῆς Ἀθηνᾶς, ἀκρόπολιν τοῦτο εἶναι. Αἰγιαλέως δὲ Εὔρωπα γενέσθαι φασίν, Εὔρωπος δὲ Τελχῖνα, Τελχῖνος δὲ Ἆπιν.

2.5.7 οὗτος ὁ Ἆπις ἐς τοσόνδε ηὐξήθη δυνάμεως, πρὶν ἢ Πέλοπα ἐς Ὀλυμπίαν ἀφικέσθαι, ὡς τὴν ἐντὸς Ἰσθμοῦ χώραν Ἀπίαν ἀπ᾽ ἐκείνου καλεῖσθαι. Ἄπιδος δὲ ἦν Θελξίων, Θελξίονος δὲ Αἴγυρος, τοῦ δὲ Θουρίμαχος, Θουριμάχου δὲ Λεύκιππος· Λευκίππῳ δὲ ἄρρενες παῖδες οὐκ ἐγένοντο, θυγάτηρ δὲ Καλχινία. ταύτῃ τῇ Καλχινίᾳ Ποσειδῶνα συγγενέσθαι φασὶ καὶ τὸν τεχθέντα ὑπ᾽ αὐτῆς ἔθρεψεν ὁ Λεύκιππος καὶ τελευτῶν παρέδωκέν οἱ τὴν ἀρχήν· ὄνομα δὲ ἦν Πέρατος τῷ παιδί.

2.5.8 τὰ δὲ ἐς Πλημναῖον τὸν Περάτου μάλιστα ἐφαίνετό μοι θαύματος ἄξια· τὰ γάρ οἱ τικτόμενα ὑπὸ τῆς γυναικὸς αὐτίκα ὁπότε πρῶτον κλαύσειεν ἠφίει τὴν ψυχήν, ἐς ὃ Δημήτηρ ἔλεον ἴσχει Πλημναίου, παραγενομένη δὲ ἐς τὴν Αἰγιάλειαν ὡς δὴ γυνὴ ξένη Πλημναίῳ παῖδα ἀνέθρεψεν Ὀρθόπολιν. Ὀρθοπόλιδι δὲ θυγάτηρ γίνεται Χρυσόρθη· ταύτην τεκεῖν νομίζουσιν ἐξ Ἀπόλλωνος καὶ ὁ παῖς ὠνομάσθη Κόρωνος, Κορώνου δὲ γίνονται Κόραξ καὶ νεώτερος Λαμέδων.

2.6.1 Κόρακος δὲ ἀποθανόντος ἄπαιδος ὑπὸ τοῦτον τὸν καιρὸν Ἐπωπεὺς ἀφικόμενος ἐκ Θεσσαλίας ἔσχε τὴν ἀρχήν. ἐπὶ τούτου βασιλεύοντος στρατόν σφισι πολέμιον λέγουσιν ἐς τὴν χώραν τότε ἐλθεῖν πρῶτον, τὰ πρὸ τοῦ πάντα τὸν χρόνον διατελέσασιν ἐν εἰρήνῃ. αἰτία δὲ ἥδε· Ἀντιόπης ἐν Ἕλλησι τῆς Νυκτέως ὄνομα ἦν ἐπὶ κάλλει, καί οἱ καὶ φήμη προσῆν Ἀσωποῦ θυγατέρα, ὃς τὴν Θηβαΐδα καὶ Πλαταιίδα ὁρίζει, καὶ οὐ Νυκτέως εἶναι.

2.6.2 ταύτην οὐκ οἶδα εἴτε γυναῖκα αἰτήσας εἴτε θρασύτερα ἐξ ἀρχῆς βουλευσάμενος Ἐπωπεὺς ἁρπάζει· ὡς δὲ οἱ Θηβαῖοι σὺν ὅπλοις ἦλθον, ἐνταῦθα τιτρώσκεται μὲν Νυκτεύς, ἐτρώθη δὲ κρατῶν τῇ μάχῃ καὶ Ἐπωπεύς. Νυκτέα μὲν δὴ κάμνοντα ὀπίσω κομίζουσιν ἐς Θήβας, καὶ ὡς ἔμελλε τελευτᾶν, Λύκον ἀδελφὸν ὄντα παραδίδωσι Θηβαίων ἐν τῷ παρόντι ἄρχειν· Λάβδακον γὰρ τὸν Πολυδώρου τοῦ Κάδμου παῖδα ἔτι αὐτός τε ἐπετρόπευεν ὁ Νυκτεὺς καὶ τότε ἀπέλιπεν ἐπιτροπεύειν ἐκείνῳ. τοῦτον οὖν τὸν Λύκον ἱκέτευσε στρατῷ μείζονι ἐπὶ τὴν Αἰγιάλειαν ἐλάσαντα τιμωρήσασθαι μὲν Ἐπωπέα, κακοῦν δὲ εἰ λάβοι καὶ αὐτὴν Ἀντιόπην.

2.6.3 Ἐπωπεὺς δὲ τὸ μὲν παραυτίκα ἐπινίκια ἔθυε καὶ Ἀθηνᾶς ᾠκοδόμει ναόν, ἐπ᾽ ἐξειργασμένῳ δὲ εὔξατο ἐνδείξασθαι τὴν θεὸν εἴ οἱ τετελεσμένος ἐστὶν ὁ ναὸς κατὰ γνώμην· μετὰ δὲ τὴν εὐχὴν ἔλαιον λέγουσι ῥυῆναι πρὸ τοῦ ναοῦ. ὕστερον δὲ καὶ Ἐπωπέα κατέλαβεν ἀποθανεῖν ὑπὸ τοῦ τραύματος ἀμεληθέντος κατ᾽ ἀρχάς, ὡς μηδὲν ἔτι Λύκῳ δεῆσαι πολέμου· Λαμέδων γὰρ ὁ Κορώνου βασιλεύσας μετὰ Ἐπωπέα ἐξέδωκεν Ἀντιόπην. ἡ δὲ ὡς ἐς Θήβας ἤγετο τὴν ἐπ᾽ Ἐλευθερῶν, ἐνταῦθα καθ᾽ ὁδὸν τίκτει.

2.6.4 καὶ ἔπη <ἐπὶ> τούτῳ πεποίηκεν Ἄσιος ὁ Ἀμφιπτολέμου·

> Ἀντιόπη δ᾽ ἔτεκε Ζῆθον καὶ Ἀμφίονα δῖον
> Ἀσωποῦ κούρη ποταμοῦ βαθυδινήεντος,
> Ζηνί τε κυσαμένη καὶ Ἐπωπέι ποιμένι λαῶν.

Ὅμηρος δὲ σφᾶς ἀνήγαγεν ἐπὶ τὸ σεμνότερον τοῦ γένους καὶ Θήβας φησὶν οἰκίσαι πρώτους, ἀποκρίνων τὴν κάτω πόλιν ἐμοὶ δοκεῖν ἀπὸ τῆς Καδμείας.

2.6.5 Λαμέδων δὲ βασιλεύσας ἔγημεν ἐξ Ἀθηνῶν γυναῖκα Φηνὼ Κλυτίου· καὶ ὕστερον γενομένου οἱ πολέμου πρὸς Ἄρχανδρον καὶ Ἀρχιτέλην τοὺς Ἀχαιοῦ συμμαχήσοντα ἐπηγάγετο Σικυῶνα ἐκ τῆς Ἀττικῆς, καὶ θυγατέρα τε συνῴκισεν αὐτῷ Ζευξίππην καὶ ἀπὸ τούτου βασιλεύσαντος ἡ γῆ Σικυωνία καὶ Σικυὼν ἀντὶ Αἰγιάλης ἡ πόλις ὠνομάσθη. Σικυῶνα δὲ οὐ Μαραθῶνος τοῦ Ἐπωπέως, Μητίονος δὲ εἶναι τοῦ Ἐρεχθέως φασίν. ὁμολογεῖ δέ σφισι καὶ Ἄσιος, ἐπεὶ Ἡσίοδός γε καὶ Ἴβυκος, ὁ μὲν ἐποίησεν ὡς Ἐρεχθέως εἴη Σικυών, Ἴβυκος δὲ εἶναι Πέλοπός φησιν αὐτόν.

2.6.6 Σικυῶνος δὲ γίνεται Χθονοφύλη, Χθονοφύλης δὲ καὶ Ἑρμοῦ Πόλυβον γενέσθαι λέγουσιν· ὕστερον δὲ αὐτὴν Φλίας ὁ Διονύσου γαμεῖ, καί οἱ παῖς Ἀνδροδάμας γίνεται. Πόλυβος δὲ Ταλαῷ τῷ Βίαντος βασιλεύοντι Ἀργείων Λυσιάνασσαν τὴν θυγατέρα ἔδωκε· καὶ ὅτε Ἄδραστος ἔφευγεν ἐξ Ἄργους, παρὰ Πόλυβον ἦλθεν ἐς Σικυῶνα καὶ ὕστερον ἀποθανόντος Πολύβου τὴν ἐν Σικυῶνι ἀρχὴν ἔσχεν. Ἀδράστου δὲ ἐς Ἄργος κατελθόντος Ἰανίσκος ἀπόγονος Κλυτίου τοῦ Λαμέδοντι κηδεύσαντος ἐλθὼν ἐκ τῆς Ἀττικῆς ἐβασίλευσεν, ἀποθανόντος δὲ Ἰανίσκου Φαῖστος τῶν Ἡρακλέους λεγόμενος παίδων καὶ οὗτος εἶναι.

2.6.7 Φαίστου δὲ κατὰ μαντείαν μετοικήσαντος ἐς Κρήτην βασιλεῦσαι λέγεται Ζεύξιππος Ἀπόλλωνος υἱὸς καὶ νύμφης Ὑλλίδος. μετὰ δὲ Ζεύξιππον τελευτήσαντα Ἀγαμέμνων στρατὸν ἤγαγεν ἐπὶ Σικυῶνα καὶ τὸν βασιλέα Ἱππόλυτον Ῥοπάλου παῖδα τοῦ Φαίστου· δείσας δὲ τὸν στρατὸν ἐπιόντα Ἱππόλυτος συνεχώρησεν Ἀγαμέμνονος κατήκοος καὶ Μυκηναίων εἶναι. Ἱππολύτου δὲ ἦν τούτου Λακεστάδης. Φάλκης {ταμφάλκης} δὲ ὁ Τημένου καταλαβὼν νύκτωρ Σικυῶνα σὺν Δωριεῦσι κακὸν μὲν ἅτε Ἡρακλείδην καὶ αὐτὸν ἐποίησεν οὐδέν, κοινωνὸν δὲ ἔσχε τῆς ἀρχῆς.

2.7.1 καὶ Δωριεῖς μὲν Σικυώνιοι γεγόνασιν ἀπὸ τούτου καὶ μοῖρα τῆς Ἀργείας· τὴν δὲ τοῦ Αἰγιαλέως ἐν τῷ πεδίῳ πόλιν Δημήτριος καθελὼν ὁ Ἀντιγόνου τῇ πάλαι ποτὲ ἀκροπόλει προσῴκισε τὴν νῦν πόλιν. ἐχόντων δὲ ἀσθενῶς ἤδη τῶν Σικυωνίων—αἰτίαν δὲ οὐκ ὀρθῶς ποιοῖ τις ἂν ζητῶν, ἀποχρῴτο δὲ τῷ Ὁμήρῳ λελεγμένῳ περὶ Διὸς

> ὃς δὴ πολλάων πολίων κατέλυσε κάρηνα

—διακειμένοις οὖν ἀδυνάτως ἐπιγενόμενος σεισμὸς ὀλίγου τὴν πόλιν ἐποίησεν ἀνδρῶν ἔρημον, πολλὰ δὲ σφᾶς καὶ τῶν ἐς ἐπίδειξιν ἀφείλετο. ἐκάκωσε δὲ καὶ περὶ Καρίαν καὶ Λυκίαν τὰς πόλεις καὶ Ῥοδίοις ἐσείσθη μάλιστα ἡ νῆσος, ὥστε καὶ τὸ λόγιον τετελέσθαι Σιβύλλῃ τὸ ἐς τὴν Ῥόδον ἔδοξεν.

2.7.2 ἐκ δὲ τῆς Κορινθίας ἐλθοῦσιν ἐς τὴν Σικυωνίαν Λύκου Μεσσηνίου μνῆμά ἐστιν, ὅστις δὴ οὗτος ὁ Λύκος· οὐ γάρ τινα Λύκον εὑρίσκω Μεσσήνιον ἀσκήσαντα πένταθλον οὐδὲ Ὀλυμπικὴν ἀνῃρημένον νίκην. τοῦτο μὲν δὴ χῶμά ἐστι γῆς, αὐτοὶ δὲ Σικυώνιοι τὰ πολλὰ <οὐχ> ἐοικότι τρόπῳ θάπτουσι. τὸ μὲν σῶμα γῇ κρύπτουσι, λίθου δὲ ἐποικοδομήσαντες κρηπῖδα κίονας ἐφιστᾶσι καὶ ἐπ᾽ αὐτοῖς ἐπίθημα ποιοῦσι κατὰ τοὺς ἀετοὺς μάλιστα τοὺς ἐν τοῖς ναοῖς· ἐπίγραμμα δὲ ἄλλο μὲν ἐπιγράφουσιν οὐδέν, τὸ δὲ ὄνομα ἐφ᾽ αὑτοῦ καὶ οὐ πατρόθεν ὑπειπόντες κελεύουσι τὸν νεκρὸν χαίρειν.

2.7.3 μετὰ δὲ τὸ μνῆμα τοῦ Λύκου διαβεβηκόσιν ἤδη τὸν Ἀσωπόν, ἔστιν ἐν δεξιᾷ τὸ Ὀλύμπιον, ὀλίγον δὲ ἔμπροσθεν ἐν ἀριστερᾷ τῆς ὁδοῦ τάφος Εὐπόλιδι Ἀθηναίῳ ποιήσαντι κωμῳδίαν. προελθοῦσι δὲ καὶ ἐπιστρέψασιν ὡς ἐπὶ τὴν πόλιν Ξενοδίκης μνῆμά ἐστιν ἀποθανούσης ἐν ὠδῖσι· πεποίηται δὲ οὐ κατὰ τὸν ἐπιχώριον τρόπον, ἀλλ' ὡς ἂν τῇ γραφῇ μάλιστα ἁρμόζοι· γραφὴ δὲ εἴπερ ἄλλη τις καὶ αὕτη ἐστὶ θέας ἀξία.

2.7.4 προελθοῦσι δὲ ἐντεῦθεν τάφος Σικυωνίοις ἐστίν, ὅσοι περὶ Πελλήνην καὶ Δύμην τὴν Ἀχαιῶν καὶ ἐν Μεγάλῃ πόλει καὶ περὶ Σελλασίαν ἐτελεύτησαν· τὰ δὲ ἐς αὐτοὺς σαφέστερον ἐν τοῖς ἐφεξῆς δηλώσω. πρὸς δὲ τῇ πύλῃ πηγή ἐστί σφισιν ἐν σπηλαίῳ, ἧς τὸ ὕδωρ οὐκ ἄνεισιν ἐκ γῆς, ἐπιρρεῖ δὲ ἐκ τοῦ ὀρόφου τοῦ σπηλαίου· καὶ καλεῖται δι' αὐτὸ Στάζουσα ἡ πηγή.

2.7.5 ἐν δὲ τῇ νῦν ἀκροπόλει Τύχης ἱερόν ἐστιν Ἀκραίας, μετὰ δὲ αὐτὸ Διοσκούρων· ξόανα δὲ οὗτοί τε καὶ τὸ ἄγαλμα τῆς Τύχης ἐστί. τοῦ θεάτρου δὲ ὑπὸ τὴν ἀκρόπολιν ᾠκοδομημένου τὸν ἐν τῇ σκηνῇ πεποιημένον ἄνδρα ἀσπίδα ἔχοντα Ἄρατόν φασιν εἶναι τὸν Κλεινίου. μετὰ δὲ τὸ θέατρον Διονύσου ναός ἐστι· χρυσοῦ μὲν καὶ ἐλέφαντος ὁ θεός, παρὰ δὲ αὐτὸν Βάκχαι λίθου λευκοῦ. ταύτας τὰς γυναῖκας ἱερὰς εἶναι καὶ Διονύσῳ μαίνεσθαι λέγουσιν. ἄλλα δὲ ἀγάλματα ἐν ἀπορρήτῳ Σικυωνίοις ἐστί· ταῦτα μιᾷ καθ' ἕκαστον ἔτος νυκτὶ ἐς τὸ Διονύσιον ἐκ τοῦ καλουμένου κοσμητηρίου κομίζουσι, κομίζουσι δὲ μετὰ δᾴδων τε ἡμμένων καὶ ὕμνων ἐπιχωρίων.

2.7.6 ἡγεῖται μὲν οὖν ὃν Βάκχειον ὀνομάζουσιν—Ἀνδροδάμας σφίσιν ὁ Φλίαντος τοῦτον ἱδρύσατο—, ἕπεται δὲ <ὁ> καλούμενος Λύσιος, ὃν Θηβαῖος Φάνης εἰπούσης τῆς Πυθίας ἐκόμισεν ἐκ Θηβῶν. ἐς δὲ Σικυῶνα ἦλθεν ὁ Φάνης, ὅτε Ἀριστόμαχος ὁ Κλεοδαίου τῆς γενομένης μαντείας ἁμαρτὼν δι' αὐτὸ καὶ καθόδου τῆς ἐς Πελοπόννησον ἥμαρτεν. ἐκ δὲ τοῦ Διονυσίου βαδίζουσιν ἐς τὴν ἀγοράν, ἔστι ναὸς Ἀρτέμιδος ἐν δεξιᾷ Λιμναίας. καὶ ὅτι μὲν κατερρύηκεν ὁ ὄροφος, δῆλά ἐστιν ἰδόντι· περὶ δὲ τοῦ ἀγάλματος οὔτε ὡς κομισθέντος ἑτέρωσε οὔτε ὅντινα αὐτοῦ διεφθάρη τρόπον εἰπεῖν ἔχουσιν.

2.7.7 ἐς δὲ τὴν ἀγορὰν ἐσελθοῦσι Πειθοῦς ἐστιν ἱερὸν οὐδὲ τοῦτο ἄγαλμα ἔχον. Πειθὼ δὲ ἐπὶ λόγῳ τοιῷδε αὐτοῖς κατέστη σέβεσθαι. Ἀπόλλων καὶ Ἄρτεμις ἀποκτείναντες Πύθωνα παρεγένοντο ἐς τὴν Αἰγιάλειαν καθαρσίων ἕνεκα. γενομένου δέ σφισι δείματος, ἔνθα καὶ νῦν Φόβον ὀνομάζουσι τὸ χωρίον, οἱ μὲν ἐς Κρήτην παρὰ Καρμάνορα ἀπετράποντο, τοὺς δὲ ἀνθρώπους ἐν τῇ Αἰγιαλείᾳ νόσος ἐπέλαβε· καὶ σφᾶς ἐκέλευον οἱ μάντεις Ἀπόλλωνα ἱλάσασθαι καὶ Ἄρτεμιν.

2.7.8 οἱ δὲ παῖδας ἑπτὰ καὶ ἴσας παρθένους ἐπὶ τὸν Σύθαν ποταμὸν ἀποστέλλουσιν ἱκετεύοντας· ὑπὸ τούτων δὲ πεισθέντας τοὺς θεούς φασιν ἐς τὴν τότε ἀκρόπολιν ἐλθεῖν, καὶ ὁ τόπος ἔνθα πρῶτον ἀφίκοντο Πειθοῦς ἐστιν ἱερόν. τούτοις δὲ ἐοικότα καὶ νῦν ἔτι ποιεῖται· καὶ γὰρ ἐπὶ τὸν Σύθαν ἴασιν οἱ παῖδες τῇ ἑορτῇ τοῦ Ἀπόλλωνος, καὶ ἀγαγόντες δὴ τοὺς θεοὺς ἐς τὸ τῆς Πειθοῦς ἱερὸν αὖθις ἀπάγειν ἐς τὸν ναόν φασι τοῦ Ἀπόλλωνος. ὁ δὲ ναὸς ἔστι μὲν ἐν τῇ νῦν ἀγορᾷ, τὸ δὲ ἐξ ἀρχῆς λέγουσιν αὐτὸν ὑπὸ Προίτου ποιηθῆναι· τὰς γάρ οἱ θυγατέρας ἐνταῦθα τῆς μανίας παύσασθαι.

2.7.9 λέγουσι δὲ καὶ τάδε, ὡς Μελέαγρος ἐς τοῦτον τὸν ναὸν ἀνέθηκε τὴν λόγχην ᾗ τὸν ὗν κατειργάσατο. καὶ αὐλοὺς ἀνατεθῆναί φασιν ἐνταῦθα τοὺς Μαρσύου· γενομένης γὰρ τῷ Σιληνῷ τῆς συμφορᾶς τὸν ποταμὸν τὸν Μαρσύαν κατενεγκεῖν αὐτοὺς ἐς τὸν Μαίανδρον, ἀναφανέντας δὲ ἐν τῷ Ἀσωπῷ καὶ κατὰ τὴν Σικυωνίαν ἐκπεσόντας ὑπὸ ποιμένος τοῦ εὑρόντος δοθῆναι τῷ Ἀπόλλωνι. τούτων τῶν ἀναθημάτων οὐδὲν ἔτι ἐλείπετο, συγκατεκαύθη γὰρ ἐμπιπραμένῳ τῷ ναῷ· τὸν δὲ ἐπ᾽ ἐμοῦ ναὸν καὶ τὸ ἄγαλμα Πυθοκλῆς ἀνέθηκεν.

2.8.1 τῷ δὲ τῆς Πειθοῦς ἱερῷ τὸ ἐγγὺς τέμενος ἀνειμένον βασιλεῦσι Ῥωμαίων οἰκία ποτὲ ἦν Κλέωνος τυράννου· Κλεισθένης μὲν γὰρ ὁ Ἀριστωνύμου τοῦ Μύρωνος ἐχόντων ἔτι τὴν κάτω πόλιν Σικυωνίων ἐτυράννησε, Κλέων δὲ ἐν τῇ νῦν πόλει. πρὸ ταύτης τῆς οἰκίας ἡρῷόν ἐστιν Ἀράτου μέγιστα Ἑλλήνων ἐργασαμένου τῶν ἐφ᾽ αὑτοῦ· ἔχει δὲ ὧδε τὰ ἐς αὐτόν.

2.8.2 μετὰ Κλέωνα μοναρχήσαντα ἐνέπεσε τῶν ἐν τέλει πολλοῖς ἐπιθυμία τυραννίδος οὕτω δή τι ἀκάθεκτος ὡς καὶ ἄνδρας δύο Εὐθύδημον καὶ Τιμοκλείδαν ὁμοῦ τυραννῆσαι. τούτους μὲν οὖν ἐξέβαλεν ὁ δῆμος, Κλεινίαν τὸν πατέρα Ἀράτου προστησάμενος· ἔτεσι δὲ ὕστερον οὐ πολλοῖς ἐτυράννησεν Ἀβαντίδας. Κλεινίᾳ μὲν οὖν συνεβεβήκει πρότερον ἔτι ἡ τελευτή· Ἄρατον δὲ Ἀβαντίδας φυγάδα ἐποίησεν, ἢ καὶ αὐτὸς ἀπεχώρησεν Ἄρατος ἐθελοντής. Ἀβαντίδαν μὲν οὖν κτείνουσιν ἄνδρες τῶν ἐπιχωρίων, τύραννος δὲ αὐτίκα ἐγεγόνει ὁ Ἀβαντίδου πατὴρ Πασέας.

2.8.3 Νικοκλῆς δὲ ἐκεῖνον ἀνελὼν ἐτυράννησεν αὐτός. ἐπὶ τοῦτον τὸν Νικοκλέα Ἄρατος ἀφικόμενος Σικυωνίων φυγάσι καὶ Ἀργείοις μισθωτοῖς τοὺς μὲν ἔλαθεν ἅτε ἐν σκότῳ—νύκτωρ γὰρ δὴ τὴν ἐπιχείρησιν ἐποιεῖτο—, τοὺς δὲ καὶ βιασάμενος τῶν φυλασσόντων ἐγένετο ἐντὸς τείχους· καὶ—ὑπέφαινε γὰρ ἕως ἤδη—προσλαβὼν τὸν δῆμον ἐπὶ τὴν οἰκίαν σπουδῇ τὴν τυραννικὴν τρέπεται. καὶ ταύτην μὲν εἷλεν οὐ χαλεπῶς, ὁ δὲ Νικοκλῆς αὐτὸς ἔλαθεν ἀποδράς. Σικυωνίοις δὲ ἀπέδωκεν Ἄρατος ἐξ ἴσου πολιτεύεσθαι διαλλάξας τοῖς φεύγουσιν, οἰκίας μὲν φυγάσι καὶ ὅσα τῶν κτημάτων ἄλλα {ἃ} ἐπέπρατο ἀποδούς, τιμὴν δὲ τοῖς πριαμένοις διέλυσεν αὐτός.

2.8.4 καὶ—ἦν γὰρ δέος τοῖς πᾶσιν Ἕλλησι Μακεδόνων καὶ Ἀντιγόνου Φίλιππον ἐπιτροπεύοντος τὸν Δημητρίου—, τοῦδε ἕνεκα τοὺς Σικυωνίους ἐς τὸ Ἀχαιῶν συνέδριον ἐσήγαγε Δωριεῖς ὄντας. αὐτίκα δὲ στρατηγὸς ὑπὸ τῶν Ἀχαιῶν ᾕρητο, καὶ σφᾶς ἐπὶ Λοκροὺς τοὺς Ἀμφισσέας ἀγαγὼν καὶ ἐς τὴν Αἰτωλῶν πολεμίων ὄντων τὴν γῆν ἐπόρθησε· Κόρινθον δὲ ἔχοντος Ἀντιγόνου καὶ φρουρᾶς Μακεδόνων ἐνούσης τοὺς Μακεδόνας τῷ αἰφνιδίῳ τῆς ἐπιθέσεως κατέπληξε καὶ ἄλλους τε κρατήσας μάχῃ διέφθειρε καὶ Περσαῖον ἐπὶ τῇ φρουρᾷ τεταγμένον, ὃς παρὰ Ζήνωνα τὸν Μνασέου κατὰ μάθησιν σοφίας ἐφοίτησεν.

2.8.5 ἐλευθερώσαντος δὲ Ἀράτου Κόρινθον προσεχώρησαν μὲν ἐς τὸ συνέδριον Ἐπιδαύριοι καὶ Τροιζήνιοι οἱ τὴν Ἀργολίδα Ἀκτὴν οἰκοῦντες καὶ τῶν ἐκτὸς ἰσθμοῦ Μεγαρεῖς, συμμαχίαν δὲ πρὸς Ἀχαιοὺς Πτολεμαῖος ἐποιήσατο. Λακεδαιμόνιοι δὲ καὶ Ἆγις ὁ Εὐδαμίδου βασιλεὺς ἔφθησαν μὲν Πελλήνην ἑλόντες ἐξ ἐπιδρομῆς, ἥκοντι δὲ Ἀράτῳ καὶ τῇ στρατιᾷ συμβαλόντες ἐκρατήθησαν καὶ τὴν Πελλήνην ἐκλιπόντες ἀναχωροῦσιν οἴκαδε ὑπόσπονδοι.

2.8.6 Ἄρατος δέ, ὥς οἱ τὰ ἐν Πελοποννήσῳ προεκεχωρήκει, δεινὸν ἡγεῖτο Πειραιᾶ καὶ Μουνυχίαν, ἔτι δὲ Σαλαμῖνα καὶ Σούνιον ἐχόμενα ὑπὸ Μακεδόνων περιοφθῆναι, καὶ—οὐ γὰρ ἤλπιζε δύνασθαι πρὸς βίαν αὐτὰ ἐξελεῖν—Διογένην πείθει τὸν ἐν τοῖς φρουροῖς ἄρχοντα ἀφεῖναι τὰ χωρία ἐπὶ ταλάντοις πεντήκοντα καὶ ἑκατόν, καὶ τῶν χρημάτων συνετέλεσεν αὐτὸς Ἀθηναίοις ἕκτον μέρος. ἔπεισε δὲ καὶ Ἀριστόμαχον τυραννοῦντα ἐν Ἄργει δημοκρατίαν ἀποδόντα Ἀργείοις ἐς τὸ Ἀχαϊκὸν συντελεῖν, Μαντίνειάν τε Λακεδαιμονίων ἐχόντων εἷλεν. ἀλλὰ γὰρ οὐ πάντα ἀνθρώπῳ τελεῖται κατὰ γνώμην, εἰ δὴ καὶ Ἄρατον κατέλαβεν ἀνάγκη γενέσθαι Μακεδόνων καὶ Ἀντιγόνου σύμμαχον· ἐγένετο δὲ οὕτως.

2.9.1 Κλεομένης ὁ Λεωνίδου τοῦ Κλεωνύμου παραλαβὼν τὴν βασιλείαν ἐν Σπάρτῃ Παυσανίαν ἐμιμεῖτο τυραννίδος τε ἐπιθυμῶν καὶ νόμοις τοῖς καθεστηκόσιν οὐκ ἀρεσκόμενος. ἅτε δὲ ὄντι αὐτῷ Παυσανίου θερμοτέρῳ καὶ οὐ φιλοψύχῳ ταχὺ τὰ πάντα ὑπὸ φρονήματος καὶ τόλμης κατείργαστο, καὶ βασιλέα τε οἰκίας τῆς ἑτέρας Εὐρυδαμίδαν παῖδα ἔτι ἀνελὼν φαρμάκῳ διὰ τῶν ἐφορευόντων ἐς Ἐπικλείδαν τὸν ἀδελφὸν μετέστησε τὴν ἀρχὴν καὶ τὸ κράτος τῆς γερουσίας καταλύσας πατρονόμους τῷ λόγῳ κατέστησεν ἀντ᾽ αὐτῶν. ἐπιθυμῶν δὲ πραγμάτων μειζόνων καὶ ἀρχῆς τῶν Ἑλλήνων, ἐπέθετο Ἀχαιοῖς πρώτοις, συμμάχους ἐλπίζων ἕξειν ἢν κρατήσῃ καὶ μάλιστα ἐμποδὼν οὐκ ἐθέλων εἶναί οἱ τοῖς δρωμένοις.

2.9.2 συμβαλὼν δὲ περὶ Δύμην τὴν ὑπὲρ Πατρῶν, Ἀράτου καὶ τότε ἡγουμένου τῶν Ἀχαιῶν, νικᾷ τῇ μάχῃ. τοῦτο Ἄρατον ἠνάγκασεν ὑπέρ τε Ἀχαιῶν καὶ αὐτῆς Σικυῶνος δείσαντα Ἀντίγονον ἐπάγεσθαι. Κλεομένους δὲ παραβάντος ἣν πρὸς Ἀντίγονον συνέθετο εἰρήνην καὶ παράσπονδα ἐκ τοῦ φανεροῦ καὶ ἄλλα δράσαντος καὶ Μεγαλοπολίτας ποιήσαντος ἀναστάτους, οὕτω διαβάντος ἐς Πελοπόννησον Ἀντιγόνου συμβάλλουσιν Ἀχαιοὶ Κλεομένει περὶ Σελλασίαν. νικησάντων δὲ τῶν Ἀχαιῶν Σελλασία τε ἠνδραποδίσθη καὶ αὐτὴ Λακεδαίμων ἑάλω. Λακεδαιμονίοις μὲν οὖν ἀπέδωκεν Ἀντίγονος καὶ Ἀχαιοὶ πολιτείαν τὴν πάτριον.

2.9.3 τῶν δὲ Λεωνίδου παίδων Ἐπικλείδας μὲν ἀπέθανεν ἐν τῇ μάχῃ, Κλεομένην δὲ φεύγοντα ἐς Αἴγυπτον καὶ τιμῆς παρὰ Πτολεμαίῳ πρῶτα ἔχοντα συνέβη δεθῆναι, καταγνωσθέντα Αἰγυπτίων ἄνδρας ἐπὶ τὸν βασιλέα συνιστάναι. καὶ ἀπέδρα μὲν ἐκ τοῦ δεσμωτηρίου καὶ τοῖς Ἀλεξανδρεῦσιν ἀρχὴν θορύβου παρέσχε· τέλος δέ, ὡς ἡλίσκετο, ἀπέσφαξεν αὑτόν. Λακεδαιμόνιοι δὲ ἄσμενοι Κλεομένους ἀπαλλαγέντες βασιλεύεσθαι μὲν οὐκέτι ἠξίωσαν, τὰ δὲ λοιπὰ καὶ ἐς τόδε διαμένει σφίσιν ἐκείνης τῆς πολιτείας. Ἀράτῳ δὲ Ἀντίγονος ἅτε ἀνδρὶ εὐεργέτῃ καὶ συγκατειργασμένῳ λαμπρὰ οὕτω διέμεινεν εὔνους.

2.9.4 Φίλιππος δὲ ὡς παρέλαβε τὴν ἀρχήν—οὐ γὰρ αὐτὸν Ἄρατος θυμῷ πολλὰ ἐς τοὺς ἀρχομένους χρώμενον ἐπῄνει, τὰ δὲ καὶ ὡρμημένον ἐπεῖχε μὴ ποιεῖν—, τούτων ἕνεκεν ἀπέκτεινεν Ἄρατον, οὐδὲν προϊδομένῳ δούς οἱ φάρμακον. καὶ τὸν μὲν ἐξ Αἰγίου—ταύτῃ γὰρ τὸ χρεὼν ἐπέλαβεν αὐτὸν—ἐς Σικυῶνα κομίσαντες θάπτουσι, καὶ τὸ ἡρῷον Ἀράτειον ἔτι ὀνομάζεται. Φιλίππῳ δὲ καὶ ἐς Εὐρυκλείδην καὶ Μίκωνα Ἀθηναίους ὅμοια εἰργάσθη· καὶ γὰρ τούσδε ὄντας ῥήτορας καὶ οὐκ ἀπιθάνους τῷ δήμῳ φαρμάκοις ἔκτεινεν.

2.9.5 ἔμελλε δὲ ἄρα καὶ αὐτῷ Φιλίππῳ τὸ ἀνδροφόνον φάρμακον ἔσεσθαι συμφορά· τὸν γάρ οἱ παῖδα Δημήτριον {ὁ νεώτερος τῶν Φιλίππου παίδων} Περσεὺς φαρμάκῳ διέφθειρε καὶ δι᾽ αὐτὸ καὶ τῷ πατρὶ ἀθυμήσαντι παρέσχεν αἰτίαν ἀποθανεῖν. παρεδήλωσα δὲ τάδε ἀπιδὼν ἐς <τὸ> Ἡσιόδου σὺν θεῷ πεποιημένον, τὸν ἐπ᾽ ἄλλῳ βουλεύοντα ἄδικα ἐς αὐτὸν πρῶτον τρέπειν.

2.9.6 μετὰ δὲ <τὸ> Ἀράτου ἡρῷον ἔστι μὲν Ποσειδῶνι Ἰσθμίῳ βωμός, ἔστι δὲ Ζεὺς Μειλίχιος καὶ Ἄρτεμις ὀνομαζομένη Πατρῴα, σὺν τέχνῃ πεποιημένα οὐδεμιᾷ· πυραμίδι δὲ ὁ Μειλίχιος, ἡ δὲ κίονί ἐστιν εἰκασμένη. ἐνταῦθα καὶ βουλευτήριόν σφισι πεποίηται καὶ στοὰ καλουμένη Κλεισθένειος ἀπὸ τοῦ οἰκοδομήσαντος· ᾠκοδόμησε δὲ ἀπὸ λαφύρων ὁ Κλεισθένης αὐτὴν τὸν πρὸς Κίρρᾳ πόλεμον συμπολεμήσας Ἀμφικτύοσι. τῆς δὲ ἀγορᾶς ἐστιν ἐν τῷ ὑπαίθρῳ Ζεὺς χαλκοῦς, τέχνη Λυσίππου, παρὰ δὲ αὐτὸν Ἄρτεμις ἐπίχρυσος.

2.9.7 πλησίον δὲ Ἀπόλλωνός ἐστιν ἱερὸν Λυκίου, κατερρυηκός τε ἤδη καὶ ἥκιστα θέας ἄξιον. φοιτώντων γὰρ λύκων σφίσιν ἐπὶ τὰς ποίμνας ὡς μηδένα εἶναι καρπὸν ἔτι ἀπ᾽ αὐτῶν, ὁ θεὸς τόπον τινὰ εἰπὼν ἔνθα ἔκειτο αὖον ξύλον, τούτου φλοιὸν ἔχρησε τοῦ ξύλου καὶ κρέας ὁμοῦ προθεῖναι τοῖς θηρίοις· καὶ τοὺς μὲν αὐτίκα ὡς ἐγεύσαντο διέφθειρεν ὁ φλοιός, τὸ ξύλον δὲ ἐκεῖνο ἔκειτο μὲν ἐν τῷ ἱερῷ τοῦ Λυκίου, ὅ τι δὲ ἦν δένδρον οὐδὲ οἱ τῶν Σικυωνίων ἐξηγηταὶ συνίεσαν.

2.9.8 τούτου δέ εἰσιν εἰκόνες ἐφεξῆς χαλκαῖ· τὰς Προίτου θυγατέρας λέγουσιν εἶναι σφᾶς, τὸ δὲ ἐπίγραμμα ἐς γυναῖκας ἄλλας εἶχεν. ἐνταῦθα Ἡρακλῆς χαλκοῦς ἐστι· Λύσιππος ἐποίησεν αὐτὸν Σικυώνιος, καὶ πλησίον Ἑρμῆς ἕστηκεν Ἀγοραῖος.

2.10.1 ἐν δὲ τῷ γυμνασίῳ τῆς ἀγορᾶς ὄντι οὐ μακρὰν Ἡρακλῆς ἀνάκειται λίθου, Σκόπα ποίημα. ἔστι δὲ καὶ ἑτέρωθι ἱερὸν Ἡρακλέους· τὸν μὲν πάντα ἐνταῦθα περίβολον Παιδιζὴν ὀνομάζουσιν, ἐν μέσῳ δέ ἐστι τῷ περιβόλῳ τὸ ἱερόν, ἐν δὲ αὐτῷ ξόανον ἀρχαῖον, τέχνη Φλιασίου Λαφάους. ἐπὶ δὲ τῇ θυσίᾳ τοιάδε δρᾶν νομίζουσι. Φαῖστον ἐν Σικυωνίᾳ λέγουσιν ἐλθόντα καταλαβεῖν Ἡρακλεῖ σφᾶς ὡς ἥρωι ἐναγίζοντας· οὔκουν ἠξίου δρᾶν οὐδὲν ὁ Φαῖστος τῶν αὐτῶν, ἀλλ᾽ ὡς θεῷ θύειν. καὶ νῦν ἔτι ἄρνα οἱ Σικυώνιοι σφάξαντες καὶ τοὺς μηροὺς ἐπὶ τοῦ βωμοῦ καύσαντες τὰ μὲν ἐσθίουσιν ὡς ἀπὸ ἱερείου, τὰ δὲ ὡς ἥρωι τῶν κρεῶν ἐναγίζουσι. τῆς ἑορτῆς δέ, ἣν ἄγουσι τῷ Ἡρακλεῖ, τὴν προτέραν τῶν ἡμερῶν * * * {ὀνόματα} ὀνομάζοντες Ἡράκλεια δὴ καλοῦσι τὴν ὑστέραν.

2.10.2 ἐντεῦθέν ἐστιν ὁδὸς ἐς ἱερὸν Ἀσκληπιοῦ. παρελθοῦσι δὲ ἐς τὸν περίβολον ἐν ἀριστερᾷ διπλοῦν ἐστιν οἴκημα· κεῖται δὲ Ὕπνος ἐν τῷ προτέρῳ, καί οἱ πλὴν τῆς κεφαλῆς ἄλλο οὐδὲν ἔτι λείπεται. τὸ ἐνδοτέρω δὲ Ἀπόλλωνι ἀνεῖται Καρνείῳ, καὶ ἐς αὐτὸ οὐκ ἔστι πλὴν τοῖς ἱερεῦσιν ἔσοδος. κεῖται δὲ ἐν τῇ στοᾷ κήτους ὀστοῦν θαλασσίου μεγέθει μέγα καὶ μετ᾽ αὐτὸ ἄγαλμα Ὀνείρου καὶ Ὕπνος κατακοιμίζων λέοντα, Ἐπιδώτης δὲ ἐπίκλησιν. ἐς δὲ τὸ Ἀσκληπιεῖον ἐσιοῦσι καθ᾽ ἑκάτερον τῆς ἐσόδου τῇ μὲν Πανὸς καθήμενον ἄγαλμά ἐστι, τῇ δὲ Ἄρτεμις ἕστηκεν.

2.10.3 ἐσελθοῦσι δὲ ὁ θεός ἐστιν οὐκ ἔχων γένεια, χρυσοῦ καὶ ἐλέφαντος, Καλάμιδος δὲ ἔργον· ἔχει δὲ καὶ σκῆπτρον καὶ ἐπὶ τῆς ἑτέρας χειρὸς πίτυος καρπὸν τῆς ἡμέρου. φασὶ δέ σφισιν ἐξ Ἐπιδαύρου κομισθῆναι τὸν θεὸν ἐπὶ ζεύγους ἡμιόνων δράκοντι εἰκασμένον, τὴν δὲ ἀγαγοῦσαν Νικαγόραν εἶναι Σικυωνίαν Ἀγασικλέους μητέρα, γυναῖκα δὲ Ἐχετίμου. ἐνταῦθα ἀγάλματά ἐστιν οὐ μεγάλα ἀπηρτημένα τοῦ ὀρόφου· τὴν δὲ ἐπὶ τῷ δράκοντι Ἀριστοδάμαν Ἀράτου μητέρα εἶναι λέγουσι καὶ Ἄρατον Ἀσκληπιοῦ παῖδα εἶναι νομίζουσιν.

2.10.4 οὗτος μὲν δὴ παρείχετο ὁ περίβολος τοσάδε ἐς μνήμην, * * * δὲ αὐτοῦ {δὲ} ἄλλος ἐστὶν Ἀφροδίτης ἱερός· ἐν δὲ αὐτῷ πρῶτον ἄγαλμά ἐστιν Ἀντιόπης· εἶναι γάρ οἱ τοὺς παῖδας Σικυωνίους καὶ δι᾽ ἐκείνους ἐθέλουσι καὶ αὐτὴν Ἀντιόπην προσήκειν σφίσι. μετὰ τοῦτο ἤδη τὸ τῆς Ἀφροδίτης ἐστὶν ἱερόν. ἐσίασι μὲν δὴ ἐς αὐτὸ γυνή τε νεωκόρος, ᾗ μηκέτι θέμις παρ᾽ ἄνδρα φοιτῆσαι, καὶ παρθένος ἱερωσύνην ἐπέτειον ἔχουσα· λουτροφόρον τὴν παρθένον ὀνομάζουσι· τοῖς δὲ ἄλλοις κατὰ ταὐτὰ καὶ ὁρᾶν ἀπὸ τῆς ἐσόδου τὴν θεὸν καὶ αὐτόθεν προσεύχεσθαι.

2.10.5 τὸ μὲν δὴ ἄγαλμα καθήμενον Κάναχος Σικυώνιος ἐποίησεν, ὃς καὶ τὸν ἐν Διδύμοις τοῖς Μιλησίων καὶ Θηβαίοις τὸν Ἰσμήνιον εἰργάσατο Ἀπόλλωνα· πεποίηται δὲ ἔκ τε χρυσοῦ καὶ ἐλέφαντος, φέρουσα ἐπὶ τῇ κεφαλῇ πόλον, τῶν χειρῶν δὲ ἔχει τῇ μὲν μήκωνα τῇ δὲ ἑτέρᾳ μῆλον. τῶν δὲ ἱερείων τοὺς μηροὺς θύουσι {δὲ} πλὴν ὑῶν, τἆλλα δὲ ἀρκεύθου ξύλοις καθαγίζουσι, καιομένοις δὲ ὁμοῦ τοῖς μηροῖς φύλλον τοῦ παιδέρωτος συγκαθαγίζουσιν.

2.10.6 ἔνεστι δὲ ὁ παιδέρως ἐν ὑπαίθρῳ τοῦ περιβόλου πόα, φύεται δὲ ἀλλαχόθι οὐδαμοῦ γῆς, οὔτε ἄλλης οὔτε τῆς Σικυωνίας. τὰ δέ οἱ φύλλα ἐλάσσονα ἢ φηγοῦ, μείζονα δέ ἐστιν ἢ πρίνου, σχῆμα δέ σφισιν οἷον τοῖς τῆς δρυός· καὶ τὸ μὲν ὑπομελαίνει, τὸ δὲ ἕτερον λευκόν ἐστι· φύλλοις δ᾽ ἂν λεύκης μάλιστα εἰκάζοις τὴν χροιάν.

2.10.7 ἀπὸ τούτων δὲ ἀνιοῦσιν ἐς τὸ γυμνάσιον, ἔστιν ἐν δεξιᾷ Φεραίας ἱερὸν Ἀρτέμιδος· κομισθῆναι δὲ τὸ ξόανον λέγουσιν ἐκ Φερῶν. τὸ δέ σφισι γυμνάσιον τοῦτο Κλεινίας ᾠκοδόμησε, καὶ παιδεύουσιν ἐνταῦθα ἔτι τοὺς ἐφήβους. κεῖται δὲ λίθου λευκοῦ καὶ Ἄρτεμις τὰ ἐς ἰξὺν μόνον εἰργασμένη καὶ Ἡρακλῆς τὰ κάτω τοῖς Ἑρμαῖς τοῖς τετραγώνοις εἰκασμένος.

2.11.1 ἐντεῦθεν δὲ ἀποτραπεῖσιν ἐπὶ πύλην καλουμένην Ἱεράν, οὐ πόρρω τῆς πύλης ναός ἐστιν Ἀθηνᾶς, ὃν Ἐπωπεύς ποτε ἀνέθηκε μεγέθει καὶ κόσμῳ τοὺς τότε ὑπερβεβλημένον. ἔδει δὲ ἄρα χρόνῳ καὶ τοῦδε ἀφανισθῆναι τὴν μνήμην· κεραυνοῖς θεὸς αὐτὸν <κατέκαυσε>, βωμὸς δὲ ἐκεῖνος—οὐ γάρ τι ἐς αὐτὸν κατέσκηψε—μένει καὶ ἐς τόδε οἷον Ἐπωπεὺς ἐποίησε. πρὸ τοῦ βωμοῦ δὲ αὐτῷ μνῆμα Ἐπωπεῖ κέχωσται, καὶ τοῦ τάφου πλησίον εἰσὶν Ἀποτρόπαιοι θεοί· παρὰ τούτοις δρῶσιν ὅσα Ἕλληνες ἐς ἀποτροπὴν κακῶν νομίζουσιν. Ἐπωπέα δὲ καὶ Ἀρτέμιδι καὶ Ἀπόλλωνι τὸ πλησίον ἱερὸν ποιῆσαι λέγουσι, τὸ δὲ μετ᾽ αὐτὸ Ἥρας Ἄδραστον· ἀγάλματα δὲ ὑπελείπετο οὐδετέρῳ. βωμοὺς δὲ ὄπισθεν τοῦ Ἡραίου τὸν μὲν Πανὶ ᾠκοδόμησεν, Ἡλίῳ δὲ λίθου λευκοῦ.

2.11.2 καταβαίνουσι δὲ ὡς ἐπὶ τὸ πεδίον, ἱερόν ἐστιν ἐνταῦθα Δήμητρος· ἱδρῦσαι δέ φασιν αὐτὸ Πλημναῖον ἀποδιδόντα χάριν τῇ θεῷ τοῦ παιδὸς τῆς τροφῆς. τοῦ δὲ ἱεροῦ τῆς Ἥρας, ἣν ἱδρύσατο Ἄδραστος, ὀλίγον ἀπωτέρω

Καρνείου ναός ἐστιν Ἀπόλλωνος·· κίονες δὲ ἑστήκασιν ἐν αὐτῷ μόνοι, τοίχους δὲ οὐκέτι οὐδὲ ὄροφον οὔτε ἐνταῦθα εὑρήσεις οὔτε ἐν τῷ τῆς Προδρομίας Ἥρας. τοῦτον γὰρ δὴ Φάλκης ἱδρύσατο ὁ Τημένου, τῆς ὁδοῦ οἱ τῆς ἐς Σικυῶνα Ἥραν φάμενος ὁδηγὸν γενέσθαι.

2.11.3 ἐκ Σικυῶνος δὲ τὴν κατ᾽ εὐθὺ ἐς Φλιοῦντα ἐρχομένοις καὶ ἐν ἀριστερᾷ τῆς ὁδοῦ δέκα μάλιστα ἐκτραπεῖσι στάδια, Πυραία καλούμενόν ἐστιν ἄλσος, ἱερὸν δὲ ἐν αὐτῷ Προστασίας Δήμητρος καὶ Κόρης. ἐνταῦθα ἐφ᾽ αὑτῶν οἱ ἄνδρες ἑορτὴν ἄγουσι, τὸν δὲ Νυμφῶνα καλούμενον ταῖς γυναιξὶν ἑορτάζειν παρείκασι· καὶ ἀγάλματα Διονύσου καὶ Δήμητρος καὶ Κόρης τὰ πρόσωπα φαίνοντα ἐν τῷ Νυμφῶνί ἐστιν. ἡ δὲ ἐς Τιτάνην ὁδὸς σταδίων μέν ἐστιν ἑξήκοντα καὶ ζεύγεσιν ἄβατος διὰ στενότητα·

2.11.4 σταδίους <δὲ> προελθοῦσιν ἐμοὶ δοκεῖν εἴκοσι καὶ ἐν ἀριστερᾷ διαβᾶσι τὸν Ἀσωπόν, ἔστιν ἄλσος πρίνων καὶ ναὸς θεῶν ἃς Ἀθηναῖοι Σεμνάς, Σικυώνιοι δὲ Εὐμενίδας ὀνομάζουσι· κατὰ δὲ ἔτος ἕκαστον ἑορτὴν ἡμέρᾳ μιᾷ σφισιν ἄγουσι θύοντες πρόβατα ἐγκύμονα, μελικράτῳ δὲ σπονδῇ καὶ ἄνθεσιν ἀντὶ στεφάνων χρῆσθαι νομίζουσιν. ἐοικότα δὲ καὶ ἐπὶ τῷ βωμῷ τῶν Μοιρῶν δρῶσιν· ὁ δέ σφισιν ἐν ὑπαίθρῳ τοῦ ἄλσους ἐστίν.

2.11.5 ἀναστρέψασι δὲ ἐς τὴν ὁδὸν διαβᾶσί τε αὖθις τὸν Ἀσωπὸν καὶ ἐς κορυφὴν ὄρους ἥξασιν, ἐνταῦθα λέγουσιν οἱ ἐπιχώριοι Τιτᾶνα οἰκῆσαι πρῶτον· εἶναι δὲ αὐτὸν ἀδελφὸν Ἡλίου καὶ ἀπὸ τούτου κληθῆναι Τιτάνην τὸ χωρίον. δοκεῖν δὲ ἐμοὶ δεινὸς ἐγένετο ὁ Τιτὰν τὰς ὥρας τοῦ ἔτους φυλάξας καὶ ὁπότε ἥλιος σπέρματα καὶ δένδρων αὔξει καὶ πεπαίνει καρπούς, καὶ ἐπὶ τῷδε ἀδελφὸς ἐνομίσθη τοῦ Ἡλίου. ὕστερον δὲ Ἀλεξάνωρ ὁ {τοῦ} Μαχάονος τοῦ Ἀσκληπιοῦ παραγενόμενος ἐς Σικυωνίαν ἐν Τιτάνῃ τὸ Ἀσκληπιεῖον ἐποίησε.

2.11.6 περιοικοῦσι μὲν δὴ καὶ ἄλλοι καὶ τὸ πολὺ οἰκέται τοῦ θεοῦ, καὶ κυπαρίσσων ἐστὶν ἐντὸς τοῦ περιβόλου δένδρα ἀρχαῖα· τὸ δὲ ἄγαλμα οὔτε ὁποίου ξύλου γέγονεν ἢ μετάλλου μαθεῖν ἔστιν οὔτε τὸν ποιήσαντα ἴσασι, πλὴν εἰ μή τις ἄρα ἐς αὐτὸν τὸν Ἀλεξάνορα ἀναφέροι. φαίνεται δὲ τοῦ ἀγάλματος πρόσωπον μόνον καὶ ἄκραι χεῖρες καὶ πόδες· χιτὼν γάρ οἱ λευκὸς ἐρεοῦς καὶ ἱμάτιον ἐπιβέβληται. καὶ Ὑγείας δ᾽ ἔστι κατὰ ταὐτὸν ἄγαλμα. καὶ οὐκ ἂν οὐδὲ τοῦτο ἴδοις ῥᾳδίως, οὕτω περιέχουσιν αὐτὸ κόμαι τε γυναικῶν αἳ κείρονται τῇ θεῷ καὶ ἐσθῆτος Βαβυλωνίας τελαμῶνες. ᾧ δ᾽ ἂν ἐνταῦθα τούτων ἱλάσασθαι θελήσῃ τις, ἀποδέδεικταί οἱ τὸ αὐτὸ σέβεσθαι τοῦτο ὃ δὴ καὶ Ὑγείαν καλοῦσι.

2.11.7 τῷ δὲ Ἀλεξάνορι καὶ Εὐαμερίωνι—καὶ γὰρτού τοις ἀγάλματά ἐστι—τῷ μὲν ὡς ἥρωι μετὰ ἥλιον δύναντα ἐναγίζουσιν, Εὐαμερίωνι δὲ ὡς θεῷ θύουσιν.

εἰ δὲ ὀρθῶς εἰκάζω, τὸν Εὐαμερίωνα τοῦτον Περγαμηνοὶ Τελεσφόρον ἐκ μαντεύματος, Ἐπιδαύριοι δὲ Ἄκεσιν ὀνομάζουσι. τῆς δὲ Κορωνίδος ἔστι μὲν καὶ ταύτης ξόανον, καθίδρυται δὲ οὐδαμοῦ τοῦ ναοῦ· θυομένων δὲ τῷ θεῷ ταύρου καὶ ἀρνὸς καὶ ὑὸς ἐς Ἀθηνᾶς ἱερὸν τὴν Κορωνίδα μετενεγκόντες ἐνταῦθα τιμῶσιν. ὁπόσα δὲ τῶν θυομένων καθαγίζουσιν, οὐδὲ ἀποχρᾷ σφισιν ἐκτέμνειν τοὺς μηρούς· χαμαὶ δὲ καίουσι πλὴν τοὺς ὄρνιθας, τούτους δὲ ἐπὶ τοῦ βωμοῦ.

2.11.8 τὰ δὲ ἐν τοῖς ἀετοῖς Ἡρακλῆς καὶ Νῖκαι πρὸς τοῖς πέρασίν εἰσιν. ἀνάκειται δὲ ἀγάλματα ἐν τῇ στοᾷ Διονύσου καὶ Ἑκάτης, Ἀφροδίτη τε καὶ {δὴ} Μήτηρ θεῶνκαὶ Τύχη· ταῦτα μὲν ξόανα, λίθου δὲ Ἀσκληπιὸς ἐπίκλησιν Γορτύνιος. παρὰ δὲ τοὺς δράκοντας ἐσιέναι τοὺς ἱεροὺς οὐκ ἐθέλουσιν ὑπὸ δείματος· καταθέντες δέ σφισι πρὸ τῆς ἐσόδου τροφὴν <οὐκ>έτι πολυπραγμονοῦσι. κεῖται δὲ χαλκοῦς ἀνὴρ ἐντὸς τοῦ περιβόλου Γρανιανὸς Σικυώνιος, <ὃς> νίκας {ἃς} ἀνείλετο Ὀλυμπίασι δύο μὲν πεντάθλου καὶ σταδίου τὴν τρίτην, διαύλου δὲ ἀμφότερα καὶ γυμνὸς καὶ μετὰ τῆς ἀσπίδος.

2.12.1 ἐν δὲ Τιτάνῃ καὶ Ἀθηνᾶς ἱερόν ἐστιν, ἐς ὃ τὴν Κορωνίδα ἀνάγουσιν· ἐν δὲ αὐτῷ ξόανον Ἀθηνᾶς ἐστιν ἀρχαῖον, κεραυνωθῆναι δὲ καὶ τοῦτο ἐλέγετο· ἐκ τούτου τοῦ λόφου καταβᾶσιν—ᾠκοδόμηται γὰρ ἐπὶ λόφῳ τὸ ἱερὸν—βωμός ἐστιν ἀνέμων, ἐφ᾽ οὗ τοῖς ἀνέμοις ὁ ἱερεὺς μιᾷ νυκτὶ ἀνὰ πᾶν ἔτος θύει. δρᾷ δὲ καὶ ἄλλα ἀπόρρητα ἐς βόθρους τέσσαρας, ἡμερούμενος τῶν πνευμάτων τὸ ἄγριον, καὶ δὴ καὶ Μηδείας ὡς λέγουσιν ἐπῳδὰς ἐπᾴδει.

2.12.2 ἐκ δὲ Τιτάνης ἐς Σικυῶνα ἀφικομένοις καὶ καταβαίνουσιν ἐς θάλασσαν ἐν ἀριστερᾷ τῆς ὁδοῦ ναός <ἐστιν>Ἥρας οὐκ ἔχων ἔτι οὔτε ἄγαλμα οὔτε ὄροφον· τὸν δὲ ἀναθέντα Προῖτον εἶναι τὸν Ἄβαντός φασι. καταβᾶσι δὲ ἐς τὸν Σικυωνίων καλούμενον λιμένα καὶ τραπεῖσιν ἐπ᾽ Ἀριστοναύτας τὸ ἐπίνειον τὸ Πελληνέων, ἔστιν ὀλίγον ὑπὲρ τὴν ὁδὸν ἐν ἀριστερᾷ Ποσειδῶνος ἱερόν· προελθοῦσι δὲ κατὰ τὴν λεωφόρον Ἑλισσών τε καλούμενος ποταμὸς καὶ μετ᾽ αὐτὸν Σύθας ἐστίν, ἐκδιδόντες ἐς θάλασσαν.

2.12.3 ἡ δὲ Φλιασία τῆς Σικυωνίων ἐστὶν ὅμορος· καὶ Τιτάνης μὲν τεσσαράκοντα σταδίους ἀπέχει μάλιστα ἡ πόλις, ἐκ Σικυῶνος δὲ ἐς αὐτὴν ὁδός ἐστιν εὐθεῖα. καὶ ὅτι μὲν Ἀρκάσι Φλιάσιοι προσήκουσιν οὐδέν, δηλοῖ τὰ ἐς τὸν Ἀρκάδων κατάλογον τῆς Ὁμήρου ποιήσεως, ὅτι οὐκ εἰσὶν Ἀρκάσι καὶ οὗτοι συγκατειλεγμένοι· ὡς δὲ Ἀργεῖοί τε ἦσαν ἐξ ἀρχῆς καὶ ὕστερον Δωριεῖς γεγόνασιν Ἡρακλειδῶν κατελθόντων ἐς Πελοπόννησον, φανεῖται προϊόντι ὁμοῦ τῷ λόγῳ. διάφορα δὲ ἐς τοὺς Φλιασίους τὰ πολλὰ εἰδὼς εἰρημένα, τοῖς μάλιστα αὐτῶν ὡμολογημένοις χρήσομαι.

2.12.4 ἐν τῇ γῇ ταύτῃ γενέσθαι πρῶτον Ἄραντά φασιν ἄνδρα αὐτόχθονα· καὶ πόλιν τε ᾤκισε περὶ τὸν βουνὸν τοῦτον, ὃς Ἀραντῖνος ἔτι καλεῖται καὶ ἐς ἡμᾶς, οὐ πολὺ ἑτέρου λόφου διεστηκώς, ἐφ᾽ οὗ Φλιασίοις ἥ τε ἀκρόπολις καὶ τῆς Ἥβης ἐστὶ τὸ ἱερόν. ἐνταῦθά τε δὴ πόλιν ᾤκισε καὶ ἀπ᾽ αὐτοῦ τὸ ἀρχαῖον ἡ γῆ καὶ ἡ πόλις Ἀραντία ἐκλήθησαν. τούτῳ βασιλεύοντι Ἀσωπὸς Κηλούσης εἶναι λεγόμενος καὶ Ποσειδῶνος ἐξεῦρε τοῦ ποταμοῦ τὸ ὕδωρ, ὅντινα οἱ νῦν ἀπὸ τοῦ εὑρόντος καλοῦσιν Ἀσωπόν. τὸ δὲ μνῆμα τοῦ Ἄραντός ἐστιν ἐν χωρίῳ Κελεαῖς, ἔνθα δὴ καὶ Δυσαύλην ἄνδρα Ἐλευσίνιον τεθάφθαι λέγουσιν.

2.12.5 Ἄραντος δὲ υἱὸς Ἄορις καὶ θυγάτηρ ἐγένετο Ἀραιθυρέα. τούτους Φλιάσιοί φασι θήρας ἐμπείρους γενέσθαι καὶ τὰ ἐς πόλεμον ἀνδρείους. προαποθανούσης δὲ Ἀραιθυρέας Ἄορις ἐς μνήμην τῆς ἀδελφῆς μετωνόμασεν Ἀραιθυρέαν τὴν χώραν· καὶ ἐπὶ τῷδε Ὅμηρος τοὺς Ἀγαμέμνονος ὑπηκόους καταλέγων τὸ ἔπος ἐποίησεν·

> Ὀρνειάς τ᾽ ἐνέμοντο Ἀραιθυρέην τ᾽ ἐρατεινήν.

τάφους δὲ τῶν Ἄραντος παίδων οὐχ ἑτέρωθι ἡγοῦμαι τῆς χώρας, ἐπὶ τῷ λόφῳ δὲ εἶναι τῷ Ἀραντίνῳ· καί σφισιν ἐπίθημα στῆλαι περιφανεῖς εἰσι, καὶ πρὸ τῆς τελετῆς ἣν τῇ Δήμητρι ἄγουσιν Ἄραντα καὶ τοὺς παῖδας καλοῦσιν ἐπὶ τὰς σπονδὰς ἐς ταῦτα βλέποντες τὰ μνήματα.

2.12.6 Φλίαντα δέ, ὃς τρίτον τοῦτο ἐποίησεν ὄνομα ἀφ᾽ αὑτοῦ τῇ γῇ, Κείσου μὲν παῖδα εἶναι τοῦ Τημένου κατὰ δὴ τὸν Ἀργείων λόγον οὐδὲ ἀρχὴν ἔγωγε προσίεμαι, Διονύσου δὲ οἶδα καλούμενον καὶ τῶν πλευσάντων ἐπὶ τῆς Ἀργοῦς καὶ τοῦτον γενέσθαι λεγόμενον. ὁμολογεῖ δέ μοι καὶ τοῦ Ῥοδίου ποιητοῦ τὰ ἔπη·

> Φλίας αὖτ᾽ ἐπὶ τοῖσιν Ἀραιθυρέηθεν ἵκανεν,
> ἔνθ᾽ ἀφνειὸς ἔναιε Διωνύσοιο ἕκητι
> πατρὸς ἑοῦ, πηγῇσιν ἐφέστιος Ἀσωποῖο.

τοῦ δὲ Φλίαντος Ἀραιθυρέαν εἶναι μητέρα, ἀλλ᾽ οὐ Χθονοφύλην· <Χθονοφύλην> δέ οἱ συνοικῆσαι καὶ Ἀνδροδάμαν γενέσθαι Φλίαντι ἐξ αὐτῆς.

2.13.1 Ἡρακλειδῶν δὲ κατελθόντων Πελοπόννησος ἐταράχθη πᾶσα πλὴν Ἀρκάδων, ὡς πολλὰς μὲν τῶν πόλεων συνοίκους ἐκ τοῦ Δωρικοῦ προσλαβεῖν, πλείονας δὲ ἔτι γενέσθαι τὰς μεταβολὰς τοῖς οἰκήτορσι. τὰ δὲ κατὰ Φλιοῦντα οὕτως ἔχει. Ῥηγνίδας ἐπ᾽ αὐτὴν ὁ Φάλκου τοῦ Τημένου Δωριεὺς ἔκ τε Ἄργους στρατεύει καὶ ἐκ τῆς Σικυωνίας. τῶν δὲ Φλιασίων τοῖς μὲν ἃ προεκαλεῖτο

Ῥηγνίδας ἐφαίνετο ἀρεστά, μένοντας ἐπὶ τοῖς αὐτῶν βασιλέα Ῥηγνίδαν καὶ τοὺς σὺν ἐκείνῳ Δωριεῖς ἐπὶ ἀναδασμῷ γῆς δέχεσθαι.

2.13.2 Ἵππασος δὲ καὶ οἱ σὺν αὐτῷ διεκελεύοντο ἀμύνεσθαι μηδὲ πολλῶν καὶ ἀγαθῶν ἀμαχεὶ τοῖς Δωριεῦσιν ἀφίστασθαι. προσεμένου δὲ τοῦ δήμου τὴν ἐναντίαν ταύτῃ γνώμην, οὕτως Ἵππασος σὺν τοῖς ἐθέλουσιν ἐς Σάμον φεύγει. Ἱππάσου δὲ τούτου τέταρτος ἦν ἀπόγονος Πυθαγόρας ὁ λεγόμενος γενέσθαι σοφός· Μνησάρχου γὰρ Πυθαγόρας ἦν τοῦ Εὔφρονος τοῦ Ἱππάσου. ταῦτα μὲν Φλιάσιοι λέγουσι περὶ αὐτῶν, ὁμολογοῦσι δέ σφισι τὰ πολλὰ καὶ Σικυώνιοι.

2.13.3 προσέσται δὲ ἤδη καὶ τῶν ἐς ἐπίδειξιν ἡκόντων τὰ ἀξιολογώτατα. ἔστι γὰρ ἐν τῇ Φλιασίων ἀκροπόλει κυπαρίσσων ἄλσος καὶ ἱερὸν ἁγιώτατον ἐκ παλαιοῦ· τὴν δὲ θεὸν ἧς ἐστι τὸ ἱερὸν οἱ μὲν ἀρχαιότατοι Φλιασίων Γανυμήδαν, οἱ δὲ ὕστερον Ἥβην ὀνομάζουσιν· ἧς καὶ Ὅμηρος μνήμην ἐποιήσατο ἐν τῇ Μενελάου πρὸς Ἀλέξανδρον μονομαχίᾳ φάμενος οἰνοχόον τῶν θεῶν εἶναι, καὶ αὖθις <ἐν> Ὀδυσσέως ἐς Ἅιδου καθόδῳ γυναῖκα Ἡρακλέους εἶπεν εἶναι. Ὠλῆνι δὲ ἐν Ἥρας ἐστὶν ὕμνῳ πεποιημένα τραφῆναι τὴν Ἥραν ὑπὸ Ὡρῶν, εἶναι δέ οἱ παῖδας Ἄρην τε καὶ Ἥβην.

2.13.4 παρὰ δὲ Φλιασίοις τῇ θεῷ ταύτῃ καὶ ἄλλαι τιμαὶ καὶ μέγιστον τὸ ἐς τοὺς ἱκέτας ἐστί. δεδώκασι γὰρ δὴ ἄδειαν ἐνταῦθα ἱκετεύουσι, λυθέντες δὲ οἱ δεσμῶται τὰς πέδας πρὸς τὰ ἐν τῷ ἄλσει δένδρα ἀνατιθέασιν. ἄγεται δὲ καὶ ἑορτή σφισιν ἐπέτειος, ἣν καλοῦσι Κισσοτόμους. ἄγαλμα δὲ οὔτε ἐν ἀπορρήτῳ φυλάσσουσιν οὐδὲν οὔτε ἐστὶν ἐν φανερῷ δεικνύμενον—ἐφ᾽ ὅτῳ δὲ οὕτω νομίζουσιν, ἱερός ἐστιν αὐτοῖς λόγος—, ἐπεὶ τῆς γε Ἥρας ἐστὶν ἐξιόντων ἐν ἀριστερᾷ ναὸς ἄγαλμα ἔχων Παρίου λίθου.

2.13.5 ἐν δὲ τῇ ἀκροπόλει καὶ ἄλλος περίβολός ἐστιν ἱερὸς Δήμητρος, ἐν δὲ αὐτῷ ναός τε καὶ ἄγαλμα Δήμητρος καὶ τῆς παιδός· τὸ δὲ τῆς Ἀρτέμιδος—ἔστι γὰρ καὶ Ἀρτέμιδος ἐνταῦθα χαλκοῦν ἄγαλμα—{ὃ} ἐφαίνετο ἀρχαῖον εἶναί μοι. κατιόντων δὲ ἐκ τῆς ἀκροπόλεώς ἐστιν Ἀσκληπιοῦ ναὸς ἐν δεξιᾷ καὶ ἄγαλμα οὐκ ἔχον πω γένεια. ὑπὸ τοῦτον τὸν ναὸν θέατρον πεποίηται· τούτου δὲ οὐ πόρρω Δήμητρός ἐστιν ἱερὸν καὶ καθήμενα ἀγάλματα ἀρχαῖα.

2.13.6 ἀνάκειται δὲ ἐπὶ τῆς ἀγορᾶς αἶξ χαλκῆ, τὰ πολλὰ ἐπίχρυσος· παρὰ δὲ Φλιασίοις τιμὰς ἐπὶ τῷδε εἴληφε. τὸ ἄστρον ἣν ὀνομάζουσιν αἶγα ἀνατέλλουσα τὰς ἀμπέλους λυμαίνεται συνεχῶς· ἵνα δὲ ἄχαρι μηδὲν ἀπ᾽ αὐτῆς γένηται, οἱ δὲ τὴν ἐπὶ τῆς ἀγορᾶς χαλκῆν αἶγα ἄλλοις τε τιμῶσι καὶ χρυσῷ τὸ ἄγαλμα ἐπικοσμοῦντες. ἐνταῦθά ἐστι καὶ Ἀριστίου μνῆμα τοῦ

Πρατίνου· τούτῳ τῷ Ἀριστίᾳ σάτυροι καὶ Πρατίνᾳ τῷ πατρί εἰσι πεποιημένοι πλὴν τῶν Αἰσχύλου δοκιμώτατοι.

2.13.7 ὄπισθεν δὲ τῆς ἀγορᾶς ἐστιν οἶκος ὀνομαζόμενος ὑπὸ Φλιασίων μαντικός. ἐς τοῦτον Ἀμφιάραος ἐλθὼν καὶ τὴν νύκτα ἐγκατακοιμηθεὶς μαντεύεσθαι τότε πρῶτον, ὡς οἱ Φλιάσιοί φασιν, ἤρξατο· τέως δὲ ἦν Ἀμφιάραος τῷ ἐκείνων λόγῳ ἰδιώτης τε καὶ οὐ μάντις. καὶ τὸ οἴκημα ἀπὸ τούτου συγκέκλεισται τὸν πάντα ἤδη χρόνον. οὐ πόρρω δέ ἐστιν ὁ καλούμενος Ὀμφαλός, Πελοποννήσου δὲ πάσης μέσον, εἰ δὴ τὰ ὄντα εἰρήκασιν. ἀπὸ δὲ τοῦ Ὀμφαλοῦ προελθοῦσι Διονύσου σφίσιν ἱερόν ἐστιν ἀρχαῖον, ἔστι δὲ καὶ Ἀπόλλωνος καὶ ἄλλο Ἴσιδος. τὸ μὲν δὴ ἄγαλμα τοῦ Διονύσου δῆλον πᾶσιν, ὡσαύτως δὲ καὶ τὸ τοῦ Ἀπόλλωνος· τὸ δὲ τῆς Ἴσιδος τοῖς ἱερεῦσι θεάσασθαι μόνον ἔστι.

2.13.8 λέγεται δὲ καὶ ὧδε ὑπὸ Φλιασίων λόγος· Ἡρακλέα, ὅτ᾽ ἐκ Λιβύης ἀνεσώθη κομίζων τὰ μῆλα τὰ Ἑσπερίδων καλούμενα, ἐς Φλιοῦντα ἐλθεῖν κατὰ δή τι ἴδιον, διαιτωμένου δὲ ἐνταῦθα Οἰνέα ἐξ Αἰτωλίας ἀφικέσθαι παρ᾽ αὐτόν· ἐγεγόνει δὲ τῷ Ἡρακλεῖ πρότερον ἔτι κηδεστής, τότε δὲ ἀφιγμένος εἱστία τὸν Ἡρακλέα ἢ αὐτὸς εἱστιᾶτο ὑπὸ ἐκείνου. Κύαθον δ᾽ οὖν παῖδα οἰνοχόον Οἰνέως οὐκ ἀρεσθεὶς τῷ δοθέντι πώματι παίει τῶν δακτύλων ἑνὶ ἐς τὴν κεφαλήν· ἀποθανόντος δὲ αὐτίκα ὑπὸ τῆς πληγῆς Φλιασίοις ἐστὶν οἴκημα ἐς μνήμην. τοῦτο ᾠκοδόμηται μὲν παρὰ τὸ ἱερὸν τοῦ Ἀπόλλωνος, ἀγάλματα δὲ λίθου πεποιημένα ἔχει, κύλικα ὀρέγοντα Ἡρακλεῖ τὸν Κύαθον.

2.14.1 τῆς δὲ πόλεως αἱ Κελεαὶ πέντε που σταδίους μάλιστα ἀπέχουσι, καὶ τῇ Δήμητρι ἐνταῦθα δι᾽ ἐνιαυτοῦ τετάρτου τὴν τελετὴν καὶ οὐ κατὰ ἔτος ἄγουσιν. ἱεροφάντης δὲ οὐκ ἐς τὸν βίον πάντα ἀποδέδεικται, κατὰ δὲ ἑκάστην τελετὴν ἄλλοτέ ἐστιν ἄλλος σφίσιν αἱρετός, λαμβάνων ἢν ἐθέλῃ καὶ γυναῖκα. καὶ ταῦτα μὲν διάφορα τῶν Ἐλευσῖνι νομίζουσι, τὰ δὲ ἐς αὐτὴν τὴν τελετὴν ἐκείνων ἐστὶν μίμησις. ὁμολογοῦσι δὲ καὶ αὐτοὶ μιμεῖσθαι Φλιάσιοι τὰ ἐν Ἐλευσῖνι δρώμενα.

2.14.2 Δυσαύλην δέ φασιν ἀδελφὸν Κελεοῦ παραγενόμενόν σφισιν ἐς τὴν χώραν καταστήσασθαι τὴν τελετήν, ἐκβληθῆναι δὲ αὐτὸν ἐξ Ἐλευσῖνος ὑπὸ Ἴωνος, ὅτε Ἴων Ἀθηναίοις ὁ Ξούθου πολέμαρχος τοῦ πρὸς Ἐλευσινίους ᾑρέθη πολέμου. τοῦτο μὲν δὴ Φλιασίοις οὐκ ἔστιν ὅπως ὁμολογήσω, κρατηθέντα μάχῃ τινὰ Ἐλευσινίων φυγάδα ἀπελαθέντα οἴχεσθαι, τοῦ πολέμου τε ἐπὶ συνθήκαις καταλυθέντος πρὶν ἢ διαπολεμηθῆναι καὶ ἐν Ἐλευσῖνι αὐτοῦ καταμείναντος Εὐμόλπου.

2.14.3 δύναιτο δ᾽ ἂν κατὰ ἄλλην τινὰ ἐνταῦθα ὁ Δυσαύλης ἀφικέσθαι πρόφασιν καὶ οὐχ ὡς οἱ Φλιάσιοί φασιν. οὐ μὴν οὐδὲ Κελεῷ προσήκων ἐμοὶ δοκεῖν οὐδὲ ἄλλως ἦν ἐν τοῖς ἐπιφανέσιν Ἐλευσινίων· οὐ γὰρ ἄν ποτε Ὅμηρος παρῆκεν αὐτὸν ἐν τοῖς ἔπεσιν. ἔστι γὰρ καὶ Ὁμήρῳ πεποιημένα ἐς Δήμητραν· ἐν δὲ αὐτοῖς καταλέγων τοὺς διδαχθέντας ὑπὸ τῆς θεοῦ τὴν τελετὴν Δυσαύλην οὐδένα οἶδεν Ἐλευσίνιον. ἔχει δὲ οὕτω τὰ ἔπη·

δεῖξεν Τριπτολέμῳ τε Διοκλεῖ τε πληξίππῳ
Εὐμόλπου τε βίῃ Κελεῷ θ᾽ ἡγήτορι λαῶν
δρησμοσύνην ἱερῶν καὶ ἐπέφραδεν ὄργια πᾶσιν.

2.14.4 οὗτος δ᾽ οὖν, ὡς οἱ Φλιάσιοί φασιν, ὁ Δυσαύλης κατεστήσατο ἐνταῦθα τὴν τελετὴν καὶ οὗτος ἦν ὁ τῷ χωρίῳ τὸ ὄνομα παραθέμενος Κελεάς· Δυσαύλου τέ ἐστιν ἐνταῦθα, ὡς εἴρηταί μοι, μνῆμα. πρότερον δὲ ἄρα ἐπεποίητο <ὁ> Ἀράντειος τάφος· ὕστερον γὰρκατὰ τὸν Φλιασίων λόγον καὶ οὐκ ἐπὶ τῆς Ἄραντος βασιλείας ἀφίκετο ὁ Δυσαύλης. Φλιάσιοι γὰρ Προμηθεῖ γενέσθαι τῷ Ἰαπετοῦ κατὰ τὸν αὐτὸν χρόνον φασὶν Ἄραντα καὶ τρισὶν ἀνθρώπων γενεαῖς Πελασγοῦ τε εἶναι πρεσβύτερον τοῦ Ἀρκάδος καὶ τῶν λεγομένων Ἀθήνησιν αὐτοχθόνων. τοῦ δὲ Ἀνακτόρου καλουμένου πρὸς τῷ ὀρόφῳ Πέλοπος ἅρμα λέγουσιν ἀνακεῖσθαι.

2.15.1 Φλιασίοις μὲν δὴ τοσαῦτα λόγου μάλιστα ἦν ἄξια· ἐκ Κορίνθου δ᾽ ἐς Ἄργος ἐρχομένῳ Κλεωναὶ πόλις ἐστὶν οὐ μεγάλη· παῖδα δὲ εἶναι Πέλοπος Κλεώνην λέγουσιν, οἱ δὲ τῷ παρὰ Σικυῶνα ῥέοντι Ἀσωπῷ θυγατέρα ἐπὶ ταῖς ἄλλαις Κλεώνην γενέσθαι· τὸ δ᾽ οὖν ὄνομα ἀπὸ τοῦ ἑτέρου τούτων ἐτέθη τῇ πόλει. ἐνταῦθά ἐστιν ἱερὸν Ἀθηνᾶς, τὸ δὲ ἄγαλμα Σκύλλιδος τέχνη καὶ Διποίνου· μαθητὰς δὲ εἶναι Δαιδάλου σφᾶς, οἱ δὲ καὶ γυναῖκα <ἐκ> Γόρτυνος ἐθέλουσι λαβεῖν Δαίδαλον καὶ τὸν Δίποινον καὶ Σκύλλιν ἐκ τῆς γυναικός οἱ ταύτης γενέσθαι. ἐν Κλεωναῖς δὲ τοῦτό ἐστι τὸ ἱερὸν καὶ μνῆμα Εὐρύτου καὶ Κτεάτου· θεωροὺς γὰρ ἐξ Ἤλιδος ἐς τὸν ἀγῶνα ἰόντας τῶν Ἰσθμίων αὐτοὺς ἐνταῦθα Ἡρακλῆς κατετόξευσεν, ἔγκλημα ποιούμενος ὅτι οἱ πρὸς Αὐγείαν πολεμοῦντι ἀντετάχθησαν.

2.15.2 ἐκ Κλεωνῶν δέ εἰσιν ἐς Ἄργος ὁδοὶ δύο, ἡ μὲν ἀνδράσιν εὐζώνοις καὶ ἔστιν ἐπίτομος, ἡ δὲ ἐπὶ τοῦ καλουμένου Τρητοῦ, στενὴ μὲν καὶ αὐτὴ περιεχόντων ὀρῶν, ὀχήμασι δέ ἐστιν ὅμως ἐπιτηδειοτέρα. ἐν τούτοις τοῖς ὄρεσι τὸ σπήλαιον ἔτιδείκνυται τοῦ λέοντος, καὶ ἡ Νεμέα τὸ χωρίον ἀπέχει σταδίους πέντε που καὶ δέκα. ἐν δὲ αὐτῇ Νεμείου τε Διὸς ναός ἐστι θέας ἄξιος, πλὴν ὅσον κατερρυήκει τε ὁ ὄροφος καὶ ἄγαλμα οὐδὲν ἔτι ἐλείπετο·

κυπαρίσσων τε ἄλσος ἐστὶ περὶ τὸν ναόν, καὶ τὸν Ὀφέλτην ἐνταῦθα ὑπὸ τῆς τροφοῦ τεθέντα ἐς τὴν πόαν διαφθαρῆναι λέγουσιν ὑπὸ τοῦ δράκοντος.

2.15.3 θύουσι δὲ Ἀργεῖοι τῷ Διὶ καὶ ἐν τῇ Νεμέᾳ καὶ Νεμείου Διὸς ἱερέα αἱροῦνται, καὶ δὴ καὶ δρόμου προτιθέασιν ἀγῶνα ἀνδράσιν ὡπλισμένοις Νεμείων πανηγύρει τῶν χειμερινῶν. ἐνταῦθα ἔστι μὲν Ὀφέλτου τάφος, περὶ δὲ αὐτὸν θριγκὸς λίθων καὶ ἐντὸς τοῦ περιβόλου βωμοί· ἔστι δὲ χῶμα γῆς Λυκούργου μνῆμα τοῦ Ὀφέλτου πατρός. τὴν δὲ πηγὴν Ἀδράστειαν ὀνομάζουσιν εἴτε ἐπ᾽ ἄλλῃ τινὶ αἰτίᾳ εἴτε καὶ ἀνευρόντος αὐτὴν Ἀδράστου· τὸ δὲ ὄνομα λέγουσι τῇ χώρᾳ Νεμέαν δοῦναι θυγατέρα Ἀσωποῦ καὶ ταύτην. καὶ ὄρος Ἀπέσας ἐστὶν ὑπὲρ τὴν Νεμέαν, ἔνθα Περσέα πρῶτον Διὶ θῦσαι λέγουσιν Ἀπεσαντίῳ.

2.15.4 ἀνελθοῦσι δὲ ἐς τὸν Τρητὸν καὶ αὖθις τὴν ἐς Ἄργος ἰοῦσίν ἐστι Μυκηνῶν ἐρείπια ἐν ἀριστερᾷ. καὶ ὅτι μὲν Περσεὺς ἐγένετο Μυκηνῶν οἰκιστής, ἴσασιν Ἕλληνες· ἐγὼ δὲ αἰτίαν τε γράψω τοῦ οἰκισμοῦ καὶ δι᾽ ἥντινα πρόφασιν Ἀργεῖοι Μυκηναίους ὕστερον ἀνέστησαν. ἐν γὰρ τῇ νῦν Ἀργολίδι ὀνομαζομένῃ τὰ μὲν ἔτι παλαιότερα οὐ μνημονεύουσιν, Ἴναχον δὲ βασιλεύοντα τόν τε ποταμὸν ἀφ᾽ αὑτοῦ λέγουσιν ὀνομάσαι καὶ θῦσαι τῇ Ἥρᾳ.

2.15.5 λέγεται δὲ καὶ ὧδε λόγος· Φορωνέα ἐν τῇ γῇ ταύτῃ γενέσθαι πρῶτον, Ἴναχον δὲ οὐκ ἄνδρα ἀλλὰ τὸν ποταμὸν πατέρα εἶναι Φορωνεῖ· τοῦτον δὲ Ποσειδῶνι καὶ Ἥρᾳ δικάσαι περὶ τῆς χώρας, σὺν δὲ αὐτῷ Κηφισόν τε καὶ Ἀστερίωνα {καὶ τὸν Ἴναχον ποταμόν}· κρινάντων δὲ Ἥρας εἶναι τὴν γῆν, οὕτω σφίσιν ἀφανίσαι τὸ ὕδωρ Ποσειδῶνα. καὶ διὰ τοῦτο οὔτε Ἴναχος ὕδωρ οὔτε ἄλλος παρέχεται τῶν εἰρημένων ποταμῶν ὅτι μὴ ὕσαντος τοῦ θεοῦ· θέρους δὲ αὖά σφισίν ἐστι τὰ ῥεύματα πλὴν τῶν ἐν Λέρνῃ. Φορωνεὺς δὲ ὁ Ἰνάχου τοὺς ἀνθρώπους συνήγαγε πρῶτον ἐς κοινόν, σποράδας τέως καὶ ἐφ᾽ ἑαυτῶν ἑκάστοτε οἰκοῦντας· καὶ τὸ χωρίον ἐς ὃ πρῶτον ἠθροίσθησαν ἄστυ ὠνομάσθη Φορωνικόν.

2.16.1 Ἄργος δὲ Φορωνέως θυγατριδοῦς βασιλεύσας μετὰ Φορωνέα ὠνόμασεν ἀφ᾽ αὑτοῦ τὴν χώραν. Ἄργου δὲ Πείρασος γίνεται καὶ Φόρβας, Φόρβαντος δὲ Τριόπας, Τριόπα δὲ Ἴασος καὶ Ἀγήνωρ. Ἰὼ μὲν οὖν Ἰάσου θυγάτηρ, εἴτε ὡς Ἡρόδοτος ἔγραψεν εἴτε καθ᾽ ὃ λέγουσιν Ἕλληνες, ἐς Αἴγυπτον ἀφικνεῖται· Κρότωπος δὲ ὁ Ἀγήνορος ἔσχε μετὰ Ἴασον τὴν ἀρχήν, Κροτώπου δὲ Σθενέλας γίνεται, Δαναὸς δ᾽ ἀπ᾽ Αἰγύπτου πλεύσας ἐπὶ Γελάνορα τὸν Σθενέλα τοὺς ἀπογόνους τοὺς Ἀγήνορος βασιλείας ἔπαυσεν. τὰ δὲ ἀπὸ τούτου καὶ οἱ πάντες ὁμοίως ἴσασι, θυγατέρων τῶν Δαναοῦ τὸ ἐς τοὺς ἀνεψιοὺς τόλμημα καὶ ὡς ἀποθανόντος Δαναοῦ τὴν ἀρχὴν Λυγκεὺς ἔσχεν.

2.16.2 οἱ δὲ Ἄβαντος τοῦ Λυγκέως παῖδες τὴν βασιλείαν ἐνείμαντο, καὶ Ἀκρίσιος μὲν αὐτοῦ κατέμεινεν ἐν τῷ Ἄργει, Προῖτος δὲ τὸ Ἡραῖον καὶ Μιδείαν καὶ Τίρυνθα ἔσχε καὶ ὅσα πρὸς θαλάσσῃ τῆς Ἀργείας· σημεῖά τε τῆς ἐν Τίρυνθι οἰκήσεως Προίτου καὶ ἐς τόδε λείπεται. χρόνῳ δὲ ὕστερον Ἀκρίσιος Περσέα αὐτόν τε περιεῖναι πυνθανόμενος καὶ ἔργα ἀποδείκνυσθαι, ἐς Λάρισαν ἀπεχώρησε τὴν ἐπὶ τῷ Πηνειῷ. Περσεὺς δὲ—ἰδεῖν γὰρ πάντως ἤθελε τὸν γονέα τῆς μητρὸς καὶ λόγοις τε χρηστοῖς καὶ ἔργοις δεξιώσασθαι—ἔρχεται παρ' αὐτὸν ἐς τὴν Λάρισαν· καὶ ὁ μὲν οἷα ἡλικίᾳ τε ἀκμάζων καὶ τοῦ δίσκου χαίρων τῷ εὑρήματι ἐπεδείκνυτο ἐς ἅπαντας, Ἀκρίσιος δὲ λανθάνει κατὰ δαίμονα ὑποπεσὼν τοῦ δίσκου τῇ ὁρμῇ.

2.16.3 καὶ Ἀκρισίῳ μὲν ἡ πρόρρησις τοῦ θεοῦ τέλος ἔσχεν, οὐδὲ ἀπέτρεψέν οἱ τὸ χρεὼν τὰ ἐς τὴν παῖδα καὶ τὸν θυγατριδοῦν παρευρήματα· Περσεὺς δὲ ὡς ἀνέστρεψεν ἐς Ἄργος—ᾐσχύνετο γὰρ τοῦ φόνου τῇ φήμῃ—, Μεγαπένθην τὸν Προίτου πείθει οἱ τὴν ἀρχὴν ἀντιδοῦναι, παραλαβὼν δὲ αὐτὸς τὴν ἐκείνου Μυκήνας κτίζει. τοῦ ξίφους γὰρ ἐνταῦθα ἐξέπεσεν ὁ μύκης αὐτῷ, καὶ τὸ σημεῖον ἐς οἰκισμὸν ἐνόμιζε συμβῆναι πόλεως. ἤκουσα δὲ καὶ ὡς διψῶντι ἐπῆλθεν ἀνελέσθαι οἱ μύκητα ἐκ τῆς γῆς, ῥυέντος δὲ ὕδατος πιὼν καὶ ἡσθεὶς Μυκήνας ἔθετο τὸ ὄνομα τῷ χωρίῳ.

2.16.4 Ὅμηρος δὲ ἐν Ὀδυσσείᾳ γυναικὸς Μυκήνης ἐν ἔπει τῷδε ἐμνήσθη·

> Τυρώ τ' Ἀλκμήνη τε ἐυστέφανός τε Μυκήνη.

ταύτην εἶναι θυγατέρα Ἰνάχου γυναῖκα δὲ Ἀρέστορος τὰ ἔπη λέγει, ἃ δὴ Ἕλληνες καλοῦσιν Ἠοίας μεγάλας· ἀπὸ ταύτης οὖν γεγονέναι καὶ τὸ ὄνομα τῇ πόλει φασίν. ὃν δὲ προσποιοῦσιν Ἀκουσι<λάῳ> λόγον, Μυκηνέα υἱὸν εἶναι Σπάρτωνος, Σπάρτωνα δὲ Φορωνέως, οὐκ ἂν ἔγωγε ἀποδεξαίμην, διότι μηδὲ αὐτοὶ Λακεδαιμόνιοι. Λακεδαιμονίοις γὰρ Σπάρτης μὲν γυναικὸς εἰκών ἐστιν ἐν Ἀμύκλαις, Σπάρτωνα δὲ Φορωνέως παῖδα θαυμάζοιεν ἂν καὶ ἀρχὴν ἀκούσαντες.

2.16.5 Μυκήνας δὲ Ἀργεῖοι καθεῖλον ὑπὸ ζηλοτυπίας. ἡσυχαζόντων γὰρ τῶν Ἀργείων κατὰ τὴν ἐπιστρατείαν τοῦ Μήδου, Μυκηναῖοι πέμπουσιν ἐς Θερμοπύλας ὀγδοήκοντα ἄνδρας, οἳ Λακεδαιμονίοις μετέσχον τοῦ ἔργου· τοῦτο ἤνεγκέ σφισι ὄλεθρόν τὸ φιλοτίμημα παροξῦναν Ἀργείους. λείπεται δὲ ὅμως ἔτι καὶ ἄλλα τοῦ περιβόλου καὶ ἡ πύλη, λέοντες δὲ ἐφεστήκασιν αὐτῇ· Κυκλώπων δὲ καὶ ταῦτα ἔργα εἶναι λέγουσιν, οἳ Προίτῳ τὸ τεῖχος ἐποίησαν ἐν Τίρυνθι.

2.16.6 Μυκηνῶν δὲ ἐν τοῖς ἐρειπίοις κρήνη τέ ἐστι καλουμένη Περσεία καὶ Ἀτρέως καὶ τῶν παίδων ὑπόγαια οἰκοδομήματα, ἔνθα οἱ θησαυροί σφισι τῶν χρημάτων ἦσαν. τάφος δὲ ἔστι μὲν Ἀτρέως, εἰσὶ δὲ καὶ ὅσους σὺν Ἀγαμέμνονι ἐπανήκοντας ἐξ Ἰλίου δειπνίσας κατεφόνευσεν Αἴγισθος. τοῦ μὲν δὴ Κασσάνδρας μνήματος ἀμφισβητοῦσι Λακεδαιμονίων οἱ περὶ Ἀμύκλας οἰκοῦντες· ἕτερον δέ ἐστιν Ἀγαμέμνονος, τὸ δὲ Εὐρυμέδοντος τοῦ ἡνιόχου, καὶ Τελεδάμου τὸ αὐτὸ καὶ Πέλοπος—

2.16.7 τούτους γὰρ τεκεῖν διδύμους Κασσάνδραν φασί, νηπίους δὲ ἔτι ὄντας ἐπικατέσφαξε τοῖς γονεῦσιν Αἴγισθος—, <Ηλέκτρας δὲ οὔ>· Πυλάδῃ γὰρ συνῴκησεν Ὀρέστου δόντος· Ἑλλάνικος δὲ καὶ τάδε ἔγραψε, Μέδοντα καὶ Στρόφιον γενέσθαι Πυλάδῃ παῖδας ἐξ Ἠλέκτρας. Κλυταιμνήστρα δὲ ἐτάφη καὶ Αἴγισθος ὀλίγον ἀπωτέρω τοῦ τείχους· ἐντὸς δὲ ἀπηξιώθησαν, ἔνθα Ἀγαμέμνων τε αὐτὸς ἔκειτο καὶ οἱ σὺν ἐκείνῳ φονευθέντες.

2.17.1 Μυκηνῶν δὲ ἐν ἀριστερᾷ πέντε ἀπέχει καὶ δέκα στάδια τὸ Ἡραῖον. ῥεῖ δὲ κατὰ τὴν ὁδὸν ὕδωρ Ἐλευθέριον καλούμενον· χρῶνται δὲ αὐτῷ πρὸς καθάρσια αἱ περὶ τὸ ἱερὸν καὶ τῶν θυσιῶν ἐς τὰς ἀπορρήτους. αὐτὸ δὲ τὸ ἱερόν ἐστιν ἐν χθαμαλωτέρῳ τῆς Εὐβοίας· τὸ γὰρ δὴ ὄρος τοῦτο ὀνομάζουσιν Εὔβοιαν, λέγοντες Ἀστερίωνι γενέσθαι τῷ ποταμῷ θυγατέρας Εὔβοιαν καὶ Πρόσυμναν καὶ Ἀκραίαν, εἶναι δὲ σφᾶς τροφοὺς τῆς Ἥρας.

2.17.2 καὶ ἀπὸ μὲν Ἀκραίας τὸ ὄρος καλοῦσι τὸ ἀπαντικρὺ τοῦ Ἡραίου, ἀπὸ δὲ Εὐβοίας ὅσον περὶ τὸ ἱερόν, Πρόσυμναν δὲ τὴν ὑπὸ τὸ Ἡραῖον χώραν. ὁ δὲ Ἀστερίων οὗτος ῥέων ὑπὲρ τὸ Ἡραῖον ἐς φάραγγα ἐσπίπτων ἀφανίζεται. φύεται δὲ αὐτοῦ πόα πρὸς ταῖς ὄχθαις· ἀστερίωνα ὀνομάζουσι καὶ τὴν πόαν· ταύτην τῇ Ἥρᾳ καὶ αὐτὴν φέρουσι καὶ ἀπὸ τῶν φύλλων αὐτῆς στεφάνους πλέκουσιν.

2.17.3 ἀρχιτέκτονα μὲν δὴ γενέσθαι τοῦ ναοῦ λέγουσιν Εὐπόλεμον Ἀργεῖον· ὁπόσα δὲ ὑπὲρ τοὺς κίονάς ἐστιν εἰργασμένα, τὰ μὲν ἐς τὴν Διὸς γένεσιν καὶ θεῶν καὶ γιγάντων μάχην ἔχει, τὰ δὲ ἐς τὸν πρὸς Τροίαν πόλεμον καὶ Ἰλίου τὴν ἅλωσιν. ἀνδριάντες τε ἑστήκασι πρὸ τῆς ἐσόδου καὶ γυναικῶν, αἳ γεγόνασιν ἱέρειαι τῆς Ἥρας, καὶ ἡρώων ἄλλων τε καὶ Ὀρέστου· τὸν γὰρ ἐπίγραμμα ἔχοντα, ὡς εἴη βασιλεὺς Αὔγουστος, Ὀρέστην εἶναι λέγουσιν. ἐν δὲ τῷ προνάῳ τῇ μὲν Χάριτες ἀγάλματά ἐστιν ἀρχαῖα, ἐν δεξιᾷ δὲ κλίνη τῆς Ἥρας καὶ ἀνάθημα ἀσπὶς ἣν Μενέλαός ποτε ἀφείλετο Εὔφορβον ἐν Ἰλίῳ.

2.17.4 τὸ δὲ ἄγαλμα τῆς Ἥρας ἐπὶ θρόνου κάθηται μεγέθει μέγα, χρυσοῦ μὲν καὶ ἐλέφαντος, Πολυκλείτου δὲ ἔργον· ἔπεστι δέ οἱ στέφανος Χάριτας ἔχων καὶ Ὥρας ἐπειργασμένας, καὶ τῶν χειρῶν τῇ μὲν καρπὸν φέρει ῥοιᾶς, τῇ δὲ σκῆπτρον. τὰ μὲν οὖν ἐς τὴν ῥοιάν—ἀπορρητότερος γάρ ἐστιν ὁ λόγος—ἀφείσθω μοι· κόκκυγα δὲ ἐπὶ τῷ σκήπτρῳ καθῆσθαί φασι λέγοντες τὸν Δία, ὅτε ἤρα παρθένου τῆς Ἥρας, ἐς τοῦτον τὸν ὄρνιθα ἀλλαγῆναι, τὴν δὲ ἅτε παίγνιον θηρᾶσαι. τοῦτον τὸν λόγον καὶ ὅσα ἐοικότα εἴρηται περὶ θεῶν οὐκ ἀποδεχόμενος γράφω, γράφω δὲ οὐδὲν ἧσσον.

2.17.5 λέγεται δὲ παρεστηκέναι τῇ Ἥρᾳ τέχνη Ναυκύδους ἄγαλμα Ἥβης, ἐλέφαντος καὶ τοῦτο καὶ χρυσοῦ· παρὰ δὲ αὐτήν ἐστιν ἐπὶ κίονος ἄγαλμα Ἥρας ἀρχαῖον. τὸ δὲ ἀρχαιότατον πεποίηται μὲν ἐξ ἀχράδος, ἀνετέθη δὲ ἐς Τίρυνθα ὑπὸ Πειράσου τοῦ Ἄργου, Τίρυνθα δὲ ἀνελόντες Ἀργεῖοι κομίζουσιν ἐς τὸ Ἡραῖον· ὃ δὴ καὶ αὐτὸς εἶδον, καθήμενον ἄγαλμα οὐ μέγα.

2.17.6 ἀναθήματα δὲ τὰ ἄξια λόγου βωμὸς ἔχων ἐπειργασμένον τὸν λεγόμενον Ἥβης καὶ Ἡρακλέους γάμον· οὗτος μὲν ἀργύρου, χρυσοῦ δὲ καὶ λίθων λαμπόντων Ἀδριανὸς βασιλεὺς ταὼν <ἀνέθηκεν>· ἀνέθηκε δέ, ὅτι τὴν ὄρνιθα ἱερὰν τῆς Ἥρας νομίζουσι. κεῖται δὲ καὶ στέφανος χρυσοῦς καὶ πέπλος πορφύρας, Νέρωνος ταῦτα ἀναθήματα.

2.17.7 ἔστι δὲ ὑπὲρ τὸν ναὸν τοῦτον τοῦ προτέρου ναοῦ θεμέλιά τε καὶ εἰ δή τι ἄλλο ὑπελίπετο ἡ φλόξ. κατεκαύθη δὲ τὴν ἱέρειαν τῆς Ἥρας Χρυσίδα ὕπνου καταλαβόντος, ὅτε ὁ λύχνος πρὸ τῶν στεφανωμάτων ἥπτετο. καὶ Χρυσὶς μὲν ἀπελθοῦσα ἐς Τεγέαν τὴν Ἀθηνᾶν τὴν Ἀλέαν ἱκέτευεν· Ἀργεῖοι δὲ καίπερ κακοῦ τηλικούτου παρόντος σφίσι τὴν εἰκόνα οὐ καθεῖλον τῆς Χρυσίδος, ἀνάκειται δὲ καὶ ἐς τόδε τοῦ ναοῦ τοῦ κατακαυθέντος ἔμπροσθεν.

2.18.1 ἐκ Μυκηνῶν δὲ ἐς Ἄργος ἐρχομένοις ἐν ἀριστερᾷ Περσέως παρὰ τὴν ὁδόν ἐστιν ἡρῷον. ἔχει μὲν δὴ καὶ ἐνταῦθα τιμὰς παρὰ τῶν προσχωρίων, μεγίστας δὲ ἔν τε Σερίφῳ καὶ παρ' Ἀθηναίοις, οἷς Περσέως τέμενος καὶ Δίκτυος καὶ Κλυμένης βωμὸς σωτήρων καλουμένων Περσέως. ἐν δὲ τῇ Ἀργείᾳ προελθοῦσιν ὀλίγον ἀπὸ τοῦ ἡρῴου τούτου Θυέστου τάφος ἐστὶν ἐν δεξιᾷ· λίθου δὲ ἔπεστιν αὐτῷ κριός, ὅτι τὴν ἄρνα ὁ Θυέστης ἔσχε τὴν χρυσῆν, μοιχεύσας τοῦ ἀδελφοῦ τὴν γυναῖκα. Ἀτρέα δὲ οὐκ ἐπέσχεν ὁ λογισμὸς μετρῆσαι τὴν ἴσην, ἀλλὰ τῶν Θυέστου παίδων σφαγὰς καὶ τὰ ᾀδόμενα δεῖπνα ἐξειργάσατο.

2.18.2 ὕστερον δὲ οὐκ ἔχω σαφῶς εἰπεῖν πότερον ἀδικίας ἦρξεν Αἴγισθος ἢ προϋπῆρξεν Ἀγαμέμνονι φόνος Ταντάλου τοῦ Θυέστου· συνοικεῖν δέ φασιν αὐτὸν Κλυταιμνήστρᾳ παρθένῳ παρὰ Τυνδάρεω λαβόντα. ἐγὼ δὲ καταγνῶναι μὲν οὐκ ἐθέλω φύσει σφᾶς γενέσθαι κακούς· εἰ δὲ ἐπὶ τοσοῦτον αὐτοῖς τὸ μίασμα τὸ Πέλοπος καὶ ὁ Μυρτίλου προστρόπαιος ἠκολούθησε, τούτοις ἦν ἄρα ὁμολογοῦντα, ἡνίκα ἡ Πυθία Γλαύκῳ τῷ Ἐπικύδους Σπαρτιάτῃ, βουλεύσαντι ἐπίορκα ὀμόσαι, καὶ τοῦδε εἶπεν ἐς τοὺς ἀπογόνους κατιέναι τὴν δίκην.

2.18.3 ἀπὸ δὲ τῶν Κριῶν—οὕτω γὰρ τοῦ Θυέστου τὸ μνῆμα ὀνομάζουσι—προελθοῦσιν ὀλίγον ἐστὶν ἐν ἀριστερᾷ χωρίον Μυσία καὶ Δήμητρος Μυσίας ἱερὸν ἀπὸ ἀνδρὸς Μυσίου τὸ ὄνομα, γενομένου καὶ τούτου, καθάπερ λέγουσιν Ἀργεῖοι, ξένου τῇ Δήμητρι. τούτῳ μὲν οὖν οὐκ ἔπεστιν ὄροφος· ἐν δὲ αὐτῷ ναός ἐστιν ἄλλος ὀπτῆς πλίνθου, ξόανα δὲ Κόρης καὶ Πλούτωνος καὶ Δήμητρός ἐστι. προελθοῦσι δὲ ποταμός ἐστιν Ἴναχος, καὶ διαβᾶσιν Ἡλίου βωμός. ἐντεῦθεν δὲ ἐπὶ πύλην ἥξεις καλουμένην ἀπὸ τοῦ πλησίον ἱεροῦ· τὸ δὲ ἱερόν ἐστιν Εἰλειθυίας.

2.18.4 μόνους δὲ Ἑλλήνων οἶδα Ἀργείους ἐς τρεῖς βασιλείας νεμηθέντας. ἐπὶ γὰρ τῆς ἀρχῆς τῆς Ἀναξαγόρου τοῦ Ἀργείου τοῦ Μεγαπένθους μανία ταῖς γυναιξὶν ἐνέπεσεν, ἐκφοιτῶσαι δὲ ἐκ τῶν οἰκιῶν ἐπλανῶντο ἀνὰ τὴν χώραν, ἐς ὃ Μελάμπους ὁ Ἀμυθάονος ἔπαυσε σφᾶς τῆς νόσου, ἐφ᾽ ᾧ τε αὐτὸς καὶ ὁ ἀδελφὸς Βίας Ἀναξαγόρᾳ τὸ ἴσον ἕξουσιν. ἀπὸ μὲν δὴ Βίαντος βασιλεύουσι πέντε ἄνδρες ἐπὶ γενεὰς τέσσαρας ἐς Κυάνιππον τὸν Αἰγιαλέως, ὄντες Νηλεῖδαι τὰ πρὸς μητρός, ἀπὸ δὲ Μελάμποδος γενεαί τε ἓξ καὶ ἄνδρες ἴσοι μέχρις Ἀμφιλόχου τοῦ Ἀμφιαράου·

2.18.5 τὸ δὲ ἐγχώριον γένος οἱ Ἀναξαγορίδαι βασιλεύουσι πλέον. Ἶφις μὲν γὰρ ὁ Ἀλέκτορος τοῦ Ἀναξαγόρου Σθενέλῳ τῷ Καπανέως ἀδελφοῦ παιδὶ ἀπέλιπε τὴν ἀρχήν· Ἀμφιλόχου δὲ μετὰ ἅλωσιν Ἰλίου μετοικήσαντος ἐς τοὺς νῦν Ἀμφιλόχους, Κυανίππου <δ᾽> ἄπαιδος τελευτήσαντος, οὕτω Κυλαράβης ὁ Σθενέλου μόνος τὴν βασιλείαν ἔσχεν. οὐ μέντοι παῖδας κατέλιπεν οὐδ᾽ οὗτος, ἀλλὰ Ὀρέστης ὁ Ἀγαμέμνονος τὸ Ἄργος κατέσχε παροικῶν τε ἐγγὺς αὐτῷ καὶ ἄνευ τῆς πατρῴας ἀρχῆς προσπεποιημένος μὲν Ἀρκάδων τοὺς πολλούς, παρειληφὼς δὲ καὶ τὴν ἐν Σπάρτῃ βασιλείαν, συμμαχικοῦ δὲ ἐκ Φωκέων ἀεί ποτε ἐπ᾽ ὠφελείᾳ ἑτοίμου παρόντος.

2.18.6 Λακεδαιμονίων δὲ ἐβασίλευσεν Ὀρέστης Λακεδαιμονίων ἐφέντων αὐτῷ· τοὺς γὰρ Τυνδάρεω θυγατριδοῦς τὴν ἀρχὴν ἔχειν {οὐκ} ἠξίουν πρὸ Νικοστράτου καὶ Μεγαπένθους Μενελάῳ γεγενημένων ἐκ δούλης. Ὀρέστου δὲ ἀποθανόντος ἔσχε Τισαμενὸς τὴν ἀρχήν, Ἑρμιόνης τῆς Μενελάου καὶ Ὀρέστου παῖς. τὸν δὲ Ὀρέστου νόθον Πενθίλον Κιναίθων ἔγραψεν <ἐν> τοῖς ἔπεσιν Ἠριγόνην τὴν Αἰγίσθου τεκεῖν.

2.18.7 ἐπὶ δὲ τοῦ Τισαμενοῦ τούτου κατίασιν ἐς Πελοπόννησον Ἡρακλεῖδαι, Τήμενος μὲν καὶ Κρεσφόντης Ἀριστομάχου, τοῦ τρίτου δὲ Ἀριστοδήμου προτεθνεῶτος εἵποντο οἱ παῖδες. Ἄργους μὲν δὴ καὶ τῆς ἐν Ἄργει βασιλείας ὀρθότατα ἐμοὶ δοκεῖν ἠμφισβήτουν, ὅτι ἦν Πελοπίδης ὁ Τισαμενός, οἱ δὲ Ἡρακλεῖδαι τὸ ἀνέκαθέν εἰσι Περσεῖδαι· Τυνδάρεω δὲ καὶ αὐτὸν ἐκπεσόντα ἀπέφαινον ὑπὸ Ἱπποκόωντος, Ἡρακλέα δὲ ἔφασαν ἀποκτείναντα Ἱπποκόωντα καὶ τοὺς παῖδας παρακαταθέσθαι Τυνδάρεῳ τὴν χώραν· τοιαῦτα δὲ καὶ περὶ τῆς Μεσσηνίας ἕτερα ἔλεγον, παρακαταθήκην Νέστορι δοθῆναι καὶ ταύτην ὑπὸ Ἡρακλέους ἑλόντος Πύλον.

2.18.8 ἐκβάλλουσιν οὖν ἐκ μὲν Λακεδαίμονος καὶ Ἄργους Τισαμενόν, ἐκ δὲ τῆς Μεσσηνίας τοὺς Νέστορος ἀπογόνους, Ἀλκμαίωνα Σίλλου τοῦ Θρασυμήδους καὶ Πεισίστρατον τὸν Πεισιστράτου καὶ τοὺς Παίονος τοῦ Ἀντιλόχου παῖδας, σὺν δὲ αὐτοῖς Μέλανθον τὸν Ἀνδροπόμπου τοῦ Βώρου τοῦ Πενθίλου τοῦ Περικλυμένου. Τισαμενὸς μὲν οὖν ἦλθε σὺν τῇ στρατιᾷ καὶ οἱ παῖδες ἐς τὴν νῦν Ἀχαΐαν.

2.18.9 οἱ δὲ Νηλεῖδαι πλὴν Πεισιστράτου—τοῦτον γὰρ οὐκ οἶδα παρ᾽ οὕστινας ἀπεχώρησεν—ἐς Ἀθήνας ἀφίκοντο οἱ λοιποί, καὶ τὸ Παιονιδῶν γένος καὶ Ἀλκμαιωνιδῶν ἀπὸ τούτων ὠνομάσθησαν. Μέλανθος δὲ καὶ τὴν βασιλείαν ἔσχεν ἀφελόμενος Θυμοίτην τὸν Ὀξύντου· Θυμοίτης γὰρ Θησειδῶν ἔσχατος ἐβασίλευσεν Ἀθηναίων.

2.19.1 τὰ μὲν οὖν Κρεσφόντου καὶ τῶν Ἀριστοδήμου παίδων οὐκ ἤπειγεν ὁ λόγος με ἐνταῦθα δηλῶσαι· Τήμενος δὲ ἐκ μὲν τοῦ φανεροῦ Δηιφόντῃ τῷ Ἀντιμάχου τοῦ Θρασυάνορος τοῦ Κτησίππου τοῦ Ἡρακλέους στρατηγῷ πρὸς τὰς μάχας ἐχρήσατο ἀντὶ τῶν υἱῶν καὶ σύμβουλον ἐς πάντα εἶχεν, ἅτε αὐτόν τε ἐκεῖνον πεποιημένος πρότερον ἔτι γαμβρὸν καὶ τῶν παίδων ἀρεσκόμενος τῇ Ὑρνηθοῖ μάλιστα, ὑπωπτεύετο δὲ ἤδη καὶ τὴν βασιλείαν ἐς ἐκείνην καὶ Δηιφόντην τρέπειν. ἐπεβουλεύθη δὲ τούτων ἕνεκα ὑπὸ τῶν υἱῶν· ἐκείνων δὲ αὐτῷ Κεῖσος πρεσβύτατος ὢν ἔσχε τὴν ἀρχήν.

2.19.2 Ἀργεῖοι δέ, ἅτε ἰσηγορίαν καὶ τὸ αὐτόνομον ἀγαπῶντες ἐκ παλαιοτάτου, τὰ τῆς ἐξουσίας τῶν βασιλέων ἐς ἐλάχιστον προήγαγον, ὡς Μήδωνι τῷ Κείσου καὶ τοῖς ἀπογόνοις τὸ ὄνομα λειφθῆναι τῆς βασιλείας μόνον. Μέλταν δὲ τὸν Λακήδου δέκατον ἀπόγονον Μήδωνος τὸ παράπαν ἔπαυσεν ἀρχῆς καταγνοὺς ὁ δῆμος.

2.19.3 Ἀργείοις δὲ τῶν ἐν τῇ πόλει τὸ ἐπιφανέστατόν ἐστιν Ἀπόλλωνος ἱερὸν Λυκίου. τὸ μὲν οὖν ἄγαλμα τὸ ἐφ᾽ ἡμῶν Ἀττάλου ποίημα ἦν Ἀθηναίου, τὸ δὲ ἐξ ἀρχῆς Δαναοῦ καὶ ὁ ναὸς καὶ τὸ ξόανον ἀνάθημα ἦν· ξόανα γὰρ δὴ τότε εἶναι πείθομαι πάντα καὶ μάλιστα τὰ Αἰγύπτια. Δαναὸς δὲ ἱδρύσατο Λύκιον Ἀπόλλωνα ἐπ᾽ αἰτίᾳ τοιαύτῃ. παραγενόμενος ἐς τὸ Ἄργος ἠμφισβήτει πρὸς Γελάνορα τὸν Σθενέλα περὶ τῆς ἀρχῆς. ῥηθέντων δὲ ἐπὶ τοῦ δήμου παρ᾽ ἀμφοτέρων πολλῶν τε καὶ ἐπαγωγῶν καὶ οὐχ ἧσσον δίκαια λέγειν τοῦ Γελάνορος δόξαντος, ὁ μὲν δῆμος ὑπερέθετο, φασὶν, ἐς τὴν ἐπιοῦσαν κρίνειν.

2.19.4 ἀρχομένης δὲ ἡμέρας ἐς βοῶν ἀγέλην νεμομένην πρὸ τοῦ τείχους ἐσπίπτει λύκος, προσπεσὼν δὲ ἐμάχετο πρὸς ταῦρον ἡγεμόνα τῶν βοῶν. παρίσταται δὴ τοῖς Ἀργείοις τῷ μὲν Γελάνορα, Δαναὸν δὲ εἰκάσαι τῷ λύκῳ, ὅτι οὔτε τὸ θηρίον τοῦτό ἐστιν ἀνθρώποις σύντροφον οὔτε Δαναός σφισιν ἐς ἐκεῖνο τοῦ χρόνου. ἐπεὶ δὲ τὸν ταῦρον κατειργάσατο ὁ λύκος, διὰ τοῦτο ὁ Δαναὸς ἔσχε τὴν ἀρχήν. οὕτω δὴ νομίζων Ἀπόλλωνα ἐπὶ τὴν ἀγέλην ἐπαγαγεῖν τῶν βοῶν τὸν λύκον, ἱδρύσατο Ἀπόλλωνος ἱερὸν Λυκίου.

2.19.5 ἐνταῦθα ἀνάκειται μὲν θρόνος Δαναοῦ, κεῖται δὲ εἰκὼν Βίτωνος, ἀνὴρ ἐπὶ τῶν ὤμων φέρων ταῦρον· ὡς δὲ Λυκέας ἐποίησεν, ἐς Νεμέαν Ἀργείων ἀγόντων θυσίαν τῷ Διὶ ὁ Βίτων ὑπὸ ῥώμης τε καὶ ἰσχύος ταῦρον ἀράμενος ἤνεγκεν. ἑξῆς δὲ τῆς εἰκόνος ταύτης πῦρ καίουσιν ὀνομάζοντες Φορωνέως εἶναι· οὐ γάρ τι ὁμολογοῦσι δοῦναι πῦρ Προμηθέα ἀνθρώποις, ἀλλὰ ἐς Φορωνέα τοῦ πυρὸς μετάγειν ἐθέλουσι τὴν εὕρεσιν.

2.19.6 τὰ δὲ ξόανα Ἀφροδίτης καὶ Ἑρμοῦ, τὸ μὲν Ἐπειοῦ λέγουσιν ἔργον εἶναι, τὸ δὲ Ὑπερμήστρας ἀνάθημα. ταύτην γὰρ τῶν θυγατέρων μόνην τὸ πρόσταγμα ὑπεριδοῦσαν ὑπήγαγεν ὁ Δαναὸς ἐς δικαστήριον, τοῦ τε Λυγκέως οὐκ ἀκίνδυνον αὑτῷ τὴν σωτηρίαν ἡγούμενος καὶ ὅτι τοῦ τολμήματος οὐ μετασχοῦσα ταῖς ἀδελφαῖς καὶ τῷ βουλεύσαντι τὸ ὄνειδος ηὔξησε. κριθεῖσα δὲ ἐν τοῖς Ἀργείοις ἀποφεύγει τε καὶ Ἀφροδίτην ἐπὶ τῷδε ἀνέθηκε Νικηφόρον.

2.19.7 τοῦ ναοῦ δέ ἐστιν ἐντὸς Λάδας ποδῶν ὠκύτητι ὑπερβαλλόμενος τοὺς ἐφ᾽ αὑτοῦ καὶ Ἑρμῆς ἐς λύρας ποίησιν χελώνην ᾐρηκώς. ἔστι δὲ ἔμπροσθεν τοῦ ναοῦ βάθρον πεποιημένα ἐν τύπῳ ταύρου μάχην ἔχον καὶ λύκου, σὺν δὲ αὐτοῖς παρθένον ἀφιεῖσαν πέτραν ἐπὶ τὸν ταῦρον· Ἄρτεμιν δὲ εἶναι νομίζουσι τὴν παρθένον. Δαναὸς δὲ ταῦτά τε ἀνέθηκε καὶ πλησίον κίονας καὶ Διὸς καὶ Ἀρτέμιδος ξόανον.

2.19.8 τάφοι δέ εἰσιν ὁ μὲν Λίνου τοῦ Ἀπόλλωνος καὶ Ψαμάθης τῆς Κροτώπου, τὸν δὲ λέγουσιν εἶναι Λίνου τοῦ ποιήσαντος τὰ ἔπη. τὰ μὲν οὖν ἐς τοῦτον οἰκειότερα ὄντα ἑτέρῳ λόγῳ παρίημι <ἐν> τῷδε, τὰ δὲ ἐς τὸν Ψαμάθης ἡ Μεγαρική μοι συγγραφὴ προεδήλωσεν. ἐπὶ τούτοις ἐστὶν Ἀπόλλων Ἀγυιεὺς καὶ βωμὸς Ὑετίου Διός, ἔνθα οἱ συσπεύδοντες Πολυνείκει τὴν ἐς Θήβας κάθοδον ἀποθανεῖσθαι συνώμοσαν, ἢν μὴ τὰς Θήβας γένηταί σφισιν ἑλεῖν. ἐς δὲ τοῦ Προμηθέως τὸ μνῆμα ἧσσόν μοι δοκοῦσιν Ὀπουντίων εἰκότα λέγειν, λέγουσι δὲ ὅμως.

2.20.1 παρέντι δὲ Κρεύγα τε εἰκόνα ἀνδρὸς πύκτου <καὶ> τρόπαιον ἐπὶ Κορινθίοις ἀνασταθέν, ἄγαλμά ἐστι καθήμενον Διὸς Μειλιχίου, λίθου λευκοῦ, Πολυκλείτου δὲ ἔργον. ποιηθῆναι δὲ ἐπυνθανόμην αὐτὸ ἐπ' αἰτίᾳ τοιαύτῃ. Λακεδαιμονίοις πολεμεῖν πρὸς Ἀργείους ἀρξαμένοις οὐδεμία ἦν ἔτι ἀπαλλαγή, πρὶν ἢ Φίλιππος σφᾶς ἠνάγκασεν ὁ Ἀμύντου μένειν ἐπὶ τοῖς καθεστηκόσιν ἐξ ἀρχῆς ὅροις τῆς χώρας. τὸν δὲ ἔμπροσθεν χρόνον οἱ Λακεδαιμόνιοι μηδὲν ἔξω Πελοποννήσου περιεργαζόμενοι τῆς Ἀργείας ἀεί τι ἀπετέμνοντο, ἢ οἱ Ἀργεῖοι τετραμμένων πρὸς πόλεμον ἐκείνων ὑπερόριον ἐν τῷ τοιούτῳ καὶ αὐτοί σφισιν ἐνέκειντο.

2.20.2 προηγμένου δὲ ἀμφοτέροις ἐς ἄκρον τοῦ μίσους ἔδοξεν Ἀργείοις λογάδας τρέφειν χιλίους· ἡγεμὼν δὲ ἐτέτακτο ἐπ' αὐτοῖς Βρύας Ἀργεῖος, ὃς ἄλλα τε ἐς ἄνδρας ὕβρισε τοῦ δήμου καὶ παρθένον κομιζομένην παρὰ τὸν νυμφίον ᾔσχυνεν ἀφελόμενος τοὺς ἄγοντας. ἐπιλαβούσης δὲ τῆς νυκτὸς τυφλοῖ τὸν Βρύαντα ἡ παῖς φυλάξασα ὑπνωμένον· φωραθεῖσα δὲ ὡς ἐπέσχεν ἡμέρα, κατέφυγεν ἱκέτις ἐς τὸν δῆμον. οὐ προεμένων δὲ αὐτὴν τιμωρήσασθαι τοῖς χιλίοις καὶ ἀπὸ τούτου προαχθέντων ἐς μάχην ἀμφοτέρων, κρατοῦσιν οἱ τοῦ δήμου, κρατήσαντες δὲ οὐδένα ὑπὸ τοῦ θυμοῦ τῶν ἐναντίων ἔλιπον. ὕστερον δὲ ἄλλα τε ἐπηγάγοντο καθάρσια ὡς ἐπὶ αἵματι ἐμφυλίῳ καὶ ἄγαλμα ἀνέθηκαν Μειλιχίου Διός.

2.20.3 πλησίον δέ εἰσιν ἐπειργασμένοι λίθῳ Κλέοβις καὶ Βίτων αὐτοί τε ἕλκοντες τὴν ἅμαξαν καὶ ἐπ' αὐτῇ ἄγοντες τὴν μητέρα ἐς τὸ Ἡραῖον. τούτων δὲ ἀπαντικρὺ Νεμείου Διός ἐστιν ἱερόν, ἄγαλμα ὀρθὸν χαλκοῦν, τέχνη Λυσίππου. μετὰ δὲ αὐτὸ προελθοῦσιν ἐν δεξιᾷ Φορωνέως τάφος ἐστίν· ἐναγίζουσι δὲ καὶ ἐς ἡμᾶς ἔτι τῷ Φορωνεῖ. πέραν δὲ τοῦ Νεμείου Διὸς Τύχης ἐστὶν ἐκ παλαιοτάτου ναός, εἰ δὴ Παλαμήδης κύβους εὑρὼν ἀνέθηκεν ἐς τοῦτον τὸν ναόν.

2.20.4 τὸ δὲ μνῆμα τὸ πλησίον Χορείας μαινάδος ὀνομάζουσι, Διονύσῳ λέγοντες καὶ ἄλλας γυναῖκας καὶ ταύτην ἐς Ἄργος συστρατεύσασθαι, Περσέα δέ, ὡς ἐκράτει τῆς μάχης, φονεῦσαι τῶν γυναικῶν τὰς πολλάς· τὰς μὲν οὖν λοιπὰς θάπτουσιν ἐν κοινῷ, ταύτῃ δὲ—ἀξιώματι γὰρ δὴ προεῖχεν—ἰδίᾳ τὸ μνῆμα ἐποίησαν.

2.20.5 ἀπωτέρω δὲ ὀλίγον Ὡρῶν ἱερόν ἐστιν. ἐπανιόντι δὲ ἐκεῖθεν ἀνδριάντες ἑστήκασι Πολυνείκους τοῦ Οἰδίποδος καὶ ὅσοι σὺν ἐκείνῳ τῶν ἐν τέλει πρὸς τὸ τεῖχος μαχόμενοι τὸ Θηβαίων ἐτελεύτησαν. τούτους τοὺς ἄνδρας ἐς μόνων ἑπτὰ ἀριθμὸν κατήγαγεν Αἰσχύλος, πλειόνων ἔκ τε Ἄργους ἡγεμόνων καὶ Μεσσήνης καί τινων καὶ Ἀρκάδων στρατευσαμένων. τούτων δὲ τῶν ἑπτὰ—

ἐπηκολουθήκασι γὰρ καὶ Ἀργεῖοι τῇ Αἰσχύλου ποιήσει—πλησίον κεῖνται καὶ οἱ τὰς Θήβας ἑλόντες Αἰγιαλεὺς Ἀδράστου καὶ Πρόμαχος ὁ Παρθενοπαίου τοῦ Ταλαοῦ καὶ Πολύδωρος Ἱππομέδοντος καὶ Θέρσανδρος καὶ οἱ Ἀμφιαράου παῖδες, Ἀλκμαίων τε καὶ Ἀμφίλοχος, Διομήδης τε καὶ Σθένελος· παρῆν δὲ ἔτι καὶ ἐπὶ τούτων Εὐρύαλος Μηκιστέως καὶ Πολυνείκους Ἄδραστος καὶ Τιμέας.

2.20.6 τῶν δὲ ἀνδριάντων οὐ πόρρω δείκνυται Δαναοῦ μνῆμα καὶ Ἀργείων τάφος κενὸς ὁπόσους ἔν τε Ἰλίῳ καὶ ὀπίσω κομιζομένους ἐπέλαβεν ἡ τελευτή. καὶ Διός ἐστιν ἐνταῦθα ἱερὸν Σωτῆρος καὶ παριοῦσίν ἐστιν οἴκημα· ἐνταῦθα τὸν Ἄδωνιν αἱ γυναῖκες Ἀργείων ὀδύρονται. ἐν δεξιᾷ δὲ τῆς ἐσόδου τῷ Κηφισῷ πεποίηται τὸ ἱερόν· τῷ δὲ ποταμῷ τούτῳ τὸ ὕδωρ φασὶν οὐ καθάπαξ ὑπὸ τοῦ Ποσειδῶνος ἀφανισθῆναι, ἀλλὰ ἐνταῦθα δὴ μάλιστα, ἔνθα καὶ τὸ ἱερόν ἐστι, συνιᾶσιν ὑπὸ γῆν ῥέοντος.

2.20.7 παρὰ δὲ τὸ ἱερὸν τοῦ Κηφισοῦ Μεδούσης λίθου πεποιημένη κεφαλή· Κυκλώπων φασὶν εἶναι καὶ τοῦτο τὸ ἔργον. τὸ δὲ χωρίον τὸ ὄπισθεν καὶ ἐς τόδε Κριτήριον ὀνομάζουσιν, Ὑπερμήστραν ἐνταῦθα ὑπὸ Δαναοῦ κριθῆναι λέγοντες. τούτου δέ ἐστιν οὐ πόρρω θέατρον· ἐν δὲ αὐτῷ καὶ ἄλλα θέας ἄξια καὶ ἀνὴρ φονεύων ἐστὶν ἄνδρα, Ὀθρυάδαν τὸν Σπαρτιάτην Περίλαος Ἀργεῖος ὁ Ἀλκήνορος· Περιλάῳ δὲ τούτῳ καὶ πρότερον ἔτι ὑπῆρχε Νεμείων ἀνῃρῆσθαι νίκην παλαίοντι.

2.20.8 ὑπὲρ δὲ τὸ θέατρον Ἀφροδίτης ἐστὶν ἱερόν, ἔμπροσθεν δὲ τοῦ ἕδους Τελέσιλλα ἡ ποιήσασα τὰ ᾄσματα ἐπείργασται στήλῃ· καὶ βιβλία μὲν ἐκεῖνα ἔρριπταί οἱ πρὸς τοῖς ποσίν, αὐτὴ δὲ ἐς κράνος ὁρᾷ κατέχουσα τῇ χειρὶ καὶ ἐπιτίθεσθαι τῇ κεφαλῇ μέλλουσα. ἦν δὲ ἡ Τελέσιλλα καὶ ἄλλως ἐν ταῖς γυναιξὶν εὐδόκιμος καὶ μᾶλλον ἐτιμᾶτο ἔτι ἐπὶ τῇ ποιήσει. συμβάντος δὲ Ἀργείοις ἀτυχῆσαι λόγου μειζόνως πρὸς Κλεομένην τὸν Ἀναξανδρίδου καὶ Λακεδαιμονίους, καὶ τῶν μὲν ἐν αὐτῇ πεπτωκότων τῇ μάχῃ, ὅσοι δὲ ἐς τὸ ἄλσος τοῦ Ἄργου κατέφευγον διαφθαρέντων καὶ τούτων, τὰ μὲν πρῶτα ἐξιόντων κατὰ ὁμολογίαν, ὡς δὲ ἔγνωσαν ἀπατώμενοι συγκατακαυθέντων τῷ ἄλσει τῶν λοιπῶν, οὕτω τοὺς Λακεδαιμονίους Κλεομένης ἦγεν ἐπὶ ἔρημον ἀνδρῶν τὸ Ἄργος.

2.20.9 Τελέσιλλα δὲ οἰκέτας μὲν καὶ ὅσοι διὰ νεότητα ἢ γῆρας ὅπλα ἀδύνατοι φέρειν ἦσαν, τούτους μὲν πάντας ἀνεβίβασεν ἐπὶ τὸ τεῖχος, αὐτὴ δὲ ὁπόσα ἐν ταῖς οἰκίαις ὑπελείπετο καὶ τὰ ἐκ τῶν ἱερῶν ὅπλα ἀθροίσασα τὰς ἀκμαζούσας ἡλικίᾳ τῶν γυναικῶν ὥπλιζεν, ὁπλίσασα δὲ ἔτασσε κατὰ τοῦτο ᾗ τοὺς πολεμίους προσιόντας ἠπίστατο. ὡς δὲ <ἐγγὺς> ἐγίνοντο οἱ Λακεδαιμόνιοι καὶ αἱ γυναῖκες οὔτε τῷ ἀλαλαγμῷ κατεπλάγησαν δεξάμεναί τε ἐμάχοντο ἐρρωμένως, ἐνταῦθα οἱ Λακεδαιμόνιοι, φρονήσαντες ὡς καὶ διαφθείρασί σφισι τὰς γυναῖκας ἐπιφθόνως τὸ κατόρθωμα ἕξει καὶ σφαλεῖσι μετὰ ὀνειδῶν γενήσοιτο ἡ συμφορά, ὑπείκουσι ταῖς γυναιξί.

2.20.10 πρότερον δὲ ἔτι τὸν ἀγῶνα τοῦτον προεσήμηνεν ἡ Πυθία, καὶ τὸ λόγιον εἴτε ἄλλως εἴτε καὶ ὡς συνεὶς ἐδήλωσεν Ἡρόδοτος·

> ἀλλ᾽ ὅταν ἡ θήλεια τὸν ἄρρενα νικήσασα
> ἐξελάσῃ καὶ κῦδος ἐν Ἀργείοισιν ἄρηται,
> πολλὰς Ἀργείων ἀμφιδρυφέας τότε θήσει.

τὰ μὲν ἐς τὸ ἔργον τῶν γυναικῶν ἔχοντα τοῦ χρησμοῦ ταῦτα ἦν.

2.21.1 κατελθοῦσι δὲ ἐντεῦθεν καὶ τραπεῖσιν αὖθις ἐπὶ τὴν ἀγοράν, ἔστι μὲν Κερδοῦς Φορωνέως γυναικὸς μνῆμα, ἔστι δὲ ναὸς Ἀσκληπιοῦ. τὸ δὲ τῆς Ἀρτέμιδος ἱερὸν ἐπίκλησιν Πειθοῦς, Ὑπερμήστρα καὶ τοῦτο ἀνέθηκε νικήσασα τῇ δίκῃ τὸν πατέρα ἣν τοῦ Λυγκέως ἕνεκα ἔφυγε. καὶ Αἰνείου ἐνταῦθα χαλκοῦς ἀνδριάς ἐστι καὶ χωρίον καλούμενον Δέλτα· ἐφ᾽ ὅτῳ δέ—οὐ γάρ μοι τὰ λεγόμενα ἤρεσκεν— ἑκὼν παρίημι.

2.21.2 πρὸ δὲ αὐτοῦ πεποίηται Διὸς Φυξίου βωμὸς καὶ πλησίον Ὑπερμήστρας μνῆμα Ἀμφιαράου μητρός, τὸ δὲ ἕτερον Ὑπερμήστρας τῆς Λαναοῦ· σὺν δὲ αὐτῇ καὶ Λυγκεὺς τέθαπται. τούτων δὲ ἀπαντικρὺ Ταλαοῦ τοῦ Βίαντός ἐστι τάφος· τὰ δὲ ἐς Βίαντα καὶ ἀπογόνους τοῦ Βίαντος ἤδη λέλεκταί μοι.

2.21.3 Ἀθηνᾶς δὲ ἱδρύσασθαι Σάλπιγγος ἱερόν φασιν Ἡγέλεων. Τυρσηνοῦ δὲ τοῦτον <τὸν> Ἡγέλεων, τὸν δὲ Ἡρακλέους εἶναι καὶ γυναικὸς λέγουσι τῆς Λυδῆς, Τυρσηνὸν δὲ σάλπιγγα εὑρεῖν πρῶτον, Ἡγέλεων δὲ τὸν Τυρσηνοῦ διδάξαι τοὺς σὺν Τημένῳ Δωριέας τοῦ ὀργάνου τὸν ψόφον καὶ δι᾽ αὐτὸ Ἀθηνᾶν ἐπονομάσαι Σάλπιγγα. πρὸ δὲ τοῦ ναοῦ τῆς Ἀθηνᾶς Ἐπιμενίδου λέγουσιν εἶναι τάφον. Λακεδαιμονίους γὰρ πολεμήσαντας πρὸς Κνωσσίους ἑλεῖν ζῶντα Ἐπιμενίδην, λαβόντας δὲ ἀποκτεῖναι, διότι σφίσιν οὐκ αἴσια ἐμαντεύετο, αὐτοὶ δὲ ἀνελόμενοι θάψαι ταύτῃ φασί.

2.21.4 τὸ δὲ οἰκοδόμημα λευκοῦ λίθου κατὰ μέσον μάλιστα τῆς ἀγορᾶς οὐ τρόπαιον ἐπὶ Πύρρῳ τῷ Ἠπειρώτῃ, καθὰ λέγουσιν οἱ Ἀργεῖοι, καυθέντος δὲ ἐνταῦθα τοῦ νεκροῦ μνῆμα καὶ τοῦτο ἂν εὕροι τις, ἐν ᾧ τά τε ἄλλα ὅσοις ὁ Πύρρος ἐχρῆτο ἐς τὰς μάχας καὶ οἱ ἐλέφαντές εἰσιν ἐπειργασμένοι. τοῦτο μὲν δὴ κατὰ τὴν πυρὰν <τὸ> οἰκοδόμημα ἐγένετο· αὐτὰ δὲ κεῖται τοῦ Πύρρου τὰ ὀστᾶ ἐν τῷ ἱερῷ τῆς Δήμητρος, παρ᾽ ᾧ συμβῆναί οἱ καὶ τὴν τελευτὴν ἐδήλωσα ἐν τῇ Ἀτθίδι συγγραφῇ. τοῦ δὲ τῆς Δήμητρος ἱεροῦ τούτου κατὰ τὴν ἔσοδον ἀσπίδα ἰδεῖν Πύρρου χαλκῆν ἔστιν ὑπὲρ τῶν θυρῶν ἀνακειμένην.

2.21.5 τοῦ δὲ ἐν τῇ ἀγορᾷ τῶν Ἀργείων οἰκοδομήματος οὐ μακρὰν χῶμα γῆς ἐστιν· ἐν δὲ αὐτῷ κεῖσθαι τὴν Μεδούσης λέγουσι τῆς Γοργόνος κεφαλήν. ἀπόντος δὲ τοῦ μύθου τάδε ἄλλα ἐς αὐτήν ἐστιν εἰρημένα· Φόρκου μὲν θυγατέρα εἶναι, τελευτήσαντος δέ οἱ τοῦ πατρὸς βασιλεύειν τῶν περὶ τὴν λίμνην τὴν Τριτωνίδα οἰκούντων καὶ ἐπὶ θήραν τε ἐξιέναι καὶ ἐς τὰς μάχας ἡγεῖσθαι τοῖς Λίβυσι καὶ δὴ καὶ τότε ἀντικαθημένην στρατῷ πρὸς τὴν Περσέως δύναμιν—ἕπεσθαι γὰρ καὶ τῷ Περσεῖ λογάδας ἐκ Πελοποννήσου—δολοφονηθῆναι νύκτωρ, καὶ τὸν Περσέα τὸ κάλλος ἔτι καὶ ἐπὶ νεκρῷ θαυμάζοντα οὕτω τὴν κεφαλὴν ἀποτεμόντα αὐτῆς ἄγειν τοῖς Ἕλλησιν ἐς ἐπίδειξιν.

2.21.6 Καρχηδονίῳ δὲ ἀνδρὶ Προκλεῖ τῷ Εὐκράτους ἕτερος λόγος ὅδε ἐφαίνετο εἶναι τοῦ προτέρου πιθανώτερος. Λιβύης ἡ ἔρημος καὶ ἄλλα παρέχεται θηρία ἀκούσασιν οὐ πιστὰ καὶ ἄνδρες ἐνταῦθα ἄγριοι καὶ ἄγριαι γίνονται γυναῖκες· ἔλεγέ τε ὁ Προκλῆς ἀπ᾽ αὐτῶν ἄνδρα ἰδεῖν κομισθέντα ἐς Ῥώμην. εἴκαζεν οὖν πλανηθεῖσαν γυναῖκα ἐκ τούτων καὶ ἀφικομένην ἐπὶ τὴν λίμνην τὴν Τριτωνίδα λυμαίνεσθαι τοὺς προσοίκους, ἐς ὃ Περσεὺς ἀπέκτεινεν αὐτήν· Ἀθηνᾶν δέ οἱ συνεπιλαβέσθαι δοκεῖν τοῦ ἔργου, ὅτι οἱ περὶ τὴν λίμνην τὴν Τριτωνίδα ἄνθρωποι ταύτης εἰσὶν ἱεροί.

2.21.7 ἐν δὲ Ἄργει παρὰ τοῦτο δὴ τὸ μνῆμα τῆς Γοργόνος Γοργοφόνης τάφος ἐστὶ τῆς Περσέως. καὶ ἐφ᾽ ὅτῳ μὲν αὐτῇ τὸ ὄνομα ἐτέθη, δῆλον εὐθὺς ἀκούσαντι· γυναικῶν δὲ πρώτην αὐτήν φασι τελευτήσαντος τοῦ ἀνδρὸς Περιήρους τοῦ Αἰόλου—τούτῳ γὰρ παρθένος συνῴκησε—, τὴν δὲ αὖθις Οἰβάλῳ γήμασθαι· πρότερον δὲ καθεστήκει ταῖς γυναιξὶν ἐπὶ ἀνδρὶ ἀποθανόντι χηρεύειν.

2.21.8 τοῦ τάφου δὲ ἔμπροσθεν τρόπαιον λίθου πεποίηται κατὰ ἀνδρὸς Ἀργείου Λαφάους· τοῦτον γὰρ—γράφω δὲ ὁπόσα λέγουσιν αὐτοὶ περὶ σφῶν Ἀργεῖοι—τυραννοῦντα ἐξέβαλεν ἐπαναστὰς ὁ δῆμος, φυγόντα δὲ ἐς Σπάρτην Λακεδαιμόνιοι κατάγειν ἐπειρῶντο ἐπὶ τυραννίδι, νικήσαντες δὲ οἱ Ἀργεῖοι τῇ μάχῃ Λαφάην τε καὶ τῶν Λακεδαιμονίων τοὺς πολλοὺς ἀπέκτειναν. τὸ δὲ ἱερὸν τῆς Λητοῦς ἔστι μὲν οὐ μακρὰν τοῦ τροπαίου, τέχνη δὲ τὸ ἄγαλμα Πραξιτέλους.

2.21.9 τὴν δὲ εἰκόνα παρὰ τῇ θεῷ τῆς παρθένου Χλῶριν ὀνομάζουσι, Νιόβης μὲν θυγατέρα εἶναι λέγοντες, Μελίβοιαν δὲ καλεῖσθαι τὸ ἐξ ἀρχῆς· ἀπολλυμένων δὲ ὑπὸ Ἀρτέμιδος καὶ Ἀπόλλωνος τῶν Ἀμφίονος παίδων περιγενέσθαι μόνην τῶν ἀδελφῶν ταύτην καὶ Ἀμύκλαν, περιγενέσθαι δὲ εὐξαμένους τῇ Λητοῖ. Μελίβοιαν δὲ οὕτω δή τι παραυτίκα τε χλωρὰν τὸ δεῖμα ἐποίησε καὶ ἐς τὸ λοιπὸν τοῦ βίου παρέμεινεν ὡς καὶ τὸ ὄνομα ἐπὶ τῷ συμβάντι ἀντὶ Μελιβοίας αὐτῇ γενέσθαι Χλῶριν.

2.21.10 τούτους δή φασιν Ἀργεῖοι τὸ ἐξ ἀρχῆς οἰκοδομῆσαι τῇ Λητοῖ τὸν ναόν· ἐγὼ δὲ—πρόσκειμαι γὰρ πλέον τι {ἢ οἱ λοιποὶ} τῇ Ὁμήρου ποιήσει—δοκῶ τῇ Νιόβῃ τῶν παίδων μηδένα ὑπόλοιπον γενέσθαι. μαρτυρεῖ δέ μοι τὸ ἔπος·

τὼ δ᾽ ἄρα καὶ δοιώ περ ἐόντ᾽ ἀπὸ πάντας ὄλεσσαν.

οὗτος μὲν δὴ τὸν οἶκον τὸν Ἀμφίονος ἐκ βάθρων ἀνατραπέντα οἶδε.

2.22.1 τῆς δὲ Ἥρας ὁ ναὸς τῆς Ἀνθείας ἐστὶ τοῦ ἱεροῦ τῆς Λητοῦς ἐν δεξιᾷ καὶ πρὸ αὐτοῦ γυναικῶν τάφος. ἀπέθανον δὲ αἱ γυναῖκες ἐν μάχῃ πρὸς Ἀργείους τε καὶ Περσέα, ἀπὸ νήσων τῶν ἐν Αἰγαίῳ Διονύσῳ συνεστρατευμέναι· καὶ διὰ τοῦτο Ἁλίας αὐτὰς ἐπονομάζουσιν. ἀντικρὺ δὲ τοῦ μνήματος τῶν γυναικῶν Δήμητρός ἐστιν ἱερὸν ἐπίκλησιν Πελασγίδος ἀπὸ τοῦ ἱδρυσαμένου Πελασγοῦ τοῦ Τριόπα, καὶ οὐ πόρρω τοῦ ἱεροῦ τάφος Πελασγοῦ.

2.22.2 πέραν δὲ τοῦ τάφου χαλκεῖόν ἐστιν οὐ μέγα, ἀνέχει δὲ αὐτὸ ἀγάλματα ἀρχαῖα Ἀρτέμιδος καὶ Διὸς καὶ Ἀθηνᾶς. Λυκέας μὲν οὖν ἐν τοῖς ἔπεσιν ἐποίησε Μηχανέως τὸ ἄγαλμα εἶναι Διός, καὶ Ἀργείων ἔφη τοὺς ἐπὶ Ἴλιον στρατεύσαντας ἐνταῦθα ὀμόσαι παραμενεῖν πολεμοῦντας, ἔστ᾽ ἂν ἢ τὸ Ἴλιον ἕλωσιν ἢ μαχομένους τελευτὴ σφᾶς ἐπιλάβῃ· ἑτέροις δέ ἐστιν εἰρημένον ὀστᾶ ἐν τῷ χαλκείῳ κεῖσθαι Ταντάλου.

2.22.3 τὸν μὲν δὴ Θυέστου παῖδα ἢ Βροτέου—λέγεται γὰρ ἀμφότερα—, ὃς Κλυταιμνήστρᾳ πρότερον ἢ Ἀγαμέμνων συνῴκησε, τοῦτον μὲν <τὸν> Τάνταλον οὐ διοίσομαι ταφῆναι ταύτῃ· τοῦ δὲ λεγομένου Διός τε εἶναι καὶ Πλουτοῦς ἰδὼν οἶδα ἐν Σιπύλῳ τάφον θέας ἄξιον. πρὸς δὲ οὐδὲ ἀνάγκη συνέπεσεν ἐκ τῆς Σιπύλου φυγεῖν αὐτόν, ὡς Πέλοπα ἐπέλαβεν ὕστερον ἐλαύνοντος Ἴλου τοῦ Φρυγὸς ἐπ᾽ αὐτὸν στρατείᾳ. τάδε μὲν ἐς τοσοῦτον ἐξητάσθω· τὰ δὲ ἐς τὸν βόθρον τὸν πλησίον δρώμενα Νικόστρατον ἄνδρα ἐπιχώριον καταστήσασθαι λέγουσιν. ἀφιᾶσι δὲ καὶ νῦν ἔτι ἐς τὸν βόθρον καιομένας λαμπάδας Κόρῃ τῇ Δήμητρος.

2.22.4 ἐνταῦθα Ποσειδῶνός ἐστιν ἱερὸν ἐπίκλησιν Προσκλυστίου· τῆς γὰρ χώρας τὸν Ποσειδῶνά φασιν ἐπικλύσαι τὴν πολλήν, ὅτι Ἥρας εἶναι καὶ οὐκ αὐτοῦ τὴν γῆν Ἴναχος καὶ οἱ συνδικάσαντες ἔγνωσαν. Ἥρα μὲν δὴ παρὰ Ποσειδῶνος εὕρετο ἀπελθεῖν ὀπίσω τὴν θάλασσαν· Ἀργεῖοι δέ, ὅθεν τὸ κῦμα ἀνεχώρησεν, ἱερὸν Ποσειδῶνι ἐποίησαν Προσκλυστίῳ.

2.22.5 προελθόντι δὲ οὐ πολὺ τάφος ἐστὶν Ἄργου Διὸς εἶναι δοκοῦντος καὶ τῆς Φορωνέως Νιόβης· μετὰ δὲ ταῦτα Διοσκούρων ναός. ἀγάλματα δὲ αὐτοί τε καὶ οἱ παῖδές εἰσιν Ἄναξις καὶ Μνασίνους, σὺν δέ σφισιν αἱ μητέρες Ἱλάειρα καὶ Φοίβη, τέχνη μὲν Διποίνου καὶ Σκύλλιδος, ξύλου δὲ ἐβένου· τοῖς δ᾽ ἵπποις τὰ μὲν πολλὰ ἐβένου καὶ τούτοις, ὀλίγα δὲ καὶ ἐλέφαντος πεποίηται.

2.22.6 πλησίον δὲ τῶν Ἀνάκτων Εἰληθυίας ἐστὶν ἱερὸν ἀνάθημα Ἑλένης, ὅτε σὺν Πειρίθῳ Θησέως ἀπελθόντος ἐς Θεσπρωτοὺς Ἄφιδνά τε ὑπὸ Διοσκούρων ἑάλω καὶ ἤγετο ἐς Λακεδαίμονα Ἑλένη. ἔχειν μὲν γὰρ αὐτὴν λέγουσιν ἐν γαστρί, τεκοῦσαν δὲ ἐν Ἄργει καὶ τῆς Εἰληθυίας ἱδρυσαμένην τὸ ἱερὸν τὴν μὲν παῖδα ἣν ἔτεκε Κλυταιμνήστρᾳ δοῦναι—συνοικεῖν γὰρ ἤδη Κλυταιμνήστραν Ἀγαμέμνονι—, αὐτὴν δὲ ὕστερον τούτων Μενελάῳ γήμασθαι.

2.22.7 καὶ ἐπὶ τῷδε Εὐφορίων Χαλκιδεὺς καὶ Πλευρώνιος Ἀλέξανδρος ἔπη ποιήσαντες, πρότερον δὲ ἔτι Στησίχορος ὁ Ἱμεραῖος, κατὰ ταὐτά φασιν Ἀργείοις Θησέως εἶναι θυγατέρα Ἰφιγένειαν. τοῦ δὲ ἱεροῦ τῆς Εἰληθυίας πέραν ἐστὶν Ἑκάτης ναός, Σκόπα δὲ τὸ ἄγαλμα ἔργον. τοῦτο μὲν λίθου· τὰ δ᾽ ἀπαντικρὺ χαλκᾶ, Ἑκάτης καὶ ταῦτα ἀγάλματα, τὸ μὲν Πολύκλειτος ἐποίησε, τὸ δὲ ἀδελφὸς Πολυκλείτου Ναυκύδης †Μόθωνος†.

2.22.8 ἐρχομένῳ δὲ ὁδὸν εὐθεῖαν ἐς γυμνάσιον Κυλάραβιν, ἀπὸ τοῦ παιδὸς ὀνομαζόμενον τοῦ Σθενέλου, τέθαπται δὴ Λικύμνιος ὁ Ἠλεκτρύωνος· ἀποθανεῖν δ᾽ αὐτὸν Ὅμηρος ὑπὸ Τληπτολέμου φησὶ τοῦ Ἡρακλέους, καὶ διὰ τὸν φόνον τοῦτον ἔφυγεν ἐξ Ἄργους Τληπτόλεμος. ὀλίγον δὲ τῆς ἐπὶ Κυλάραβιν καὶ τὴν ταύτῃ πύλην ἀποτραπεῖσι Σακάδα μνῆμά ἐστιν, ὃς τὸ αὔλημα τὸ Πυθικὸν πρῶτος ηὔλησεν ἐν Δελφοῖς·

2.22.9 καὶ τὸ ἔχθος τὸ Ἀπόλλωνι διαμένον ἐς τοὺς αὐλητὰς ἔτι ἀπὸ Μαρσύου καὶ τῆς ἁμίλλης τοῦ Σιληνοῦ παυθῆναι διὰ τοῦτον δοκεῖ τὸν Σακάδαν. ἐν δὲ τῷ γυμνασίῳ τῷ Κυλαράβου καὶ Πανία ἐστὶν Ἀθηνᾶ καλουμένη καὶ τάφον Σθενέλου δεικνύουσι, τὸν δὲ αὐτοῦ Κυλαράβου. πεποίηται δὲ οὐ πόρρω τοῦ γυμνασίου πολυάνδριον τοῖς μετὰ Ἀθηναίων πλεύσασιν Ἀργείοις ἐπὶ καταδουλώσει Συρακουσῶν τε καὶ Σικελίας.

2.23.1 ἐντεῦθεν ἐρχομένοις ὁδὸν καλουμένην <Κοίλην> ναός ἐστιν ἐν δεξιᾷ Διονύσου· τὸ δὲ ἄγαλμα εἶναι λέγουσιν ἐξ Εὐβοίας. συμβάσης γὰρ τοῖς Ἕλλησιν, ὡς ἐκομίζοντο ἐξ Ἰλίου, τῆς πρὸς τῷ Καφηρεῖ ναυαγίας, τοὺς δυνηθέντας ἐς τὴν γῆν διαφυγεῖν τῶν Ἀργείων ῥῖγός τε πιέζει καὶ λιμός. εὐξαμένοις δὲ θεῶν τινα ἐν τοῖς παροῦσιν ἀπόροις γενέσθαι σωτῆρα, αὐτίκα ὡς προῄεσαν ἐφάνη σφίσι Διονύσου σπήλαιον, καὶ ἄγαλμα ἦν ἐν τῷ σπηλαίῳ τοῦ θεοῦ· τότε δὲ αἶγες ἄγριαι φεύγουσαι τὸν χειμῶνα ἐς αὐτὸ ἦσαν ἠθροισμέναι. ταύτας οἱ Ἀργεῖοι σφάξαντες τά τε κρέα ἐδείπνησαν καὶ δέρμασιν ἐχρήσαντο ἀντὶ ἐσθῆτος. ἐπεὶ δὲ ὁ χειμὼν ἐπαύσατο καὶ ἐπισκευάσαντες τὰς ναῦς οἴκαδε ἐκομίζοντο, ἐπάγονται τὸ ἐκ τοῦ σπηλαίου ξόανον·

2.23.2 καὶ διατελοῦσιν ἐς τόδε τιμῶντες ἔτι. τοῦ Διονύσου δὲ ἐγγυτάτω οἰκίαν ὄψει τὴν Ἀδράστου καὶ ἀπωτέρω ταύτης ἱερὸν Ἀμφιαράου καὶ τοῦ ἱεροῦ πέραν Ἐριφύλης μνῆμα. ἑξῆς δὲ τούτων ἐστὶν Ἀσκληπιοῦ τέμενος καὶ μετὰ ταῦτα ἱερὸν Βάτωνος. ἦν δὲ ὁ Βάτων γένους Ἀμφιαράῳ τοῦ αὐτοῦ τῶν Μελαμποδιδῶν καὶ ἐς μάχην ἐξιόντι ἡνιόχει τοὺς ἵππους· γενομένης δὲ τῆς τροπῆς ἀπὸ τοῦ Θηβαίων τείχους χάσμα γῆς Ἀμφιάραον καὶ τὸ ἅρμα ὑποδεξάμενον ἠφάνισεν ὁμοῦ καὶ τοῦτον τὸν Βάτωνα.

2.23.3 ἐπανιόντι δὲ ἐκ τῆς Κοίλης Ὑρνηθοῦς τάφον λέγουσιν εἶναι. εἰ μὲν δὴ κενὸν καὶ ἄλλως ἐς μνήμην τῆς γυναικός, εἰκότα λέγουσιν· εἰ δὲ τῆς Ὑρνηθοῦς κεῖσθαι τὸν νεκρὸν νομίζουσιν ἐνταῦθα, ἐγὼ μέν σφισιν οὐ πείθομαι, πειθέσθω δὲ ὅστις τὰ Ἐπιδαυρίων οὐ πέπυσται.

2.23.4 τὸ δ' ἐπιφανέστατον Ἀργείοις τῶν Ἀσκληπιείων ἄγαλμα ἐφ' ἡμῶν ἔχει καθήμενον Ἀσκληπιὸν λίθου λευκοῦ, καὶ παρ' αὐτὸν ἕστηκεν Ὑγεία· κάθηνται δὲ καὶ οἱ ποιήσαντες τὰ ἀγάλματα Ξενόφιλος καὶ Στράτων. ἐξ ἀρχῆς δὲ ἱδρύσατο Σφῦρος τὸ ἱερόν, Μαχάονος μὲν υἱός, ἀδελφὸς δὲ Ἀλεξάνορος τοῦ παρὰ Σικυωνίοις ἐν Τιτάνῃ τιμὰς ἔχοντος.

2.23.5 τῆς δὲ Ἀρτέμιδος τῆς Φεραίας—σέβουσι γὰρ καὶ Ἀργεῖοι Φεραίαν Ἄρτεμιν κατὰ ταὐτὰ Ἀθηναίοις καὶ Σικυωνίοις—τὸ ἄγαλμα καὶ οὗτοί φασιν ἐκ Φερῶν τῶν ἐν Θεσσαλίᾳ κομισθῆναι. τάδε δὲ αὐτοῖς οὐχ ὁμολογῶ· λέγουσι γὰρ Ἀργεῖοι Δηιανείρας ἐν Ἄργει μνῆμα εἶναι τῆς Οἰνέως τό τε Ἑλένου τοῦ Πριάμου, καὶ ἄγαλμα κεῖσθαι παρὰ σφίσιν Ἀθηνᾶς τὸ ἐκκομισθὲν ἐξ Ἰλίου καὶ ἁλῶναι ποιῆσαν Ἴλιον. τὸ μὲν δὴ Παλλάδιον—καλεῖται γὰρ οὕτω—δῆλόν ἐστιν ἐς Ἰταλίαν κομισθὲν ὑπὸ Αἰνείου· Δηιανείρᾳ δὲ τὴν τελευτὴν περὶ Τραχῖνα ἴσμεν καὶ οὐκ ἐν Ἄργει γενομένην, καὶ ἔστιν ὁ τάφος αὐτῇ πλησίον Ἡρακλείας τῆς ὑπὸ τῇ Οἴτῃ.

2.23.6 τὰ δὲ ἐς Ἕλενον τὸν Πριάμου δεδήλωκεν ὁ λόγος ἤδη μοι, μετὰ Πύρρου τοῦ Ἀχιλλέως αὐτὸν ἐλθεῖν ἐς Ἤπειρον καὶ ἐπιτροπεῦσαί τε τοὺς Πύρρου παῖδας συνοικοῦντα Ἀνδρομάχῃ καὶ τὴν Κεστρίνην καλουμένην ἀπὸ Κεστρίνου τοῦ Ἑλένου λαβεῖν τὸ ὄνομα. οὐ μὴν οὐδὲ αὐτῶν λέληθεν Ἀργείων τοὺς ἐξηγητὰς ὅτι μὴ πάντα ἐπ' ἀληθείᾳ λέγεταί σφισι, λέγουσι δὲ ὅμως· οὐ γάρ τι ἕτοιμον μεταπεῖσαι τοὺς πολλοὺς ἐναντία ὧν δοξάζουσιν.

2.23.7 ἄλλα δέ ἐστιν Ἀργείοις θέας ἄξια· κατάγεων οἰκοδόμημα, ἐπ' αὐτῷ δὲ ἦν ὁ χαλκοῦς θάλαμος, ὃν Ἀκρίσιός ποτε ἐπὶ φρουρᾷ τῆς θυγατρὸς ἐποίησε· Περίλαος δὲ καθεῖλεν αὐτὸν τυραννήσας. τοῦτό τε οὖν τὸ οἰκοδόμημά ἐστι καὶ Κροτώπου μνῆμα καὶ Διονύσου ναὸς Κρησίου. Περσεῖ γὰρ πολεμήσαντα αὐτὸν καὶ αὖθις ἐλθόντα ἐς λύσιν τοῦ ἔχθους τά τε ἄλλα τιμηθῆναι μεγάλως λέγουσιν ὑπὸ Ἀργείων καὶ τέμενός οἱ δοθῆναι τοῦτο ἐξαίρετον·

2.23.8 Κρησίου δὲ ὕστερον ὠνομάσθη, διότι Ἀριάδνην ἀποθανοῦσαν ἔθαψεν ἐνταῦθα. Λυκέας δὲ λέγει κατασκευαζομένου δεύτερον τοῦ ναοῦ κεραμέαν εὑρεθῆναι σορόν, εἶναι δὲ Ἀριάδνης αὐτήν· καὶ αὐτός τε καὶ ἄλλους Ἀργείων ἰδεῖν ἔφη τὴν σορόν. πλησίον δὲ τοῦ Διονύσου καὶ Ἀφροδίτης ναός ἐστιν Οὐρανίας.

2.24.1 τὴν δὲ ἀκρόπολιν Λάρισαν μὲν καλοῦσιν ἀπὸ τῆς Πελασγοῦ θυγατρός· ἀπὸ ταύτης δὲ καὶ δύο τῶν ἐν Θεσσαλίᾳ πόλεων, ἥ τε ἐπὶ θαλάσσῃ καὶ ἡ παρὰ τὸν Πηνειόν, ὠνομάσθησαν. ἀνιόντων δὲ ἐς τὴν ἀκρόπολιν ἔστι μὲν τῆς Ἀκραίας Ἥρας τὸ ἱερόν, ἔστι δὲ καὶ ναὸς Ἀπόλλωνος, ὃν Πυθαεὺς πρῶτος παραγενόμενος ἐκ Δελφῶν λέγεται ποιῆσαι. τὸ δὲ ἄγαλμα τὸ νῦν χαλκοῦν ἐστιν ὀρθόν, Δειραδιώτης Ἀπόλλων καλούμενος, ὅτι καὶ ὁ τόπος οὗτος καλεῖται Δειράς. ἡ δέ οἱ μαντική—μαντεύεται γὰρ ἔτι καὶ ἐς ἡμᾶς—καθέστηκε τρόπον τοῦτον. γυνὴ μὲν προφητεύουσά ἐστιν, ἀνδρὸς εὐνῆς εἰργομένη· θυομένης δὲ ἐν νυκτὶ ἀρνὸς κατὰ μῆνα ἕκαστον, γευσαμένη δὴ τοῦ αἵματος ἡ γυνὴ κάτοχος ἐκ τοῦ θεοῦ γίνεται.

2.24.2 τοῦ Δειραδιώτου δὲ Ἀπόλλωνος ἔχεται μὲν ἱερὸν Ἀθηνᾶς Ὀξυδερκοῦς καλουμένης, Διομήδους ἀνάθημα, ὅτι οἱ μαχομένῳ ποτὲ ἐν Ἰλίῳ τὴν ἀχλὺν ἀφεῖλεν ἡ θεὸς ἀπὸ τῶν ὀφθαλμῶν· ἔχεται δὲ τὸ στάδιον, ἐν ᾧ τὸν ἀγῶνα τῷ Νεμείῳ Διὶ καὶ τὰ Ἡραῖα ἄγουσιν. ἐς δὲ τὴν ἀκρόπολιν ἰοῦσίν ἐστιν ἐν ἀριστερᾷ τῆς ὁδοῦ τῶν Αἰγύπτου παίδων καὶ ταύτῃ μνῆμα. χωρὶς μὲν γὰρ ἀπὸ τῶν σωμάτων ἐνταῦθα αἱ κεφαλαί, χωρὶς δὲ ἐν Λέρνῃ σώματα τὰ λοιπά· ἐν Λέρνῃ γὰρ καὶ ὁ φόνος ἐξειργάσθη τῶν νεανίσκων, ἀποθανόντων δὲ ἀποτέμνουσιν αἱ γυναῖκες τὰς κεφαλὰς ἀπόδειξιν πρὸς τὸν πατέρα ὧν ἐτόλμησαν.

2.24.3 ἐπ᾽ ἄκρᾳ δέ ἐστι τῇ Λαρίσῃ Διὸς ἐπίκλησιν Λαρισαίου ναός, οὐκ ἔχων ὄροφον· τὸ δὲ ἄγαλμα ξύλου πεποιημένον οὐκέτι ἑστηκὸς ἦν ἐπὶ τῷ βάθρῳ. καὶ Ἀθηνᾶς δὲ ναός ἐστι θέας ἄξιος· ἐνταῦθα ἀναθήματα κεῖται καὶ ἄλλα καὶ Ζεὺς ξόανον, δύο μὲν ᾗ πεφύκαμεν ἔχον ὀφθαλμούς, τρίτον δὲ ἐπὶ τοῦ μετώπου. τοῦτον τὸν Δία Πριάμῳ φασὶν εἶναι τῷ Λαομέδοντος πατρῷον ἐν ὑπαίθρῳ τῆς αὐλῆς ἱδρυμένον, καὶ ὅτε ἡλίσκετο ὑπὸ Ἑλλήνων Ἴλιον, ἐπὶ τούτου κατέφυγεν ὁ Πρίαμος τὸν βωμόν. ἐπεὶ δὲ τὰ λάφυρα ἐνέμοντο, λαμβάνει Σθένελος ὁ Καπανέως αὐτόν, καὶ ἀνάκειται μὲν διὰ τοῦτο ἐνταῦθα·

2.24.4 τρεῖς δὲ ὀφθαλμοὺς ἔχειν ἐπὶ τῷδε ἄν τις τεκμαίροιτο αὐτόν. Δία γὰρ ἐν οὐρανῷ βασιλεύειν, οὗτος μὲν λόγος κοινὸς πάντων ἐστὶν ἀνθρώπων. ὃν δὲ ἄρχειν φασὶν ὑπὸ γῆς, ἔστιν ἔπος τῶν Ὁμήρου Δία ὀνομάζον καὶ τοῦτον·

Ζεύς τε καταχθόνιος καὶ ἐπαινὴ Περσεφόνεια.

Αἰσχύλος δὲ ὁ Εὐφορίωνος καλεῖ Δία καὶ τὸν ἐν θαλάσσῃ. τρισὶν οὖν ὁρῶντα ἐποίησεν ὀφθαλμοῖς ὅστις δὴ ἦν ὁ ποιήσας, ἅτε ἐν ταῖς τρισὶ ταῖς λεγομέναις λήξεσιν ἄρχοντα τὸν αὐτὸν τοῦτον θεόν.

2.24.5 ὁδοὶ δὲ ἐξ Ἄργους καὶ κατ᾽ ἄλλα εἰσὶ τῆς Πελοποννήσου καὶ πρὸς Ἀρκαδίας ἐπὶ Τεγέαν. ἐν δεξιᾷ δὲ ὄρος ἐστὶν ἡ Λυκώνη, δένδρα κυπαρίσσου μάλιστα ἔχουσα. ᾠκοδόμηται δὲ ἐπὶ κορυφῇ τοῦ ὄρους Ἀρτέμιδος Ὀρθίας ἱερόν, καὶ ἀγάλματα Ἀπόλλωνος καὶ Λητοῦς καὶ Ἀρτέμιδος πεποίηται λευκοῦ λίθου· Πολυκλείτου δέ φασιν εἶναι ἔργα. καταβάντων δὲ ἐκ τοῦ ὄρους αὖθίς ἐστιν ἐν ἀριστερᾷ τῆς λεωφόρου ναὸς Ἀρτέμιδος.

2.24.6 ὀλίγον δὲ ἀπωτέρω <ἐν> δεξιᾷ τῆς ὁδοῦ Χάον ἐστὶν ὄρος ὀνομαζόμενον, ὑπὸ δὲ αὐτῷ δένδρα πέφυκεν ἥμερα καὶ ἄνεισι τοῦ Ἐρασίνου φανερὸν ἐνταῦθα δὴ τὸ ὕδωρ· τέως δὲ ἐκ Στυμφάλου ῥεῖ τῆς Ἀρκάδων ὥσπερ ἐξ Εὐρίπου κατὰ Ἐλευσῖνα καὶ τὴν ταύτῃ θάλασσαν οἱ Ῥειτοί. πρὸς δὲ τοῦ Ἐρασίνου ταῖς κατὰ τὸ ὄρος ἐκβολαῖς Διονύσῳ καὶ Πανὶ θύουσι, τῷ Διονύσῳ δὲ καὶ ἑορτὴν ἄγουσι καλουμένην Τύρβην.

2.24.7 ἐπανελθοῦσι δὲ ἐς τὴν ἐπὶ Τεγέας ὁδόν ἐστιν ἐν δεξιᾷ τοῦ ὀνομαζομένου Τρόχου Κεγχρεαί. τὸ δὲ ὄνομα ἐφ᾽ ὅ<τῳ> τῷ χωρίῳ γέγονεν, οὐ λέγουσι, πλὴν εἰ μὴ καὶ τοῦτο ἄρα ὠνομάσθη διὰ τὸν Πειρήνης παῖδα Κεγχρίαν. καὶ πολυάνδρια ἐνταῦθά ἐστιν Ἀργείων νικησάντων μάχῃ Λακεδαιμονίους περὶ Ὑσίας. τὸν δὲ ἀγῶνα τοῦτον συμβάντα εὕρισκον Ἀθηναίοις ἄρχοντος Πεισιστράτου, τετάρτῳ δὲ ἔτει τῆς <ἑβδόμης καὶ εἰκοστῆς> Ὀλυμπιάδος ἣν Εὐρύβοτος Ἀθηναῖος ἐνίκα στάδιον. καταβάντι δὲ ἐς τὸ χθαμαλώτερον ἐρείπια Ὑσιῶν ἐστι πόλεώς ποτε ἐν τῇ Ἀργολίδι, καὶ τὸ πταῖσμα Λακεδαιμονίοις ἐνταῦθα γενέσθαι λέγουσιν.

2.25.1 ἡ δ᾽ ἐς Μαντίνειαν ἄγουσα ἐξ Ἄργους ἐστὶν οὐχ ἥπερ καὶ ἐπὶ Τεγέαν, ἀλλὰ ἀπὸ τῶν πυλῶν τῶν πρὸς τῇ Δειράδι. ἐπὶ δὲ τῆς ὁδοῦ ταύτης ἱερὸν διπλοῦν πεποίηται, καὶ πρὸς ἡλίου δύνοντος ἔσοδον καὶ κατὰ ἀνατολὰς ἑτέραν ἔχον. κατὰ μὲν δὴ τοῦτο Ἀφροδίτης κεῖται ξόανον, πρὸς δὲ ἡλίου δυσμὰς Ἄρεως· εἶναι δὲ τὰ ἀγάλματα Πολυνείκους λέγουσιν ἀναθήματα καὶ Ἀργείων, ὅσοι τιμωρήσοντες αὐτῷ συνεστρατεύοντο.

2.25.2 προελθοῦσι δὲ αὐτόθεν διαβάντων ποταμὸν χείμαρρον Χάραδρον καλούμενον ἔστιν Οἰνόη, τὸ ὄνομα ἔχουσα, ὡς Ἀργεῖοί φασιν, ἀπὸ Οἰνέως.

Οἰνέα γὰρ τὸν βασιλεύσαντα ἐν Αἰτωλίᾳ λέγουσιν ὑπὸ τῶν Ἀγρίου παίδων ἐκβληθέντα τῆς ἀρχῆς παρὰ Διομήδην ἐς Ἄργος ἀφικέσθαι. ὁ δὲ τὰ μὲν ἄλλα ἐτιμώρησεν αὐτῷ στρατεύσας ἐς τὴν Καλυδωνίαν, παραμένειν δὲ οὐκ ἔφη οἱ δύνασθαι· συνακολουθεῖν δέ, εἰ βούλοιτο, ἐς Ἄργος ἐκεῖνον ἐκέλευεν. ἀφικόμενον δὲ τά τε ἄλλα ἐθεράπευεν, ὡς πατρὸς θεραπεύειν πατέρα εἰκὸς ἦν, καὶ ἀποθανόντα ἔθαψεν ἐνταῦθα. ἀπὸ τούτου μὲν Οἰνόη χωρίον ἐστὶν Ἀργείοις·

2.25.3 ὑπὲρ δὲ Οἰνόης ὄρος ἐστὶν Ἀρτεμίσιον καὶ ἱερὸν Ἀρτέμιδος ἐπὶ κορυφῇ τοῦ ὄρους. ἐν τούτῳ δέ εἰσι τῷ ὄρει καὶ αἱ πηγαὶ τοῦ Ἰνάχου· πηγαὶ γὰρ δὴ τῷ ὄντι εἰσὶν αὐτῷ, τὸ δὲ ὕδωρ οὐκ ἐπὶ πολὺ ἐξικνεῖται τῆς γῆς.

2.25.4 ταύτῃ μὲν δὴ θέας οὐδὲν ἔτι ἦν ἄξιον· ἑτέρα δὲ ὁδὸς ἀπὸ τῶν πυλῶν τῶν πρὸς τῇ Δειράδι ἐστὶν ἐπὶ Λύρκειαν. ἐς τοῦτο λέγεται τὸ χωρίον Λυγκέα ἀποσωθῆναι τῶν πεντήκοντα ἀδελφῶν μόνον· καὶ ἡνίκα ἐσώθη, πυρσὸν ἀνέσχεν ἐντεῦθεν. συνέκειτο δὲ ἄρα αὐτῷ πρὸς τὴν Ὑπερμήστραν ἀνασχεῖν τὸν πυρσόν, ἢν διαφυγὼν Δαναὸν ἐς ἀσφαλὲς ἀφίκηταί ποι· τὴν δὲ καὶ αὐτὴν ἀνάψαι λέγουσιν ἕτερον ἀπὸ τῆς Λαρίσης, δῆλα καὶ ταύτην ποιοῦσαν ὅτι ἐν οὐδενὶ οὐδὲ αὐτὴ καθέστηκεν ἔτι κινδύνῳ. ἐπὶ τούτῳ δὲ Ἀργεῖοι κατὰ ἔτος ἕκαστον πυρσῶν ἑορτὴν ἄγουσι.

2.25.5 τὸ δὲ χωρίον τότε μὲν Λυγκεία ἐκαλεῖτο, οἰκήσαντος δὲ ὕστερον ἐν αὐτῷ Λύρκου—παῖς δὲ ἦν Ἄβαντος νόθος—τὸ ὄνομα δι᾽ αὐτὸν ἔσχηκε· καὶ ἄλλα τέ ἐστιν οὐκ ἀξιόλογα ἐν τοῖς ἐρειπίοις καὶ εἰκὼν ἐπὶ στήλῃ τοῦ Λύρκου. ἐς μὲν δὴ ταύτην ἐστὶν ἐξ Ἄργους ἑξήκοντα μάλιστά που στάδια, ἐκ δὲ Λυρκείας ἕτερα τοσαῦτα ἐς Ὀρνεάς. Λυρκείας μὲν δὴ πόλεως, ἅτε ἠρημωμένης ἤδη κατὰ τὴν Ἑλλήνων στρατείαν ἐπὶ Ἴλιον, οὐκ ἐποιήσατο Ὅμηρος ἐν καταλόγῳ μνήμην· Ὀρνεὰς δέ—ἔτι γὰρ ᾠκοῦντο—, ὥσπερ τῷ τόπῳ τῆς Ἀργείας ἔκειντο, οὕτω καὶ ἐν τοῖς ἔπεσι προτέρας ἢ Φλιοῦντά τε καὶ Σικυῶνα κατέλεξεν.

2.25.6 ἐκαλοῦντο δὲ ἀπὸ Ὀρνέως τοῦ Ἐρεχθέως· τοῦ δὲ Ὀρνέως ἦν τούτου Πετεώς, τοῦ δὲ Μενεσθεύς, ὃς Ἀγαμέμνονι μετὰ Ἀθηναίων τὴν Πριάμου συγκαθεῖλεν ἀρχήν. ἀπὸ μὲν δὴ τούτου τὸ ὄνομα ἐγένετο τῇ πόλει, Ἀργεῖοι δὲ ὕστερον τούτων Ὀρνεάτας ἀνέστησαν· ἀναστάντες δὲ σύνοικοι γεγόνασιν Ἀργείοις. ἔστι δὲ ἐν ταῖς Ὀρνεαῖς Ἀρτέμιδός τε ἱερὸν καὶ ξόανον ὀρθὸν καὶ ἕτερος ναὸς θεοῖς πᾶσιν ἐς κοινὸν ἀνειμένος. τὰ δὲ ἐπέκεινα Ὀρνεῶν ἥ τε Σικυωνία καὶ ἡ Φλιασία ἐστίν.

2.25.7 ἐρχομένοις δὲ ἐξ Ἄργους ἐς τὴν Ἐπιδαυρίαν ἐστὶν οἰκοδόμημα ἐν δεξιᾷ πυραμίδι μάλιστα εἰκασμένον, ἔχει δὲ ἀσπίδας σχῆμα Ἀργολικὰς ἐπειργασμένας. ἐνταῦθα Προίτῳ περὶ τῆς ἀρχῆς πρὸς Ἀκρίσιον μάχη γίνεται, καὶ τέλος μὲν ἴσον τῷ ἀγῶνι συμβῆναί φασι καὶ ἀπ᾽ αὐτοῦ διαλλαγὰς ὕστερον, ὡς οὐδέτεροι βεβαίως κρατεῖν ἐδύναντο· συμβάλλειν δὲ σφᾶς λέγουσιν ἀσπίσι πρῶτον τότε καὶ αὐτοὺς καὶ τὸ στράτευμα ὡπλισμένους. τοῖς δὲ πεσοῦσιν ἀφ᾽ ἑκατέρων—πολῖται γὰρ καὶ συγγενεῖς ἦσαν—ἐποιήθη ταύτῃ μνῆμα ἐν κοινῷ.

2.25.8 προϊοῦσι δὲ ἐντεῦθεν καὶ ἐκτραπεῖσιν ἐς δεξιὰν Τίρυνθός ἐστιν ἐρείπια. ἀνέστησαν δὲ καὶ Τιρυνθίους Ἀργεῖοι, συνοίκους προσλαβεῖν καὶ τὸ Ἄργος ἐπαυξῆσαι θελήσαντες. Τίρυνθα δὲ ἥρωα, ἀφ᾽οὗ τῇ πόλει τὸ ὄνομα ἐγένετο, παῖδα Ἄργου τοῦ Διὸς εἶναι λέγουσι. τὸ δὲ τεῖχος, ὃ δὴ μόνον τῶν ἐρειπίων λείπεται, Κυκλώπων μέν ἐστιν ἔργον, πεποίηται δὲ ἀργῶν λίθων, μέγεθος ἔχων ἕκαστος λίθος ὡς ἀπ᾽ αὐτῶν μηδ᾽ ἂν ἀρχὴν κινηθῆναι τὸν μικρότατον ὑπὸ ζεύγους ἡμιόνων· λιθία δὲ ἐνήρμοσται πάλαι, ὡς μάλιστα αὐτῶν ἕκαστον ἁρμονίαν τοῖς μεγάλοις λίθοις εἶναι.

2.25.9 καταβάντων δὲ ὡς ἐπὶ θάλασσαν, ἐνταῦθα οἱ θάλαμοι τῶν Προίτου θυγατέρων εἰσίν· ἐπανελθόντων δὲ ἐς τὴν λεωφόρον, ἐπὶ Μήδειαν ἐς ἀριστερὰν ἥξεις. βασιλεῦσαι δέ φασιν Ἠλεκτρύωνα ἐν τῇ Μηδείᾳ τὸν πατέρα Ἀλκμήνης· ἐπ᾽ ἐμοῦ δὲ Μηδείας πλὴν τὸ ἔδαφος ἄλλο οὐδὲν ἐλείπετο.

2.25.10 κατὰ δὲ τὴν <ἐς>Ἐπίδαυρον εὐθεῖάν ἐστι κώμη Λῆσσα, ναὸς δὲ Ἀθηνᾶς ἐν αὐτῇ καὶ ξόανον οὐδέν τι διάφορον ἢ τὸ ἐν ἀκροπόλει τῇ Λαρίσῃ. ἔστι δὲ ὄρος ὑπὲρ τῆς Λήσσης τὸ Ἀραχναῖον, πάλαι δὲ †σάπυς ἐλάτων† ἐπὶ Ἰνάχου τὸ ὄνομα εἰλήφει. βωμοὶ δέ εἰσιν ἐν αὐτῷ Διός τε καὶ Ἥρας· δεῆσαν ὄμβρου σφίσιν ἐνταῦθα θύουσι.

2.26.1 κατὰ δὲ τὴν Λῆσσαν ἔχεται τῆς Ἀργείας ἡ Ἐπιδαυρίων· πρὶν δὲ ἢ κατὰ ταύτην γενέσθαι τὴν πόλιν, ἐπὶ τὸ ἱερὸν ἀφίξῃ τοῦ Ἀσκληπιοῦ. ταύτην τὴν χώραν οὐκ οἶδα οἵτινες πρότερον ᾤκησαν πρὶν Ἐπίδαυρον ἐλθεῖν ἐς αὐτήν· οὐ μὴν οὐδὲ τοὺς ἀπογόνους Ἐπιδαύρου πυθέσθαι παρὰ τῶν ἐπιχωρίων ἐδυνάμην. τελευταῖον δὲ πρὶν ἢ παραγενέσθαι Δωριέας ἐς Πελοπόννησον βασιλεῦσαί φασι Πιτυρέα Ἴωνος ἀπόγονον τοῦ Ξούθου. τοῦτον παραδοῦναι λέγουσιν ἀμαχεὶ τὴν γῆν Δηιφόντῃ καὶ Ἀργείοις·

2.26.2 καὶ ὁ μὲν ἐς Ἀθήνας ὁμοῦ τοῖς πολίταις ἀφικόμενος ἐνταῦθα ᾤκησε, Δηιφόντης δὲ καὶ Ἀργεῖοι τὴν Ἐπιδαυρίαν ἔσχον. ἀπεσχίσθησαν δὲ οὗτοι τῶν ἄλλων Ἀργείων Τημένου τελευτήσαντος, Δηιφόντης μὲν καὶ Ὑρνηθὼ κατ᾽ ἔχθος τῶν Τημένου παίδων, ὁ δὲ σὺν αὐτοῖς στρατὸς Δηιφόντῃ καὶ Ὑρνηθοῖ πλέον ἢ Κείσῳ καὶ τοῖς ἀδελφοῖς νέμοντες. Ἐπίδαυρος δέ, ἀφ᾽ οὗ τὸ ὄνομα τῇ γῇ ἐτέθη, ὡς μέν φασιν Ἠλεῖοι, Πέλοπος ἦν· κατὰ δὲ Ἀργείων δόξαν καὶ τὰ ἔπη τὰς μεγάλας Ἠοίας ἦν Ἐπιδαύρῳ πατὴρ Ἄργος ὁ Διός· Ἐπιδαύριοι δὲ Ἀπόλλωνι Ἐπίδαυρον παῖδα προσποιοῦσιν.

2.26.3 Ἀσκληπιοῦ δὲ ἱερὰν μάλιστα εἶναι τὴν γῆν ἐπὶ λόγῳ συμβέβηκε τοιῷδε. Φλεγύαν Ἐπιδαύριοί φασιν ἐλθεῖν ἐς Πελοπόννησον πρόφασιν μὲν ἐπὶ θέᾳ τῆς χώρας, ἔργῳ δὲ κατάσκοπον πλήθους τῶν ἐνοικούντων καὶ εἰ τὸ πολὺ μάχιμον εἴη τῶν ἀνθρώπων. ἦν γὰρ δὴ Φλεγύας πολεμικώτατος τῶν τότε καὶ ἐπιὼν ἑκάστοτε ἐφ᾽ οὓς τύχοι τοὺς καρποὺς ἔφερε καὶ ἤλαυνε τὴν λείαν.

2.26.4 ὅτε δὲ παρεγένετο ἐς Πελοπόννησον, εἵπετο ἡ θυγάτηρ αὐτῷ, λεληθυῖα ἔτι τὸν πατέρα ὅτι ἐξ Ἀπόλλωνος εἶχεν ἐν γαστρί. ὡς δὲ ἐν τῇ γῇ τῇ Ἐπιδαυρίων ἔτεκεν, ἐκτίθησι τὸν παῖδα ἐς τὸ ὄρος τοῦτο ὃ δὴ Τίτθιον ὀνομάζουσιν ἐφ᾽ ἡμῶν, τηνικαῦτα δὲ ἐκαλεῖτο Μύρτιον· ἐκκειμένῳ δὲ ἐδίδου μέν οἱ γάλα μία τῶν περὶ τὸ ὄρος {τῶν} ποιμαινομένων αἰγῶν, ἐφύλασσε δὲ ὁ κύων ὁ τοῦ αἰπολίου φρουρός.

2.26.5 Ἀρεσθάνας δὲ—ὄνομα γὰρ τῷ ποιμένι τοῦτο ἦν—ὡς τὸν ἀριθμὸν οὐχ εὕρισκεν ὁμολογοῦντα τῶν αἰγῶν καὶ ὁ κύων ἅμα ἀπεστάτει τῆς ποίμνης, οὕτω τὸν Ἀρεσθάναν ἐς πᾶν φασιν ἀφικνεῖσθαι ζητήσεως, εὑρόντα δὲ ἐπιθυμῆσαι τὸν παῖδα ἀνελέσθαι· καὶ ὡς ἐγγὺς ἐγίνετο, ἀστραπὴν ἰδεῖν ἐκλάμψασαν ἀπὸ τοῦ παιδός, νομίσαντα δὲ εἶναι θεῖόν τι, ὥσπερ ἦν, ἀποτραπέσθαι. ὁ δὲ αὐτίκα ἐπὶ γῆν καὶ θάλασσαν πᾶσαν ἠγγέλλετο τά τε ἄλλα ὁπόσα βούλοιτο εὑρίσκειν ἐπὶ τοῖς κάμνουσι καὶ ὅτι ἀνίστησι τεθνεῶτας.

2.26.6 λέγεται δὲ καὶ ἄλλος ἐπ᾽ αὐτῷ λόγος, Κορωνίδα κύουσαν Ἀσκληπιὸν Ἴσχυι τῷ Ἐλάτου συγγενέσθαι, καὶ τὴν μὲν ἀποθανεῖν ὑπὸ Ἀρτέμιδος ἀμυνομένης τῆς ἐς τὸν Ἀπόλλωνα ὕβρεως, ἐξημμένης δὲ ἤδη τῆς πυρᾶς ἁρπάσαι λέγεται τὸν παῖδα Ἑρμῆς ἀπὸ τῆς φλογός.

2.26.7 ὁ δὲ τρίτος τῶν λόγων ἥκιστα ἐμοὶ δοκεῖν ἀληθής ἐστιν, Ἀρσινόης ποιήσας εἶναι τῆς Λευκίππου παῖδα Ἀσκληπιόν. Ἀπολλοφάνει γὰρ τῷ Ἀρκάδι ἐς Δελφοὺς ἐλθόντι καὶ ἐρομένῳ τὸν θεὸν εἰ γένοιτο ἐξ Ἀρσινόης Ἀσκληπιὸς καὶ Μεσσηνίοις πολίτης εἴη, ἔχρησεν ἡ Πυθία·

> ὦ μέγα χάρμα βροτοῖς βλαστὼν Ἀσκληπιὲ πᾶσιν,
> ὃν Φλεγυηὶς ἔτικτεν ἐμοὶ φιλότητι μιγεῖσα
> ἱμερόεσσα Κορωνὶς ἐνὶ κραναῇ Ἐπιδαύρῳ.

οὗτος ὁ χρησμὸς δηλοῖ μάλιστα οὐκ ὄντα Ἀσκληπιὸν Ἀρσινόης, ἀλλὰ Ἡσίοδον ἢ τῶν τινα ἐμπεποιηκότων ἐς τὰ Ἡσιόδου τὰ ἔπη συνθέντα ἐς τὴν Μεσσηνίων χάριν.

2.26.8 μαρτυρεῖ δέ μοι καὶ τόδε ἐν Ἐπιδαύρῳ τὸν θεὸν γενέσθαι· τὰ γὰρ Ἀσκληπιεῖα εὑρίσκω <ὄντα> τὰ ἐπιφανέστατα γεγονότα ἐξ Ἐπιδαύρου. τοῦτο μὲν γὰρ Ἀθηναῖοι, τῆς τελετῆς λέγοντες Ἀσκληπιῷ μεταδοῦναι, τὴν ἡμέραν ταύτην Ἐπιδαύρια ὀνομάζουσι καὶ θεὸν ἀπ' ἐκείνου φασὶν Ἀσκληπιόν σφισι νομισθῆναι· τοῦτο δὲ Ἀρχίας ὁ Ἀρισταίχμου, τὸ συμβὰν σπάσμα θηρεύοντί οἱ περὶ τὸν Πίνδασον ἰαθεὶς ἐν τῇ Ἐπιδαυρίᾳ, τὸν θεὸν ἐπηγάγετο ἐς Πέργαμον.

2.26.9 ἀπὸ δὲ τοῦ Περγαμηνῶν Σμυρναίοις γέγονεν ἐφ' ἡμῶν Ἀσκληπιεῖον τὸ ἐπὶ θαλάσσῃ. τὸ δ' ἐν Βαλάκραις ταῖς Κυρηναίων ἐστὶν Ἀσκληπιὸς καλούμενος Ἰατρὸς ἐξ Ἐπιδαύρου καὶ οὗτος. ἐκ δὲ τοῦ παρὰ Κυρηναίοις τὸ ἐν Λεβήνῃ τῇ Κρητῶν ἐστιν Ἀσκληπιεῖον. διάφορον δὲ Κυρηναίοις τοσόνδε ἐς Ἐπιδαυρίους ἐστίν, ὅτι αἶγας οἱ Κυρηναῖοι θύουσιν, Ἐπιδαυρίοις οὐ καθεστηκότος.

2.26.10 θεὸν δὲ Ἀσκληπιὸν νομισθέντα ἐξ ἀρχῆς καὶ οὐκ ἀνὰ χρόνον λαβόντα τὴν φήμην τεκμηρίοις καὶ ἄλλοις εὑρίσκω καὶ Ὁμήρου μαρτυρεῖ μοι τὰ περὶ Μαχάονος ὑπὸ Ἀγαμέμνονος εἰρημένα·

> Ταλθύβι', ὅττι τάχιστα Μαχάονα δεῦρο κάλεσσον
> φῶτ' Ἀσκληπιοῦ υἱόν,

ὡς ἂν εἰ λέγοι θεοῦ παῖδα ἄνθρωπον.

2.27.1 τὸ δὲ ἱερὸν ἄλσος τοῦ Ἀσκληπιοῦ περιέχουσιν ὅροι πανταχόθεν· οὐδὲ ἀποθνήσκουσιν <ἄνθρωποι> οὐδὲ τίκτουσιν αἱ γυναῖκές σφισιν ἐντὸς τοῦ περιβόλου, καθὰ καὶ ἐπὶ Δήλῳ τῇ νήσῳ τὸν αὐτὸν νόμον. τὰ δὲ θυόμενα, ἤν τέ τις Ἐπιδαυρίων αὐτῶν ἤν τε ξένος ὁ θύων ᾖ, καταναλίσκουσιν ἐντὸς τῶν ὅρων· τὸ δὲ αὐτὸ γινόμενον οἶδα καὶ ἐν Τιτάνῃ.

2.27.2 τοῦ δὲ Ἀσκληπιοῦ τὸ ἄγαλμα μεγέθει μὲν τοῦ Ἀθήνησιν Ὀλυμπίου Διὸς ἥμισυ ἀποδεῖ, πεποίηται δὲ ἐλέφαντος καὶ χρυσοῦ· μηνύει δὲ ἐπίγραμμα τὸν εἰργασμένον εἶναι Θρασυμήδην Ἀριγνώτου Πάριον. κάθηται δὲ ἐπὶ θρόνου βακτηρίαν κρατῶν, τὴν δὲ ἑτέραν τῶν χειρῶν ὑπὲρ κεφαλῆς ἔχει τοῦ δράκοντος, καί οἱ καὶ κύων παρακατακείμενος πεποίηται. τῷ θρόνῳ δὲ ἡρώων ἐπειργασμένα Ἀργείων ἐστὶν ἔργα, Βελλεροφόντου τὸ ἐς τὴν Χίμαιραν καὶ Περσεὺς ἀφελὼν τὴν Μεδούσης κεφαλήν. τοῦ ναοῦ δέ ἐστι πέραν ἔνθα οἱ ἱκέται τοῦ θεοῦ καθεύδουσιν.

2.27.3 οἴκημα δὲ περιφερὲς λίθου λευκοῦ καλούμενον Θόλος ᾠκοδόμηται πλησίον, θέας ἄξιον. ἐν δὲ αὐτῷ Παυσίου γράψαντος βέλη μὲν καὶ τόξον ἐστὶν ἀφεικὼς Ἔρως, λύραν δὲ ἀντ᾽ αὐτῶν ἀράμενος φέρει. γέγραπται δὲ ἐνταῦθα καὶ Μέθη, Παυσίου καὶ τοῦτο ἔργον, ἐξ ὑαλίνης φιάλης πίνουσα· ἴδοις δὲ κἂν <ἐν> τῇ γραφῇ φιάλην τε ὑάλου καὶ δι᾽ αὐτῆς γυναικὸς πρόσωπον. στῆλαι δὲ εἱστήκεσαν ἐντὸς τοῦ περιβόλου τὸ μὲν ἀρχαῖον καὶ πλέονες, ἐπ᾽ ἐμοῦ δὲ ἓξ λοιπαί· ταύταις ἐγγεγραμμένα καὶ ἀνδρῶν καὶ γυναικῶν ἐστιν ὀνόματα ἀκεσθέντων ὑπὸ τοῦ Ἀσκληπιοῦ, προσέτι δὲ καὶ νόσημα ὅ τι ἕκαστος ἐνόσησε καὶ ὅπως ἰάθη· γέγραπται δὲ φωνῇ τῇ Δωρίδι.

2.27.4 χωρὶς δὲ ἀπὸ τῶν ἄλλων ἐστὶν ἀρχαία στήλη· ἵππους δὲ Ἱππόλυτον ἀναθεῖναι τῷ θεῷ φησιν εἴκοσι. ταύτης τῆς στήλης τῷ ἐπιγράμματι ὁμολογοῦντα λέγουσιν Ἀρικιεῖς, ὡς τεθνεῶτα Ἱππόλυτον ἐκ τῶν Θησέως ἀρῶν ἀνέστησεν Ἀσκληπιός· ὁ δὲ ὡς αὖθις ἐβίω, οὐκ ἠξίου νέμειν τῷ πατρὶ συγγνώμην, ἀλλὰ ὑπεριδὼν τὰς δεήσεις ἐς Ἰταλίαν ἔρχεται παρὰ τοὺς Ἀρικιεῖς, καὶ ἐβασίλευσέ τε αὐτόθι καὶ ἀνῆκε τῇ Ἀρτέμιδι τέμενος, ἔνθα ἄχρι ἐμοῦ μονομαχίας ἆθλα ἦν καὶ ἱερᾶσθαι τῇ θεῷ τὸν νικῶντα. ὁ δὲ ἀγὼν ἐλευθέρων μὲν προέκειτο οὐδενί, οἰκέταις δὲ ἀποδρᾶσι τοὺς δεσπότας.

2.27.5 Ἐπιδαυρίοις δέ ἐστι θέατρον ἐν τῷ ἱερῷ μάλιστα ἐμοὶ δοκεῖν θέας ἄξιον· τὰ μὲν γὰρ Ῥωμαίων πολὺ δή τι καὶ ὑπερῆρκε τῶν πανταχοῦ τῷ κόσμῳ, μεγέθει δὲ Ἀρκάδων τὸ ἐν Μεγάλῃ πόλει· ἁρμονίας δὲ ἢ κάλλους ἕνεκα ἀρχιτέκτων ποῖος ἐς ἅμιλλαν Πολυκλείτῳ γένοιτ᾽ ἂν ἀξιόχρεως; Πολύκλειτος γὰρ καὶ θέατρον τοῦτο καὶ οἴκημα τὸ περιφερὲς ὁ ποιήσας ἦν. ἐντὸς δὲ τοῦ ἄλσους ναός τέ ἐστιν Ἀρτέμιδος καὶ ἄγαλμα Ἠπιόνης καὶ Ἀφροδίτης ἱερὸν καὶ Θέμιδος καὶ στάδιον, οἷα Ἕλλησι τὰ πολλὰ γῆς χῶμα, καὶ κρήνη τῷ τε ὀρόφῳ καὶ κόσμῳ τῷ λοιπῷ θέας ἀξία.

2.27.6 ὁπόσα δὲ Ἀντωνῖνος ἀνὴρ τῆς συγκλήτου βουλῆς ἐφ᾽ ἡμῶν ἐποίησεν, ἔστι μὲν Ἀσκληπιοῦ λουτρόν, ἔστι δὲ ἱερὸν θεῶν οὓς Ἐπιδώτας ὀνομάζουσιν· ἐποίησε δὲ καὶ Ὑγείᾳ ναὸν καὶ Ἀσκληπιῷ καὶ Ἀπόλλωνι ἐπίκλησιν Αἰγυπτίοις. καὶ—ἦν γὰρ στοὰ καλουμένη Κότυος, καταρρυέντος δέ οἱ τοῦ ὀρόφου διέφθαρτο ἤδη πᾶσα ἅτε ὠμῆς τῆς πλίνθου ποιηθεῖσα—ἀνῳκοδόμησε καὶ ταύτην. Ἐπιδαυρίων δὲ οἱ περὶ τὸ ἱερὸν μάλιστα ἐταλαιπώρουν, ὅτι μήτε αἱ γυναῖκες ἐν σκέπῃ σφίσιν ἔτικτον καὶ ἡ τελευτὴ τοῖς κάμνουσιν ὑπαίθριος ἐγίνετο· ὁ δὲ καὶ ταῦτα ἐπανορθούμενος κατεσκευάσατο οἴκησιν· ἐνταῦθα ἤδη καὶ ἀποθανεῖν ἀνθρώπῳ καὶ τεκεῖν γυναικὶ ὅσιον.

2.27.7 ὄρη δέ ἐστιν ὑπὲρ τὸ ἄλσος τό τε Τίτθιον καὶ ἕτερον ὀνομαζόμενον Κυνόρτιον, Μαλεάτου δὲ Ἀπόλλωνος ἱερὸν ἐν αὐτῷ. τοῦτο μὲν δὴ τῶν ἀρχαίων· τὰ δὲ ἄλλα ὅσα περὶ τὸ ἱερὸν τοῦ Μαλεάτου καὶ ἔλυτρον κρήνης, ἐς ὃ τὸ ὕδωρ συλλέγεταί σφισι τὸ ἐκ τοῦ θεοῦ, Ἀντωνῖνος καὶ ταῦτα Ἐπιδαυρίοις ἐποίησεν.

2.28.1 δράκοντες δὲ, οἱ λοιποὶ καὶ ἕτερον γένος, ἐς τὸ ξανθότερον ῥέπον τῆς χρόας, ἱεροὶ μὲν τοῦ Ἀσκληπιοῦ νομίζονται καὶ εἰσὶν ἀνθρώποις ἥμεροι, τρέφει δὲ μόνη σφᾶς ἡ τῶν Ἐπιδαυρίων γῆ. τὸ δὲ αὐτὸ εὑρίσκω καὶ ἄλλαις χώραις συμβεβηκός· Λιβύη μέν γε μόνη κροκοδείλους τρέφει χερσαίους διπήχεων οὐκ ἐλάσσονας, παρὰ δὲ Ἰνδῶν μόνων ἄλλα τε κομίζεται καὶ ὄρνιθες οἱ ψιττακοί. τοὺς δὲ ὄφεις οἱ Ἐπιδαύριοι τοὺς μεγάλους ἐς πλέον πηχῶν καὶ τριάκοντα προήκοντας, οἷοι παρά τε Ἰνδοῖς τρέφονται καὶ ἐν Λιβύῃ, ἄλλο δή τι γένος φασὶν εἶναι καὶ οὐ δράκοντας.

2.28.2 ἐς δὲ τὸ ὄρος ἀνιοῦσι τὸ Κορυφαῖον, ἔστι καθ᾽ ὁδὸν Στρεπτῆς καλουμένης ἐλαίας φυτόν, αἰτίου τοῦ περιαγαγόντος τῇ χειρὶ Ἡρακλέους ἐς τοῦτο τὸ σχῆμα. εἰ δὲ καὶ Ἀσιναίοις τοῖς ἐν τῇ Ἀργολίδι ἔθηκεν ὅρον τοῦτον, οὐκ ἂν ἔγωγε εἰδείην, ἐπεὶ μηδὲ ἑτέρωθι ἀναστάτου γενομένης χώρας τὸ σαφὲς ἔτι οἷόν τε τῶν ὅρων ἐξευρεῖν. ἐπὶ δὲ τῇ ἄκρᾳ τοῦ ὄρους Κορυφαίας ἐστὶν ἱερὸν Ἀρτέμιδος, οὗ καὶ Τελέσιλλα ἐποιήσατο ἐν ᾄσματι μνήμην.

2.28.3 κατιοῦσι δὲ ἐς τῶν Ἐπιδαυρίων τὴν πόλιν χωρίον ἐστὶ πεφυκυίας ἀγριελαίους ἔχον· Ὑρνήθιον δὲ καλοῦσι τὸ χωρίον. τὰ δὲ ἐς αὐτό, ὡς Ἐπιδαύριοί τε λέγουσι καὶ εἰκὸς ἔχει, γράψω. Κεῖσος καὶ οἱ λοιποὶ Τημένου παῖδες μάλιστα ᾔδεσαν Δηιφόντην λυπήσοντες, εἰ διαλῦσαί πως ἀπ᾽ αὐτοῦ τὴν Ὑρνηθὼ δυνηθεῖεν. ἀφίκοντο οὖν ἐς Ἐπίδαυρον Κερύνης καὶ Φάλκης· Ἀγραίῳ γὰρ τῷ νεωτάτῳ τὰ ποιούμενα οὐκ ἤρεσκεν. οὗτοι δὲ στήσαντες τὸ ἅρμα ὑπὸ τὸ τεῖχος κήρυκα ἀποστέλλουσι παρὰ τὴν ἀδελφήν, ἐλθεῖν δῆθεν ἐς λόγους αὐτῇ βουλόμενοι.

2.28.4 ὡς δὲ ὑπήκουσε καλοῦσιν, ἐνταῦθα οἱ νεανίσκοι πολλὰ μὲν Δηιφόντου κατηγόρουν, πολλὰ δὲ αὐτὴν ἱκέτευον ἐκείνην ἐπανήκειν ἐς Ἄργος, ἄλλα τε ἐπαγγελλόμενοι καὶ ἀνδρὶ δώσειν αὐτὴν Δηιφόντου τὰ πάντα ἀμείνονι καὶ ἀνθρώπων πλειόνων καὶ γῆς ἄρχοντι εὐδαιμονεστέρας. Ὑρνηθὼ δὲ τοῖς λεχθεῖσιν ἀλγήσασα ἀπεδίδου σφίσι τὴν ἴσην, Δηιφόντην μὲν αὐτῇ τε ἄνδρα ἀρεστὸν εἶναι φήσασα καὶ Τημένῳ γενέσθαι γαμβρὸν οὐ μεμπτόν, ἐκείνοις δὲ Τημένου προσήκειν σφαγεῦσιν ὀνομάζεσθαι μᾶλλον ἢ παισίν.

2.28.5 καὶ τὴν μὲν οὐδὲν ἔτι ἀποκρινάμενοι συλλαμβάνουσιν, ἀναθέντες δὲ ἐς τὸ ἅρμα ἀπήλαυνον· Δηιφόντῃ δὲ ἀγγέλλει τις τῶν Ἐπιδαυρίων ὡς Κερύνης καὶ Φάλκης ἄγοντες οἴχοιντο ἄκουσαν Ὑρνηθώ. ὁ δὲ αὐτός τε ὡς τάχους εἶχεν ἤμυνε καὶ οἱ Ἐπιδαύριοι πυνθανόμενοι προσεβοήθουν. Δηιφόντης δὲ Κερύνην μὲν ὡς κατελάμβανεν ἀναιρεῖ βαλών, Φάλκην δὲ ἐχόμενον Ὑρνηθοῦς βαλεῖν μὲν ἔδεισε, μὴ ἁμαρτὼν γένοιτο αὐτῆς ἐκείνης φονεύς, συμπλακεὶς δὲ ἐπειρᾶτο ἀφαιρεῖσθαι. Φάλκης δὲ ἀντεχόμενος καὶ ἕλκων βιαιότερον ἀπέκτεινεν ἔχουσαν ἐν γαστρί.

2.28.6 καὶ ὁ μὲν συνείς, οἷα ἐς τὴν ἀδελφὴν ἐξειργασμένος ἔργα ἦν, ἤλαυνε τὸ ἅρμα ἀφειδέστερον, προλαβεῖν τῆς ὁδοῦ σπεύδων πρὶν ἢ πάντας ἐπ᾽ αὐτὸν συλλεχθῆναι τοὺς Ἐπιδαυρίους· Δηιφόντης δὲ σὺν τοῖς παισίν—ἐγεγόνεσαν γὰρ καὶ παῖδες αὐτῷ πρότερον ἔτι υἱοὶ μὲν Ἀντιμένης καὶ Ξάνθιππός τε καὶ Ἀργεῖος, θυγάτηρ δὲ Ὀρσοβία· ταύτην Πάμφυλον τὸν Αἰγιμίου λέγουσιν ὕστερον γῆμαι—τότε δὲ ἀναλαβόντες τὸν νεκρὸν τῆς Ὑρνηθοῦς κομίζουσιν ἐς τοῦτο τὸ χωρίον τὸ ἀνὰ χρόνον Ὑρνήθιον κληθέν.

2.28.7 καί οἱ ποιήσαντες ἡρῷον τιμὰς καὶ ἄλλας δεδώκασι καὶ ἐπὶ τοῖς πεφυκόσιν ἐλαίοις, καὶ εἰ δή τι ἄλλο δένδρον ἔσω, καθέστηκε νόμος τὰ θραυόμενα μηδένα ἐς οἶκον φέρεσθαι μηδὲ χρᾶσθαί σφισιν ἐς μηδέν, κατὰ χώραν <δ᾽> αὐτοῦ λείπουσιν ἱερὰ εἶναι τῆς Ὑρνηθοῦς.

2.28.8 οὐ πόρρω δὲ τῆς πόλεως Μελίσσης μνῆμά ἐστιν, ἣ Περιάνδρῳ συνῴκησε τῷ Κυψέλου, καὶ ἕτερον Προκλέους πατρὸς τῆς Μελίσσης. ἐτυράννει δὲ καὶ οὗτος Ἐπιδαυρίων, καθὰ δὴ καὶ ὁ γαμβρός οἱ Περίανδρος Κορίνθου.

2.29.1 αὐτὴ δὲ τῶν Ἐπιδαυρίων ἡ πόλις παρείχετο ἐς μνήμην τάδε ἀξιολογώτατα· τέμενος δή ἐστιν Ἀσκληπιοῦ καὶ ἀγάλματα ὁ θεὸς αὐτὸς καὶ Ἠπιόνη, γυναῖκα δὲ εἶναι τὴν Ἠπιόνην Ἀσκληπιοῦ φασι· ταῦτά ἐστιν ἐν ὑπαίθρῳ λίθου Παρίου. ναοὶ δὲ ἐν τῇ πόλει καὶ Διονύσου καὶ Ἀρτέμιδός ἐστιν ἄλσος· εἰκάσαις ἂν θηρευούσῃ τὴν Ἄρτεμιν. Ἀφροδίτης τε ἱερὸν πεποίηται· τὸ δὲ πρὸς τῷ λιμένι ἐπὶ ἄκρας ἀνεχούσης ἐς θάλασσαν λέγουσιν Ἥρας εἶναι. τὴν δὲ Ἀθηνᾶν ἐν τῇ ἀκροπόλει, ξόανον θέας ἄξιον, Κισσαίαν ἐπονομάζουσιν.

2.29.2 Αἰγινῆται δὲ οἰκοῦσιν ἔχοντες τὴν νῆσον ἀπαντικρὺ τῆς Ἐπιδαυρίας. ἀνθρώπους δ᾽ οὐκ εὐθὺς ἐξ ἀρχῆς λέγουσιν ἐν αὐτῇ γενέσθαι· Διὸς δὲ ἐς ἔρημον κομίσαντος Αἴγιναν τὴν Ἀσωποῦ τῇ μὲν τὸ ὄνομα ἐτέθη τοῦτο ἀντὶ Οἰνώνης, Αἰακοῦ δὲ αἰτήσαντος ὡς ηὐξήθη παρὰ Διὸς οἰκήτορας, οὕτω οἱ τὸν Δία ἀνεῖναι τοὺς ἀνθρώπους φασὶν ἐκ τῆς γῆς. βασιλεύσαντα δὲ ἐν τῇ γῇ πλὴν Αἰακὸν οὐδένα εἰπεῖν ἔχουσιν, ἐπεὶ μηδὲ τῶν Αἰακοῦ παίδων τινὰ ἴσμεν καταμείναντα, Πηλεῖ μὲν συμβὰν καὶ Τελαμῶνι ἐπὶ φόνῳ φεύγειν τῷ Φώκου, τῶν δὲ αὖ Φώκου παίδων περὶ τὸν Παρνασσὸν οἰκησάντων ἐν τῇ νῦν καλουμένῃ Φωκίδι.

2.29.3 τὸ δὲ ὄνομα προϋπῆρχεν ἤδη τῇ χώρᾳ, Φώκου τοῦ Ὀρνυτίωνος γενεᾷ πρότερον ἐς αὐτὴν ἐλθόντος. ἐπὶ μὲν δὴ Φώκου τούτου <ἡ> περὶ Τιθορέαν τε καὶ Παρνασσὸν ἐκαλεῖτο {ἡ} Φωκίς· ἐπὶ δὲ τοῦ Αἰακοῦ καὶ πᾶσιν ἐξενίκησεν, ὅσοι Μινύαις τέ εἰσιν Ὀρχομενίοις ὅμοροι καὶ ἐπὶ Σκάρφειαν τὴν Λοκρῶν καθήκουσι.

2.29.4 γεγόνασι δὲ ἀπὸ μὲν Πηλέως οἱ ἐν Ἠπείρῳ βασιλεῖς, Τελαμῶνος δὲ τῶν παίδων Αἴαντος μέν ἐστιν ἀφανέστερον γένος οἷα ἰδιωτεύσαντος ἀνθρώπου, πλὴν ὅσον Μιλτιάδης, ὃς Ἀθηναίοις ἐς Μαραθῶνα ἡγήσατο, καὶ Κίμων ὁ Μιλτιάδου προῆλθον ἐς δόξαν· οἱ δὲ Τευκρίδαι βασιλεῖς διέμειναν Κυπρίων ἄρχοντες ἐς Εὐαγόραν. Φώκῳ δὲ Ἄσιος ὁ τὰ ἔπη ποιήσας γενέσθαι φησὶ Πανοπέα καὶ Κρῖσον· καὶ Πανοπέως μὲν ἐγένετο Ἐπειὸς ὁ τὸν ἵππον τὸν δούρειον, ὡς Ὅμηρος ἐποίησεν, ἐργασάμενος, Κρίσου δὲ ἦν ἀπόγονος τρίτος Πυλάδης, Στροφίου τε ὢν τοῦ Κρίσου καὶ Ἀναξιβίας ἀδελφῆς Ἀγαμέμνονος. γένη μὲν τοσαῦτα τῶν καλουμένων Αἰακιδῶν, ἐξεχώρησε δὲ ἑτέρωσε ἀπ᾽ ἀρχῆς.

2.29.5 χρόνῳ δὲ ὕστερον μοῖρα Ἀργείων τῶν Ἐπίδαυρον ὁμοῦ Δηιφόντῃ κατασχόντων, διαβᾶσα ἐς Αἴγιναν καὶ Αἰγινήταις τοῖς ἀρχαίοις γενόμενοι σύνοικοι, τὰ Δωριέων ἔθη καὶ φωνὴν κατεστήσαντο ἐν τῇ νήσῳ. προελθοῦσι δὲ Αἰγινήταις ἐς μέγα δυνάμεως, ὡς Ἀθηναίων γενέσθαι ναυσὶν ἐπικρατεστέρους καὶ ἐν τῷ Μηδικῷ πολέμῳ παρασχέσθαι πλοῖα μετά γε Ἀθηναίους πλεῖστα, οὐ παρέμεινεν ἐς ἅπαν ἡ εὐδαιμονία, γενόμενοι δὲ ὑπὸ Ἀθηναίων ἀνάστατοι Θυρέαν τὴν ἐν τῇ Ἀργολίδι Λακεδαιμονίων δόντων ᾤκησαν. καὶ ἀπέλαβον μὲν τὴν νῆσον, ὅτε περὶ Ἑλλήσποντον αἱ Ἀθηναίων τριήρεις ἐλήφθησαν, πλούτου δὲ ἢ δυνάμεως οὐκέτι ἐξεγένετο ἐς ἴσον προελθεῖν σφισιν.

2.29.6 προσπλεῦσαι δὲ Αἴγινά ἐστι νήσων τῶν Ἑλληνίδων ἀπορωτάτη· πέτραι τε γὰρ ὕφαλοι περὶ πᾶσαν καὶ χοιράδες ἀνεστήκασι. μηχανήσασθαι δὲ ἐξεπίτηδες ταῦτα Αἰακόν φασι λῃστειῶν τῶν ἐκ θαλάσσης φόβῳ, καὶ πολεμίοις ἀνδράσι μὴ ἄνευ κινδύνου εἶναι. πλησίον δὲ τοῦ λιμένος ἐν ᾧ μάλιστα ὁρμίζονται ναός ἐστιν Ἀφροδίτης, ἐν ἐπιφανεστάτῳ δὲ τῆς πόλεως τὸ Αἰάκειον καλούμενον, περίβολος τετράγωνος λευκοῦ λίθου.

2.29.7 ἐπειργασμένοι δέ εἰσι κατὰ τὴν ἔσοδον οἱ παρὰ Αἰακόν ποτε ὑπὸ τῶν Ἑλλήνων σταλέντες· αἰτίαν δὲ τὴν αὐτὴν Αἰγινήταις καὶ οἱ λοιποὶ λέγουσιν. αὐχμὸς τὴν Ἑλλάδα ἐπὶ χρόνον ἐπίεζε καὶ οὔτε τὴν ἐκτὸς ἰσθμοῦ χώραν οὔτε Πελοποννησίοις ὗεν ὁ θεός, ἐς ὃ ἐς Δελφοὺς ἀπέστειλαν ἐρησομένους τὸ αἴτιον ὅ τι εἴη καὶ αἰτήσοντας ἅμα λύσιν τοῦ κακοῦ. τούτοις ἡ Πυθία εἶπε Δία ἱλάσκεσθαι, χρῆναι δέ, εἴπερ ὑπακούσει σφίσιν, Αἰακὸν τὸν ἱκετεύσαντα εἶναι.

2.29.8 οὕτως Αἰακοῦ δεησομένους ἀποστέλλουσιν ἀφ᾽ ἑκάστης πόλεως· καὶ ὁ μὲν τῷ Πανελληνίῳ Διὶ θύσας καὶ εὐξάμενος τὴν Ἑλλάδα γῆν ἐποίησεν ὕεσθαι, τῶν δὲ ἐλθόντων ὡς αὐτὸν εἰκόνας ταύτας ἐποιήσαντο οἱ Αἰγινῆται.

τοῦ περιβόλου δὲ ἐντὸς ἐλαῖαι πεφύκασιν ἐκ παλαιοῦ καὶ βωμός ἐστιν οὐ πολὺ ἀνέχων ἐκ τῆς γῆς· ὡς δὲ καὶ μνῆμα οὗτος ὁ βωμὸς εἴη Αἰακοῦ, λεγόμενόν ἐστιν ἐν ἀπορρήτῳ.

2.29.9 παρὰ δὲ τὸ Αἰάκειον Φώκου τάφος χῶμά ἐστι περιεχόμενον κύκλῳ κρηπῖδι, ἐπίκειται δέ οἱ λίθος τραχύς· καὶ ἡνίκα Φῶκον Τελαμὼν καὶ Πηλεὺς προηγάγοντο ἐς ἀγῶνα πεντάθλου καὶ περιῆλθεν ἐς Πηλέα ἀφεῖναι τὸν λίθον—οὗτος γὰρ ἀντὶ δίσκου σφίσιν ἦν—, ἑκὼν τυγχάνει τοῦ Φώκου. ταῦτα δὲ ἐχαρίζοντο τῇ μητρί· αὐτοὶ μὲν γὰρ ἐγεγόνεσαν ἐκ τῆς Σκίρωνος θυγατρός, Φῶκος δὲ οὐκ ἐκ τῆς αὐτῆς, ἀλλ᾽ ἐξ ἀδελφῆς Θέτιδος ἦν, εἰ δὴ τὰ ὄντα λέγουσιν Ἕλληνες. Πυλάδης τέ μοι καὶ διὰ ταῦτα φαίνεται καὶ οὐκ Ὀρέστου φιλίᾳ μόνον βουλεῦσαι Νεοπτολέμῳ τὸν φόνον.

2.29.10 τότε δὲ ὡς τῷ δίσκῳ πληγεὶς ἀπέθανεν ὁ Φῶκος, φεύγουσιν ἐπιβάντες νεὼς οἱ Ἐνδηίδος παῖδες· Τελαμὼν δὲ ὕστερα κήρυκα ἀποστέλλων ἠρνεῖτο μὴ βουλεῦσαι Φώκῳ θάνατον. Αἰακὸς δὲ ἐς μὲν τὴν νῆσον ἀποβαίνειν αὐτὸν οὐκ εἴα, ἑστηκότα δὲ ἐπὶ νεώς, εἰ δὲ ἐθέλοι, χῶμα ἐν τῇ θαλάσσῃ χώσαντα ἐκέλευεν ἐντεῦθεν ἀπολογήσασθαι. οὕτως ἐς τὸν Κρυπτὸν καλούμενον λιμένα ἐσπλεύσας νύκτωρ ἐποίει χῶμα. καὶ τοῦτο μὲν ἐξεργασθὲν καὶ ἐς ἡμᾶς ἔτι μένει· καταγνωσθεὶς δὲ οὐκ ἀναίτιος εἶναι Φώκῳ τῆς τελευτῆς, τὸ δεύτερον ἐς Σαλαμῖνα ἀπέπλευσε.

2.29.11 τοῦ λιμένος δὲ οὐ πόρρω τοῦ Κρυπτοῦ θέατρόν ἐστι θέας ἄξιον, κατὰ τὸ Ἐπιδαυρίων μάλιστα μέγεθος καὶ ἐργασίαν τὴν λοιπήν. τούτου δὲ ὄπισθεν ᾠκοδόμηται σταδίου πλευρὰ μία, ἀνέχουσά τε αὐτὴ τὸ θέατρον καὶ ἀντὶ ἐρείσματος ἀνάλογον ἐκείνῳ χρωμένη.

2.30.1 ναοὶ δὲ οὐ πολὺ ἀλλήλων ἀφεστηκότες ὁ μὲν Ἀπόλλωνός ἐστιν, ὁ δὲ Ἀρτέμιδος, Διονύσῳ δὲ αὐτῶν ὁ τρίτος. Ἀπόλλωνι μὲν δὴ ξόανον γυμνόν ἐστι τέχνης τῆς ἐπιχωρίου, τῇ δὲ Ἀρτέμιδί ἐστιν ἐσθής, κατὰ ταὐτὰ δὲ καὶ τῷ Διονύσῳ· καὶ γένεια Διόνυσος ἔχων πεποίηται. τοῦ δὲ Ἀσκληπιοῦ τὸ ἱερὸν ἔστι μὲν ἑτέρωθι καὶ οὐ ταύτῃ, λίθου δὲ ἄγαλμα καθήμενον.

2.30.2 θεῶν δὲ Αἰγινῆται τιμῶσιν Ἑκάτην μάλιστα καὶ τελετὴν ἄγουσιν ἀνὰ πᾶν ἔτος Ἑκάτης, Ὀρφέα σφίσι τὸν Θρᾷκα καταστήσασθαι τὴν τελετὴν λέγοντες. τοῦ περιβόλου δὲ ἐντὸς ναός ἐστι, ξόανον δὲ ἔργον Μύρωνος, ὁμοίως ἓν πρόσωπόν τε καὶ τὸ λοιπὸν σῶμα. Ἀλκαμένης δὲ ἐμοὶ δοκεῖν πρῶτος ἀγάλματα Ἑκάτης τρία ἐποίησε προσεχόμενα ἀλλήλοις, ἣν Ἀθηναῖοι καλοῦσιν Ἐπιπυργιδίαν· ἕστηκε δὲ παρὰ τῆς Ἀπτέρου Νίκης τὸν ναόν.

2.30.3 ἐν Αἰγίνῃ δὲ πρὸς τὸ ὄρος τοῦ Πανελληνίου Διὸς ἰοῦσιν, ἔστιν Ἀφαίας ἱερόν, ἐς ἣν καὶ Πίνδαρος ᾆσμα Αἰγινήταις ἐποίησε. φασὶ δὲ οἱ Κρῆτες—τούτοις γάρ ἐστι τὰ ἐς αὐτὴν ἐπιχώρια—Καρμάνορος τοῦ καθήραντος Ἀπόλλωνα ἐπὶ φόνῳ τῷ Πύθωνος παῖδα Εὔβουλον εἶναι, Διὸς δὲ καὶ Κάρμης τῆς Εὐβούλου Βριτόμαρτιν γενέσθαι· χαίρειν δὲ αὐτὴν δρόμοις τε καὶ θήραις καὶ Ἀρτέμιδι μάλιστα φίλην εἶναι· Μίνω δὲ ἐρασθέντα φεύγουσα ἔρριψεν ἑαυτὴν ἐς δίκτυα ἀφειμένα ἐπ᾽ ἰχθύων θήρᾳ. ταύτην μὲν θεὸν ἐποίησεν Ἄρτεμις, σέβουσι δὲ οὐ Κρῆτες μόνον ἀλλὰ καὶ Αἰγινῆται, λέγοντες φαίνεσθαί σφισιν ἐν τῇ νήσῳ τὴν Βριτόμαρτιν. ἐπίκλησις δέ οἱ παρά τε Αἰγινήταις ἐστὶν Ἀφαία καὶ Δίκτυννα ἐν Κρήτῃ.

2.30.4 τὸ δὲ Πανελλήνιον, ὅτι μὴ τοῦ Διὸς τὸ ἱερόν, ἄλλο τὸ ὄρος ἀξιόλογον εἶχεν οὐδέν. τοῦτο δὲ τὸ ἱερὸν λέγουσιν Αἰακὸν ποιῆσαι τῷ Διί· τὰ δὲ ἐς τὴν Αὐξησίαν καὶ Δαμίαν, ὡς οὐχ ὗεν ὁ θεὸς Ἐπιδαυρίοις, ὡς τὰ ξόανα ταῦτα ἐκ μαντείας ἐποιήσαντο ἐλαίας παρ᾽ Ἀθηναίων λαβόντες, ὡς Ἐπιδαύριοι μὲν οὐκ ἀπέφερον ἔτι Ἀθηναίοις ἃ ἐτάξαντο οἷα Αἰγινητῶν ἐχόντων τὰ ἀγάλματα, Ἀθηναίων δὲ ἀπώλοντο οἱ διαβάντες διὰ ταῦτα ἐς Αἴγιναν, ταῦτα εἰπόντος Ἡροδότου καθ᾽ ἕκαστον αὐτῶν ἐπ᾽ ἀκριβὲς οὔ μοι γράφειν κατὰ γνώμην ἦν εὖ προειρημένα, πλὴν τοσοῦτό γε ὅτι εἶδόν τε τὰ ἀγάλματα καὶ ἔθυσά σφισι κατὰ <τὰ> αὐτὰ καθὰ δὴ καὶ Ἐλευσῖνι θύειν νομίζουσιν.

2.30.5 Αἰγίνης μὲν δὴ Αἰακοῦ ἕνεκα καὶ ἔργων ὁπόσα ἀπεδείξατο ἐς τοσόνδε ἔστω μνήμη· τῆς δὲ Ἐπιδαυρίας ἔχονται Τροιζήνιοι, σεμνύνοντες εἴπερ καὶ ἄλλοι τινὲς τὰ ἐγχώρια· φασὶ δὲ Ὧρον γενέσθαι σφίσιν ἐν τῇ γῇ πρῶτον. ἐμοὶ μὲν οὖν Αἰγύπτιον φαίνεται καὶ οὐδαμῶς Ἑλληνικὸν ὄνομα Ὧρος εἶναι· βασιλεῦσαι δ᾽ οὖν φασιν αὐτὸν καὶ Ὡραίαν ἀπ᾽ αὐτοῦ καλεῖσθαι τὴν γῆν, Ἄλθηπον δὲ Ποσειδῶνος παῖδα καὶ Ληίδος τῆς Ὥρου, παραλαβόντα μετὰ Ὧρον τὴν ἀρχήν, Ἀλθηπίαν ὀνομάσαι τὴν γῆν.

2.30.6 ἐπὶ τούτου βασιλεύοντος Ἀθηνᾶν καὶ Ποσειδῶνα ἀμφισβητῆσαι λέγουσι περὶ τῆς χώρας, ἀμφισβητήσαντας δὲ ἔχειν ἐν κοινῷ· προστάξαι γὰρ οὕτω Δία σφίσι. καὶ διὰ τοῦτο Ἀθηνᾶν τε σέβουσι Πολιάδα καὶ Σθενιάδα ὀνομάζοντες τὴν αὐτὴν καὶ Ποσειδῶνα Βασιλέα ἐπίκλησιν· καὶ δὴ καὶ νόμισμα αὐτοῖς τὸ ἀρχαῖον ἐπίσημα ἔχει τρίαιναν καὶ Ἀθηνᾶς πρόσωπον.

2.30.7 μετὰ δὲ Ἄλθηπον Σάρων ἐβασίλευσεν. ἔλεγον δὲ ὅτι οὗτος τῇ Σαρωνίδι τὸ ἱερὸν Ἀρτέμιδι ᾠκοδόμησεν ἐπὶ θαλάσσῃ τελματώδει καὶ ἐπιπολῆς μᾶλλον, ὥστε καὶ Φοιβαία λίμνη διὰ τοῦτο ἐκαλεῖτο. Σάρωνα δὲ—θηρεύειν γὰρ δὴ μάλιστα ἥρητο—κατέλαβεν ἔλαφον διώκοντα ἐς θάλασσαν συνεσπεσεῖν φευγούσῃ· καὶ ἥ τε ἔλαφος ἐνήχετο ἀπωτέρω τῆς γῆς καὶ ὁ Σάρων εἴχετο τῆς ἄγρας, ἐς ὃ ὑπὸ προθυμίας ἀφίκετο ἐς τὸ πέλαγος· ἤδη δὲ κάμνοντα αὐτὸν καὶ ὑπὸ τῶν κυμάτων κατακλυζόμενον ἐπέλαβε τὸ χρεών. ἐκπεσόντα δὲ τὸν νεκρὸν κατὰ τὴν Φοιβαίαν λίμνην ἐς τὸ ἄλσος τῆς Ἀρτέμιδος ἐντὸς τοῦ ἱεροῦ περιβόλου θάπτουσι, καὶ λίμνην ἀπὸ τούτου Σαρωνίδα τὴν ταύτῃ θάλασσαν καλοῦσιν ἀντὶ Φοιβαίας.

2.30.8 τοὺς δὲ ὕστερον βασιλεύσαντας οὐκ ἴσασιν ἄχρι Ὑπέρητος καὶ Ἄνθα· τούτους δὲ εἶναι Ποσειδῶνος καὶ Ἀλκυόνης Ἄτλαντος θυγατρός, καὶ πόλεις αὐτοὺς ἐν τῇ χώρᾳ φασὶν Ὑπέρειάν τε καὶ Ἄνθειαν οἰκίσαι· Ἀέτιον δὲ τὸν Ἄνθα τοῦ πατρὸς καὶ τοῦ θείου παραλαβόντα τὴν ἀρχὴν τὴν ἑτέραν τῶν πόλεων Ποσειδωνιάδα ὀνομάσαι. Τροίζηνος δὲ καὶ Πιτθέως παρὰ Ἀέτιον ἐλθόντων βασιλεῖς μὲν τρεῖς ἀντὶ ἑνὸς ἐγένοντο, ἴσχυον δὲ οἱ παῖδες μᾶλλον οἱ Πέλοπος.

2.30.9 σημεῖον δέ· ἀποθανόντος γὰρ Τροίζηνος Πιτθεὺς <ἐς> τὴν νῦν πόλιν συναγαγὼν τοὺς ἀνθρώπους ὠνόμασεν ἀπὸ τοῦ ἀδελφοῦ Τροίζηνα, συλλαβὼν <Ὑπέρειάν τε> καὶ Ἄνθειαν. πολλοῖς <δὲ> ἔτεσιν ὕστερον ἐς ἀποικίαν ἐκ Τροιζῆνος σταλέντες Ἁλικαρνασσὸν ἐν τῇ Καρίᾳ καὶ Μύνδον ἀπῴκισαν <οἱ> γεγονότες ἀπ᾽ Ἀετίου τοῦ Ἄνθα. Τροίζηνος δὲ οἱ παῖδες Ἀνάφλυστος καὶ Σφῆττος μετοικοῦσιν ἐς τὴν Ἀττικήν, καὶ οἱ δῆμοι τὰ ὀνόματα ἔχουσιν ἀπὸ τούτων. τὰ δὲ ἐς Θησέα θυγατριδοῦν Πιτθέως εἰδόσι τὰ ἐς αὐτὸν οὐ γράφω, δεῖ δέ με τοσόνδε ἔτι δηλῶσαι.

2.30.10 Ἡρακλειδῶν γὰρ κατελθόντων ἐδέξαντο καὶ οἱ Τροιζήνιοι συνοίκους Δωριέων τῶν ἐξ Ἄργους καὶ πρότερον ἔτι Ἀργείων ὄντες κατήκοοι· καὶ σφᾶς καὶ Ὅμηρος ἐν καταλόγῳ φησὶν ὑπὸ Διομήδους ἄρχεσθαι. Διομήδης γὰρ καὶ Εὐρύαλος ὁ Μηκιστέως Κυάνιππον τὸν Αἰγιαλέως παῖδα ὄντα ἐπιτροπεύοντες Ἀργείων ἡγήσαντο ἐς Τροίαν. Σθένελος δέ, ὡς ἐδήλωσα ἐν τοῖς πρότερον, οἰκίας τε ἦν ἐπιφανεστέρας, τῶν Ἀναξαγοριδῶν καλουμένων, καὶ ἡ βασιλεία τούτῳ μάλιστα ἦν ἡ Ἀργείων προσήκουσα. τοσαῦτα Τροιζηνίοις ἐχόμενα ἱστορίας ἦν, παρὲξ ἢ ὅσαι πόλεις παρ᾽ αὐτῶν φασιν ἀποικισθῆναι· κατασκευὴν δὲ ἱερῶν καὶ ὅσα ἄλλα ἐς ἐπίδειξιν, τὸ ἐντεῦθεν ἐπέξειμι.

2.31.1 ἐν τῇ ἀγορᾷ Τροιζηνίων ναὸς καὶ ἀγάλματα Ἀρτέμιδός ἐστι Σωτείρας· Θησέα δὲ ἐλέγετο ἱδρύσασθαι καὶ ὀνομάσαι Σώτειραν, ἡνίκα Ἀστερίωνα τὸν Μίνω καταγωνισάμενος ἀνέστρεψεν ἐκ τῆς Κρήτης. ἀξιολογώτατον δὲ εἶναι τοῦτο ἔδοξέν οἱ τῶν κατειργασμένων, οὐ τοσοῦτον ἐμοὶ δοκεῖν ὅτι ἀνδρείᾳ τοὺς ἀποθανόντας ὑπὸ Θησέως ὑπερέβαλεν ὁ Ἀστερίων, ἀλλὰ τό τε ἐκ τοῦ λαβυρίνθου δυσέξοδον καὶ <τὸ> λαθόντα ἀποδρᾶναι μετὰ τὸ ἔργον ἐποίησεν εἰκότα τὸν λόγον ὡς προνοίᾳ θείᾳ καὶ αὐτὸς ἀνασωθείη Θησεὺς καὶ οἱ σὺν αὐτῷ.

2.31.2 ἐν τούτῳ δέ εἰσι τῷ ναῷ βωμοὶ θεῶν τῶν λεγομένων ὑπὸ γῆν ἄρχειν, καί φασιν ἐξ Ἅιδου Σεμέλην τε ὑπὸ Διονύσου κομισθῆναι ταύτῃ καὶ ὡς Ἡρακλῆς ἀναγάγοι τὸν κύνα τοῦ Ἅιδου· ἐγὼ δὲ Σεμέλην μὲν οὐδὲ ἀποθανεῖν ἀρχὴν πείθομαι Διός γε οὖσαν γυναῖκα, τὰ δὲ ἐς τὸν ὀνομαζόμενον Ἅιδου κύνα ἑτέρωθι ἔσται μοι δῆλα ὁποῖα εἶναί μοι δοκεῖ.

2.31.3 ὄπισθεν δὲ τοῦ ναοῦ Πιτθέως μνῆμά ἐστι, τρεῖς δὲ ἐπ᾽ αὐτῷ θρόνοι κεῖνται λίθου λευκοῦ· δικάζειν δὲ Πιτθέα καὶ ἄνδρας δύο σὺν αὐτῷ λέγουσιν ἐπὶ τῶν θρόνων. οὐ πόρρω δὲ ἱερὸν Μουσῶν ἐστι, ποιῆσαι δὲ ἔλεγον αὐτὸ Ἄρδαλον παῖδα Ἡφαίστου· καὶ αὐλόν τε εὑρεῖν νομίζουσι τὸν Ἄρδαλον τοῦτον καὶ τὰς Μούσας ἀπ᾽ αὐτοῦ καλοῦσιν Ἀρδαλίδας. ἐνταῦθα Πιτθέα διδάξαι λόγων τέχνην φασί, καί τι βιβλίον Πιτθέως δὴ σύγγραμμα ὑπὸ ἀνδρὸς ἐκδοθὲν Ἐπιδαυρίου καὶ αὐτὸς ἐπελεξάμην. τοῦ Μουσείου δὲ <οὐ> πόρρω βωμός ἐστιν ἀρχαῖος, Ἀρδάλου καὶ τοῦτον ὥς φασιν ἀναθέντος· ἐπὶ δὲ αὐτῷ Μούσαις καὶ Ὕπνῳ θύουσι, λέγοντες τὸν Ὕπνον θεὸν μάλιστα εἶναι φίλον ταῖς Μούσαις.

2.31.4 πλησίον δὲ τοῦ θεάτρου Λυκείας ναὸν Ἀρτέμιδος ἐποίησεν Ἱππόλυτος· ἐς δὲ τὴν ἐπίκλησιν οὐδὲν εἶχον πυθέσθαι παρὰ τῶν ἐξηγητῶν, ἀλλὰ ἢ λύκους ἐφαίνετό μοι τὴν Τροιζηνίαν λυμαινομένους ἐξελεῖν ὁ Ἱππόλυτος ἢ Ἀμαζόσι, παρ᾽ ὧν τὰ πρὸς μητρὸς ἦν, ἐπίκλησις τῆς Ἀρτέμιδός ἐστιν αὕτη· εἴη δ᾽ ἂν ἔτι καὶ ἄλλο οὐ γινωσκόμενον ὑπὸ ἐμοῦ. τὸν δὲ ἔμπροσθεν τοῦ ναοῦ λίθον, καλούμενον δὲ ἱερόν, εἶναι λέγουσιν ἐφ᾽ οὗ ποτε ἄνδρες Τροιζηνίων ἐννέα Ὀρέστην ἐκάθηραν ἐπὶ τῷ φόνῳ τῆς μητρός.

2.31.5 εἰσὶ δὲ οὐ μακρὰν τῆς Λυκείας Ἀρτέμιδος βωμοὶ διεστηκότες οὐ πολὺ ἀπ᾽ ἀλλήλων· ὁ μὲν πρῶτός ἐστιν αὐτῶν Διονύσου κατὰ δή τι μάντευμα ἐπίκλησιν Σαώτου, δεύτερος δὲ Θεμίδων ὀνομαζόμενος· Πιτθεὺς τοῦτον ἀνέθηκεν, ὡς λέγουσιν. Ἡλίου δὲ Ἐλευθερίου καὶ σφόδρα εἰκότι λόγῳ δοκοῦσί μοι ποιῆσαι βωμόν, ἐκφυγόντες δουλείαν ἀπὸ Ξέρξου τε καὶ Περσῶν.

2.31.6 τὸ δὲ ἱερὸν τοῦ Ἀπόλλωνος τοῦ Θεαρίου κατασκευάσαι μὲν Πιτθέα ἔφασαν, ἔστι δὲ ὧν οἶδα παλαιότατον. ἀρχαῖος μὲν οὖν καὶ Φωκαεῦσι τοῖς ἐν Ἰωνίᾳ ναός ἐστιν Ἀθηνᾶς, ὃν Ἅρπαγός ποτε ὁ Μῆδος ἐνέπρησεν, ἀρχαῖος δὲ καὶ {ὁ} Σαμίοις Ἀπόλλωνος Πυθίου· πλὴν πολύ γε ὕστερον τοῦ παρὰ Τροιζηνίοις ἐποιήθησαν. ἄγαλμα δέ ἐστι τὸ ἐφ᾽ ἡμῶν ἀνάθημα Αὐλίσκου, τέχνη δὲ Ἕρμωνος Τροιζηνίου· τοῦ δὲ Ἕρμωνος τούτου καὶ τὰ τῶν Διοσκούρων ξόανά ἐστι.

2.31.7 κεῖνται δὲ ἐν στοᾷ τῆς ἀγορᾶς γυναῖκες λίθου καὶ αὐταὶ καὶ οἱ παῖδες. εἰσὶ δὲ ἃς Ἀθηναῖοι Τροιζηνίοις γυναῖκας καὶ τέκνα ἔδωκαν σώζειν, ἐκλιπεῖν σφισιν ἀρέσαν τὴν πόλιν μηδὲ στρατῷ πεζῷ τὸν Μῆδον ἐπιόντα ὑπομεῖναι. λέγονται δὲ οὐ πασῶν τῶν γυναικῶν—οὐ γὰρ δὴ πολλαί τινες ἐκεῖναι—, ὁπόσαι δὲ ἀξιώματι προεῖχον, τούτων εἰκόνας ἀναθεῖναι μόνων.

2.31.8 τοῦ δὲ ἱεροῦ τοῦ Ἀπόλλωνός ἐστιν οἰκοδόμημα ἔμπροσθεν, Ὀρέστου καλούμενον σκηνή. πρὶν γὰρ ἐπὶ τῷ αἵματι καθαρθῆναι τῆς μητρός, Τροιζηνίων οὐδεὶς πρότερον ἤθελεν αὐτὸν οἴκῳ δέξασθαι· καθίσαντες δὲ ἐνταῦθα ἐκάθαιρον καὶ εἱστίων, ἐς ὃ ἀφήγνισαν. καὶ νῦν ἔτι οἱ ἀπόγονοι τῶν καθηράντων ἐνταῦθα δειπνοῦσιν ἐν ἡμέραις ῥηταῖς. κατορυχθέντων δὲ ὀλίγον ἀπὸ τῆς σκηνῆς τῶν καθαρσίων φασὶν ἀπ᾽ αὐτῶν ἀναφῦναι δάφνην, ἣ δὴ καὶ ἐς ἡμᾶς ἔστιν, ἡ πρὸ τῆς σκηνῆς ταύτης.

2.31.9 καθῆραι δέ φασιν Ὀρέστην καθαρσίοις καὶ ἄλλοις καὶ ὕδατι <τῷ> ἀπὸ τῆς Ἵππου κρήνης. ἔστι γὰρ καὶ Τροιζηνίοις Ἵππου καλουμένη κρήνη, καὶ ὁ λόγος ἐς αὐτὴν <οὐ> διαφόρως τῷ Βοιωτῶν ἔχει· Πηγάσῳ γὰρ τῷ ἵππῳ καὶ οὗτοι λέγουσι τὸ ὕδωρ ἀνεῖναι τὴν γῆν θιγόντι τοῦ ἐδάφους τῇ ὁπλῇ, Βελλεροφόντην δὲ ἐλθεῖν ἐς Τροιζῆνα γυναῖκα αἰτήσοντα Αἴθραν παρὰ Πιτθέως, πρὶν δὲ γῆμαι συμβῆναί οἱ φυγεῖν ἐκ Κορίνθου.

2.31.10 καὶ Ἑρμῆς ἐνταῦθά ἐστι Πολύγιος καλούμενος. πρὸς τούτῳ τῷ ἀγάλματι τὸ ῥόπαλον θεῖναί φασιν Ἡρακλέα· καὶ—ἦν γὰρ κοτίνου—τοῦτο μὲν ὅτῳ πιστὰ ἐνέφυ τῇ γῇ καὶ ἀνεβλάστησεν αὖθις καὶ ἔστιν ὁ κότινος πεφυκὼς ἔτι, τὸν δὲ Ἡρακλέα λέγουσιν ἀνευρόντα τὸν πρὸς τῇ Σαρωνίδι κότινον ἀπὸ τούτου τεμεῖν ῥόπαλον. ἔστι δὲ καὶ Διὸς ἱερὸν ἐπίκλησιν Σωτῆρος· ποιῆσαι δὲ αὐτὸ βασιλεύοντα Ἀέτιον τὸν Ἄνθα λέγουσιν. ὕδωρ δὲ ὀνομάζουσι Χρυσορόαν· αὐχμοῦ δὲ ἐπὶ ἔτη συμβάντος σφίσιν ἐννέα, ἐν οἷς οὐχ ὗεν <ὁ> θεός, τὰ μὲν ἄλλα ἀναξηρανθῆναί φασιν ὕδατα, τὸν δὲ Χρυσορόαν τοῦτον καὶ τότε ὁμοίως διαμεῖναι ῥέοντα.

2.32.1 Ἱππολύτῳ δὲ τῷ Θησέως τέμενός τε ἐπιφανέστατον ἀνεῖται καὶ ναὸς ἐν αὐτῷ καὶ ἄγαλμά ἐστιν ἀρχαῖον. ταῦτα μὲν Διομήδην λέγουσι ποιῆσαι καὶ προσέτι θῦσαι τῷ Ἱππολύτῳ πρῶτον· Τροιζηνίοις δὲ ἱερεὺς μέν ἐστιν Ἱππολύτου τὸν χρόνον τοῦ βίου πάντα ἱερώμενος καὶ θυσίαι καθεστήκασιν ἐπέτειοι, δρῶσι δὲ καὶ ἄλλο τοιόνδε· ἑκάστη παρθένος πλόκαμον ἀποκείρεταί οἱ πρὸ γάμου, κειραμένη δὲ ἀνέθηκεν ἐς τὸν ναὸν φέρουσα. ἀποθανεῖν δὲ αὐτὸν οὐκ ἐθέλουσι συρέντα ὑπὸ τῶν ἵππων οὐδὲ τὸν τάφον ἀποφαίνουσιν εἰδότες· τὸν δὲ ἐν οὐρανῷ καλούμενον ἡνίοχον, τοῦτον εἶναι νομίζουσιν ἐκεῖνον Ἱππόλυτον τιμὴν παρὰ θεῶν ταύτην ἔχοντα.

2.32.2 τούτου δὲ ἐντὸς τοῦ περιβόλου ναός ἐστιν Ἀπόλλωνος Ἐπιβατηρίου, Διομήδους ἀνάθημα ἐκφυγόντος τὸν χειμῶνα ὃς τοῖς Ἕλλησιν ἐπεγένετο ἀπὸ Ἰλίου κομιζομένοις· καὶ τὸν ἀγῶνα τῶν Πυθίων Διομήδην πρῶτον θεῖναί φασι τῷ Ἀπόλλωνι. ἐς δὲ τὴν Δαμίαν καὶ Αὐξησίαν—καὶ γὰρ Τροιζηνίοις <μέτ>εστιν αὐτῶν—οὐ τὸν αὐτὸν λέγουσιν ὃν Ἐπιδαύριοι καὶ Αἰγινῆται λόγον, ἀλλὰ ἀφικέσθαι παρθένους ἐκ Κρήτης· στασιασάντων δὲ ὁμοίως τῶν ἐν τῇ πόλει ἁπάντων καὶ ταύτας φασὶν ὑπὸ τῶν ἀντιστασιωτῶν καταλευσθῆναι, καὶ ἑορτὴν ἄγουσί σφισι Λιθοβόλια ὀνομάζοντες.

2.32.3 κατὰ δὲ τὸ ἕτερον τοῦ περιβόλου μέρος στάδιόν ἐστιν Ἱππολύτου καλούμενον καὶ ναὸς ὑπὲρ αὐτοῦ Ἀφροδίτης Κατασκοπίας· αὐτόθεν γάρ, ὁπότε γυμνάζοιτο ὁ Ἱππόλυτος, ἀπέβλεπεν ἐς αὐτὸν ἐρῶσα ἡ Φαίδρα. ἐνταῦθα ἔτι πεφύκει ἡ μυρσίνη, τὰ φύλλα ὡς καὶ πρότερον ἔγραψα ἔχουσα τετρυπημένα· καὶ ἡνίκα ἠπορεῖτο ἡ Φαίδρα καὶ ῥᾳστώνην τῷ ἔρωτι οὐδεμίαν εὕρισκεν, ἐς ταύτης τὰ φύλλα ἐσιναμώρει τῆς μυρσίνης.

2.32.4 ἔστι δὲ καὶ τάφος Φαίδρας, ἀπέχει δὲ οὐ πολὺ τοῦ Ἱππολύτου μνήματος· τὸ δὲ οὐ πόρρω κέχωσται τῆς μυρσίνης. τοῦ δὲ Ἀσκληπιοῦ τὸ ἄγαλμα ἐποίησε μὲν Τιμόθεος, Τροιζήνιοι δὲ οὐκ Ἀσκληπιὸν ἀλλὰ εἰκόνα Ἱππολύτου φασὶν εἶναι. καὶ οἰκίαν ἰδὼν οἶδα Ἱππολύτου· πρὸ δὲ αὐτῆς ἐστιν Ἡράκλειος καλουμένη κρήνη, τὸ ὕδωρ ὡς οἱ Τροιζήνιοι λέγουσιν ἀνευρόντος Ἡρακλέους.

2.32.5 ἐν δὲ τῇ ἀκροπόλει τῆς Σθενιάδος καλουμένης ναός ἐστιν Ἀθηνᾶς, αὐτὸ δὲ εἰργάσατο τῆς θεοῦ τὸ ξόανον Κάλλων Αἰγινήτης· μαθητὴς δὲ ὁ Κάλλων ἦν Τεκταίου καὶ Ἀγγελίωνος, οἳ Δηλίοις ἐποίησαν τὸ ἄγαλμα τοῦ Ἀπόλλωνος· ὁ δὲ Ἀγγελίων καὶ Τεκταῖος παρὰ Διποίνῳ καὶ Σκύλλιδι ἐδιδάχθησαν.

2.32.6 κατιόντων δὲ αὐτόθεν Λυτηρίου Πανός ἐστιν ἱερόν· Τροιζηνίων γὰρ τοῖς τὰς ἀρχὰς ἔχουσιν ἔδειξεν ὀνείρατα ἃ εἶχεν ἄκεσιν λοιμοῦ πιέσαντος τὴν Τροιζηνίαν, Ἀθηναίους {δὲ} μάλιστα. διαβάντος δὲ καὶ ἐς τὴν Τροιζηνίαν * * * ναὸν <ἂν> ἴδοις Ἴσιδος καὶ ὑπὲρ αὐτὸν Ἀφροδίτης Ἀκραίας· τὸν μὲν ἅτε ἐν μητροπόλει τῇ Τροιζῆνι Ἁλικαρνασσεῖς ἐποίησαν, τὸ δὲ ἄγαλμα τῆς Ἴσιδος ἀνέθηκε Τροιζηνίων δῆμος.

2.32.7 ἰοῦσι δὲ τὴν διὰ τῶν ὀρέων ἐς Ἑρμιόνην πηγή τέ ἐστι τοῦ Ὑλλικοῦ ποταμοῦ, Ταυρίου δὲ τὸ ἐξ ἀρχῆς καλουμένου, καὶ πέτρα Θησέως ὀνομαζομένη, μεταβαλοῦσα καὶ αὐτὴ τὸ ὄνομα ἀνελομένου Θησέως ὑπ᾽ αὐτῇ κρηπῖδας τὰς Αἰγέως καὶ ξίφος· πρότερον δὲ βωμὸς ἐκαλεῖτο Σθενίου Διός. τῆς δὲ πέτρας πλησίον Ἀφροδίτης ἐστὶν ἱερὸν Νυμφίας, ποιήσαντος Θησέως ἡνίκα ἔσχε γυναῖκα Ἑλένην.

2.32.8 ἔστι δὲ ἔξω τείχους καὶ Ποσειδῶνος ἱερὸν Φυταλμίου· μηνίσαντα γάρ σφισι τὸν Ποσειδῶνα ποιεῖν φασιν ἄκαρπον τὴν χώραν ἅλμης ἐς τὰ σπέρματα καὶ τῶν φυτῶν τὰς ῥίζας καθικνουμένης, ἐς ὃ θυσίαις τε εἴξας καὶ εὐχαῖς οὐκέτι ἅλμην ἀνῆκεν ἐς τὴν γῆν. ὑπὲρ δὲ τοῦ Ποσειδῶνος τὸν ναόν ἐστι Δημήτηρ Θεσμοφόρος, Ἀλθήπου καθὰ λέγουσιν ἱδρυσαμένου.

2.32.9 καταβαίνουσι δὲ ἐπὶ τὸν πρὸς τῇ Κελενδέρει καλουμένῃ λιμένα χωρίον ἐστὶν ὃ Γενέθλιον ὀνομάζουσι, τεχθῆναι Θησέα ἐνταῦθα λέγοντες. πρὸ δὲ τοῦ χωρίου τούτου ναός ἐστιν Ἄρεως, Θησέως καὶ ἐνταῦθα Ἀμαζόνας μάχῃ κρατήσαντος· αὗται δ' ἂν εἴησαν τῶν ἐν τῇ Ἀττικῇ πρὸς Θησέα καὶ Ἀθηναίους ἀγωνισαμένων.

2.32.10 ἐπὶ θάλασσαν δὲ τὴν Ψιφαίαν πορευομένοις κότινος πέφυκεν ὀνομαζόμενος ῥᾶχος στρεπτός. ῥάχους μὲν δὴ καλοῦσι Τροιζήνιοι πᾶν ὅσον ἄκαρπον ἐλαίας, κότινον καὶ φυλλίαν καὶ ἔλαιον· στρεπτὸν δὲ ἐπονομάζουσι τοῦτον, ὅτι ἐνσχεθεισῶν αὐτῷ τῶν ἡνιῶν ἀνετράπη τοῦ Ἱππολύτου τὸ ἅρμα. τούτου δὲ οὐ πολὺ τῆς Σαρωνίας Ἀρτέμιδος ἀφέστηκε τὸ ἱερόν, καὶ τὰ ἐς αὐτὸ ἐμήνυσεν ὁ λόγος ἤδη μοι. τοσόνδε δὲ ἔτι δηλώσω· Σαρώνια γὰρ δὴ κατὰ ἔτος τῇ Ἀρτέμιδι ἑορτὴν ἄγουσι.

2.33.1 νῆσοι δέ εἰσι Τροιζηνίοις μία μὲν πλησίον τῆς ἠπείρου, καὶ διαβῆναι ποσὶν ἐς αὐτήν ἐστιν· αὕτη Σφαιρία ὀνομαζομένη πρότερον Ἱερὰ δι' αἰτίαν ἐκλήθη τοιαύτην. ἔστιν ἐν αὐτῇ Σφαίρου μνῆμα· Πέλοπος δὲ ἡνίοχον εἶναι λέγουσι τὸν Σφαῖρον. τούτῳ κατὰ δή τι ἐξ Ἀθηνᾶς ὄνειρον κομίζουσα Αἴθρα {ἐς} χοὰς διέβαινεν ἐς τὴν νῆσον, διαβάσῃ δὲ ἐνταῦθα λέγεται Ποσειδῶνα μιχθῆναι. ἱδρύσατο μὲν διὰ τοῦτο Αἴθρα ναὸν ἐνταῦθα Ἀθηνᾶς Ἀπατουρίας καὶ Ἱερὰν ἀντὶ Σφαιρίας ὠνόμασε τὴν νῆσον· κατεστήσατο δὲ καὶ ταῖς Τροιζηνίων παρθένοις ἀνατιθέναι πρὸ γάμου τὴν ζώνην τῇ Ἀθηνᾷ τῇ Ἀπατουρίᾳ.

2.33.2 Καλαύρειαν δὲ Ἀπόλλωνος ἱερὰν τὸ ἀρχαῖον εἶναι λέγουσιν, ὅτε περ ἦσαν καὶ οἱ Δελφοὶ Ποσειδῶνος· λέγεται δὲ καὶ τοῦτο, ἀντιδοῦναι τὰ χωρία σφᾶς ἀλλήλοις. φασὶ δὲ ἔτι καὶ λόγιον μνημονεύουσιν·

> Ἶσόν τοι Δῆλόν τε Καλαύρειάν τε νέμεσθαι
> Πυθώ τ' ἠγαθέην καὶ Ταίναρον ἠνεμόεσσαν.

ἔστι δ' οὖν Ποσειδῶνος ἱερὸν ἐνταῦθα ἅγιον, ἱερᾶται δὲ αὐτῷ παρθένος, ἔστ' ἂν ἐς ὥραν προέλθῃ γάμου.

2.33.3 τοῦ περιβόλου δὲ ἐντὸς καὶ τὸ Δημοσθένους μνῆμά ἐστι. καί μοι τὸ δαιμόνιον δεῖξαι μάλιστα ἐπὶ τούτου δοκεῖ καὶ Ὁμήρου πρότερον ὡς εἴη βάσκανον, εἰ δὴ Ὅμηρον μὲν προδιεφθαρμένον τοὺς ὀφθαλμοὺς ἐπὶ τοσούτῳ κακῷ κακὸν δεύτερον πενία πιέζουσα ἐπὶ πᾶσαν γῆν πτωχεύοντα ἦγε, Δημοσθένει δὲ φυγῆς τε συνέπεσεν ἐν γήρᾳ λαβεῖν πεῖραν καὶ ὁ θάνατος ἐγένετο οὕτω βίαιος. εἴρηται μὲν οὖν περὶ αὐτοῦ καὶ ἄλλοις καὶ αὐτῷ Δημοσθένει πλεῖστα, ἦ μὴν τῶν χρημάτων ἃ ἐκ τῆς Ἀσίας ἤγαγεν Ἅρπαλος μὴ μεταλαβεῖν αὐτόν·

2.33.4 τὸ δὲ ὕστερον λεχθὲν ἐπέξειμι ὁποῖον ἐγένετο. Ἅρπαλος μὲν ὡς ἐξ Ἀθηνῶν ἀπέδρα διαβὰς ναυσὶν ἐς Κρήτην, οὐ πολὺ ὕστερον ὑπὸ τῶν θεραπευόντων ἀπέθανεν οἰκετῶν· οἱ δὲ ὑπὸ ἀνδρὸς Μακεδόνος Παυσανίου δολοφονηθῆναί φασιν αὐτόν. τὸν δέ οἱ τῶν χρημάτων διοικητὴν φυγόντα ἐς Ῥόδον Φιλόξενος Μακεδὼν συνέλαβεν, ὃς καὶ αὐτὸν παρὰ Ἀθηναίων ἐξῄτησεν Ἅρπαλον. τὸν δὲ παῖδα τοῦτον ἔχων ἤλεγχεν ἐς ὃ πάντα ἐπύθετο, ὅσοι τῶν Ἁρπάλου τι ἔτυχον εἰληφότες·

2.33.5 μαθὼν δὲ ἐς Ἀθήνας γράμματα ἐπέστελλεν. ἐν τούτοις τοῖς γράμμασι τοὺς λαβόντας παρὰ Ἁρπάλου καταριθμῶν καὶ αὐτοὺς καὶ ὁπόσον αὐτῶν ἔλαβεν ἕκαστος οὐδὲ ἐμνημόνευσεν ἀρχὴν Δημοσθένους, Ἀλεξάνδρῳ τε ἐς τὰ μάλιστα ἀπεχθανομένου καὶ αὐτὸς ἰδίᾳ προσκρούσας. Δημοσθένει μὲν οὖν τιμαὶ καὶ ἑτέρωθι τῆς Ἑλλάδος <καὶ> παρὰ τῶν Καλαυρείας εἰσὶν οἰκητόρων.

2.34.1 τῆς δὲ Τροιζηνίας γῆς ἐστιν ἰσθμὸς ἐπὶ πολὺ διέχων ἐς θάλασσαν, ἐν δὲ αὐτῷ πόλισμα οὐ μέγα ἐπὶ θαλάσσῃ Μέθανα ᾤκισται. Ἴσιδος δὲ ἐνταῦθα ἱερόν ἐστι καὶ ἄγαλμα ἐπὶ τῆς ἀγορᾶς Ἑρμοῦ, τὸ δὲ ἕτερον Ἡρακλέους. τοῦ δὲ πολίσματος τριάκοντά που στάδια ἀπέχει θερμὰ λουτρά· φασὶ δὲ Ἀντιγόνου τοῦ Δημητρίου Μακεδόνων βασιλεύοντος τότε πρῶτον τὸ ὕδωρ φανῆναι, φανῆναι δὲ οὐχ ὕδωρ εὐθὺς ἀλλὰ πῦρ ἀναζέσαι πολὺ ἐκ τῆς γῆς, ἐπὶ δὲ τούτῳ μαρανθέντι ῥυῆναι τὸ ὕδωρ, ὃ δὴ καὶ ἐς ἡμᾶς ἄνεισι θερμόν τε καὶ δεινῶς ἁλμυρόν. λουσαμένῳ δὲ ἐνταῦθα οὔτε ὕδωρ ἐστὶν ἐγγὺς ψυχρὸν οὔτε ἐσπεσόντα ἐς τὴν θάλασσαν ἀκινδύνως νήχεσθαι· θηρία γὰρ καὶ ἄλλα καὶ κύνας παρέχεται πλείστους.

2.34.2 ὃ δὲ ἐθαύμασα ἐν τοῖς Μεθάνοις μάλιστα, γράψω καὶ τοῦτο. ἄνεμος ὁ Λὶψ βλαστανούσαις ταῖς ἀμπέλοις ἐμπίπτων ἐκ τοῦ Σαρωνικοῦ κόλπου τὴν βλάστην σφῶν ἀφαυαίνει· κατιόντος οὖν ἔτι τοῦ πνεύματος ἀλεκτρυόνα τὰ πτερὰ ἔχοντα διὰ παντὸς λευκὰ διελόντες ἄνδρες δύο ἐναντίοι περιθέουσι τὰς ἀμπέλους, ἥμισυ ἑκάτερος τοῦ ἀλεκτρυόνος φέρων· ἀφικόμενοι δ᾽ ἐς τὸ αὐτὸ ὅθεν ὡρμήθησαν, κατορύσσουσιν ἐνταῦθα.

2.34.3 τοῦτο μὲν πρὸς τὸν Λίβα σφίσιν ἐστὶν εὑρημένον· τὰς δὲ νησῖδας αἳ πρόκεινται τῆς χώρας ἀριθμὸν ἐννέα οὔσας Πέλοπος μὲν καλοῦσι, τοῦ θεοῦ δὲ ὕοντος μίαν ἐξ αὐτῶν οὔ φασιν ὕεσθαι. τοῦτο δὲ εἰ τοιοῦτόν ἐστιν οὐκ οἶδα, ἔλεγον δὲ οἱ περὶ τὰ Μέθανα, ἐπεὶ χάλαζάν γε ἤδη θυσίαις εἶδον καὶ ἐπῳδαῖς ἀνθρώπους ἀποτρέποντας.

2.34.4 τὰ μὲν δὴ Μέθανα ἰσθμός ἐστι τῆς Πελοποννήσου· ἐντὸς δὲ τοῦ ἰσθμοῦ τῆς Τροιζηνίων ὅμορός ἐστιν Ἑρμιόνη. οἰκιστὴν δὲ τῆς ἀρχαίας πόλεως Ἑρμιονεῖς γενέσθαι φασὶν Ἑρμίονα Εὔρωπος. τὸν δὲ Εὔρωπα—ἦν γὰρ δὴ Φορωνέως—Ἡροφάνης ὁ Τροιζήνιος ἔφασκεν εἶναι νόθον· οὐ γὰρ ἄν ποτε ἐς Ἄργον τὸν Νιόβης θυγατριδοῦν ὄντα Φορωνέως τὴν ἐν Ἄργει περιελθεῖν ἂν ἀρχὴν παρόντος Φορωνεῖ γνησίου παιδός.

2.34.5 ἐγὼ δέ, εἰ καὶ γνήσιον ὄντα Εὔρωπα πρότερον τὸ χρεὼν ἢ Φορωνέα ἐπέλαβεν, εὖ οἶδα ὡς οὐκ ἔμελλεν ὁ παῖς αὐτῷ Νιόβης παιδὶ ἴσα οἴσεσθαι Διός γε εἶναι δοκοῦντι. ἐπῴκησαν δὲ καὶ Ἑρμιόνα ὕστερον Δωριεῖς οἱ ἐξ Ἄργους· πόλεμον δὲ οὐ δοκῶ γενέσθαι σφίσιν, ἐλέγετο γὰρ ἂν ὑπὸ Ἀργείων.

2.34.6 ἔστι δὲ ὁδὸς ἐς Ἑρμιόνα ἐκ Τροιζῆνος κατὰ τὴν πέτραν ἣ πρότερον μὲν ἐκαλεῖτο Σθενίου Διὸς βωμός, μετὰ δὲ Θησέα ἀνελόμενον τὰ γνωρίσματα ὀνομάζουσιν οἱ νῦν Θησέως αὐτήν. κατὰ ταύτην οὖν τὴν πέτραν ἰοῦσιν ὀρεινὴν ὁδόν, ἔστι μὲν Ἀπόλλωνος ἐπίκλησιν Πλατανιστίου ναός, ἔστι δὲ Εἰλεοὶ χωρίον, ἐν δὲ αὐτῷ Δήμητρος καὶ Κόρης {τῆς Δήμητρος} ἱερά· τὰ δὲ πρὸς θάλασσαν ἐν ὅροις τῆς Ἑρμιονίδος ἱερὸν Δήμητρός ἐστιν ἐπίκλησιν Θερμασίας.

2.34.7 σταδίους δὲ ὀγδοήκοντα ἀπέχει μάλιστα ἄκρα Σκυλλαῖον ἀπὸ τῆς Νίσου καλουμένη θυγατρός. ὡς γὰρ δὴ τὴν Νίσαιαν ὁ Μίνως καὶ τὰ Μέγαρα εἷλεν ἐκείνης προδούσης, οὔτε γυναῖκα ἕξειν αὐτὴν ἔτι ἔφασκε καὶ προσέταξε τοῖς Κρησὶν ἐκβάλλειν τῆς νεώς· ἀποθανοῦσαν δὲ ἀπέρριψεν ἐς τὴν ἄκραν ταύτην ὁ κλύδων. τάφον δὲ οὐκ ἀποφαίνουσιν αὐτῆς, ἀλλὰ περιοφθῆναι τὸν νεκρόν φασι διαφορηθέντα ὑπὸ τῶν ἐκ θαλάσσης ὀρνίθων.

2.34.8 ἀπὸ δὲ Σκυλλαίου πλέοντι ὡς ἐπὶ τὴν πόλιν ἄκρα τέ ἐστιν ἑτέρα Βουκέφαλα καὶ μετὰ τὴν ἄκραν νῆσοι, πρώτη μὲν Ἁλιοῦσσα—παρέχεται δὲ αὕτη λιμένα ἐνορμίσασθαι ναυσὶν ἐπιτήδειον—, μετὰ δὲ Πιτυοῦσσα, τρίτη δὲ ἣν Ἀριστερὰν ὀνομάζουσι. ταύτας δὲ παραπλεύσαντί ἐστιν αὖθις ἄκρα Κωλυεργία ἀνέχουσα ἐκ τῆς ἠπείρου, μετὰ δὲ αὐτὴν νῆσος Τρίκρανα καλουμένη καὶ ὄρος ἐς θάλασσαν ἀπὸ τῆς Πελοποννήσου προβεβλημένον Βούπορθμος. ἐν Βουπόρθμῳ δὲ πεποίηται μὲν ἱερὸν Δήμητρος καὶ τῆς παιδός, πεποίηται δὲ Ἀθηνᾶς· ἐπίκλησις δέ ἐστι τῇ θεῷ Προμαχόρμα.

2.34.9 πρόκειται δὲ Βουπόρθμου νῆσος Ἀπεροπία καλουμένη, τῆς δὲ Ἀπεροπίας ἀφέστηκεν οὐ πολὺ ἑτέρα νῆσος Ὑδρέα. μετὰ ταύτην αἰγιαλός τε παρήκει τῆς ἠπείρου μηνοειδὴς καὶ ἀκτὴ μετὰ τὸν αἰγιαλὸν ἐπὶ Ποσείδιον, ἐκ θαλάσσης μὲν ἀρχομένη τῆς πρὸς ἀνατολάς, προήκουσα δὲ ὡς ἐπὶ τὴν ἑσπέραν· ἔχει δὲ καὶ λιμένας ἐν αὐτῇ. μῆκος μὲν δὴ τῆς ἀκτῆς ἐστιν ἑπτά που στάδια, πλάτος δὲ ᾗ πλατυτάτη σταδίων τριῶν οὐ πλέον.

2.34.10 ἐνταῦθα ἡ προτέρα πόλις τοῖς Ἑρμιονεῦσιν ἦν. ἔστι δέ σφισι καὶ νῦν ἔτι ἱερὰ αὐτόθι, Ποσειδῶνος μὲν ἐπὶ τῆς ἀκτῆς τῇ ἀρχῇ, προελθοῦσι δὲ ἀπὸ θαλάσσης ἐς τὰ μετέωρα ναὸς Ἀθηνᾶς, παρὰ δὲ αὐτῷ σταδίου θεμέλια· ἐν δὲ αὐτῷ τοὺς Τυνδάρεω παῖδας ἀγωνίσασθαι λέγουσιν. ἔστι δὲ καὶ ἕτερον οὐ μέγα τῆς Ἀθηνᾶς ἱερόν, ὁ δὲ ὄροφος κατερρύηκεν αὐτῷ. καὶ Ἡλίῳ ναὸς καὶ ἄλλος Χάρισιν, ὁ δὲ Σαράπιδι ᾠκοδόμηται καὶ Ἴσιδι· καὶ περίβολοι μεγάλων λίθων λογάδων εἰσίν, ἐντὸς δὲ αὐτῶν ἱερὰ δρῶσιν ἀπόρρητα Δήμητρι.

2.34.11 τοσαῦτα μὲν Ἑρμιονεῦσίν ἐστιν ἐνταῦθα· ἡ δὲ ἐφ᾽ ἡμῶν πόλις ἀπέχει μὲν τῆς ἄκρας, ἐφ᾽ ᾗ τοῦ Ποσειδῶνος τὸ ἱερόν, τέσσαρας μάλιστα σταδίους, κειμένη δὲ ἐν ὁμαλῷ τὰ πρῶτα ἠρέμα ἐς πρόσαντες ἄνεισι, τὸ δέ ἐστιν ἤδη τοῦ Πρωνός· Πρῶνα γὰρ τὸ ὄρος τοῦτο ὀνομάζουσι. τεῖχος μὲν δὴ περὶ πᾶσαν τὴν Ἑρμιόνα ἕστηκε· τὰ δὲ ἐς συγγραφὴν καὶ ἄλλα παρείχετο καὶ ὧν αὐτὸς ποιήσασθαι μάλιστα ἠξίωσα μνήμην, Ἀφροδίτης ναός ἐστιν ἐπίκλησιν Ποντίας καὶ Λιμενίας τῆς αὐτῆς, ἄγαλμα δὲ λευκοῦ λίθου μεγέθει τε μέγα καὶ ἐπὶ τῇ τέχνῃ θέας ἄξιον.

2.34.12 καὶ ναὸς ἕτερός ἐστιν Ἀφροδίτης· αὕτη καὶ ἄλλας ἔχει παρὰ Ἑρμιονέων τιμάς, καὶ ταῖς παρθένοις καὶ ἣν γυνὴ χηρεύουσα παρὰ ἄνδρα μέλλῃ φοιτᾶν, ἁπάσαις πρὸ γάμου θύειν καθέστηκεν ἐνταῦθα. Δήμητρος δὲ ἱερὰ πεποίηται Θερμασίας, τὸ μὲν ἐπὶ τοῖς πρὸς τὴν Τροιζηνίαν ὅροις, ὥς ἐστιν εἰρημένον ἤδη μοι, τὸ δὲ καὶ ἐν αὐτῇ τῇ πόλει.

2.35.1 πλησίον δὲ αὐτοῦ Διονύσου ναὸς Μελαναίγιδος· τούτῳ μουσικῆς ἀγῶνα κατὰ ἔτος ἕκαστον ἄγουσι, καὶ ἁμίλλης κολύμβου καὶ πλοίων τιθέασιν ἆθλα· καὶ Ἀρτέμιδος ἐπίκλησιν Ἰφιγενείας ἐστὶν ἱερὸν καὶ Ποσειδῶν χαλκοῦς τὸν ἕτερον πόδα ἔχων ἐπὶ δελφῖνος. παρελθοῦσι δὲ ἐς τὸ τῆς Ἑστίας, ἄγαλμα μέν ἐστιν οὐδέν, βωμὸς δέ· καὶ ἐπ᾽ αὐτοῦ θύουσιν Ἑστίᾳ.

2.35.2 Ἀπόλλωνος δέ εἰσι ναοὶ τρεῖς καὶ ἀγάλματα τρία· καὶ τῷ μὲν οὐκ ἔστιν ἐπίκλησις, τὸν δὲ Πυθαέα {οὕτως} ὀνομάζουσι, καὶ Ὅριον τὸν τρίτον. τὸ μὲν δὴ τοῦ Πυθαέως ὄνομα μεμαθήκασι παρὰ Ἀργείων· τούτοις γὰρ Ἑλλήνων πρώτοις ἀφικέσθαι Τελέσιλλά φησι τὸν Πυθαέα ἐς τὴν χώραν Ἀπόλλωνος παῖδα ὄντα· τὸν δὲ Ὅριον ἐφ᾽ ὅτῳ καλοῦσιν, σαφῶς μὲν οὐκ ἂν ἔχοιμι εἰπεῖν, τεκμαίρομαι δὲ περὶ γῆς ὅρων πολέμῳ σφᾶς ἢ δίκῃ νικήσαντας ἐπὶ τῷδε τιμὰς Ἀπόλλωνι Ὁρίῳ νεῖμαι.

2.35.3 τὸ δὲ ἱερὸν τῆς Τύχης νεώτατον μὲν λέγουσιν Ἑρμιονεῖς τῶν παρά σφισιν εἶναι, λίθου δὲ Παρίου κολοσσὸς ἕστηκεν. κρήνας δὲ τὴν μὲν σφόδρα ἔχουσιν ἀρχαίαν, ἐς δὲ αὐτὴν οὐ φανερῶς τὸ ὕδωρ κάτεισιν, ἐπιλείποι δὲ οὐκ ἄν ποτε, οὐδ᾽ εἰ πάντες καταβάντες ὑδρεύοιντο ἐξ αὐτῆς· τὴν δὲ ἐφ᾽ ἡμῶν πεποιήκασιν, ὄνομα δέ ἐστιν τῷ χωρίῳ Λειμών, ὅθεν ῥεῖ τὸ ὕδωρ ἐς αὐτήν.

2.35.4 τὸ δὲ λόγου μάλιστα ἄξιον ἱερὸν Δήμητρός ἐστιν ἐπὶ τοῦ Πρωνός. τοῦτο τὸ ἱερὸν Ἑρμιονεῖς μὲν Κλύμενον Φορωνέως παῖδα καὶ ἀδελφὴν Κλυμένου Χθονίαν τοὺς ἱδρυσαμένους φασὶν εἶναι. Ἀργεῖοι δέ, ὅτε ἐς τὴν Ἀργολίδα ἦλθε Δημήτηρ, τότε Ἀθέραν μὲν λέγουσι καὶ Μύσιον ὡς ξενίαν παρασχόντας τῇ θεῷ * * *, Κολόνταν δὲ οὔτε οἴκῳ δέξασθαι τὴν θεὸν οὔτε ἀπονεῖμαί τι ἄλλο ἐς τιμήν· ταῦτα δὲ οὐ κατὰ γνώμην Χθονίᾳ τῇ θυγατρὶ ποιεῖν αὐτόν. Κολόνταν μὲν οὖν φασιν ἀντὶ τούτων συγκαταπρησθῆναι τῇ οἰκίᾳ, Χθονίαν δὲ κομισθεῖσαν ἐς Ἑρμιόνα ὑπὸ Δήμητρος Ἑρμιονεῦσι ποιῆσαι τὸ ἱερόν.

2.35.5 Χθονία δ᾽ οὖν ἡ θεός τε αὐτὴ καλεῖται καὶ Χθόνια ἑορτὴν κατὰ ἔτος ἄγουσιν ὥρᾳ θέρους, ἄγουσι δὲ οὕτως. ἡγοῦνται μὲν αὐτοῖς τῆς πομπῆς οἵ τε ἱερεῖς τῶν θεῶν καὶ ὅσοι τὰς ἐπετείους ἀρχὰς ἔχουσιν, ἕπονται δὲ καὶ γυναῖκες καὶ ἄνδρες. τοῖς δὲ καὶ παισὶν ἔτι οὖσι καθέστηκεν ἤδη τὴν θεὸν τιμᾶν τῇ πομπῇ· οὗτοι λευκὴν ἐσθῆτα καὶ ἐπὶ ταῖς κεφαλαῖς ἔχουσι στεφάνους. πλέκονται δὲ οἱ στέφανοί σφισιν ἐκ τοῦ ἄνθους ὃ καλοῦσιν οἱ ταύτῃ κοσμοσάνδαλον, ὑάκινθον ἐμοὶ δοκεῖν ὄντα καὶ μεγέθει καὶ χρόᾳ· ἔπεστι δέ οἱ καὶ τὰ ἐπὶ τῷ θρήνῳ γράμματα.

2.35.6 τοῖς δὲ τὴν πομπὴν πέμπουσιν ἕπονται θήλειαν ἐξ ἀγέλης βοῦν ἄγοντες διειλημμένην δεσμοῖς τε καὶ ὑβρίζουσαν ἔτι ὑπὸ ἀγριότητος. ἐλάσαντες δὲ πρὸς τὸν ναὸν οἱ μὲν ἔσω φέρεσθαι τὴν βοῦν ἐς τὸ ἱερὸν ἀνῆκαν ἐκ τῶν δεσμῶν, ἕτεροι δὲ ἀναπεπταμένας ἔχοντες τέως τὰς θύρας, ἐπειδὰν τὴν βοῦν ἴδωσιν ἐντὸς τοῦ ναοῦ, προσέθεσαν τὰς θύρας.

2.35.7 τέσσαρες δὲ ἔνδον ὑπολειπόμεναι γρᾶες, αὗται τὴν βοῦν εἰσιν αἱ κατεργαζόμεναι· δρεπάνῳ γὰρ ἥτις ἂν τύχῃ τὴν φάρυγγα ὑπέτεμε τῆς βοός. μετὰ δὲ αἱ θύραι ἠνοίχθησαν καὶ προσελαύνουσιν οἷς ἐπιτέτακται βοῦν {δὲ} δευτέραν καὶ τρίτην ἐπὶ ταύτῃ καὶ ἄλλην τετάρτην. κατεργάζονταί τε δὴ πάσας κατὰ ταὐτὰ αἱ γρᾶες καὶ τόδε ἄλλο πρόσκειται τῇ θυσίᾳ θαῦμα· ἐφ᾽ ἥντινα γὰρ ἂν πέσῃ τῶν πλευρῶν ἡ πρώτη βοῦς, ἀνάγκη πεσεῖν καὶ πάσας.

2.35.8 θυσία μὲν δρᾶται τοῖς Ἑρμιονεῦσι τὸν εἰρημένον τρόπον· πρὸ δὲ τοῦ ναοῦ γυναικῶν ἱερασαμένων τῇ Δήμητρι εἰκόνες ἑστήκασιν οὐ πολλαί, καὶ παρελθόντι ἔσω θρόνοι τέ εἰσιν, ἐφ᾽ ὧν αἱ γρᾶες ἀναμένουσιν ἐσελαθῆναι καθ᾽ ἑκάστην τῶν βοῶν, καὶ ἀγάλματα οὐκ ἄγαν ἀρχαῖα Ἀθηνᾶ καὶ Δημήτηρ. αὐτὸ δὲ ὃ σέβουσιν ἐπὶ πλέον ἢ τἄλλα, ἐγὼ μὲν οὐκ εἶδον, οὐ μὴν οὐδὲ ἀνὴρ ἄλλος οὔτε ξένος οὔτε Ἑρμιονέων αὐτῶν· μόναι δὲ ὁποῖόν τί ἐστιν αἱ γρᾶες ἴστωσαν.

2.35.9 ἔστι δὲ καὶ ἄλλος ναός· εἰκόνες δὲ περὶ πάντα ἑστήκασιν αὐτόν. οὗτος ὁ ναός ἐστιν ἀπαντικρὺ τοῦ τῆς Χθονίας, καλεῖται δὲ Κλυμένου, καὶ τῷ Κλυμένῳ θύουσιν ἐνταῦθα. Κλύμενον δὲ οὐκ ἄνδρα Ἀργεῖον ἐλθεῖν ἔγωγε ἐς Ἑρμιόνα ἡγοῦμαι, τοῦ θεοῦ δέ ἐστιν ἐπίκλησις, ὅντινα ἔχει λόγος βασιλέα ὑπὸ γῆν εἶναι.

2.35.10 παρὰ μὲν δὴ τοῦτόν ἐστιν ἄλλος ναὸς καὶ ἄγαλμα Ἄρεως, τοῦ δὲ τῆς Χθονίας ἐστὶν ἱεροῦ στοὰ κατὰ τὴν δεξιάν, Ἠχοῦς ὑπὸ τῶν ἐπιχωρίων καλουμένη· φθεγξαμένῳ δὲ ἀνδρὶ τὰ ὀλίγιστα ἐς τρὶς ἀντιβοῆσαι πέφυκεν. ὄπισθεν δὲ τοῦ ναοῦ τῆς Χθονίας χωρία ἐστὶν ἃ καλοῦσιν Ἑρμιονεῖς τὸ μὲν Κλυμένου, τὸ δὲ Πλούτωνος, τὸ τρίτον δὲ αὐτῶν λίμνην Ἀχερουσίαν. περιείργεται μὲν δὴ πάντα θριγκοῖς λίθων, ἐν δὲ τῷ τοῦ Κλυμένου καὶ γῆς χάσμα· διὰ τούτου δὲ Ἡρακλῆς ἀνῆγε τοῦ Ἅιδου τὸν κύνα κατὰ τὰ λεγόμενα ὑπὸ Ἑρμιονέων.

2.35.11 πρὸς δὲ τῇ πύλῃ, καθ᾽ ἣν ὁδὸς εὐθεῖά ἐστιν ἄγουσα ἐπὶ Μάσητα, Εἰλειθυίας ἐστὶν ἐντὸς τοῦ τείχους ἱερόν. ἄλλως μὲν δὴ κατὰ ἡμέραν ἑκάστην καὶ θυσίαις καὶ θυμιάμασι μεγάλως τὴν θεὸν ἱλάσκονται καὶ ἀναθήματα δίδοται πλεῖστα τῇ Εἰλειθυίᾳ· τὸ δὲ ἄγαλμα οὐδενὶ πλὴν εἰ μὴ ἄρα ταῖς ἱερείαις ἔστιν ἰδεῖν.

2.36.1 κατὰ δὲ τὴν ἐπὶ Μάσητα εὐθεῖαν προελθοῦσιν ἑπτά που σταδίους καὶ ἐς ἀριστερὰν ἐκτραπεῖσιν, ἐς Ἁλίκην ἐστὶν ὁδός. ἡ δὲ Ἁλίκη τὰ μὲν ἐφ᾽ ἡμῶν ἐστιν ἔρημος, ᾠκεῖτο δὲ καὶ αὕτη ποτέ, καὶ Ἁλικῶν λόγος ἐν στήλαις ἐστὶ ταῖς Ἐπιδαυρίων αἳ τοῦ Ἀσκληπιοῦ τὰ ἰάματα ἐγγεγραμμένα ἔχουσιν· ἄλλο δὲ σύγγραμμα οὐδὲν οἶδα ἀξιόχρεων, ἔνθα ἢ πόλεως Ἁλίκης ἢ ἀνδρῶν ἐστιν Ἁλικῶν μνήμη. ἔστι δ᾽ οὖν ὁδὸς καὶ ἐς ταύτην, τοῦ τε Πρωνὸς μέση καὶ ὄρους ἑτέρου Θόρνακος καλουμένου τὸ ἀρχαῖον· ἀπὸ δὲ τῆς Διὸς ἐς κόκκυγα τὸν ὄρνιθα ἀλλαγῆς λεγομένης ἐνταῦθα γενέσθαι μετονομασθῆναι τὸ ὄρος φασίν.

2.36.2 ἱερὰ δὲ καὶ ἐς τόδε ἐπὶ ἄκρων τῶν ὀρῶν, ἐπὶ μὲν τῷ Κοκκυγίῳ Διός, ἐν δὲ τῷ Πρωνί ἐστιν Ἥρας· καὶ τοῦ γε Κοκκυγίου πρὸς τοῖς πέρασι ναός ἐστι, θύραι δὲ οὐκ ἐφεστήκασιν οὐδὲ ὄροφον εἶχεν οὐδέ οἵ τι ἐνῆν ἄγαλμα· εἶναι δὲ ἐλέγετο ὁ ναὸς Ἀπόλλωνος. παρὰ δὲ αὐτὸν ὁδός ἐστιν ἐπὶ Μάσητα τοῖς ἐκτραπεῖσιν ἐκ τῆς εὐθείας. Μάσητι δὲ οὔσῃ πόλει τὸ ἀρχαῖον, καθὰ καὶ Ὅμηρος ἐν Ἀργείων καταλόγῳ πεποίηκεν, ἐπινείῳ καθ᾽ ἡμᾶς ἐχρῶντο Ἑρμιονεῖς.

2.36.3 ἀπὸ Μάσητος δὲ ὁδὸς ἐν δεξιᾷ ἐστιν ἐπὶ ἄκραν καλουμένην Στρουθοῦντα. στάδιοι δὲ ἀπὸ τῆς ἄκρας ταύτης κατὰ τῶν ὀρῶν τὰς κορυφὰς †πεντήκοντά εἰσι καὶ διακόσιοι† ἐς Φιλανόριόν τε καλούμενον καὶ ἐπὶ Βολεούς· οἱ δὲ Βολεοὶ οὗτοι λίθων εἰσὶ σωροὶ λογάδων. χωρίον δὲ ἕτερον, ὃ Διδύμους ὀνομάζουσι, στάδια εἴκοσιν αὐτόθεν ἀφέστηκεν· ἐνταῦθα ἔστι μὲν ἱερὸν Ἀπόλλωνος, ἔστι δὲ Ποσειδῶνος, ἐπὶ δὲ αὐτοῖς Δήμητρος, ἀγάλματα δὲ ὀρθὰ λίθου λευκοῦ.

2.36.4 τὸ δὲ ἐντεῦθέν ἐστιν Ἀργείων ἥ ποτε Ἀσιναία καλουμένη, καὶ Ἀσίνης ἐστὶν <ἐρείπια> ἐπὶ θαλάσσῃ. Λακεδαιμονίων δὲ καὶ τοῦ βασιλέως Νικάνδρου τοῦ Χαρίλλου τοῦ Πολυδέκτου τοῦ Εὐνόμου τοῦ Πρυτάνιδος τοῦ Εὐρυπῶντος ἐς τὴν Ἀργολίδα ἐσβαλόντων στρατιᾷ συνεσέβαλόν σφισιν οἱ Ἀσιναῖοι, καὶ ἐδῄωσαν σὺν ἐκείνοις τῶν Ἀργείων τὴν γῆν. ὡς δὲ ὁ στόλος τῶν Λακεδαιμονίων ἀπῆλθεν οἴκαδε, στρατεύουσιν ἐπὶ τὴν Ἀσίνην οἱ Ἀργεῖοι καὶ ὁ βασιλεὺς αὐτῶν Ἔρατος.

2.36.5 καὶ χρόνον μέν τινα ἀπὸ τοῦ τείχους ἠμύναντο οἱ Ἀσιναῖοι καὶ ἀποκτείνουσιν ἄλλους τε καὶ Λυσίστρατον ἐν τοῖς δοκιμωτάτοις ὄντα Ἀργείων· ἁλισκομένου δὲ τοῦ τείχους οὗτοι μὲν γυναῖκας ἐς τὰ πλοῖα ἐνθέμενοι καὶ παῖδας ἐκλείπουσι τὴν αὑτῶν, Ἀργεῖοι δὲ ἐς ἔδαφος καταβαλόντες τὴν Ἀσίνην καὶ τὴν γῆν προσορισάμενοι τῇ σφετέρᾳ Πυθαέως τε Ἀπόλλωνος ὑπελίποντο <τὸ> ἱερὸν—καὶ νῦν ἔτι δῆλόν ἐστι—καὶ τὸν Λυσίστρατον πρὸς αὐτῷ θάπτουσιν.

2.36.6 ἀπέχει δὲ Ἀργείων τῆς πόλεως τεσσαράκοντα καὶ οὐ πλείω στάδια ἡ κατὰ Λέρναν θάλασσα. κατιόντων δὲ ἐς Λέρναν πρῶτον μὲν καθ᾽ ὁδόν ἐστιν ὁ Ἐρασῖνος, ἐκδίδωσι δὲ ἐς τὸν Φρίξον, ὁ Φρίξος δὲ ἐς τὴν θάλασσαν τὴν μεταξὺ Τημενίου καὶ Λέρνης. ἀπὸ δὲ Ἐρασίνου τραπεῖσιν ἐς ἀριστερὰ σταδίους ὅσον ὀκτώ, Διοσκούρων ἱερόν ἐστιν Ἀνάκτων· πεποίηται δέ σφισι κατὰ ταὐτὰ καὶ ἐν τῇ πόλει τὰ ξόανα.

2.36.7 ἀναστρέψας δὲ ἐς τὴν εὐθεῖαν τόν τε Ἐρασῖνον διαβήσῃ καὶ ἐπὶ τὸν Χείμαρρον ποταμὸν ἀφίξῃ. πλησίον δὲ αὐτοῦ περίβολός ἐστι λίθων, καὶ τὸν Πλούτωνα ἁρπάσαντα ὡς λέγεται Κόρην τὴν Δήμητρος καταβῆναι ταύτῃ φασὶν ἐς τὴν ὑπόγεων νομιζομένην ἀρχήν. ἡ δὲ Λέρνα ἐστίν, ὡς καὶ τὰ πρότερα ἔχει μοι τοῦ λόγου, πρὸς θαλάσσῃ, καὶ τελετὴν Λερναίᾳ ἄγουσιν ἐνταῦθα Δήμητρι.

2.36.8 ἔστι δὲ ἄλσος ἱερὸν ἀρχόμενον μὲν ἀπὸ ὄρους ὃ καλοῦσι Ποντῖνον, τὸ δὲ ὄρος ὁ Ποντῖνος οὐκ ἐᾷ τὸ ὕδωρ ἀπορρεῖν τὸ ἐκ τοῦ θεοῦ, ἀλλὰ ἐς αὐτὸ καταδέχεται· ῥεῖ δὲ καὶ ποταμὸς ἀπ᾽ αὐτοῦ Ποντῖνος. καὶ ἐπὶ κορυφῇ τοῦ ὄρους ἱερόν τε Ἀθηνᾶς Σαΐτιδος, ἐρείπια ἔτι μόνα, καὶ θεμέλια οἰκίας ἐστὶν Ἱππομέδοντος, ὃς Πολυνείκει τῷ Οἰδίποδος τιμωρήσων ἦλθεν ἐς Θήβας.

2.37.1 ἀπὸ δὴ τοῦ ὄρους τούτου τὸ ἄλσος ἀρχόμενον πλατάνων τὸ πολὺ ἐπὶ τὴν θάλασσαν καθήκει. ὅροι δὲ αὐτοῦ τῇ μὲν ποταμὸς ὁ Ποντῖνος, τῇ δὲ ἕτερος ποταμός· Ἀμυμώνη δὲ ἀπὸ τῆς Δαναοῦ θυγατρὸς ὄνομα τῷ ποταμῷ. ἐντὸς δὲ τοῦ ἄλσους ἀγάλματα ἔστι μὲν Δήμητρος Προσύμνης, ἔστι δὲ Διονύσου, καὶ Δήμητρος καθήμενον ἄγαλμα οὐ μέγα·

2.37.2 ταῦτα μὲν λίθου πεποιημένα, ἑτέρωθι δ᾽ ἐν ναῷ Διόνυσος Σαώτης καθήμενον ξόανον καὶ Ἀφροδίτης ἄγαλμα ἐπὶ θαλάσσῃ λίθου· ἀναθεῖναι δὲ αὐτὸ τὰς θυγατέρας λέγουσι τὰς Δαναοῦ, Δαναὸν δὲ αὐτὸν τὸ ἱερὸν ἐπὶ Ποντίνῳ ποιῆσαι τῆς Ἀθηνᾶς. καταστήσασθαι δὲ τῶν Λερναίων τὴν τελετὴν Φιλάμμωνά φασι. τὰ μὲν οὖν λεγόμενα ἐπὶ τοῖς δρωμένοις δῆλά ἐστιν οὐκ ὄντα ἀρχαῖα·

2.37.3 ἃ δὲ ἤκουσα ἐπὶ τῇ καρδίᾳ γεγράφθαι τῇ πεποιημένῃ τοῦ ὀρειχάλκου, οὐδὲ ταῦτα ὄντα Φιλάμμωνος Ἀρριφῶν εὗρε, τὸ μὲν ἀνέκαθεν Τριχωνιεὺς τῶν ἐν Αἰτωλίᾳ, τὰ δὲ ἐφ᾽ ἡμῶν Λυκίων τοῖς μάλιστα ὁμοίως δόκιμος, δεινὸς δὲ ἐξευρεῖν ἃ μή τις πρότερον εἶδε, καὶ δὴ καὶ ταῦτα φωρᾶσαι ἐπὶ τῷδε. τὰ ἔπη, καὶ ὅσα οὐ μετὰ μέτρου μεμιγμένα ἦν τοῖς ἔπεσι, τὰ πάντα Δωριστὶ ἐπεποίητο· πρὶν δὲ Ἡρακλείδας κατελθεῖν ἐς Πελοπόννησον, τὴν αὐτὴν ἠφίεσαν Ἀθηναίοις οἱ Ἀργεῖοι φωνήν· ἐπὶ δὲ Φιλάμμωνος οὐδὲ τὸ ὄνομα τῶν Δωριέων ἐμοὶ δοκεῖν ἐς ἅπαντας ἠκούετο Ἕλληνας.

2.37.4 ταῦτα μὲν δὴ ἀπέφαινεν οὕτως ἔχοντα, τῆς δὲ Ἀμυμώνης πέφυκεν ἐπὶ τῇ πηγῇ πλάτανος· ὑπὸ ταύτῃ τὴν ὕδραν τραφῆναι τῇ πλατάνῳ φασίν. ἐγὼ δὲ τὸ θηρίον πείθομαι τοῦτο καὶ μεγέθει διενεγκεῖν ὑδρῶν ἄλλων καὶ τὸν ἰὸν οὕτω δή τι ἔχειν ἀνίατον ὡς τὸν Ἡρακλέα ἀπὸ τῆς χολῆς αὐτοῦ τὰς ἀκίδας φαρμακεῦσαι τῶν ὀϊστῶν· κεφαλὴν δὲ εἶχεν ἐμοὶ δοκεῖν μίαν καὶ οὐ πλείονας, Πείσανδρος δὲ ὁ Καμιρεύς, ἵνα τὸ θηρίον τε δοκοίη φοβερώτερον {τε} καὶ αὐτῷ γίνηται ἡ ποίησις ἀξιόχρεως μᾶλλον, ἀντὶ τούτων τὰς κεφαλὰς ἐποίησε τῇ ὕδρᾳ τὰς πολλάς.

2.37.5 εἶδον δὲ καὶ πηγὴν Ἀμφιαράου καλουμένην καὶ τὴν Ἀλκυονίαν λίμνην, δι᾽ ἧς φασιν Ἀργεῖοι Διόνυσον ἐς τὸν Ἅιδην ἐλθεῖν Σεμέλην ἀνάξοντα, τὴν δὲ ταύτῃ κάθοδον δεῖξαί οἱ Πόλυμνον. τῇ δὲ Ἀλκυονίᾳ πέρας τοῦ βάθους οὐκ ἔστιν οὐδέ τινα οἶδα ἄνθρωπον ἐς τὸ τέρμα αὐτῆς οὐδεμιᾷ μηχανῇ καθικέσθαι δυνηθέντα, ὅπου καὶ Νέρων σταδίων πολλῶν κάλους ποιησάμενος καὶ συνάψας ἀλλήλοις, ἀπαρτήσας {τε} καὶ μόλυβδον ἀπ᾽ αὐτῶν καὶ εἰ δή τι χρήσιμον ἄλλο ἐς τὴν πεῖραν, οὐδὲ οὗτος οὐδένα ἐξευρεῖν <ἐδυνήθη> ὅρον τοῦ βάθους.

2.37.6 καὶ τόδε ἤκουσα ἄλλο· τὸ ὕδωρ τῆς λίμνης ὡς ἰδόντα εἰκάσαι γαληνόν ἐστι καὶ ἠρεμαῖον, παρεχόμενον δὲ ὄψιν τοιαύτην διανήχεσθαι τολμήσαντα πάντα τινὰ καθέλκειν πέφυκε καὶ ἐς βυθὸν ὑπολαβὸν ἀπήνεγκε. περίοδος δὲ τῆς λίμνης ἐστὶν οὐ πολλή, ἀλλὰ ὅσον τε σταδίου τρίτον· ἐπὶ δὲ τοῖς χείλεσιν αὐτῆς πόα καὶ σχοῖνοι πεφύκασι. τὰ δὲ ἐς αὐτὴν Διονύσῳ δρώμενα ἐν νυκτὶ κατὰ ἔτος ἕκαστον οὐχ ὅσιον ἐς ἅπαντας ἦν μοι γράψαι.

2.38.1 ἐκ Λέρνης δὲ ἰοῦσιν ἐς Τημένιον—τὸ δὲ Τημένιόν ἐστιν Ἀργείων, ὠνομάσθη δὲ ἀπὸ Τημένου τοῦ Ἀριστομάχου· καταλαβὼν γὰρ καὶ ἐχυρωσάμενος τὸ χωρίον ἐπολέμει σὺν τοῖς Δωριεῦσιν αὐτόθεν τὸν πρὸς Τισαμενὸν καὶ Ἀχαιοὺς πόλεμον—ἐς τοῦτο οὖν τὸ Τημένιον ἰοῦσιν ὅ τε Φρίξος ποταμὸς ἐκδίδωσιν ἐς θάλασσαν καὶ Ποσειδῶνος ἱερὸν ἐν Τημενίῳ πεποίηται καὶ Ἀφροδίτης ἕτερον καὶ μνῆμά ἐστι Τημένου τιμὰς ἔχον παρὰ Δωριέων τῶν ἐν Ἄργει.

2.38.2 Τημενίου δὲ ἀπέχει Ναυπλία πεντήκοντα ἐμοὶ δοκεῖν σταδίους, τὰ μὲν ἐφ᾽ ἡμῶν ἔρημος, οἰκιστὴς δὲ ἐγένετο αὐτῆς Ναύπλιος Ποσειδῶνος λεγόμενος καὶ Ἀμυμώνης εἶναι. λείπεται δὲ καὶ τειχῶν ἔτι ἐρείπια, καὶ Ποσειδῶνος ἱερὸν καὶ λιμένες εἰσὶν ἐν Ναυπλίᾳ καὶ πηγὴ Κάναθος καλουμένη· ἐνταῦθα τὴν Ἥραν φασὶν Ἀργεῖοι κατὰ ἔτος λουμένην παρθένον γίνεσθαι.

2.38.3 οὗτος μὲν δή σφισιν ἐκ τελετῆς, ἣν ἄγουσι τῇ Ἥρᾳ, λόγος τῶν ἀπορρήτων ἐστίν· τὰ δὲ ὑπὸ τῶν ἐν Ναυπλίᾳ λεγόμενα ἐς τὸν ὄνον, ὡς ἐπιφαγὼν ἀμπέλου κλῆμα ἀφθονώτερον ἐς τὸ μέλλον ἀπέφηνε τὸν καρπόν—καὶ ὄνος σφίσιν ἐν πέτρᾳ πεποιημένος διὰ τοῦτό ἐστιν ἅτε ἀμπέλων διδάξας τομήν—, παρίημι οὐκ ἀξιόλογα ἡγούμενος.

2.38.4 ἔστι δὲ ἐκ Λέρνης καὶ ἑτέρα παρ᾽ αὐτὴν ὁδὸς τὴν θάλασσαν ἐπὶ χωρίον ὃ Γενέσιον ὀνομάζουσι· πρὸς θαλάσσῃ δὲ τοῦ Γενεσίου Ποσειδῶνος ἱερόν ἐστιν οὐ μέγα. τούτου δ᾽ ἔχεται χωρίον ἄλλο Ἀπόβαθμοι· γῆς δὲ ἐνταῦθα πρῶτον τῆς Ἀργολίδος Δαναὸν σὺν ταῖς παισὶν ἀποβῆναι λέγουσιν. ἐντεῦθεν διελθοῦσιν Ἀνιγραῖα καλούμενα ὁδὸν καὶ στενὴν καὶ ἄλλως δύσβατον, ἔστιν ἐν ἀριστερᾷ μὲν καθήκουσα ἐπὶ θάλασσαν καὶ δένδρα—ἐλαίας μάλιστα—ἀγαθὴ τρέφειν γῆ.

2.38.5 ἰόντι δὲ ἄνω πρὸς τὴν ἤπειρον <ἀπ᾽> αὐτῆς χωρίον ἐστίν, ἔνθα δὴ ἐμαχέσαντο ὑπὲρ τῆς γῆς ταύτης λογάδες Ἀργείων τριακόσιοι πρὸς ἄνδρας Λακεδαιμονίων ἀριθμόν τε ἴσους καὶ ἐπιλέκτους ὁμοίως. ἀποθανόντων δὲ ἁπάντων πλὴν ἑνὸς Σπαρτιάτου καὶ δυοῖν Ἀργείων, τοῖς μὲν ἀποθανοῦσιν ἐχώσθησαν ἐνταῦθα οἱ τάφοι, τὴν χώραν δὲ οἱ Λακεδαιμόνιοι γενομένου πανδημεί σφισιν ἀγῶνος πρὸς Ἀργείους κρατήσαντες βεβαίως αὐτοί τε παραυτίκα ἐκαρποῦντο καὶ ὕστερον Αἰγινήταις ἔδοσαν ἐκπεσοῦσιν ὑπὸ Ἀθηναίων ἐκ τῆς νήσου. τὰ δὲ ἐπ᾽ ἐμοῦ τὴν Θυρεᾶτιν ἐνέμοντο Ἀργεῖοι· φασὶ δὲ ἀνασώσασθαι δίκῃ νικήσαντες.

2.38.6 ἀπὸ δὲ τῶν πολυανδρίων ἰόντι Ἀνθήνη τέ <ἐστιν>, ἐς ἣν Αἰγινῆταί ποτε ᾤκησαν, καὶ ἑτέρα κώμη Νηρίς, τρίτη δὲ Εὔα μεγίστη τῶν κωμῶν· καὶ ἱερὸν τοῦ Πολεμοκράτους ἐστὶν ἐν ταύτῃ. ὁ δὲ Πολεμοκράτης ἐστὶ καὶ οὗτος Μαχάονος υἱός, ἀδελφὸς δὲ Ἀλεξάνορος, καὶ ἰᾶται τοὺς ταύτῃ καὶ τιμὰς παρὰ τῶν προσοίκων ἔχει.

2.38.7 ἀνατείνει δὲ ὑπὲρ τὰς κώμας ὄρος Πάρνων, καὶ Λακεδαιμονίων ἐπ᾽ αὐτοῦ πρὸς Ἀργείους ὅροι καὶ Τεγεάτας εἰσίν· ἑστήκασι δὲ ἐπὶ τοῖς ὅροις Ἑρμαῖ λίθου, καὶ τοῦ χωρίου τὸ ὄνομά ἐστιν {δὲ} ἀπ᾽ αὐτῶν. ποταμὸς δὲ καλούμενος Τάναος—εἷς γὰρ δὴ οὗτος ἐκ τοῦ Πάρνωνος κάτεισι—ῥέων διὰ τῆς Ἀργείας {καὶ} ἐκδίδωσιν ἐς τὸν Θυρεάτην κόλπον.

Commentary

Mythical History of Corinth

2.1.1 **ἡ δὲ Κορινθία χώρα μοῖρα οὖσα τῆς Ἀργείας:** although this book deals with the whole of the Argolid, the manuscripts label the book Κορινθιακά after Corinth, the first city that P. treats in it. The two territories have always been closely associated in both ancient and modern times. Most of the territories that P. describes in this book were parts of the Homeric kingdoms of Argos and Mycenae, and all of them had a Dorian heritage. So P. considered all the places in book 2 parts of Ἀργεία or Ἀργολίς, terms he uses interchangeably (Hutton 2005, 70). **Κορίνθου:** the eponymous hero of Corinth and Corinthia. The names of the city of Corinth and its hero are identical except that the former is fem. and the latter masc. **ἔσχηκε:** < ἔχω, perf. act. indicative. **Διὸς δὲ εἶναι Κόρινθον:** indirect statement depending on οὐδένα . . . εἰπόντα, itself an indirect statement depending on οἶδα. The first is acc. with the infinitive, while the latter is acc. with the participle, which is the construction that οἶδα regularly takes (S 2106). The expression Διὸς Κόρινθος was employed ironically in antiquity to mock someone who often repeats a boast (Roux 85). **οὐδένα . . . εἰπόντα πω:** "no one ever said" (v. *LSJ* πω II). **σπουδῇ:** "seriously" (v. *LSJ* IV.3). **πλὴν . . . τῶν πολλῶν:** πλήν is sometimes used as a preposition with the gen. (S 1700). **Κορινθίων:** partitive gen. with τῶν πολλῶν. P. disputes the local tradition about Corinthus. **Εὔμηλός:** Eumelus is a Greek epic poet traditionally dated to the 8th c. BCE but probably living later. He is credited with a number of epics, including three—*Titanomachy*, *Corinthiaca*, and *Europia*—that may have formed a sort of Corinthian epic cycle. Cf. M. L. West, "Eumelos: A Corinthian Epic Cycle?," *JHS* 122 (2002): 109–33. P. often uses local poets as sources for local mythology and history. Some are known only from him. **Βακχιδῶν:** the Bacchidae (or Bacchiadae, according to H. 5.92.β, where their rule is termed an ὀλιγαρχία) were an aristocratic clan who ruled Corinth in the 8th c. and 7th c. BCE. They claimed descent from Heracles, and their name is derived from an early king of Corinth named Bacchis. Cf. 2.4.4; Salmon 1984, 55–74. **τὰ ἔπη . . . ποιῆσαι:** "to have composed the epic poem" (v. *LSJ* ποιέω A.I.4.a). **εἰ δὴ Εὐμήλου γε ἡ συγγραφή:** P. employs many literary sources in his work and often comments on their authenticity. He places the gen. of possession first and emphasizes it with the restrictive particle γε (S 2821), and he qualifies the conditional clause with δή (S 2843): "if indeed it is *Eumelus*' work." The term συγγραφή is chiefly used of prose works (v. *LSJ* II.1), so this may be a prose version of an original verse *Corinthiaca*. **Ἐφύραν . . . μετονομασθῆναι:** the rest of the paragraph is an indirect statement dependent on φησίν; it can be divided into four parts: (1) Ephyra's settlement of Corinthia; (2) Marathon's flight to and settlement on the Attic coast; (3) his division of land in the Peloponnesus among his sons; and (4) the renaming of Asopia and Ephyraea after Marathon's sons. **πρῶτον:** adv.; i.e., she settled there first. **Μαραθῶνα:** the eponymous hero of the Attic town Marathon, site of the famous battle between the Athenians and Persians in 490 BCE. **ἀνομίαν καὶ ὕβριν τοῦ πατρὸς:** cf. 2.6.1–3 for Epopeus' reign. Details about Epopeus' behavior toward Marathon are not preserved. **ἐς τὰ παραθαλάσσια . . . τῆς Ἀττικῆς:** "to the coastal areas of Attica." **ἀφικόμενον . . . καὶ . . . διανείμαντα . . . ἀναχωρῆσαι:** the subject of these two participles and the infinitive is αὐτόν (i.e., Marathon) below. **ἀπὸ μὲν Σικυῶνος τὴν Ἀσωπίαν, ἀπὸ δὲ Κορίνθου τὴν Ἐφυραίαν:** P. sets in parallel the two instances of renaming and links Corinth to its W neighbor Sicyon. **Ἀσωπίαν:** Sicyon was originally named after the nearby river Asopus, which appears often in book 2 (e.g., 2.5.1–4). **Ἐφυραίαν:** P. omitted the original naming of the land after Ephyra. **μετονομασθῆναι:** the naming of places and the changing of their names are an important feature of mythological history that P. often notes (e.g., 2.5.2, 2.12.5, 2.36.1).

City of Corinth

2.1.2 **οἰκοῦσι:** this verb is pl. despite the technically sg. subject, perhaps because of the pl. partitive gen. **Κορινθίων μὲν οὐδεὶς ἔτι τῶν ἀρχαίων, ἔποικοι δὲ:** P. avoids parallelism in his framing of the two different sets of inhabitants. Note also the partitive gen. with οὐδείς (S 1317). After Mummius destroyed Corinth in 146 BCE (cf. just below), the territory of the city was partly divided between Sicyon and Argos and partly declared an *ager publicus* owned by the Roman state (Roux 85). **ἀποσταλέντες:** < ἀποστέλλω, aor. passive participle. **αἴτιον . . . τὸ συνέδριον τὸ Ἀχαιῶν:** the Achaean League was a loose alliance of poleis of Achaea that was founded in the 5th c.

BCE. In the early 3rd c. BCE, it grew stronger, spread beyond the borders of Achaea, and became a potent military force in Greece under the leadership of Aratus of Sicyon, whose brilliant career P. treats with a special excursus at 2.8.2–2.9.4. **συντελοῦντες . . . ἐς αὐτό:** "as contributors (i.e., members) to it" (v. *LSJ* II.1). **οἱ Κορίνθιοι μετέσχον:** < μετέχω, aor. act. indicative. Aratus freed Corinth from a Macedonian garrison in 243 BCE, as P. relates at 2.8.4. **τοῦ πολέμου:** gen. object of μετέσχον; the gen. is often used with verbs of sharing (S 1343). The war began in 147/146 BCE. **ὃν . . . γένεσθαι:** acc. with infinitive, object of παρεσκεύασε (S 1991–94). **Κριτόλαος:** Critolaus of Megalopolis was *strategos* (the annually elected head) of the Achaean League in 147/146 BCE and died fighting the Romans at the Battle of Scarpheia. P. postpones fuller treatment of the end of old Corinth and the Achaean League to his seventh book, on Achaea (7.14–18). See also Erich Gruen, "The Origins of the Achaean War," *JHS* 96 (1976): 46–69. **στρατηγεῖν . . . ἀποδειχθεὶς:** "elected to be *strategos*" (v. *LSJ* ἀποδείκνυμι II.1). **Ἀχαιῶν:** gen. object of a verb of commanding (S 1370). **ἀποδειχθεὶς:** < ἀποδείκνυμι, aor. passive participle. **τούς τε Ἀχαιοὺς . . . καὶ . . . τοὺς πολλούς:** acc. direct objects of ἀναπείσας. **ἀποστῆναι:** < ἀφίστημι, 2nd aor. act. infinitive, "to revolt" (v. *LSJ* B.I.2); this aor. form is intransitive. **τῶν ἔξω Πελοποννήσου:** partitive gen. with τοὺς πολλούς. **τῷ πολέμῳ:** instrumental dat. with ἐκράτησαν (S 1506; v. *LSJ* κρατέω II.1.a). **τῶν ἄλλων Ἑλλήνων:** gen. of separation with παρείλοντο (S 1392). **παρείλοντο . . . περιεῖλον:** P. uses two different but related compound verbs for removal, each precisely appropriate to its object; he uses the first for the removal of (side)arms (v. *LSJ* παραιρέω II.2), the second for the removal of walls from around cities (v. *LSJ* περιαιρέω I.1). **τείχη . . . τετειχισμέναι:** close use of cognates. **(τόσων/τοσούτων πολέων) ὅσαι . . . πόλεις:** P. omits the antecedent of the correlative dependent relative clause (S 340). **ἀνάστατον:** objective complement of Κόρινθον; both are the objects of the participle ποιήσαντος (i.e., "having laid waste Corinth"; v. *LSJ* ἀνάστατος A.I.2) and of the infinitive ἀνοικίσαι in indirect discourse. **Μομμίου:** Lucius Mummius, later given the agnomen *Achaicus* for his victory over the Greeks, was Roman consul in 146 BCE. He defeated the Achaean *strategos* Diaeus and then captured, sacked, and destroyed Greek Corinth. **τῶν ἐπὶ στρατοπέδου Ῥωμαίων:** "the Romans in camp," i.e., the Roman army in the field; gen. object of ἡγουμένου. **ἀνοικίσαι . . . ἀνοικίσαι:** anaphora, "recolonize" (v. *LSJ* II). **πολιτείαν . . . τὴν ἐφ᾽ ἡμῶν κατεστήσατο:** "he established the current constitution" of the Roman imperium, i.e., the principate (v. *LSJ* πολιτεία A.III.1, καθίστημι A.II.2.b). **Καρχηδόνα:** Carthage was destroyed by Publius Cornelius Scipio Aemilianus in the same year that Mummius destroyed Corinth. Julius Caesar refounded Carthage in 49–44 BCE and Corinth in 44 BCE, the latter as Laus Iulia Corinthiensis (that name means "Corinthian Colony, Glory of Julius"). After Caesar's assassination, Augustus completed the city's refoundation. The city that P. saw was the result of extensive rebuilding after a disastrous earthquake in 77 CE. In gratitude for the aid of the Flavian emperor Vespasian, the Corinthians renamed their city Colonia Julia Flavia Augusta Corinthiensis. Cf. Donald Engels, *Roman Corinth: An Alternative Model for the Classical City* (Chicago: University of Chicago Press, 1990), 19–20. **ἐπὶ τῆς ἀρχῆς τῆς αὐτοῦ:** "during his time in power," as dictator (October 49–March 15, 44 BCE).

Crommyon

2.1.3 τῆς . . . Κορινθίας . . . γῆς: chorographic gen. (S 1311). P. shifts from the history of Corinth to the E end of the Corinthia, near the territory of Megara, to begin his journey. **Κρομυὼν:** Crommyon is on the coast of the Saronic Gulf, on the W edge of the Megarid, which P. treated at the very end of book 1. **Κρόμου τοῦ Ποσειδῶνος:** the sole mention of the eponymous hero Cromos in ancient literature (MT 208). **<Φαιάν>:** *Phaea* was the name of the Crommyonian Sow (here τὴν ὗν) defeated by the Attic hero Theseus. P. included her in a list of fabulous beasts defeated by heroes at 1.27.9. According to ps.-Apollod. *epit.* 1.1, *Phaea* was also the name of the old woman who bred the sow, which was the offspring of Echidna and Typhon. **τῶν λεγομένων Θησέως (ἔργων):** Theseus completed six labors, in comparison with Heracles' twelve. Traditionally, Theseus' labors were killing Periphetes (2.1.4), Sinis (1.37.4, 2.1.4), the Crommyonian Sow (here), Sciron (1.44.8), Cercyon (1.39.3), and Procrustes (1.38.5). These events took place during his journey from Troezen, his birthplace, to Athens, where his father, Aegeus, ruled as king. **προϊοῦσι:** < πρόειμι, a directional participle in the dat. (S 1497) and the first one in this book. P. is beginning his journey in book 2 right where he left off at the end of book 1. **ἡ πίτυς:** this may be the famous pine tree used by Sinis, the brigand who dispatched his victims by tying them to two bent pine trees and then releasing the trees, as P. describes just below. **ἄχρι γε ἐμοῦ:** "still . . . at the time of my visit" (Loeb). P. frequently ties the past to the present through surviving physical objects. **Μελικέρτου:** Melicertes, the son of Ino and Athamas, fell into the sea with his mother while they were pursued by his father during a bout of insanity. The two were subsequently transformed into sea deities—Melicertes into Palaemon, Ino into Leucothea. P. treated them at the end of his previous book, at 1.44.7–8, and describes Palaemon's temple at 2.2.1. **ἐς τοῦτον**

τὸν τόπον . . . τὸν παῖδα ὑπὸ δελφῖνος: Melicertes and the dolphin were a common image on Corinthian coins, especially during the imperial period. Two coins from the reign of Hadrian (*RPC*, vol. 3, nos. 232, 240) and several from the reign of Marcus Aurelius (*RPC*, vol. 4, nos. 7885, 8389, 9486) show Melicertes lying on a dolphin under a pine tree. **Σίσυφον:** Sisyphus was a king of Ephyra/Corinth and later was condemned to push a rock up a mountain in Hades because of his various misdeeds. P. mentions his grave at 2.2.2, his receiving the kingship from Medea at 2.3.11, and his extorting a fountain from a river god at 2.5.1. **τὸν ἀγῶνα . . . τῶν Ἰσθμίων:** the biennial Panhellenic festival of the Isthmian Games. In ancient sources, the founder of these games is variously identified as Sisyphus, his son Glaucus (father of Bellerophon), Theseus, and even Poseidon himself (Roux 87).

2.1.4 ἐπὶ τοῦ ἰσθμοῦ τῆς ἀρχῆς: = ἐπὶ τῆς τοῦ ἰσθμοῦ ἀρχῆς. **(τὸ χώριον) ἔνθα:** "(the place) where . . ." (S 2498). **ὁ λῃστὴς Σίνις:** Sinis was known as the Πιτυκάμπτης, "Pine-bender." **λαμβανόμενος πιτύων:** gen. with a verb of grasping (S 1345). **ὁπόσων . . . μάχῃ κρατήσειεν:** optative in the relative protasis of a past general condition (S 2340). The gen. here is the object of a verb of mastering (S 1370). **ὁπόσων . . . ἀπ' αὐτῶν δήσας:** "tying (the trees) to them (i.e., the defeated men)." In Greek, one ties someone or something "from" (ἐκ or ἀπό) something, rather than "to" it as in English. **ἀφῆκεν:** < ἀφίημι, 2nd aor. 3rd sg. act. indicative (S 777). **ἀφῆκεν ἂν τὰ δένδρα ἄνω φέρεσθαι:** the ἄν with the aor. indicative does not indicate the apodosis of a past contrary-to-fact condition; rather, it is the iterative aor. (S 2341). **ἑκάτερα . . . μηδετέρωσε . . . ἀμφοτέρωθεν:** the adj. and advs. indicate here precisely the number of trees and directions involved in this inventive but gruesome type of dismemberment. **τὸν δεθέντα . . . ὁ δεδεμένος:** P. varies the description of Sinis' victim slightly. Like δήσας above, all three forms are derived from δέω (A). **τοῦ δεσμοῦ μηδετέρωσε εἴκοντος:** for the gen. absolute, P. uses the negative μή that would mark the sentence as conditional in classical Greek, though it is merely causal here (S 2731). **ἐπ' ἴσης:** "equally" (v. *LSJ* ἴσος IV.2). **τοιούτῳ διεφθάρη τρόπῳ καὶ αὐτὸς ὑπὸ Θήσεως ὁ Σίνις:** the sentence is as disordered as the limbs of Sinis' victims and eventually of Sinis himself. **ἐκάθηρε:** < καθαιρέω, aor. act. indicative. **τῶν κακούργων . . . οὕς τε . . . καὶ Περιφήτην:** P. identifies the "evildoers" in the relative clause. The noun is the gen. of separation with the compound verb καθαιρέω (S 1392). **ἐν Ἐπιδαύρῳ τῇ ἱερᾷ:** P. describes Epidaurus and its famous Asclepieion at 2.26.1–2.29.1. **(παῖδα) Ἡφαίστου νομιζόμενον:** Periphetes was the son of Hephaestus and Anticleia (cf. ps.-Apollod. 3.16.1).

2.1.5 **καθήκει:** "comes down to" (v. *LSJ* A.I.2). **τῇ μὲν . . . τῇ δὲ:** "this way . . . this way" (S 346), a use of the article as a demonstrative. Cenchreae and Lechaeum are the two ports of Corinth and flank the Isthmus of Corinth; the former is to the SE of the city, the latter to the N, for westbound traffic. **ἤπειρον:** acc. complement of τὴν ἔντος χώραν. **ὃς . . . ἐπεχείρησε . . . νῆσον:** the Roman emperor Nero began his project to dig a canal across the Isthmus of Corinth in 67 CE, but it was never finished. Many other rulers and aristocrats over the centuries are said to have considered the same project: e.g., the tyrant Periander (7th c. BCE), Alexander the Great and Demetrius Poliorcetes (both 4th c. BCE), Julius Caesar (1st c. BCE), Caligula (1st c. CE), and Herodes Atticus (2nd c. CE). The modern canal was completed in 1893 (MT 208). In the absence of a canal, ancient merchants used a paved trackway called the Diolkos to move boats over land across the isthmus from 600 BCE onward. Periander is said to have built it (Salmon 1984, 136–37). **διορύσσων:** supplementary participle with a verb of ceasing (S 2098). **(τὸ χώριον) ὅθεν . . . δῆλόν ἐστιν** **ἐς . . . τὸ πετρῶδες:** i.e., during their digging. **οὐ . . . ἀρχήν:** "not at all" (v. *LSJ* ἀρχή I.1.c). **προεχώρησαν . . . προεχώρησε:** P. repeats the same verb with different subjects (first the human workers, second the ἔργον) and two different meanings ("proceeded" and "turned out well"; v. *LSJ* I.1, II.1). **ὢν:** supplementary participle with a verb of enduring (S 2098). **Ἀλεξάνδρῳ τε . . . τῷ Φιλίππου:** i.e., Alexander III, or Alexander the Great (r. 336–323 BCE), son of Philip II. Pliny *NH* 5.116 describes Alexander's plan. The single τε is sometimes used to connect sentences, usually the last item in a series (D 500). Here, however, it introduces a second example of a failed canal, and the following δέ clause gives a third example that involves the divine. **Μίμαντα:** Mimas is a promontory in Ionia that faces the island of Chios and lay between Teos and Clazomenae. It was named after a giant slain by Hephaestus during the Gigantomachy. **μόνον:** not the adv. "only," as often (v. 2.1.6), but an adj. agreeing with τοῦτο . . . ἔργων. **Κνιδίους:** Cnidus was at the end of a long peninsula in Asia Minor. P. is referring to a story told by H. at 1.17.3–6. **ἡ Πυθία . . . ἔπαυσεν:** H. gives the oracle the Cnidians received, one clearer than most of the divine utterances of the Pytho: Ἰσθμὸν δὲ μὴ πυργοῦτε μηδ' ὀρύσσετε· Ζεὺς γάρ κ' ἔθηκε νῆσον, εἴ γ' ἐβόυλετο. κέ = ἄν (S 1761). **ὀρύσσοντας:** supplementary participle with a verb of ceasing (S 2098). **οὕτω χαλεπὸν ἀνθρώπῳ τὰ θεῖα βιάσασθαι:** one of P.'s frequent musings on the human condition. Violations of divine law or the cosmic order or societal conventions prompt comment from him, a mannerism he picked up from H. **βιάσασθαι:** "to alter by violence" (Loeb).

2.1.6 τὸ δὲ . . . εἰρημένον: the legend of a divine dispute over land rights that P. will tell now. **οὐ Κορινθίοις μόνον . . . ἀλλὰ . . . Ἀθηναῖοι:** both the Corinthians and the Athenians had stories about gods contending for suzerainty over their cities. In the case of Athens, it was Athena and Poseidon; in the case of Corinth, Poseidon and Helios, as P. retells here. Again P. avoids strict parallelism, using a dat. of possession for the Corinthians and a nom. subject for the Athenians. He omits the καί in the second part of the usual phrase "not only . . . but also." MT (209) points out that Poseidon is often on the losing end of such divine competitions, e.g., losing Athens to Athena (1.24.5), Argos to Hera (2.15.5), and Troezen to Athena (2.30.6). Here, however, Poseidon gets half. **ἐμοὶ δοκεῖν:** "as it seems to me," absolute infinitive (S 2012d). **ἐλθεῖν . . . ἐς ἀμφισβήτησιν:** = ἀμφισβητῆσαι (v. *LSJ* I.2). **Βριάρεων:** Briareos, along with Cottus and Gyges, was one of the Hundred-Handers who assisted the gods in their battle against the Titans. Cf. ps-Apollod. 1.1.1. **ἰσθμὸν . . . καὶ ὅσα ταύτῃ (ἐστιν):** "the Isthmus and the parts adjoining" (Loeb). **δικάσαντα . . . δόντα:** both participles modify Βριαρέων and govern different constructions that have a similar meaning here. **δικάσαντα:** this participle governs an objective infinitive clause, "judging that the isthmus . . . belonged to . . ." **τὴν ἄκραν . . . τὴν ὑπὲρ τῆς πόλεως:** i.e., the Acrocorinth (v. 2.5.1). **Ἡλίῳ:** dat. of indirect object with δόντα. **ἀπὸ . . . τούτου:** "from this time on" (S 1684.1a).

2.1.7 θέας . . . ἄξια: "worth seeing." Like any good guide—and following H. as well—P. professes to include only worthwhile λόγοι and θεωρήματα in his work. **αὐτόθι:** P. prefers this adv. to its more Attic counterpart αὐτοῦ, "here" (S 342). **θέατρον:** the theater is a Hellenistic structure. Nero had its stage and cavea refaced, perhaps after his victory in a musical contest there in 67 CE. He also gave a speech at the theater that is also preserved on stone there (Dittenberger *ILS* 8794 = *SIG*³ 814; MT 209) **στάδιον:** the stadium was built in the time of Alexander and Philip and extensively restored in Roman times (MT 209). **λίθου λευκοῦ:** "white stone" is often understood as marble (as in the Loeb translation), but archaeologists have found that the stadium was actually built with white limestone from Acrocorinth (MT 209–10). This is an example of gen. of material (S 1323), which P. frequently employs in his descriptions. **ἐλθόντι:** P. is guiding us into the sanctuary of Poseidon at the Isthmus of Cornith, the site of the Isthmian Games, with another directional participle. **τοῦτο μὲν . . . τοῦτο δὲ:** adverbial use of the demonstrative pronouns, "on this side . . . on the other side" (S 1256). **ἀθλητῶν νικησάντων τὰ Ἴσθμια:** "the athletes who won victories at the Isthmian Games." The verb regularly takes the acc. pl. of the Panhellenic competitions, e.g., the Nemean, Isthmian, Olympic, and

Pythian Games (v. *LSJ* A.I.1). **πιτύων δένδρα:** "pine trees," a rare gen. of explanation (S 1322). **ἐπὶ στοίχου:** "in a row" (v. *LSJ* στοίχος). **τὰ πολλὰ . . . αὐτῶν:** "the majority of them" (S 1189). **τῷ ναῷ:** the original temple was built in the mid-7th c. BCE and replaced with the current one in the 460s BCE (MT 210). A coin of Marcus Aurelius (*RPC*, vol. 4, no. 9482) shows the temple. **μέγεθος:** acc. of respect (S 1601b) with οὐ μείζονι. **Τρίτωνες χαλκοῖ:** these were *acroteria*, small statues placed on the roof of a building. **ἀγάλματα . . . δύο μὲν Ποσειδῶνος, τρίτον δὲ Ἀμφιτρίτης, καὶ Θάλασσα:** a great example of P.'s dogged avoidance of parallelism. In enumerating the statues within the sanctuary of Poseidon, P. varies the construction in each clause: (1) cardinal number and gen. of the god, (2) ordinal number and gen. of the goddess, and (3) nom. of the personification. **Ἀμφιτρίτης:** Amphitrite was the daughter of either Nereus and Doris (Hesiod *Theogony* 243) or Oceanus and Tethys (ps.-Apollod. 1.11) and was the wife of Poseidon. **Ἡρώδης Ἀθηναῖος:** Herodes Atticus (101–77 CE) was the wealthiest and arguably the most cultured Athenian of his age and was responsible for a number of lavish public benefactions throughout Greece, especially in his home city of Athens. See Jennifer Tobin, *Herodes Attikos and the City of Athens: Patronage and Conflict under the Antonines* (Amsterdam, 1997). **πλὴν τῶν ὁπλῶν:** improper preposition with the gen. (S 1700), as at the beginning of 2.1.1. The noun here—ὁπλή, "hoof"—is not to be confused with ὅπλον, "tool, implement."

2.1.8 **παρὰ τοὺς ἵππους:** although no motion is involved, the preposition παρά is here used to denote parallel extent with a verb of rest (S 1692.3a), "alongside the horses." **τὰ μετ' ἰξὺν:** acc. of respect, "below the waist." P. uses an equivalent expression at the end of 2.1.9. **Παλαίμων:** the name of the deified Melicertes whom P. mentioned at 2.1.3. **τῷ βάθρῳ:** dat. with ἐπείργασται. **ἐφ' οὗ τὸ ἅρμα (ἐστιν)** **μέση:** "the middle (statue)," agreeing with Θάλασσα. **ἐπείργασται:** "there are carved in relief . . ." (v. *LSJ* ἐπεργάζομαι A.II). **Ἀφροδίτην:** Aphrodite was connected with the sea, as Hesiod's description of her birth from sea foam attests (*Theogony* 173–206). **Νηρηΐδες:** the Nereids are sea nymphs, the 50 daughters of sea deities Nereus and Doris. Ps.-Apollod. 1.2.7 gives a list of their names, as do several other ancient authors (e.g., Homer *Iliad* 18.38–49; Hesiod *Theogony* 240–64). **ἑτέρωθι τῆς Ἑλλάδος:** "in other places in Greece," adv. with chorographic gen. (S 1311; v. *LSJ* ἑτέρωθι A.II). **βωμοὺς . . . ὄντας:** the verb οἶδα typically takes a supplementary participle instead of the infinitive in indirect discourse (S 2106), as noted at 2.1.1. Here P. digresses briefly about the worship of the Nereids in the Greek world. **τοὺς δὲ (Ἑλλήνων):** "some (of the Greeks)." **ἀναθέντας:** < ἀνατίθημι, aor. act.

participle. **σφίσιν:** i.e., the Nereids. **ἔνθα καὶ Ἀχιλλεῖ τιμαί:** Achilles was the son of Peleus and the Nereid Thetis. **Δωτοῦς:** Doto was one of the Nereids. **Γαβάλοις:** Gabala was a town on the coast of Syria (modern Jableh). P. occasionally interrupts his narrative to refer to cities outside of mainland Greece, especially concerning matters of cult. **πέπλος ἔτι ἐλείπετο:** P. may be implying, with the imperf. tense, that the peplos was no longer there in his time. **Ἐριφύλην:** Eriphyle was the wife of Amphiaraus and the brother of Adrastus, king of Argos. When Adrastus was organizing the Seven against Thebes, Eriphyle took Harmonia's necklace from Polyneices as a bribe to convince her clairvoyant husband to take part despite his foreknowledge of its failure. After his death, she took Harmonia's robe as a bribe to convince her son Alcmaeon to join the expedition of the Epigoni. Upon his return, he murdered his mother, in accordance with his father's (and probably his own) wish. **ἐπὶ τῷ παιδὶ . . . Ἀλκμαίωνι:** "in the matter of her son Alcmaeon" (S 1689.2c); "was bribed to wrong her son" (Loeb).

2.1.9 **οἱ Τυνδάρεω παῖδες:** the sons of Tyndareus were Castor and Polydeuces, who famously enjoy immortality and mortality on alternate days. They were known as the Dioscouri, "Young Lads of Zeus." **ὅτι δὴ:** "obviously because" (S 2841); i.e., P. implies that their presence in a sanctuary of Poseidon should surprise no one. **ἀνθρώπων . . . ναυτιλλομένων:** "sea travelers"; I thank the anonymous referee who pointed out to me that this expression is not really just the equivalent of ναυτῶν. **ἀνάκειται:** "there are dedicated." This verb is regularly used as the passive counterpart of ἀνατίθημι, "to dedicate" (v. *LSJ* ἀνακεῖμαι A.1.a). **Γαλήνης ἄγαλμα καὶ Θαλάσσης καὶ ἵππος:** P. once again varies the constructions in a list of statues. **τὰ μετὰ τὸ στέρνον:** acc. of respect, "the parts after (i.e., below) the waist." **Ἰνώ:** Ino was the mother of Melicertes/Palaemon; see commentary on 2.1.3. **Βελλεροφόντης καὶ ὁ ἵππος ὁ Πήγασος:** Bellerophon was a famous Corinthian hero and is often depicted with his winged horse Pegasus. P. gives more information about him at 2.4.1–2. The two appear frequently on coins of the Roman era: e.g., *RPC*, vol. 3, nos. 133–35 (Hadrianic).

2.2.1 **τοῦ περιβόλου . . . ἐντὸς:** postpositive position of the improper preposition (S 1665, 1700). **Παλαίμονας . . . ναός:** this temple lies in a tripartite enclosure S of the *temenos* of Poseidon. It had a domed roof, according to Roman era coinage (e.g., *RPC*, vol. 4, nos. 10084, 4660, from the reign of Marcus Aurelius) (MT 212). **ἄλλο (ἱερόν):** it should refer to ναός but may be agreeing with Ἄδυτον here. This should be identified with the NE grotto and not the ἔσχαρα (pit for sacrificial ashes) near the temple of Palaemon (MT 212–13). **ἔνθα δὴ:** "in which very place," an intensive use of the particle (S 2843). **κεκρύφθαι:** < κρύπτω, perf. middle/passive infinitive **ὃς δ' ἂν . . . ὀμόσῃ:** protasis of a present general relative clause (S 2567). **ἐπίορκα:** internal acc. with ὀμόσῃ, "swears falsely" (v. *LSJ* ἐπίορκος I). **ἐστίν οἱ:** οἱ here is the enclitic dat. masc. sg. pronoun, not the proclitic nom. masc. pl. article (S 325). **τοῦ ὅρκου:** gen. of separation (S 1392) with διαφυγεῖν. Classical usage requires the acc. **καὶ δὴ:** this collocation of particles introduces a climax in the description (S 2847). **Κύκλωψι:** this dat. pl. is the object of θύουσιν and does not agree with αὐτῷ, which refers to the altar. Because the Cyclops Polyphemus, whom Odysseus famously encountered in book 9 of the *Odyssey*, was a son of Poseidon, an altar to him is appropriate here.

2.2.2 **<τάφους δὲ> Σισύφου καὶ Νηλέως:** this phrase is the direct object of the verb ζητοίη below. **Νηλέως:** Neleus was a son of Poseidon and fathered the Homeric hero Nestor. Ps.-Apollod. 2.7.3 says Heracles slew Neleus and his sons (save Nestor) in Pylos after Neleus refused to purify him of the murder of Eurytus. **οὐκ ἂν οἶδ' εἰ . . . :** "I do not know whether . . ." (v. *LSJ* B.6). The ἄν is transposed from the optative ζητοίη. The main verb governs a subordinated future-less-vivid condition in indirect discourse (S 2329). **ζητοίη τις (ἂν τοὺς τάφους):** "someone would look (for the tombs)," the apodosis of the condition set up by the preceding phrase. **ἐπιλεξάμενος τὰ Εὐμήλου:** P. substitutes this participial phrase for the main verb of the protasis of the future-less-vivid condition; "if he read the poems of Eumelus" (S 2344). Cf. 2.1.1 and commentary. **(τῶν τάφων) Νηλέως μὲν γὰρ . . . μνῆμα . . . (τῶν ἀνδρῶν) Σίσυφον δὲ ταφῆναι:** P. describes the circumstances of both graves but, as usual, avoids strict parallelism, augmenting the first section with a γάρ clause and elaborating the second section with a further set of μὲν . . . δέ clauses. **χρῆναι:** this impersonal verb sets up an acc. and infinitive noun clause (S 1985b). **τὸν δέ οἱ τάφον:** "his tomb"; οἱ is not the masc. pl. nom. article but the enclitic dat. masc. sg. semireflexive personal pronoun (S 325). **τῶν ἐφ' αὐτοῦ Κορινθίων:** "of the Corinthians in his own time." **τοὺς εἰδότας:** < οἶδα, perf. act. participle (S 794). **ἐξέλιπεν:** < ἐκλείπω, aor. act. indicative intransitive, "it ceased" (v. *LSJ* A.II.4). **ὅσον μέν χρόνον ἠρήμωτο ἡ πόλις:** i.e., after the sack of the city by Mummius in 146 BCE, which P. referenced in 2.1.2. **Σικυωνίοις:** after its destruction by the Romans, the territory of Corinth was divided between Sicyon and Argos. **ἐπετέτραπτο:** < ἐπιτρέπω, pluperf. middle/passive indicative, "it was entrusted" (v. *LSJ* A.I.3). The subject of the verb is the infinitive phrase ἄγειν . . . τὰ Ἴσθμια, and Σικυωνίοις is an indirect object (S 1748). **οἰκισθείσης αὖθις (πόλεως):** gen. absolute. **τοὺς νῦν οἰκήτορας:** the inhabitants of rebuilt Roman Corinth; the original Roman colonists were freedmen, according to Strabo 8.380–81. **περιῆλθεν:** < περιέρχομαι, aor. act. indicative, "it came around (to)" (v. *LSJ* A.II.1), i.e., "it came back (to)." Corinth recovered the games in 6 or 2 BCE. Cf. Donald Engels, *Roman Corinth: An Alternative Model for the Classical City* (Chicago: University of Chicago Press, 1990) 19.

Harbors of Corinth

2.2.3 **Λέχης καὶ Κεγχρίας:** a coin of Corinth under Hadrian depicts the two harbors personified as nymphs holding rudders (*RPC*, vol. 3, no. 197); P. regards them as male heroes. **πεποίηται:** "it is written (in the poem)" (v. *LSJ* A.I.4.a); this sets up the indirect statement after the citation of the source. **ἐν Ἠοίαις μεγάλαις:** the *Great Eoiae*, an important but now fragmentary poem about the genealogy of heroes, is ascribed to Hesiod. Here P. contrasts the oral tradition (λεγόμενοι) with the poetic (πεποίηται). For this poem, see Glenn Most (ed.), Hesiod, *The Shield. Catalogue of Women. Other Fragments*, Loeb Classical Library 503 (Cambridge, MA: Harvard University Press, 2007). **Οἰβάλου:** Oebalus was the king of Sparta and the second husband of Gorgophone, Perseus' daughter (cf. 2.21.7). Oebalus was the son of Perieres and fathered Tyndareus, Hippocoon, and Icarius with the naiad Batia, according to ps.-Apollod. 3.10.4. **Λεχαίῳ:** Lechaeum was one of the biggest ports in Greece and was physically joined to Corinth with long walls, just as the Peiraeus was to Athens. It was mostly deserted in the early imperial period (MT 214–15). **τὴν . . . ἐς Κεγχρέας (ὁδὸν) ἰόντων ἐξ ἰσθμοῦ:** a directional participle in the gen. that takes the acc. of the route P. guides the reader along. **ἐπὶ τῷ ἐρύματι τῷ διὰ τῆς θαλάσσης:** i.e., a mole serving as a breakwater for the harbor at Cenchreae. The port was shaped like a semicircle and is depicted on a coin of the reign of Antoninus Pius (*RPC*, vol. 4, no. 5097). **Ἴσιδος ἱερά:** Isis was an ancient Egyptian goddess Hellenized by the Ptolemaic rulers of Egypt. Her worship spread throughout the Mediterranean during the Roman Republic and early Roman Empire; e.g., note the near-contemporary scene of Isis at Cenchreae in book 11 of Apuleius' *Metamorphoses*. **Κεγχρεῶν . . . ἀπαντικρὺ:** preposition with object preceding due to anastrophe. **τὸ Ἑλένης . . . λουτρόν:** this bath, and a similarly titled spring of Helen on Chios, may have played a role in the cult of Helen and even had an "initiatory" function. See Lowell Edmunds, *Stealing*

Helen: The Myths of the Abducted Wife in Comparative Perspective (Princeton, NJ: Princeton University Press, 2016), 177. **ὕδατι . . . ἀρχομένῳ θερμαίνεσθαι:** i.e., tepid water.

Entering Corinth

2.2.4 **ἄλλα . . . μνήματα καὶ . . . Διογένης:** ἄλλος often precedes the particular thing with which it is contrasted (S 1273). **Διογένης . . . ὁ Σινωπεύς:** Diogenes of Sinope was a follower of Antisthenes, the founder of the ancient Cynic school of philosophy. According to a story related by many authors, Alexander the Great was once in Corinth and went to meet Diogenes, who was lying in the sun at the time. Alexander greeted Diogenes and asked if he wanted anything, and Diogenes replied, ἀπὸ τοῦ ἡλίου μετάστηθι, "Move out of the way of the sun" (Plutarch *Life of Alexander* 14.3). **ἄλσος . . . Κράνειον:** the grove had a gymnasium, the site of Alexander's encounter with Diogenes (Diogenes Laertius 6.79). **Ἀφροδίτης . . . Μελαινίδος:** "Aphrodite the Black" (v. *LSJ* μελαινίς I). P. explains this epithet for the goddess at 8.6.5 by stating that humans have sexual intercourse at night. **τάφος Λαΐδος:** there were two courtesans with the name *Lais*, one of the archaic period buried in Corinth, the other of the classical period in Thessaly. The *Suda* (v. Πειρήνη) preserves the epitaph in elegiac verse in Corinth: Λαΐδ' ἔχω πολιῆτιν ἐϋζώνοιο Κορίνθου / Πειρήνης λευκῶν φαιδροτέραν λιβάδων, "I hold Lais, a citizen of well-girt Corinth; / she shown brighter than the white waters of Peirene." **ᾧ δὴ:** "which indeed"; intensive δή, which often is paired with relative pronouns (S 2843). Its antecedent is τάφος, but it is a dat. of possession (S 1476). **ἐπίθημά:** this noun stands in apposition with λέαινα.

2.2.5 **ἄλλο . . . Λαΐδος φάμενον μνῆμα εἶναι:** "another tomb that says it is Lais." The middle forms of φημί are act. in meaning and rare in Attic but common in H. (S 786D). **Ἱπποστράτου:** gen. object with ἐρασθεῖσα (S 1349). ἔραμαι is a middle deponent verb; the aor. is passive in form but act. in meaning (S 811; v. *LSJ*); ἐράω supplies the present and imperf. forms in prose. **τὸ . . . ἐξ ἀρχῆς:** "originally"; a prepositional phrase that could otherwise stand alone is given an article and used as an adverbial acc. **αὐτὴν:** i.e., Lais, who is the subject of the series of participles and infinitives that follow. **λέγεται:** this verb sets up the indirect statement that consists of the rest of this long sentence. **Νικίου καὶ Ἀθηναίων:** i.e., during the fateful Sicilian Expedition in 415–413 BCE. The Athenians captured Hycara and sold all the inhabitants into slavery. **ἁλῶναι:** < ἁλίσκομαι, 2nd aor. act. infinitive (S 687). **πραθεῖσαν:** < πιπράσκω, aor. passive participle. **οὕτω . . . ὡς ἀμφισβητεῖν . . . :** a clause of natural result takes an acc. and infinitive construction (S 2251). **ἀμφισβητεῖν:** "lay claim to," with gen. object (v. *LSJ* A.I.3.a).

Agora of Corinth

2.2.6 λόγου . . . ἄξια . . . τὰ μὲν λειπόμενα ἔτι τῶν ἀρχαίων . . . τὰ δὲ πολλὰ αὐτῶν ἐπὶ τῆς ἀκμῆς . . . τῆς ὕστερον: P. explains the dearth of antiquities in Corinth and the consequent brevity of his account. He has little interest in the Roman-era sights of the city (e.g., in the agora), even though Corinth was the capital of the Roman province of Achaea. **ἔστιν οὖν ἐπὶ τῆς ἀγορᾶς . . . :** for the important question of P.'s route in the Corinthian agora and the identification of the buildings there, see MT 217–20. P. may omit buildings or imply the existence of them while mentioning statues, but most scholars agree that he usually respects topographical sequence. **ἐπίκλησιν:** this noun appears only in the acc. of respect, with the meaning "surnamed" (S 1601b; v. *LSJ*). It is used twice more at 2.2.8. **ἀλοιφῇ . . . ἐρυθρᾷ:** "red paint" (v. *LSJ* ἀλοιφή I.3). **Λύσιον δέ, τὸν δὲ Βάκχειον:** two of the very many epithets of Dionysus. P. includes the article with the second title and not the first. Both are syntactically predicates.

2.2.7 τὰ . . . λεγόμενα ἐς τὰ ξόανα: P. now adds a λόγος to explain the two statues. **Πενθέα:** Pentheus, grandson of Cadmus, was king of Thebes. Euripides used the dire events P. recapitulates here as the subject of his tragedy *Bacchae*. **λέγουσι . . . λέγουσιν:** P. uses the same verb to indicate, first, the larger poetic tradition and, second, the local oral tradition (MT 221). **τὰς δέ (γυναῖκας) ἐφώρασαν:** < φωράω not ἐφοράω. **ἄλλο (μέρος) ἄλλην (γυναῖκα) τοῦ σώματος:** "one (woman) tore off one (part) of his body, another, another (part)"; when two forms of ἄλλος are used, the second half of the statement is omitted (S 1274). P. transposes the order of the forms. **χρᾷ:** < χράω, "directs (them) to" (v. *LSJ* (B) A.I). **σφισιν ἀνευρόντας:** both terms refer to the same people, the Corinthians; the pronoun is the dat. of the indirect object with χρᾷ, and the acc. participle is the subject of the infinitive in the objective clause established by χρᾷ. **ἴσα τῷ θεῷ:** adverbial acc. of measure (S 1609), "equally with the god" (v. *LSJ* ἴσος IV.1). The acc. object of the infinitive and participle is τὸ δένδρον ἐκεῖνο. **ἀπ' αὐτοῦ (δένδρου).**

2.2.8 **Τύχης ναός:** under the Romans, Tyche was associated with the cult of Fortuna Augusta. **θεοῖς πᾶσίν ἐστι ἱερόν:** Agrippa, Augustus' admiral, built a Pantheon in Rome in 29–19 BCE (which Hadrian restored) and this one in Corinth. Hadrian built a Pantheon in Athens too (P. mentions it at 1.5.5 and 1.18.8). **κρήνη:** not the fountain proper but its water basin. **ἀφιεὶς:** < ἀφίημι, present act. participle, agreeing with δελφίς. **Κλάριος:** Claros was a sanctuary of Apollo near Colophon in Ionia. A famous oracle of the god operated at this site, which flourished in P.'s time. **Ἑρμογένους Κυθηρίου:** because this artist is not mentioned in any other source, it is difficult even to define what century he lived in—but he may belong to the Roman era (MT 221). **Ἑρμοῦ . . . ἀγάλματα χαλκοῦ μὲν καὶ ὀρθὰ ἀμφότερα, τῷ δὲ ἑτέρῳ (ἀγάλματι) . . . :** "both . . . one of them . . ." **τὸ μὲν (ἄγαλμα) . . . τὸν δὲ αὐτῶν (Δία) . . . τὸν τρίτον . . . :** P. separates the three statues into two clauses and varies his syntax to make one the subject of the verb (εἶχε) in the first clause and to make the other two the objects of the verb (καλοῦσιν) in the second clause; he also changes the gender from neut. (statue) to masc. (god).

2.3.1 **ὑπὲρ . . . τὴν ἀγοράν:** i.e., on a high foundation overlooking the agora. **Ὀκταβίας . . . ἀδελφῆς Αὐγούστου βασιλεύσαντος Ῥωμαίων:** Octavia was the full sister of Octavian, who was later Augustus Caesar, and she was the fourth wife of his rival, the triumvir Mark Antony. Although P. considers this building, known to modern archaeologists as Temple E, the temple of Octavia and, thus, a building dedicated to the Roman imperial cult, it was probably the Corinthian Capitolium, i.e., the temple of Jupiter, Juno, and Minerva. Cf. Mary E. Hoskins Walbank, "Pausanias, Octavia, and Temple E at Corinth," *Annual of the British School at Athens* 84 (1989): 361–94. For emperor worship in general, see I. Gradel, *Emperor Worship and Roman Religion* (Oxford: Clarendon Press, 2002).

Road to Lechaeum

2.3.2 **ἐκ . . . τῆς ἀγορᾶς ἐξιόντων τὴν ἐπὶ Λεχαίου (ὁδόν):** directional participle in the gen.; there is another directional participle just below in this subsection, **ἐξιοῦσιν,** although it is in the dat. **προπύλαιά:** numismatic evidence shows an arch surmounted by Helius on a chariot but varies between one fornix (Neronian) and three (Antonine) (MT 223). **Φαέθοντα:** this son of Helios famously perished while attempting to drive his father's chariot. **Ἥλιον αὐτὸν:** this is the intensive use of the pronoun (S 1206b). **φέρον:** present act. participle modifying τὸ μὲν (ἅρμα) and τὸ δὲ (ἅρμα). **ὀλίγον:** adverbial acc. with ἀπωτέρω. **τῆς Πειρήνης:** P. mentioned Peirene at 2.2.3. She appears frequently on Corinthian coins (e.g., *RPC*, vol. 3, no. 214, from the reign of Hadrian). **λέγουσιν ὡς . . . γένοιτο:** optative in indirect statement. Although the main verb is in a primary tense, the optative may still be used when it is implied that the thought quoted has been expressed in the past (S 2627). Several imperial-era coins show the fountain (e.g., *RPC*, vol. 4, no. 9494, from the reign of Lucius Verus), and many of these depict a prominent statue of Scylla within it. **ὑπὸ δακρύων:** gen. of cause, "because of tears" (S 1698.1b). P. then explains this with the phrase τὸν παῖδα ὀδυρομένη . . . **Κεγχρίαν ὑπὸ Ἀρτέμιδος ἀκούσης ἀποθανόντα:** P. mentioned Cenchrias at 2.2.3, as the eponymous hero of the port of Cenchreae.

2.3.3 **κεκόσμηται δὲ ἡ πηγὴ λίθῳ λευκῷ:** P. is describing a marble elaboration of the fountain house that a certain Antonius Sospes paid for in the late 1st c. or early 2nd c. CE. He was an agonothete of the Isthmian Games and a friend of Plutarch, and he appears in Plutarch's dialogue collection "Table Talk." Cf. Betsey A. Robinson, *Histories of Peirene: A Corinthian Fountain in Three Millennia* (Princeton, NJ: American School of Classical Studies, 2011), 207ff. **σπηλαίοις κατὰ ταὐτά (= τὰ αὐτά):** "in the same way as caves." **ἐπεὶ χαλκός γε οὐκ ἔστι Κορινθίοις:** some editors hold that there is a lacuna here after χαλκός; cf. Rocha-Pereira 1989–90, ad loc. Archaeologists have found foundries within the *peribolos* of Apollo just below (MT 223). **ἔτι γε δή:** "and furthermore" (D 245; v. *LSJ* ἔτι II.1). **τὸ Ὀδυσσέως ἐς τοὺς μνηστῆρας . . . τόλημα:** i.e., his slaughtering of the suitors in book 22 of the *Odyssey*, a subject popular with ancient Greek artists. τόλημα is the direct object of ἔχουσα, which agrees with γραφή. Perhaps this painting was a fresco in the exedra of the enclosure, which was built in the age of Augustus and rebuilt ca. 77 CE (MT 223).

2.3.4 **τὴν εὐθεῖαν (ὁδόν)** **καθήμενός ἐστιν Ἑρμῆς, παρέστηκε δέ οἱ κριός:** this pairing is found on Corinthian coins: e.g., *RPC*, vol. 3, nos. 114, 239 (Hadrianic). **θεῶν:** partitive gen. **Ὅμηρος ἐν Ἰλιάδι ἐποίησεν:** *Iliad* 14.490–91. **υἱὸν Φόρβαντος:** Ilioneus was the son of Phorbas and was the victim of Peneleos' martial prowess. **τόν:** Homer uses the article as a relative pronoun when the antecedent is definite (S 1105). **ῥα:** this enclitic Homeric form of the particle ἄρα often appears after monosyllables (S 2787). **Τρώων:** partitive gen. **ἐν τελετῇ Μητρός (θεῶν):** the rites of the Mother of the Gods, i.e., Cybele. **ἐπὶ Ἑρμῇ . . . καὶ τῷ κριῷ:** the preposition governs both phrases. **λόγον ἐπιστάμενος οὐ λέγω:** P. sometimes declines to explain a story or monument because of some religious prohibition, which is implied here by the fact that the λόγος belongs to sacred rites.

2.3.5 λουτρὰ . . . καὶ ἄλλα, τὰ μὲν . . . τὸ δὲ . . . τὸ δὲ: P. divides the baths in Corinth into three categories. **ἀπὸ τοῦ κοινοῦ:** "at the public expense" (v. *LSJ* κοινός A.II.3). **βασιλέως Ἀδριανοῦ:** the philhellenic Roman emperor Hadrian (r. 117–38 CE) was famous for his extensive travels throughout the empire and his widespread benefactions to cities large and small. P. frequently mentions his gifts to Greeks. Cf. Mary Boatwright, *Hadrian and the Cities of the Roman Empire* (Princeton, NJ: Princeton University Press, 2000). **Εὐρυκλῆς . . . Σπαρτιάτης:** Gaius Julius Eurycles was an ally of Octavian at the Battle of Actium in 31 BCE. In reward for his service, he received Roman citizenship and the title ἡγεμὼν Λακεδαιμονίων. His descendant C. Julius Eurycles Herculanus built this bath complex in the 2nd c. CE. Cf. G. Steinhauer, "C. Iulius Eurycles and the Spartan Dynasty of the Euryclids," in *Roman Peloponnese, vol. 3, Society, Economy, and Culture under the Roman Empire: Continuity and Innovation*, ed. A. D. Rizakis and Cl. E. Lepenioti (Athens: the National Hellenic Research Foundation Institute for Greek and Roman Antiquity, 2010), 75–88. Cf. also MT 224. **λίθοις . . . καὶ ἄλλοις καὶ (λίθῳ) ὃν ἐν Κροκεαῖς χώρας τῆς Λακωνικῆς ὀρύσσουσιν:** Croceae was a village to the S of Sparta along the road to Gytheion, Sparta's port (Roux 118). This is a highly prized work of *verde antico*. **ἅτε ἀφθόνου ῥέοντός . . . ὕδατος:** the particle ἅτε with a participle denotes cause (S 2085). **(ὕδωρ) ὃ δὴ . . . ἐσήγαγεν ἐκ Στυμφήλου:** i.e., an aqueduct. Remains of it can be seen in the area of Phlius (MT 224–25). **θέας . . . μάλιστα ἀξία <ἡ> (κρήνη):** P. signals the most noteworthy of the fountains. **καί οἱ Βελλεροφόντης ἔπεστι καὶ τὸ ὕδωρ:** the fountain house of Bellerophontes appears on Corinthian coins (e.g., *BMC* 653, from the reign of Septimius Severus).

Road to Sicyon

2.3.6 ἑτέραν (ὁδὸν) . . . τὴν ἐπὶ Σικυῶνα ἐρχομένοις: directional participle. **ἔστιν ἰδεῖν . . . ναὸς καὶ ἄγαλμα:** "it is possible to see a temple and statue"; P. begins with an impersonal construction (S 1985; v. *LSJ* εἰμί (A) A.VI; e.g., ἔστιν ἰδεῖν . . . ναὸν καὶ ἄγαλμα) and transitions into a personal one (e.g., εἰσὶν ναὸς καὶ ἄγαλμα, "there are a temple and statue"). **ὀλίγον ἀπωτέρω:** "a little further away," an adverbial acc. modifying a comparative adv. **Γλαύκης:** Glauce was the daughter of Creon, king of Corinth. **τῶν Μηδείας . . . φαρμάκων . . . ἴαμα:** Jason repudiated Medea to marry Glauce, and as Euripides describes in his *Medea*, the heroine retaliated by giving Glauce a poisoned robe and by killing her own children. In Euripides' play, however, Glauce does not throw herself into the well (MT 226). **τὸ καλούμενον Ὠιδεῖον:** this huge hall (it had 7,000 seats) was built under Nero. After a fire in the 2nd c. CE, it was rebuilt by Herodes Atticus. It lies NW of the fountain of Glauce (MT 225). **καταλιθωθῆναι δὲ ὑπὸ Κορινθίων:** ps.-Apollod. 1.9.28 says she left the infants on the altar of Hera, from which the Corinthians removed and killed them. **τῶν δώρων ἕνεκα ὧν (= ἅ):** an instance of the attraction of the relative pronoun ἅ into the case of its antecedent (S 2522).

2.3.7 **οὐ σὺν τῷ δικαίῳ:** i.e., ἀδίκου; an instance of litotes. **τὰ τέκνα . . . τὰ νήπια:** P. specifies that they were young children (v. *LSJ* νήπιος I.1). **αὐτῶν:** i.e., the children of Medea; dat. of indirect object. They are referred to in this sentence and the next with the pronouns αὐτοῖς (twice) and σφισιν. **πρὶν ἤ . . . ἐπεστάθη:** the tenses of the main verb (ἐφθείρετο) and of the verbs in this clause indicate that the deaths continued to happen (imperf. tense) until decisive steps were taken (aor. tense). In prose, use of πρίν to mean "until" usually takes the indicative after negative sentences or those implying a negative (G 634–35). Classical examples that seem to contradict this rule (v. S 2441c) all have a leading verb in the imperf., which emphasizes the continuation of the action up to the point of time expressed by the subordinate clause, as in "they did not cease to die until . . ." **θυσίαι . . . κατέστησαν . . . ἐκεῖναι καθεστήκασιν:** P. uses two forms of καθίστημι, 2nd aor. act. indicative and perf. act. indicative, both intransitive (v. S 420 for the paradigm of the verb, 819 for the use of the tenses). **(ἄγαλμα) Δεῖμα ἐπεστάθη:** < ἐφίστημι, aor. passive indicative, "(a statue of) Deima was set up" (v. *LSJ* A.III). **τοῦτο μὲν δή:** the particle δή here may be considered as either connecting this sentence with the previous one (the pronoun τοῦτο also serves in epanalepsis) or strengthening the μέν, for P. will shortly contrast the survival of the statue of Fear with the falling of the rites into abeyance, in the δέ clause following (D 258–59). **ἐς τὸ φοβερώτερον:** "so as to have a more fearful appearance" (S 1686.1d). **Κορίνθου . . . γενομένης ὑπὸ Ῥωμαίων καὶ . . . Κορινθίων . . . ἀπολομένων:** two consecutive gen. absolutes hammer home the end of Greek Corinth. **ἀπολομένων:** < ἀπόλλυμι, aor. middle participle. **οὐκέτι . . . καθεστήκασιν . . . αἱ θυσίαι:** P. again highlights the cultural discontinuity caused by the destruction of Corinth by Mummius. **παρὰ τῶν ἐποίκων:** "by the colonists" (S 1692.1b). **ἀποκείρονταί:** "they cut their hair" (in mourning).

2.3.8 **συνῴκησεν:** < συνοικέω, aor. act. indicative, "she married" (v. *LSJ* I.2). **χρόνῳ . . . ὕστερον:** "later," adv. with a pleonastic dat. of manner (S 1516). **φωραθεῖσα ἐπιβουλεύειν:** "caught plotting"; the verb φωράω can take an acc. object with a participle or an infinitive, and the passive construction here retains the infinitive (e.g., "they discovered her plotting . . . ," ἐφώρασαν αὐτὴν ἐπιβουλεύειν). **τὴν λεγομένην τότε Ἀρίαν:** Aria was a region of the Persian Achaemenid Empire in Western Afghanistan, but it was often confused by classical authors with the larger region of Ariana, of which Aria was a part. **τοῖς ἀνθρώποις ἔδωκε τὸ ὄνομα καλεῖσθαι Μήδους:** "she brought it about that the men were called Medes" (G 747; *LSJ* δίδωμι III.1). The men are both the dat. indirect object of ἔδωκε and the implied acc. subject of καλεῖσθαι, and τὸ ὄνομα serves both as the acc. direct object of ἔδωκε and as an acc. of respect. According to ps.-Apollod. 1.9.28, Medus conquered and named the land Media but died in an expedition against the Indians. **ἐπήγετο:** < ἐπάγω, "she brought with herself" (v. *LSJ* A.II.5). **ὄνομα δέ οἱ Μῆδον εἶναι:** acc. subject of an infinitive in indirect discourse. **Ἑλλάνικος:** Hellanicus of Mitylene was a Greek writer and historian in the 5th c. BCE (*FGrH* 324).

2.3.9 **ἔπη . . . Ναυπάκτια ὀνομαζόμενα:** this epic poem, attributed to Carcinus, was written in the 6th or 5th c. BCE and formed part of the Epic Cycle. Due to the paucity of surviving fragments, it is difficult to form an opinion of the whole work, but it appears to have included stories of Jason and the Argonauts. See M. L. West, *Greek Epic Fragments: From the Seventh to the Fifth Centuries BC, Loeb Classical Library 497* (Cambridge, MA: Harvard University Press, 2003). **μετὰ τὸν Πελίου θάνατον:** Pelias was the son of Tyro and Poseidon; Aeson, the father of Jason, was his half brother, the son of Tyro and Cretheus. Pelias seized power in Thessaly and imprisoned Aeson; Pelias later sent Jason on his quest for the Golden Fleece. Medea brought about the death of Pelias by convincing Pelias' daughters to subject him to an ultimately fatal rejuvenation process. **ἐν τῇ πέραν ἠπείρῳ:** "on the mainland opposite" (v. *LSJ* πέραν I.1); the mainland opposite Corcyra was Epirus. **Φέρητι . . . οὐδέν . . . προσκείμενον:** "nothing pertaining to Pheres" (v. *LSJ* προσκεῖμαι III.1). **Κιναίθων . . . ὁ Λακεδαιμόνιος:** Cinaethon was a Greek poet said to have written parts of the Epic Cycle, including the *Oedipodea*, *Little Iliad*, and *Telegonia*. See West, *op. cit.* **πέρα . . . οὐδὲ τούτῳ πεποιημένα ἐστίν:** "nothing more has been written by this man either" (v. *LSJ* πέρα I.1). **ἐς τοὺς παῖδας:** "about the children."

2.3.10 **Εὔμηλος:** P. mentioned this Corinthian poet in 2.1.1, as a source for the mythology of the city. The information he gives here supplements the information given there. **ἔφη . . . τὴν ἀρχήν:** this verb governs all the acc. forms and infinitives in indirect discourse until the end of the next subsection. However, the verbs in the dependent clause (i.e., ἐπεὶ . . . ἐτελεύτησεν) remain unchanged in the indicative. **Ἀλωεῖ μὲν τὴν Ἀσωπίαν, Αἰήτῃ δὲ τὴν Ἐφυραίαν:** in 2.1.1, P. noted that *Asopia* and *Ephyraea* were the original names for Sicyon and Corinth respectively. He also mentioned there that Aloeus was the son of Helios. Aeëtes too was a son of Helios, and so we see the divine father divide his lands among his mortal sons. **Αἰήτην ἀπιόντα ἐς Κόλχους:** Aeëtes founded Aea in Colchis and was the ruler there when Jason and the Argonauts later arrived in search of the Golden Fleece. **Βούνῳ:** P. mentions this obscure hero again at 2.4.7, for his piety toward Hera. **Ἐπωπέα τὸν Ἀλωέως:** P. stated in 2.1.1 that Epopeus' violence drove his son Marathon out into Attica and that Marathon later returned and divided the area between his sons Corinthus and Sicyon. P. now explains why both cities were under the power of Epopeus and his son. **σχεῖν:** < ἔχω, 2nd aor. act. infinitive **Κορίνθου . . . ὑπολειπομένου:** gen. absolute. **τοὺς Κορινθίους Μήδειαν μεταπεμψαμένους ἐξ Ἰωλκοῦ:** Medea was the daughter of Aeëtes and thus had a claim to the throne, as P. declares with the phrase δι' αὐτήν just below.

2.3.11 **βασιλεύειν μὲν δὴ:** here the δή strengthens the μέν (v. 2.3.7). **τό . . . ἀεὶ τικτόμενον (τέκνον) . . . αὐτὸ:** "(each) child as it was born" (v. *LSJ* ἀεὶ A.I). This phrase is the direct object of κατακρύπτειν and φέρουσα. **κατακρύπτειν . . . κατακρύπτειν:** an instance of pseudanaphora; the subject of each infinitive is Medea. **(Μήδειαν) φέρουσαν . . . νομίζουσαν** **μαθεῖν ὡς ἡμαρτήκοι:** here P. employs the optative mood in an indirect statement. The optative is justified because the immediate governing verb is an aor. infinitive representing an aor. indicative (e.g., "finally she learned that"), a secondary tense (S 2619). **τῆς ἐλπίδος:** gen. object of a verb of failing (S 1392). **φωραθεῖσαν:** an echo of 2.3.8, where Medea was caught plotting against Aegeus in Athens. **οὐ γὰρ αὐτὸν . . . οἴχεσθαι:** a parenthetical sentence in indirect discourse like the rest of the passage. **ἔχειν . . . συγγνώμην:** "to pardon," with the dat. of person (v. *LSJ* συγγνώμη A.I.a). **Σισύφῳ:** P. mentioned this hero at 2.1.3, as discovering the body of Melicertes.

2.4.1 **τάδε μὲν οὕτως ἔχοντα ἐπελεξάμην:** P. combines a form of ὅδε and the adverbial form of οὗτος to sum up the previous subsection. Usually the pronoun ὅδε points forward and οὗτος points backward

(S 1247), but P. frequently ignores this classical distinction. **τοῦ μνήματος:** P. is referring back to the tomb of Medea's children that was mentioned in 2.3.6, which was the occasion of the lengthy digression that followed. **Χαλινίτιδος Ἀθηνᾶς:** "Athena the Bridler" (v. *LSJ*). This was the most ancient aspect of Athena. She helped Bellerophon tame Pegasus, as P. notes (MT 227). **Βελλεροφόντῃ . . . τὸν Πήγασόν:** P. mentioned them at 2.1.9 and 2.3.5. **φασὶ:** P. artfully places the governing verb of the two indirect statements between them, deftly separating the acc. and infinitive construction from the ὡς with the optative construction. **ἐνθεῖσα . . . χαλινόν:** < ἐντίθημι, aor. act. participle, "putting the bridle (on the horse)." **ξόανόν . . . πρόσωπον δὲ καὶ χεῖρες καὶ ἀκρόποδες εἰσὶ λευκοῦ λίθου:** an acrolithic statue, i.e., a statue where the prominent features are made of stone and the rest of wood. **ἀκρόποδες:** i.e., πόδες.

2.4.2 **οὐκ αὐτοκράτορα ὄντα βασιλεύειν:** the noun αὐτοκράτωρ could denote the Roman emperor during the imperial period, but here, as occasionally, it indicates an absolute ruler of any time period, including mythical ones. Using Bellerophon as a starting point, P. gives an overview (in this and the following subsections) of the other royal dynasties of Corinth: Helios to Corinthus, the Sisyphides, Heracles to Aletes (i.e., the Dorians), and Aletes to Bacchis. **εἶναι δὲ ἐπὶ Προίτῳ καὶ Ἀργείοις:** "but was under the power of Proetus and the Argives" (v. S 1689.2c for dependence). Proetus was the son of Lynceus and the Danaid Hypermnestra and was ruler of Argos. P. explains Proetus' role in the history of Argos at 2.16.2–3. **ἐγώ τε . . . καὶ ὅστις . . . ἐπελέξατο:** P. again emphasizes his own research and superior knowledge, just as he did at 2.2.2. He invites the reader to think of himself or herself as being in the latter category. **πείθομαι:** this verb governs the preceding acc. and infinitive indirect statement. **ὅστις τὰ Ὁμήρου . . . ἐπελέξατο:** relative clause with indefinite antecedents take μή (not οὐ) when negative (S 2705d). P. refers here to the narrative at *Iliad* 6.155–203, which encapsulates the life and labors of Bellerophon. **μὴ πάρεργον:** this adverbial phrase is based on the classical μὴ παρέργως. **Βελλεροφόντου μετοικήσαντος ἐς Λυκίαν:** gen. absolute. **τῶν ἐν Ἄργει δυναστῶν ἢ Μυκήναις:** ὑπακόυω may take either a gen. or dat. object (S 1366, 1465), and P. uses both here. **ἰδίᾳ:** "on their own" (v. *LSJ* VI.2). **ἰδίᾳ τε οὐδένα . . . :** τε here connects this sentence to the previous one and has the sense of "and as a result" (S 2968); cf. this use to ἐγώ τε . . . καὶ ὅστις just above. **συντεταγμένοι δὲ Μυκηναίοις καὶ ὅσων ἄλλων Ἀγαμέμνων ἡγεῖτο:** the participle ("arrayed with") takes the dat. Μυκηναίοις and an original ἄλλοις that has been attracted into the relative clause and thus into the case of the relative pronoun ὅσων. **τοῦ στόλου:** gen. with verb of sharing (S 1343).

2.4.3 οὔτι . . . μόνον . . . ἀλλὰ καί: "not only . . . but also"; P. employs a phrase common in Greek but adds his own bit of emphasis with the adv. τι (v. *LSJ* οὔτις I.2). **Γλαῦκος:** this Glaucus should not be confused with the great-grandson of the same name who appears at *Iliad* 6.155ff.: Glaucus fathered Bellerophon, who begat Hippolochus, who sired the Homeric hero Glaucus II. **ἐπὶ . . . αὐτῷ:** "in addition to him" (S 1689.2c). **Φῶκος:** the eponymous hero of Phocis, whom P. alludes to in the phrase τῆς νῦν καλουμένης Φωκίδος just below. **Ποσειδῶνος δὲ ἐπίκλησιν:** ἐπίκλησις was used in the sense of a surname at 2.2.6 and 2.2.8, but here it means "by repute," i.e., λόγῳ. There was some ambiguity over who was his real father. **Προπόδα:** gen. sg. masc. of the 1st declension in Aeolic and Doric (S 214D5). **Δωρεῖς:** the so-called Dorian invasion was linked by historians in antiquity with the mythical return of the Heraclidae, the sons of Heracles, who were driven from the Peloponnese by Eurystheus and whose descendants returned after three generations. P. carefully gives the genealogy of Aletes here, tracing him back to the son of Zeus, his great-great-grandfather. Modern scholars are skeptical about this invasion as a historical event. **αὐτοῦ:** adv., "in the very place" (S 342). **ἐξέπεσεν:** < ἐκπίπτω, aor. act. indicative, "(the Corinthian people) were expelled" (v. *LSJ* 3). Because this verb is very often used as the passive of ἐκβάλλω (the act. form of which appears in the next subsection), it can logically take a gen. of personal agent with ὑπό (S 1752). This upheaval in population resembles that caused by Mummius (2.1.2, 2.2.2). It is interesting that the Corinthian people disregarded their kings' resignations and continued to oppose the invaders.

2.4.4 Βάκχιν: the founder of the Bacchiadae family, to which Eumelus belonged (v. 2.1.1). **ἐπὶ γενεὰς πέντε . . . (ἐπὶ) πέντε ἄλλας γενεάς:** "for five generations . . . for another five." The preposition ἐπί with the acc. can refer to duration of time (S 1689.3b), but the simple acc. can do the same. See Diodorus 7.9 for another version of these successions. **κατὰ ἔχθος:** "because of hatred" (S 1690.2c). Arieus and Perantas deposed Telestes but kept the political power in the clan. **Κύψελος τυραννήσας ὁ Ἠετίωνος:** Cypselus was the first tyrant of Corinth and ruled ca. 657–627 BCE; his son Periander, often included in ancient lists of the Seven Wise Men, succeeded him and ruled ca. 627–587 BCE. Periander was succeeded by his nephew Psammetichus, who was overthrown and killed after three years. For a discussion of the tyrants of Corinth and their importance in Corinthian history, see Salmon 1984, 186–230. **Μέλανα . . . στρατεύοντα:** the acc. direct object of ἐκέλευσεν. **τὸ μὲν παραυτίκα . . . ὕστερον δέ . . . :** "at first . . . but later . . ." **ἁμαρτὼν τοῦ χρησμοῦ:** gen. with verbs of reaching (or failing to do so) (S 1350), "mistaking the oracle" (Loeb). **δέχεται (αὐτὸν) σύνοικον:** P. includes only the predicate complement. **Τοιαῦτα μὲν ἐς τοὺς Κορινθίων βασιλέας συμβάντα εὕρισκον:** Ending the digression, P. again signals his research before moving on to the sights near the sanctuary of Athena Chalinitis, which he described at 2.4.1.

2.4.5 τῷ θεάτρῳ: this ancient theater was thoroughly restored under Hadrian (MT 230). **Δαιδάλου:** Daedalus is known from mythology as the father of Icarus and the creator of the Labyrinth, but many wooden cult figures around Greece were attributed to him. Their antiquity often garners notice from P. **τέχνην:** "the artwork (of Daedalus)" (v. *LSJ* IV). **Δαίδαλος:** despite its position, this noun is the subject not of the sentence but of the relative clause ὁπόσα εἰργάσατο, which is itself the subject of the sentence. **ἐπιπρέπει δὲ ὅμως τι καὶ ἔνθεον τούτοις:** P. attributes a degree of divine craftsmanship to the statue. **Διὸς Καπετωλίου φωνῇ τῇ Ῥωμαίων:** i.e., Jupiter Capitolinus, the most important Roman cult imported by the Roman colonists. **φωνῇ τῇ Ῥωμαίων· κατὰ Ἑλλάδα . . . γλῶσσαν:** a noteworthy instance of P.'s drive to avoid parallelism and achieve variety of expression. **Κορυφαῖος ὀνομάζοιτο ἄν:** potential optative with ἄν (S 1824). **γυμνάσιον τὸ ἀρχαῖον:** this vast structure actually dates to the Roman period (MT 230–31). **Λέρνα:** this Lerna is not to be confused with the area and lake of the same name that P. describes at 2.36.6 and 2.37.6. **ἀναψύχειν:** a rare infinitive of purpose with πεποίηνται (S 2008). **ὥρᾳ θέρους:** i.e., "in the summertime," pleonastic for θέρει. **ἀγάλματα Ἀσκληπιὸς μὲν καὶ Ὑγεία . . . τὸ δὲ τοῦ Διός . . . :** more *variatio.*

Acrocorinth

2.4.6 ἀνιοῦσιν δὲ ἐς τὸν Ἀκροκόρινθον . . . ἐς δὴ τὸν Ἀκροκόρινθον τοῦτον ἀνιοῦσίν: due to the length of the parenthetical sentence, P. repeats the directional participle and its prepositional phrase in epanalepsis and chiasmus. The second time, he emphasizes the destination with both the particle δή and the demonstrative adj. οὗτος: "well, to *this* very Acrocorinth . . ." **Βριάρεω . . . Ἡλίῳ δόντος αὐτὴν:** P. refers to the dispute between Poseidon and Helios that he described at 2.1.6. **Ἴσιδος τεμένη ὧν τὴν μὲν Πελαγίαν, τὴν δὲ Αἰγυπτίαν αὐτῶν ἐπονομάζουσιν:** sanctuaries of Isis were common in Greek cities in the imperial age; P. noted one at 2.2.3. **καὶ δύο Σαράπιδος, ἐν Κανώβῳ καλουμένου τὸ ἕτερον:** Serapis was the husband/brother of Isis. Canopus was an ancient Egyptian coastal town and the site of a temple to Serapis. **τὸ ἕτερον (τέμενος):** "one (of the two)." **καὶ Ἀνάγκης καὶ Βίας ἐστιν ἱερόν:** this sanctuary may be appropriate near the altars of Helius, who was regarded as the protector of oaths and fate (MT 231–32). **ἐσιέναι . . . ἐς αὐτὸ οὐ νομίζουσιν:** "they do not consider it customary to enter it" (v. *LSJ* νομίζω I.1), i.e., out of religious scruple.

2.4.7 **Μητρὸς θεῶν ναός ἐστι καὶ στήλη καὶ θρόνος:** some editors delete the phrase καὶ στήλη. The stele in question was probably a bas-relief of the goddess (Roux 128). The Anatolian goddess Cybele entered Greek culture in the 6th c. BCE and was connected with Rhea, Artemis, and Demeter. **αὐτὴ (ἡ θεός):** i.e., the goddess' εἰκών, or cult image. **ὁ δὲ τῶν Μοιρῶν καὶ <ὁ> Δήμητρος καὶ Κόρης (ναός)** **οὐ φανερὰ . . . τὰ ἀγάλματα:** the images are presumably kept within secluded areas of the temples. **Βούνου τοῦ Ἑρμοῦ:** P. mentioned him at 2.3.10, as the man to whom Aeëtes entrusted Sicyon before leaving for Colchis.

2.5.1 **ἀνελθοῦσι δὲ ἐς τὸν Ἀκροκόρινθον:** note the tense of the directional participle; "once you have reached the summit." **ὡπλισμένη:** < ὁπλίζω, perf. middle/passive participle. **Ἔρως ἔχων τόξον:** the usual depiction of Eros/Cupid. **δῶρον μὲν Ἀσωποῦ λέγουσιν εἶναι, δοθῆναι δὲ Σισύφῳ:** an instance of pseudanaphora, as P. expands a single action into two clauses, instead of simply writing ταύτην Ἀσωπὸν Σισύφῳ δοῦναι λέγουσιν *vel sim.* **Ζεὺς ἡρπακὼς Αἴγιναν θυγατέρα Ἀσωποῦ:** P. returns to the story at 2.29.2, when he begins his survey of the island of Aegina. **μὴ πρότερον φάναι . . . μηνύσειν:** verbs of saying or thinking regularly take οὐ with the infinitive in indirect discourse, but μή may be substituted in emphatic declarations (S 2722–23). The wily Sisyphus is adamant that he will not disclose the information before Asopus yields. **(Ἀσωπῷ) ζητοῦντι** **πρὶν ἤ. . . . . . γένοιτο:** πρίν never takes the optative unless it occurs in indirect discourse with a principal negative clause and a verb in a secondary tense or its equivalent (S 2448–49). **δόντος δὲ Ἀσωποῦ μηνύει . . . δίδωσιν:** P. abruptly switches from acc. with the infinitive in indirect discourse to the historical present in the indicative, to finish the story with a vivid flourish (S 1883). **ὅτῳ πιστὰ:** = εἴ τις ἐστιν ὅτῳ τάδε πιστά ἐστιν. P. signals his doubt parenthetically. Ancient authors give various reasons for Sisyphus' punishment in Hades, including putting death himself in chains. **(τινῶν) φαμένων:** the phrase is the gen. object of ἤκουσα.

Like H., P. emphasizes his personal research into the matter. **ταύτην (τὴν πηγήν)** **αὐτόθεν:** "from the very place" (v. *LSJ* I.1).

2.5.2 **ἐκδίδωσιν:** "empties itself (into)" (v. *LSJ* II.1). **Φλιασίας:** P. describes the city and territory of Phlius at 2.12.3–2.13.8. **ἀπὸ μὲν δὴ Κορκύρας . . . :** for this collocation of particles, see 2.3.7; δή likely acts as a connector here. **Αἰγίνης:** P. describes Aegina at 2.29.2–2.30.4. **Σχερίαν:** the name Homer gives to the island of the Phaeacians in the *Odyssey*. **τὴν ὑπὸ τῇ Καδμείᾳ (πόλιν)** **Θηβαῖοι δὲ οὐχ ὁμολογοῦσι:** P., like his model H. (cf. *Histories* 1.5, 1.171), takes the opportunity to register conflicting traditions. **τοῦ Βοιωτίου . . . Ἀσωποῦ:** there were actually four different rivers with the name *Asopus* in Greece, the Boeotian and Phliasian ones named here and others in Thessaly and Trachis.

2.5.3 **ἔπηλυ:** "immigrant," as opposed to αὐτόχθων, which P. employs at 2.5.6 (v. *LSJ* II). For the declension of this "one-ending adj.," see S 312. **Μαίανδρον . . . κατιόντα . . . καὶ ἐκδιδόντα . . . ποιεῖν τὸν Ἀσωπόν:** as a native of Asia Minor (so scholars conjecture), P. often takes the opportunity to bring in pertinent references to his homeland. Cf., e.g., 1.21.3, 2.22.3. **Δηλίων:** gen. object of ἀκούσας. **τοιοῦτο . . . ἕτερον:** the acc. direct object of οἶδα; it is explained by the acc. and infinitive indirect statement directly following, "another such (story)." **καὶ δὴ καὶ:** "and what is more" (S 2890). P. adds another example, this time the greatest river in the ancient world. **ἔχει . . . λόγος:** "and there is a story," with acc. and infinitive indirect statement following. The expression is equivalent to λέγουσι, which is common in P.'s text. **Ἀσωποῦ . . . πέρι:** an instance of anastrophe with a preposition (S 175); note the shifting of the accent on the preposition from oxytone to paroxytone.

Tenea

2.5.4 **τραπεῖσι:** < τρέπω, aor. passive participle, here used as a directional participle. **τὴν ὀρεινὴν (ὁδόν):** internal acc. object of the participle (S 1567). **ἑξήκοντα . . . μάλιστα στάδια:** acc. of extent with ἀπέχει (S 1581). **ταύτῃ:** adverbial use of the pronoun, "here" (v. *LSJ* οὗτος C.VIII.4.a). **ἡ καλουμένη Τενέα:** this city took the side of the Romans in the Achaean War and thus did not suffer destruction along with its neighbor Corinth in 146 BCE (Roux 131). According to Strabo 8.6.22, the Teneans claimed kinship with Tenedos through Tennes, the son of Cycnus. **καὶ διὰ τοῦτο . . . Ἀπόλλωνα τιμῶσιν:** Strabo 8.6.22 mentions a sanctuary of Apollo, which P. only implies here. The role of Apollo in the resettlement of the Teneans remains vague. **θεῶν:** partitive gen.

2.5.5 τὴν ἐπὶ Σικυῶνα (ὁδόν) ἐμπεπρησμένος: < πίμπρημι, perf. passive participle. **γεγόνασι μὲν δὴ . . . ἀλλὰ . . . :** an unusual marshaling of particles on P.'s part. The δή connects the sentence to the previous one (D 392), while the usual contrastive construction μὲν . . . δέ is here slightly energized by replacing the second member with ἀλλά (D 5). **τοῦτόν γε τὸν ναὸν Ἀπόλλωνος:** this temple has not yet been identified (MT 235). **λέγουσι:** P. uses two kinds of indirect statement here (as is his wont), an acc. with infinitive and a dependent clause with ὅτι and the optative. **ὅτι Πύρρος κατακαύσειεν ὁ Ἀχιλλέως αὐτόν:** Pyrrhus held a grudge against the god for his father's death and is said to have been killed at Delphi. At 1.4.4, P. explains how Pyrrhus' ghost later assisted the Delphians during a Gallic invasion in the 3rd c. BCE and so received divine honors. Ps.-Apollod. *epit.* 6.14 says that Pyrrhus plundered the votive offerings at Delphi and set the temple there on fire. **ἄλλο τοιόνδε:** this expression is immediately explicated in an indirect statement with ὡς and the optative. P. used a similar expression and explanation in 2.5.3 (τοιοῦτο ἀκούσας ἕτερον) but has altered it here deliberately, for little reason apart from *variatio.* **ποθὲν:** "from some place"; the oxytone accentuation indicates that this is an indefinite adv. and not the interrogative πόθεν, "from where?" (S 346). A dissylabic enclitic following a word (πῦρ) accented with a circumflex on the last syllable (here the only syllable) retains its accent (S 183d).

Mythical History of Sicyon

2.5.6 περὶ τῆς χώρας τῆς σφετέρας: "about their own land" (S 330). **λέγουσιν:** this verb governs the ὡς and optative clause and several acc. and infinitive constructions thereafter. It is now believed that the ultimate source of the Sicyonian king list was Menaechmus of Sicyon (*FGrH* 131), a poet of the 4th c. BCE who wrote a lost epic *Sicyonia,* along with other works (MT 236–37). **Αἰγιαλεὺς:** ps.-Apollod. 2.1.1 says that Aegialeus was the son of Inachus and the Oceanid Melia. P. here begins his account of Sicyon with an extensive mythical history of the place, focusing on the succession of kings and dynasties. For a nice summary list and genealogical chart of the 23 Sicyonian kings P. covers in this chapter and following chapters, see Roux 132. Unfortunately, most of these figures are little more than names to us now. **(τόσον) Πελοποννήσου δὲ ὅσον . . . Αἰγιαλὸς . . . ὀνομασθῆναι Αἰγιάλειαν . . . πόλιν:** the direct object of οἰκίσαι. **οὗ . . . ἐστι νῦν σφισι τὸ ἱερὸν τῆς Ἀθηνᾶς:** a dependent local clause introduced by the relative adv. οὗ, "where" (S 346, 2498); its referent is the pronoun τοῦτο following.

2.5.7 ἐς τοσόνδε . . . δυνάμεως: "to such a degree of power (that)," partitive gen. with a substantive adj. (S 1314). **πρὶν ἢ . . . ἀφικέσθαι:** after an affirmative clause, πρίν usually takes the infinitive and means "before" (S 2431). **ὡς . . . καλεῖσθαι:** clause of natural result (S 2258) set up by τοσόνδε. **τοῦ (Αἰγύρου) δὲ Θουρίμαχος:** to avoid monotony, P. slightly alters the third in a series of four regal successions. **συγγενέσθαι:** < συγγίγνομαι, aor. middle infinitive, "to have sexual intercourse with" (v. *LSJ* II.3). **τὸν τεχθέντα (παῖδα):** < τίκτω, aor. passive participle. **ὄνομα δὲ ἦν Πέρατος τῷ παιδί:** in such phrases, the name is placed in the same case as the ὄνομα, with an accompanying dat. of the person who bears it (S 1478).

2.5.8 τὰ δὲ ἐς Πλημναῖον τὸν Περάτου μάλιστα ἐφαίνετό μοι θαύματος ἄξια: P. signals that he has a noteworthy story. **τὰ γὰρ τικτόμενα:** See the similar phrase, in a quite different situation, at 2.3.11. **αὐτίκα ὁπότε κλαύσειεν, ἠφίει τὴν ψυχήν:** a past general temporal clause, with an optative (without ἄν) in the dependent clause and a secondary tense in the main clause. **ἠφίει:** < ἀφίημι, imperf. act. indicative (S 777). **ἐς ὅ:** temporal clause denoting time subsequent to that of the principal verb (S 2383C and note), "until." **ἔλεον ἴσχει Πλημναίου:** ἴσχω is a reduplicated form of ἔχω that exists only in the present (as here) and imperf. (v. *LSJ*); "(she) has pity on Plemnaios." **ὡς δὴ γυνὴ ξένη:** "pretending to be a foreign woman"; the δή perhaps highlights that the goddess could not very well appear in her own divine manifestation. That kind of visitation often has fatal consequences, as in the case of Zeus and Semele.

2.6.1 Ἐπωπεὺς: P. stated at 2.3.10 that Epopeus, king of Sicyon/Aegialea, took over Corinth too. **στρατόν . . . πολέμιον . . . πρῶτον:** treat as one phrase, "first hostile army." **τὰ πρὸ τοῦ:** "before this (i.e., the invasion)." The article τοῦ is being used here as a demonstrative; the phrase is common in H. See *LSJ* πρό A.II. **διατελέσασιν:** aor. act. participle agreeing with σφισι; i.e., the Sicyonians. **αἰτία δὲ ἥδε:** i.e., the narrative that follows. **Ἀντιόπης . . . τῆς Νυκτέως:** Antiope was the mother of Amphion and Zethus, who built the walls of Thebes. Cf. 2.6.4 and ps.-Apollod. 3.5.5, which differs in some details. **ὄνομα ἦν ἐπὶ κάλλει:** i.e., she was famous for her beauty (v. *LSJ* ὄνομα II). **καί οἱ καὶ φήμη προσῆν:** "and there was also a rumor about her that"; this phrase sets up the acc. and infinitive construction that follows.

2.6.2 οὐκ οἶδα εἴτε . . . εἴτε . . . βουλευσάμενος: this long parenthetical phrase interrupts the main clause of the sentence, i.e., ταύτην . . . Ἐπωπεὺς ἁρπάζει. **Λύκον ἀδελφὸν ὄντα:** this Lycus is not to be confused with the Theban tyrant Lycus who menaces Heracles' wife and children in Euripides' *Hercules furens*. **παραδίδωσι:** "he permitted," with acc. and infinitive construction (v. *LSJ* II). **Λάβδακον . . . τὸν Πολυδώρου τοῦ Κάδμου:** Cadmus founded Thebes after his unsuccessful search for his sister Europa, whom Zeus abducted. Polydorus was his oldest son; Pentheus, whose death P. described at 2.2.7, was the son of Agave, the daughter of Cadmus. Polydorus married Nykteis, daughter of Nykteus; when Polydorus died, Nykteus became the guardian for their son Labdacus, who was the grandfather of Oedipus. **ἐπετρόπευεν . . . ἐπιτροπεύειν:** pseudanaphora, "to act as regent" (v. *LSJ* I.3.b). **στρατῷ μείζονι:** dat. of military accompaniment (S 1526). **κακοῦν δὲ εἰ λάβοι καὶ αὐτὴν Ἀντιόπην:** conditional clauses in indirect discourse change the mood of their verbs to the optative after main verbs setting up secondary sequence (here the aor. ἱκέτευσε). The original verb form in direct discourse was in the subjunctive, e.g., ἐὰν λάβῃς, "if you seize Antiope too, punish her" (S 2621). The particle ἄν is discarded with the switch to the optative.

2.6.3 τὸ . . . παραυτίκα: pleonastic use of the article. **ἐπινίκια ἔθυε:** "he conducted sacrifices for his victory" (v. *LSJ* ἐπινίκιος II.2.a). **ἐπ' ἐξειργασμένῳ:** "after it (the sacrifice) was done." **κατέλαβεν:** impersonal verb with acc. and infinitive construction, "it happened that . . ." (v. *LSJ* II.3). **ὡς μηδὲν ἔτι Λύκῳ δεῆσαι πολέμου:** natural result clause. **Λαμέδων . . . ὁ Κορώνου:** Lamedon was the younger son of Coronus; his brother Corax became king, as mentioned at 2.5.8. **τὴν ἐπ' Ἐλευθερῶν (ὁδόν):** Eleutherae is on the border between Boeotia and Attica, NW of Athens (see 1.38.8–9). **ἐνταῦθα καθ' ὁδὸν τίκτει:** at 1.38.9, P. describes the cave where Antiope abandoned her children.

2.6.4 πεποίηκεν: "he composed (the following verses)" (v. *LSJ* A.I.3). **Ἄσιος ὁ Ἀμφιπτολέμου:** Asius of Samos was a Greek epic poet in the 6th c. BCE. Cf. M. Davies, ed., *Epicorum Graecorum Fragmenta* (Göttingen: Vandenhoek und Ruprecht, 1988), 88–91. **σφᾶς:** i.e., Amphion and Zethus. **ἀνήγαγεν:** "he brought them back," i.e., "traced their descent" (Loeb). Homer mentions Antiope and her sons at *Odyssey* 11.260–65, as part of a review of the notable dead during Odysseus' *nekyia*. **ἐπὶ τὸ σεμνότερον (μέρος):** i.e., to Zeus. **τῆς Καδμείας:** the upper city or citadel of Thebes.

2.6.5 Ἄρχανδρον καὶ Ἀρχιτέλην τοὺς Ἀχαιοῦ: these two men were not only the sons of Achaeus (son of Xuthus and founder of the Achaean race) but also husbands of the Danaids Scaea and Automate (cf. 7.1.6). **Σικυῶνα δὲ οὐ Μαραθῶνος τοῦ Ἐπωπέως, Μητίονος δὲ εἶναι τοῦ Ἐρεχθέως φασίν:** P. records four different sources about the parentage of Sicyon: Eumelus (at 2.1.1, P. described Sicyon as the son of Marathon), the Sicyonians themselves (a tradition they shared with Asius), Hesiod, and the Greek poet Ibycus from the 6th c. BCE. Erechtheus was a mythical king of Athens. **ἐπεὶ Ἡσίοδός γε καὶ Ἴβυκος:** here ἐπεί means "although" rather than "since" (v. *LSJ* B.1). **ὁ μὲν ἐποίησεν ὡς . . . Ἴβυκος δὲ . . . φησιν:** P. studiously avoids parallelism here, varying the references to the two poets and the constructions of indirect discourse.

2.6.6 Ταλαῷ τῷ Βίαντος βασιλεύοντι Ἀργείων: P. explains at 2.18.4 how Melampus and his brother Bias each received a third of the kingdom of Argos. **Ἄδραστος ἔφευγεν ἐξ Ἄργους:** Adrastus was the son-in-law of Talaus and the brother-in-law of Amphiaraus, who married Eriphyle. When Amphiaraus killed Talaus, Adrastus went into exile. He was later reconciled with Amphiaraus and took part in the expedition of the Seven against Thebes. **παρὰ Πόλυβον ἦλθεν ἐς Σικυῶνα:** the expression "to" denoting movement varies in Greek depending on whether the object is a person or place. **Κλυτίου τοῦ Λαμέδοντι κηδεύσαντος:** Clytius, father of Pheno, was just mentioned at 2.6.5.

2.6.7 κατὰ μαντείαν: "in obedience to an oracle" (Loeb). **Ἱππόλυτον Ῥοπάλου παῖδα τοῦ Φαίστου:** not the more famous Hippolytus, son of Theseus and Hippolyta. **συνεχώρησεν:** "he agreed," with infinitive construction following. **Φάλκης . . . ὁ Τημένου:** Phalces later plays a major role in the story of Deiphontes and Hyrnetho (daughter of Temenus); cf. 2.28.3–6. Temenus was a son of Aristomachus, son of Cleodaeus, son of Hyllus, son of Heracles. **κακὸν μὲν ἅτε Ἡρακλείδην καὶ (ὄντα) αὐτὸν (Λακεστάδην) ἐποίησεν οὐδέν:** "he did him no wrong inasmuch as he (Lacestades) was also a descendant of Heracles"; Lacestades was Heracles' great-great-grandson. **κοινωνὸν δὲ ἔσχε (αὐτὸν) τῆς ἀρχῆς.**

2.7.1 ἀπὸ τούτου (τοῦ χρόνου) μοῖρα τῆς Ἀργείας: as MT (238) notes very perceptively, this phrase recalls the same one used at 2.1.1; and similar phrases occurring at the end of the book (διὰ τῆς Ἀργείας, 2.38.7) and at 2.29.5 (μοῖρα Ἀργείων). It serves to emphasize the centrality of Argos to the region. **Δημήτριος . . . ὁ Ἀντιγόνου:** Demetrius I Poliorcetes (son of Antigonus I Monophthalmus) destroyed the lower city in 303 BCE during a war with Ptolemy I, and he transferred the people of the city to the acropolis, which he renamed Demetrias. Cf. Lolos (2011) 72. **αἰτίαν δὲ οὐκ ὀρθῶς ποιοῖ τις ἂν ζητῶν, ἀποχρῴτο δὲ:** potential optative followed by perhaps an imperative optative (S 1820), "one would be wrong to seek a reason this way, but let him be content." **τῷ Ὁμήρῳ λελεγμένῳ περὶ Διὸς:** *Iliad* 2.117. **διακειμένοις οὖν (Σικυωνίοις) ἀδυνάτως:** this phrase resumes the ἐχόντων . . . Σικυωνίων just above. **σεισμὸς:** this earthquake probably happened during the reign of Antoninus Pius (138–61 CE). P. seems to refer to the same event at 8.43.4 (MT 238–39). **ὀλίγου (δεῖν):** gen. of quantity (S 1399), "nearly." **πολλὰ δὲ σφᾶς . . . ἀφείλετο:** direct object with double acc. **τῶν ἐς ἐπίδειξιν:** partitive gen. with πολλά, "many of their famous sights" (Loeb). **τὸ λόγιον τετελέσθαι Σιβύλλῃ τὸ ἐς τὴν Ῥόδον ἔδοξεν:** Sibylline Oracles 7.1–3 (ed. Rzach).

Road from Corinth to Sicyon

2.7.2 ὅστις δὴ οὗτος ὁ Λύκος: one may detect a bit of frustration here, because P.'s research, as he notes, was in vain. MT (239) speculates that this was a late classical or Hellenistic athlete. **ἀνῃρημένον:** < ἀναιρέω, perf. middle participle, "who won." **τὰ πολλὰ:** "generally, for the most part" (v. *LSJ* III.1.a). **τὸ μὲν σῶμα . . . λίθου δὲ . . . ἐπίγραμμα δὲ . . . :** P. transitions from a particular instance of burial at Sicyon to a description of their funerary custom; he deals with first the body, then the edifice on top, and finally the laconic inscription. **ἐπίγραμμα . . . ἐπιγράφουσιν:** cognate acc. **οὐ πατρόθεν:** i.e., no patronymic, contrary to the usual Greek custom.

2.7.3 διαβεβηκόσιν: < διαβαίνω, perf. act. participle, a directional participle, like προελθοῦσι and ἐπιστρέψασιν just below. **Εὐπόλιδι Ἀθηναίῳ ποιήσαντι κωμῳδίαν:** Eupolis (ca. 466–411 BCE) was a comic poet and a contemporary of Aristophanes. Aelian (*De natura animalium* 10.41) says he was buried on Aegina. **ὡς ἂν τῇ γραφῇ μάλιστα ἁρμόζοι:** potential optative within a purpose clause (S 2202b), "so that it might especially befit the painting." **τῇ γραφῇ . . . γραφὴ δέ:** resumptive. **εἴπερ ἄλλη τις (γραφὴ ἀξία θέας ἐστιν):** i.e., if any painting is worth seeing, this one is.

2.7.4 τὰ δὲ ἐς αὐτοὺς σαφέστερον ἐν τοῖς ἐφεξῆς δηλώσω: At 2.8.5ff., P. discusses the exciting events at Pallene and Dyme in Achaea, Megalopolis in Arcadia, and Sellasia in Laconia in the war between Cleomenes III and the Achaean League. **ἄνεισι:** < ἄνειμι, present act. indicative 3rd sg. (S

773). **πρὸς . . . τῇ πύλῃ:** i.e., of Sicyon. Demetrius Poliorcetes created it in 303 BCE when he moved the city (MT 240). Cf. 2.7.1.

2.7.5 τὸ ἄγαλμα τῆς Τύχης: a colossal head of Tyche was found in the city baths and appears to be a copy of the original 4th c. BCE cult statue (MT 241). Tyche appears on Corinthian coins, usually with a cornucopia (e.g., *RPC*, vol. 3, nos. 116, 177, 231). **τοῦ θεάτρου δὲ . . . ᾠκοδομημένου:** either a gen. absolute or possessive with ἐν τῇ σκήνῃ. The theater was built after the refoundation of the city and restored in the Hellenistic and Roman periods (MT 241). **Ἄρατον . . . τὸν Κλεινίου:** Aratus of Sicyon (271–213 BCE) was the city's most famous native son; P. describes Aratus' life and achievements in 2.8.1–2.9.5. This is the oldest surviving example of placing the heroic statue of a local dynast on the *scaenae frons* of a theater (MT 241). **χρυσοῦ μὲν καὶ ἐλέφαντος ὁ θεός, παρὰ δὲ αὐτὸν Βάκχαι λίθου λευκοῦ:** chiastic order. **κοσμητηρίου:** the office of the κοσμήτης, the director of the rites. **κομίζουσι, κομίζουσι δέ:** anastrophe. Moving statues during cult rituals was not uncommon in ancient Greece. P. describes similar rituals for Peitho (2.7.8) and during the Athenian Arrhephoria (1.27.3). **ἡμμένων:** < ἅπτω, perf. passive participle.

2.7.6 ἡγεῖται μὲν οὖν (ὁ Διόνυσος) ὃν Βάκχειον ὀνομάζουσιν . . . <ὁ> καλούμενος Λύσιος: P. describes the secret statues on their yearly journey. Dionysus bore the same cult titles at Corinth, as P. indicated at 2.2.6. **Ἀνδροδάμας . . . ὁ Φλίαντος:** Phlias is the son of Dionysus mentioned at 2.6.6; he was one of the Argonauts. **εἰπούσης τῆς Πυθίας:** "when the Pythia commanded (it)." **Ἀριστόμαχος ὁ Κλεοδαίου:** cf. commentary on 2.6.7. **τῆς γενομένης μαντείας:** the Delphic oracle told Hyllus, son of Heracles, to "wait for the third fruit and then return" to the Peloponnesus. The god meant the third generation after Hyllus, so the intervening attempts of Hyllus, Cleodaeus, and Aristomachus failed. **ἁμαρτὼν . . . ἥμαρτεν:** pseudanaphora. **βαδίζουσιν:** directional participle. **ναὸς Ἀρτέμιδος . . . Λιμναίας:** this temple may be an archaic one found to the NE of the theater (MT 242). **ἐν δεξιᾷ:** mild hyperbaton. **δῆλά:** this refers to the ὅτι clause. **οὔτε ὡς κομισθέντος ἑτέρωσε οὔτε ὅντινα . . . διεφθάρη τρόπον:** *variatio*, "neither whether it (i.e., the cult statue) was carried away to another place nor how it was destroyed." **αὐτοῦ:** adv., "right there."

2.7.7 ἐπὶ λόγῳ τοιῷδε: "for the following reason"; this deictic connects to the next sentence, where P. tells how Apollo and Artemis came to Sicyon. **αὐτοῖς:** i.e., the Sicyonians. **Πύθωνα:** Python was the big snake of Gaia that guarded Delphi before Apollo slew it and claimed the land as his own. **ἐς τὴν Αἰγιάλειαν:** the original name of Sicyon (2.5.6). **οἱ μὲν:** Apollo and Artemis. The masc. οἱ is used for the joint masc. and fem. subject. **Καρμάνορα:** Carmanor was a Cretan of Tarrha. P. returns to him at 2.30.3. **ἀπετράποντο:** < ἀποτρέπω, not imperf. middle/passive but 2nd aor. middle.

2.7.8 οἱ δὲ παῖδας ἑπτὰ . . . : the Athenians sent seven boys and seven girls to Crete as their annual tribute to King Minos. **ἴσας παρθένους:** "an equal number of maidens." **τὸν Σύθαν ποταμὸν:** the river Sythas formed the W boundary of Sicyonia with the area of Pellene. **ἀγαγόντες δὴ:** "having brought, as they pretend" (Loeb). The particle is perhaps used ironically here. **τὸ . . . ἐξ ἀρχῆς:** "originally," contrasted with the νῦν. **αὐτὸν:** i.e., ναόν. **Προίτου:** The daughters of King Proetus of Tiryns were driven mad, for which the sources give various reasons. P. sees their statues in the agora at 2.9.8 and tells their story more fully at 2.18.4–5.

2.7.9 ἐς τοῦτον τὸν ναὸν ἀνέθηκε: the *Liber memorialis* of Ampelius (probably 3rd c. CE) lists a number of incredible offerings at this temple (8.5)—e.g., the shield and sword of Agamemnon, the cloak and breastplate of Odysseus, the bow and arrow of Teucer, the skin of Marsyas, and the oars of the Argonauts. P. does not mention a colossal statue of King Attalus I of Pergamum (which Polybius 17.16 says stood nearby), but he includes here some interesting mythical memorabilia that disappeared, as he explains below. **τὸν ὗν:** i.e., the Calydonian Boar. **γενομένης . . . τῷ Σιληνῷ τῆς συμφορᾶς:** i.e., Marsyas. He challenged Apollo to a musical contest, pipes versus lyre. When Apollo won, the god had Marsyas flayed alive. Silenus, the father of satyrs, was a companion of Dionysus, but older satyrs, like Marsyas, were also called Sileni. **ἀναφανέντας:** < ἀναφαίνω, aor. passive participle. **τῷ Ἀσωπῷ:** the river mentioned at 2.5.1–2. **ἐμπιπραμένῳ:** < ἐμπίπρημι, present passive participle. **Πυθοκλῆς:** it is unclear to whom P. refers here; a Pythocles of Sicyon won the *stadion* at the 136th Olympiad (236 BCE), but P. could be referencing a sculptor mentioned by Pliny the Elder (*NH* 34.52).

2.8.1 τῷ . . . τῆς Πειθοῦς ἱερῷ: perhaps dat. with ἐγγύς, which usually takes the gen. **ἀνειμένον:** < ἀνίημι, perf. passive participle (S 777). **βασιλεῦσι Ῥωμαίων:** dat. with ἀνειμένον; i.e., the Roman emperors. **Κλέωνος τυράννου:** Cleon was the tyrant of Sicyon in the first half of the 3rd c. BCE, probably before 274 (MT 244). **Κλεισθένης:** this is not the famous Athenian who set the stage for the democracy of the 5th c.

BCE but his maternal grandfather, the tyrant of Sicyon (ca. 600–570 BCE). Cleisthenes was a member of the Orthagorid family that ruled Sicyon in the 7th c. and 6th c. BCE (MT 245). Ca. 580 BCE, his daughter Agariste married the Athenian Megacles, the grandson of the Megacles who crushed the coup of Cylon in 632 BCE. Cf. H. 5.67, 6.126ff. **ἐν τῇ νῦν πόλει:** i.e., the upper city founded by Demetrius Poliorcetes (2.7.1). **ἡρῷόν . . . Ἀράτου:** P. mentioned Aratus at 2.7.5 but reserved a long narrative of his eventful life for this discussion of his hero shrine. Plutarch (*Life of Aratus* 53.4–5) explains that the shrine was called the Ἀράτειον and that yearly sacrifices were made there on the day Aratus freed the city from tyranny and on his birthday. **μέγιστα (ἔργα) Ἑλλήνων . . . τῶν ἐφ' αὑτοῦ.**

Aratus

2.8.2 **τῶν ἐν τέλει:** a partitive gen. with πολλοῖς, the dat. object of ἐνέπεσεν. **ἐπιθυμία τυραννίδος οὕτω δή τι ἀκάθεκτος:** this phrase sets up the result clause and explains the sad history of Sicyon at this time, hence P.'s emphasis here. In *Life of Aratus* 1–9, Plutarch tells the early history of Aratus and his experiences under the Sicyonian tyrants. **ἐξέβαλεν:** P. uses a different phrase for exile just below, φυγάδα ἐποίησεν. **προστησάμενος:** < προτίθημι, aor. middle participle, "who made (him) their champion" (Loeb). **Κλεινίᾳ . . . συνεβεβήκει πρότερον ἔτι ἡ τελευτή:** Plutarch says that Abantidas killed Cleinias and killed or exiled his kin, including Aratus (*Life of Aratus* 2.2–3), in 264 BCE. **συνεβεβήκει:** < συμβαίνω, pluperf. act. indicative. **Ἄρατον . . . Ἀβαντίδας φυγάδα ἐποίησεν, ἢ καὶ αὐτὸς ἀπεχώρησεν Ἄρατος:** chiasmus. **ἄνδρες τῶν ἐπιχωρίων:** according to Plutarch (*Life of Aratus* 3.3), these were Deinias and Aristotle the logician, who assassinated Abantidas when he attended one of their public disputations. **ἐγεγόνει:** < γίγνομαι, pluperf. act. indicative.

2.8.3 **Νικοκλῆς:** Nicocles killed Paseas in 252/251 BCE. **Ἄρατος:** Aratus is the subject of the participles (ἀφικόμενος, βιασάμενος, προσλαβών) and the main verb (τρέπεται). **Σικυωνίων φυγάσι καὶ Ἀργείοις μισθωτοῖς:** dat. of military accompaniment (S 1526). **τοὺς μὲν . . . τοὺς δὲ . . . τῶν φυλασσόντων:** partitive gen. **ἔλαθεν:** λανθάνω does not always have an accompanying participle, as it does below (ἔλαθεν ἀποδράς). **ἅτε ἐν σκότῳ (ὤν)** **νύκτωρ γὰρ δὴ τὴν ἐπιχείρησιν ἐποιεῖτο . . . ὑπέφαινε γὰρ ἕως ἤδη:** the two explanatory parenthetical sentences that break up this long and dramatic sentence; Plutarch tells the dramatic episode in much greater detail in *Life of Aratus* 5–9. Sicyon was liberated by Aratus in 251 BCE. **τοὺς . . . βιασάμενος:** "overpowered" (v. *LSJ* II.1). **ἕως:** not the adv. but the nom. Attic form of ἠώς, "dawn." **ἀπέδωκεν . . . ἐξ ἴσου πολιτεύεσθαι:** "he restored equality of political rights" (Loeb); i.e., he abolished the tyranny so that citizens could engage in politics on an equal basis. P. uses the same phrase at 1.3.3 when he discusses the idea (erroneous in his mind) that Theseus established democracy in Athens. **διαλλάξας τοις φεύγουσιν (Σικυωνίους):** "reconciling (the Sicyonians) with the exiles." **τοῖς φεύγουσιν . . . φυγάσι:** *variatio.* **τῶν κτημάτων:** partitive gen. with ὅσα . . . ἄλλα. νύκτωρ **ἐπέπρατο:** < πρίαμαι, pluperf. passive indicative. **τιμὴν . . . διέλυσεν:** "he paid the price" (v. *LSJ* διαλύω I.7). **αὐτός:** "himself," i.e., "out of his own purse" (Loeb).

2.8.4 **Ἀντιγόνου:** objective gen. with δέος. **Ἀντιγόνου Φίλιππον ἐπιτροπεύοντος τὸν Δημητρίου:** synchysis, or *abab* word order. P. is confusing Antigonus II Gonatas (king of Macedonia ca. 272–239 BCE and son of Demetrius I Poliorcetes) with Antigonus III Doson (king of Macedonia ca. 229–221 BCE, son of Demetrius the Fair, and grandson of Demetrius I Poliorcetes). Antigonus III was the half cousin of Demetrius II Aetolicus (king of Macedonia ca. 239–229 BCE) and guardian of Demetrius' son, the future Philip V (king of Macedonia ca. 221–179 BCE), who was only nine at the time of his father's death. However, Antigonus II was king when Aratus freed Sicyon (MT 246). **(Ἄρατος) ἐσήγαγε τὸ Ἀχαιῶν συνέδριον:** the Achaean League was a regional association of Greek poleis that existed as early as the 5th c. BCE but only became a potent political and military force between 280 and 146 BCE, especially under the leadership of Aratus. **στρατηγὸς:** Aratus was elected *strategos* of the Achaean League in 245 BCE. P. first mentioned the league at 2.1.2. **ᾕρητο:** < αἱρέω, pluperf. passive indicative. **τῷ αἰφνιδίῳ τῆς ἐπιθέσεως:** = τῇ αἰφνιδίᾳ ἐπιθέσει. **Κόρινθον:** the common object for both gen. absolutes, ἔχοντος Ἀντιγόνου and φρουρᾶς Μακεδόνων ἐνούσης. Aratus liberated Corinth in 243 BCE. **παρὰ Ζήνωνα τὸν Μνασέου κατὰ μάθησιν σοφίας ἐφοίτησεν:** "he studied philosophy under Zeno" (v. *LSJ* I.4). Note the periphrasis for "philosophy." **Ζήνωνα τὸν Μνασέου:** this is Zeno of Citium (ca. 334–262 BCE), the founder of the Stoic school of philosophy.

2.8.5 **Πτολεμαῖος:** both Ptolemy II Philadelphus (king of Egypt in 283–246 BCE) and Ptolemy III (king of Egypt in 246–222 BCE) were supporters of Aratus. The latter was named honorary *strategos* of the Achaean League in 243 BCE. Cf. Peter Green, *The Hellenistic Age: A Short History* (New York: Modern Library, 2008), 71. **Ἆγις ὁ Εὐδαμίδου βασιλεὺς:** Agis

IV (son of Eudamidas II) was the Eurypontid king of Sparta ca. 265–241 BCE. **ἔφθησαν . . . ἑλόντες:** supplementary participle with verb φθάνω (S 2096); an aor. participle used with a verb in any tense except present and imperf. usually coincides in time with the verb (S 1873). **Πελλήνην:** at 2.7.4, P. notes the grave of the Sicyonians who died at this engagement at Pellene, a small city just to the E of Sicyon, over its border with Achaea. **ἐξ ἐπιδρομῆς:** "by a sudden attack." **ἀναχωροῦσιν οἴκαδε ὑπόσπονδοι:** P. switches to the present tense after ἔφθησαν and ἐκρατήθησαν. The Spartan king Agis IV was deposed and later murdered after his defeat at Pellene.

2.8.6 προεκεχωρήκει: < προχωρέω, pluperf. act. indicative, "had turned out well" (v. *LSJ* II.1). **ἡγεῖτο:** this verb takes an object and a predicate, δεινὸν and Πειραιᾶ . . . περιοφθῆναι; "he considered terrible (the fact) that . . ." **ἐχόμενα ὑπὸ Μακεδόνων:** "the places held by the Macedonians." The participle is neut. pl. to comprise several nouns of various genders—masc. (Piraeus), neut. (Sunium), and fem. (Salamis and Munychia). The pronoun αὐτά below, which refers to the group, is neut. too. **οὐ γὰρ ἤλπιζε δύνασθαι:** Aratus attacked Athens in 233 BCE but only reached the Academy. **πρὸς βίαν:** "by force." **ἀφεῖναι:** < ἀφίημι, 2nd aor. act. infinitive (S 777). **ἐπὶ ταλάντοις πεντήκοντα καὶ ἑκατόν:** ἐπί with dat. can denote price (v. *LSJ* B.III.4); "for 150 talents." **τῶν χρημάτων . . . ἕκτον μέρος:** i.e., 25 talents. **συνετέλεσεν:** this verb is used in two senses in this passage; it means "contributed" here (v. *LSJ* II), whereas συντελεῖν below means "to belong" (v. *LSJ* III). **Ἀριστόμαχον τυραννοῦντα ἐν Ἄργει:** Aristomachus became tyrant in 235 BCE but resigned in 229. Aratus had attacked the city in 235 also (MT 246). **δημοκρατίαν ἀποδόντα:** cf. the phrasing at 2.8.3. Athens was liberated in 229 BCE. **Μαντίνειάν . . . εἷλεν:** Cleomenes III took the Arcadian city in 229 BCE, but Aratus seized it in 226 (MT 245). **ἀλλὰ γὰρ οὐ πάντα ἀνθρώπῳ τελεῖται κατὰ γνώμην:** P. reflects on the uncertain nature of fortune. As he relates just below, the threat from the new king of Sparta proved galvanizing and made Antigonus III and Aratus partners for a time. **εἰ δὴ καὶ:** this phrase introduces the specific example P. has at hand. **κατέλαβεν ἀνάγκη:** "necessity forced him to . . ." (v. *LSJ* καταλαμβάνω V.4).

2.9.1 Κλεομένης ὁ Λεωνίδου τοῦ Κλεωνύμου: Cleomenes III (Agiad king of Sparta in 235–222 BCE) was the son of Leonidas II; he also married Agiatis, the widow of Agis IV, who reportedly inspired him with dreams of a maximalist kingship at Sparta and the revival of the old Lycurgan constitution. **Παυσανίαν ἐμιμεῖτο:** P. is probably referring to the

Spartan general Pausanias who led the Greeks to victory at Plataea in 479 BCE but was later condemned for treason. **ἅτε . . . ὄντι αὐτῷ (i.e., Κλεομένει) . . . θερμοτέρῳ καὶ οὐ φιλοψύχῳ:** dat. of agent with κατείργαστο. **Εὐρυδαμίδαν:** Eurydamidas was the son of Agis IV and Agiatis and served as Eurypontid king for a short time late in the reign of Leonidas II. After his death, Cleomenes recalled Archidamus V (brother of Agis IV) in 228 BCE; Archidamus ruled for a year before he was assassinated. **Ἐπικλείδαν:** Epicleidas, Cleomenes' brother, later died at the Battle of Sellasia in 222 BCE, as P. notes at 2.9.3. **τῆς γερουσίας:** the Gerousia was the senate of the Sparta state. It consisted of 30 members, 28 of which were Spartans over the age of 60; the other two were the ruling kings. It had the power to put even the kings on trial. **πατρονόμους:** this board of six elders replaced the traditional five elected ephors, whom P. refers to above as the οἱ ἐφορεύοντες. **τῷ λόγῳ:** "nominally." **ἐλπίζων ἕξειν:** verbs of hoping, expecting, and so on take future infinitives. **ἢν κρατήσῃ:** protasis of future-more-vivid condition. **ἐμποδὼν οὐκ ἐθέλων εἶναί οἱ τοῖς δρωμένοις:** ἐμποδών takes a double dat., "not wanting (the Achaeans) to be a hindrance to him for his activities."

2.9.2 **νικᾷ τῇ μάχῃ:** Cleomenes beat the Achaeans at Dyme in 226 BCE. At 2.7.4, P. mentioned the graves of the fallen in this battle. **δείσαντα:** construe with Ἄρατον. **ἐπάγεσθαι:** "to bring in as an ally" (v. *LSJ* II.2), in 225 BCE. P. does not give the reader a good idea of how dire matters had become for Aratus and the Achaeans: even Ptolemy III switched his support to Cleomenes in 226; cf. Cf. Peter Green, *The Hellenistic Age: A Short History* (New York: Modern Library 2008) 138. As Plutarch (*Life of Aratus* 40–42) relates, Aratus was nearly captured by Corinthian partisans of Cleomenes, who handed over their city to the Spartan king. Cleomenes also invaded Sicyonia and besieged Aratus in his hometown, before Aratus escaped to Aegium and convinced the league assembly to ally with Antigonus and promise the Macedonian king the Acrocorinth in exchange for his aid. **Κλεομένους δὲ παραβάντος . . . δράσαντος . . . ποιήσαντος:** long gen. absolute. **παραβάντος . . . παράσπονδα:** P. emphasizes the transgressions of Cleomenes with the prefix παρα-. **ἣν πρὸς Ἀντίγονον συνέθετο εἰρήνην:** P. shows the limits of the relative clause by placing the antecedent at the end. **Μεγαλοπολίτας ποιήσαντος ἀναστάτους:** this occurred in 224 or 223 BCE (MT 247). **περὶ Σελλασίαν:** the Battle of Sellasia took place in 222 BCE. The town lay NE of Sparta. **ἑάλω:** < ἁλίσκομαι, 2nd aor. act. indicative with passive meaning and no thematic vowel (S 687). Antigonus III Doson became the first Macedonian to occupy

Sparta. **πολιτείαν τὴν πάτριον:** thus they undid Cleomenes' political reforms. He had tried to reestablish the old equality of property among Spartan citizens and to restore the traditional Lycurgan discipline.

2.9.3 **τιμῆς . . . πρῶτα ἔχοντα:** "enjoying the first (rank) of honor." **Πτολεμαίῳ:** Ptolemy III Euergetes (r. 246–221 BCE) favored the Spartans in the battle against Antigonus and the Achaeans, but Ptolemy IV Philopator (r. 221–204 BCE) soon suspected Cleomenes of conspiracy. P. does not distinguish between these two kings. **καταγνωσθέντα . . . συνιστάναι:** "convicted of combining the Egyptians against the king" (v. *LSJ* συνίστημι A.I). This was no idle concern; Upper Egypt actually seceded in 205 BCE and became a separate kingdom under the native Egyptian leader Hugronaphor; it was independent until 185 BCE. **συνιστάναι:** < συνίστημι, present act. infinitive. **ἀπέδρα:** < ἀποδιδράσκω; like ἑάλω in 2.9.2, this is an athematic 2nd aor. act. indicative (S 687). **ἀρχὴν θορύβου παρέσχε:** Cleomenes tried to incite a revolt upon his escape in 219 BCE. **τὰ . . . λοιπὰ . . . ἐκείνης τῆς πολιτείας:** the monarchy soon lapsed, and Sparta was ruled by a succession of tyrants. After the last one, Nabis, was assassinated in 192 BCE, Sparta was forced into the Achaean League. **Ἀράτῳ . . . ἅτε ἀνδρὶ εὐεργέτῃ καὶ συγκατειργασμένῳ λαμπρὰ:** dat. with εὔνους. **οὕτω διέμεινεν εὔνους:** Aratus even renamed Mantineia Antigoneia in honor of his ally. Philip V initially continued Antigonus' close relationship with Aratus, and they became very close.

2.9.4 **Φίλιππος:** Philip V (r. 221–179 BCE) succeeded Antigonus III Doson when the latter died during a battle defending Macedonia from an Illyrian invasion. Philip was mentioned as the ward of Antigonus at 2.8.4. **αὐτὸν . . . θυμῷ πολλὰ ἐς τοὺς ἀρχομένους χρώμενον:** direct object of ἐπῄνει. **θυμῷ . . . χρώμενον:** "exhibiting wrath" (v. *LSJ* θυμός II.4). **πολλὰ:** adv., "many times." **ἐπεῖχε μὴ ποιεῖν:** redundant μή with verbs of negative meaning (S 2740), "he tried to keep (him) from doing." Among other matters, Philip fomented civil war in Messenia and seduced Aratus' daughter-in-law (Plutarch *Life of Aratus* 49–50). **τούτων ἕνεκα:** P. refers to the parenthetical sentence he just ended. **προϊδομένῳ:** < προοράω, 2nd aor. middle participle. **τὸν μὲν (Ἄρατον)** **ἐξ Αἰγίου:** Aegium was the assembly place and capital of the Achaean League. **τὸ χρεὼν:** i.e., fate, necessity, and especially death. **τὸ ἡρῷον:** P. brings the narrative back to where it began at 2.8.1. **Φιλίππῳ:** dat. of agent with εἰργάσθη (S 1488). **Εὐρυκλείδην καὶ Μίκωνα:** Plutarch (*Life of Aratus* 41) names them as preventing the Athenians from helping Aratus against Cleomenes. **οὐκ ἀπιθάνους:** litotes.

2.9.5 ἔμελλε . . . ἔσεσθαι: μέλλω takes an infinitive to create a periphrastic future (S 1959); the subject of the phrase is τὸ ἀνδρόφονον φάρμακον. **ἄρα:** this particle marks "a new perception" here (S 2795); as Philip poisoned others, he too was affected by poisoning in his own life. **Δημήτριον {ὁ νεώτερος τῶν Φιλίππου παίδων} Περσεὺς:** Demetrius was actually Philip's younger son, and he had been a hostage at Rome since the end of the Second Macedonian War in 198 BCE. The favor that the Romans and Macedonians showed him made his brother Perseus jealous, and Perseus contrived to have Demetrius killed in 180 BCE, so that Perseus could succeed his father without incident. **φαρμάκῳ διέφθειρε:** P. has slightly altered the phrase φαρμάκοις ἔκτεινεν just above. **τῷ πατρὶ ἀθυμήσαντι παρέσχεν αἰτίαν ἀποθανεῖν:** "(Perseus) offered the cause for his father, having lost heart, to die"; Philip died in 179 BCE, soon after Demetrius' death. **ἐς <τὸ> Ἡσιόδου σὺν θεῷ πεποιημένον:** i.e., Hesiod *Works and Days* 265. This phrase sets up the acc. and infinitive in indirect discourse that follows. **σὺν θεῷ:** by emphasizing the idea that Hesiod's verse was divinely inspired (*Works and Days* 1–4), P. gives added weight to the maxim. **πρῶτον:** adv., "first."

Sicyon Proper: The Agora

2.9.6 Ποσειδῶνι Ἰσθμίῳ: the Sicyonians administered the Isthmian Games from 146 to 7 BCE (MT 248). **σὺν τέχνῃ πεποιημένα οὐδεμιᾷ:** P. obviously was dissatisfied with the artistry of the statues. These are aniconic images (or betyls). Zeus Meilichius was worshipped in an aniconic form at Lebadeia too (MT 248). See Milette Gaifman, *Aniconism in Greek Antiquity* (Oxford: Oxford University Press, 2012). **πυραμίδι δὲ ὁ Μειλίχιος, ἡ (Ἄρτεμις) δὲ κίονί ἐστιν εἰκασμένη:** chiastic order (*abba*). **βουλευτήριόν . . . καὶ στοὰ καλουμένη Κλεισθένειος:** the council chamber and a Hellenistic-era stoa have been found. The latter could be either a reconstruction of the archaic stoa of Cleisthenes or a *stoa poikile* built by Lamia, the lover of Demetrius Poliorcetes (MT 248). **Κλεισθένης:** this is Cleisthenes, the tyrant of Sicyon, whom P. mentioned at 2.8.1. **τὸν πρὸς Κίρρᾳ πόλεμον:** the First Sacred War arose because the Kirrhaeans harassed pilgrims on their way to Delphi and encroached on sacred land. The conflict lasted from ca. 595–585 BCE. P. narrates the war and its causes at 10.37.4–8. **Ἀμφικτύοσι:** the Delphic Amphictyonic League was a very ancient religious association organized to manage and protect the temple of Apollo at Delphi and the temple of Demeter at Anthele near Thermopylae. **τῆς . . . ἀγορᾶς:** chorographic gen. (S

1311). **Λυσίππου:** the famous sculptor Lysippus, one of Sicyon's most famous native sons, lived during the time of Alexander the Great.

2.9.7 κατερρυηκός: < κατερρύω, perf. act. participle. **ἥκιστα θέας ἄξιον:** for P., the temple may not be worth seeing, but its *logos* is worth hearing. **σφίσιν:** i.e., the people of Sicyon. **ὡς μηδένα . . . αὐτῶν:** clause of natural result with negative μή. **καρπὸν:** not "fruit" but "profit (from their flocks)" (v. *LSJ* II). **τόπον τινὰ . . . ἔνθα ἔκειτο αὖον ξύλον:** dependent adverbial clause. **τούτου φλοιὸν . . . τοῦ ξύλου καὶ κρέας ὁμοῦ:** direct objects of προθεῖναι. **ὅ τι δὲ ἦν δένδρον:** direct object of συνίεσαν. **οὐδὲ οἱ τῶν Σικυωνίων ἐξηγηταὶ:** P. has stumped his local guides with a question. **συνίεσαν:** < συνίημι, imperf. act. indicative (S 777).

2.9.8 τούτου . . . ἐφεξῆς: "right after this"; rare gen. with ἐφεξῆς (v. *LSJ* I.2). **τὰς Προίτου θυγατέρας:** P. mentioned the daughters of Proetus at 2.7.8. **τὸ δὲ ἐπίγραμμα ἐς γυναῖκας ἄλλας εἶχον:** an instance of metonomasia, or change of names, on an inscription. See another example at 2.17.3. **Λύσιππος . . . Σικυώνιος:** the sculptor just mentioned at 2.9.6.

Gymnasium and Sanctuary of Heracles

2.10.1 ἐν . . . τῷ γυμνασίῳ: archaeologists have found a large Hellenistic building with porticoed terraces and fountains in the location (MT 249). **τῆς ἀγορᾶς:** construe with οὐ μακράν. **Σκόπα:** Scopas of Paros (ca. 395–350 BCE) was a famous Greek sculptor; like Lysippus, he is considered a successor of Praxiteles. **Φλιασίου Λαφάους:** Laphaës of Phliasia is not otherwise known. **ἐπὶ δὲ τῇ θυσίᾳ τοιάδε δρᾶν νομίζουσι:** "their custom is to do . . ." Cf. commentary on 2.4.7. **Φαῖστον:** Phaestus, the son of Heracles, previously appeared at 2.6.7, where he succeeded Ianiscus as king of Sicyon before moving on to Crete, where he founded the city of Phaestus. **ἐναγίζοντας:** the Greeks distinguish between rites in honor of the dead and heroes (ἐναγίζειν) and those in honor of a god (θύειν). See Gunnell Ekroth, *The Sacrificial Rites of Greek Hero-Cults in the Archaic to the Early Hellenistic Periods* (Liège: Presses universitaires de Liège 2013). **οὔκουν:** "So (Phaestus did) not" (S 2953). Note the accentuation of the negative prefix: οὔκουν strongly emphasizes the negative, whereas οὐκοῦν is merely inferential and almost equivalent to οὖν (S 2952). **ἠξίου:** < ἀξιόω, imperf. act. indicative. **οὐδὲν . . . τῶν αὐτῶν:** compounded negative after οὔκουν. **τὰ μὲν . . . ὡς ἀπὸ ἱερείου, τὰ δὲ ὡς ἥρωι:** again

P. notes the distinction between divine rites and heroic ones. At 1.32.4, P. states that the Marathonians were the first Greeks to worship Heracles as a god. **τὴν προτέραν τῶν ἡμερῶν * * * {ὀνόματα} ὀνομάζοντες:** a textual problem here remains unsolved. It is clear that the name of the first day of the festival has fallen out and that a dittography (ὀνόματα) has replaced it.

Asclepieion

2.10.2 διπλοῦν . . . οἴκημα: "building with two rooms" (Loeb). **ἐν τῷ προτέρῳ . . . τὸ ἐνδοτέρω δὲ:** P. uses comparatives because there are only two rooms, the outer (literally, "the foreroom") and the inner. He uses an adj. and an adv. for the sake of *variatio*. **Ὕπνος:** a statue of Sleep is appropriate because the god reveals his answers and remedies for ailments to the sick who sleep in his sanctuaries. **Ἀπόλλωνι . . . Καρνείῳ:** Apollo bears this title in the Peloponnesus, for the Dorians held a festival in his honor during the month of Κάρνειος (v. *LSJ*). **ἀνεῖται:** < ἀνίημι, perf. passive indicative (S 777). **κήτους . . . θαλασσίου:** a whalebone in the stoa; the Greeks not infrequently dedicated marvels of nature in temples or public places. Anything marvelous belongs to the gods. **Ἐπιδώτης:** "the Bountiful"; this epithet is applied also to Zeus at Mantinea (v. *LSJ*). **καθ' ἑκάτερον τῆς ἐσόδου:** "on each side of the entrance"; this phrase sets up the construction τῇ μὲν . . . τῇ δέ . . . (S 1111).

2.10.3 ὁ θεός: i.e., Asclepius. **Καλάμιδος:** P. does not specify whether this is Calamis the Elder (second quarter of the 5th c. BCE) or Calamis the Younger (first quarter of the 4th c. BCE). Cf. Lolos (2011) 383. **πίτυος καρπὸν τῆς ἡμέρου:** i.e., a pinecone. **τὸν θεὸν . . . δράκοντι εἰκασμένον:** certain serpents were sacred to Asclepius and inhabited his sanctuaries (cf. 2.11.8, 2.28.1). **ἐπὶ ζεύγους ἡμιόνων:** "on a pair of mules." **Νικαγόραν . . . Σικυωνίαν Ἀγασικλέους μητέρα, γυναῖκα δὲ Ἐχετίμου:** no more is known about this myth. According to Lolos (283), since the cult was introduced from Epidaurus, it must postdate the middle of the 5th c. BCE. **ἀπηρτημένα:** < ἀπαρτάομαι, perf. middle/passive participle with gen. following. **τὴν . . . Ἀριστοδάμαν Ἀράτου μητέρα:** she does not appear in Plutarch's *Life of Aratus*. **Ἄρατον Ἀσκληπιοῦ παῖδα:** his human father, Cleinias, was mentioned by P. at 2.8.2. The sculpture supports the fanciful notion that Aratus was fathered by a god in the shape of a serpent; this was told of other great men in antiquity, most notably Alexander the Great.

2.10.4 οὗτος μὲν δὴ . . . τοσάδε: P. transitions from the enclosure of Asclepius to that of Aphrodite. **Ἀντιόπης:** Antiope, the daughter of Nycteus and the mother of Amphion and Zethus, was mentioned at 2.6.1–4, where P. explained how Epopeus abducted Antiope from Thebes and sparked an international crisis. **Ἀντιόπην προσήκειν σφίσι:** "that Antiope is related to them" (v. *LSJ* προσήκω II.1.b). **ἐσίασι:** < εἴσειμι, present act. indicative. **γυνὴ . . . νεωκόρος:** "female warden of the temple." **ᾗ μηκέτι θέμις:** μή is used with the infinitive in prohibitions (S 2715). **παρ' ἄνδρα φοιτῆσαι:** "to have sex with a man" (v. *LSJ* φοιτάω A.I.3). This is a different use of the verb from than at 2.8.4.

2.10.5 Κάναχος Σικυώνιος: Canachus was a sculptor in the latter half of the 6th c. BCE. P. names many of his works (e.g., 1.16.3). **ἐν Διδύμοις τοῖς Μιλησίων:** Didyma, by Miletus in Asia Minor, was second only to Delphi in importance as an oracle and sanctuary of Apollo. **Ἰσμήνιον . . . Ἀπόλλωνα:** a giant serpent guarded the Ismenian Spring in Boeotia until Cadmus killed it (ps.-Apollod. 3.2.2). The river Ismenus lies near the temple and oracle of Apollo. It was said to be the son of the river Asopus and Metope (ps.-Apollod. 3.12.6). Alternatively, P. cites at 9.10.6 an Ismenus who was the son of Apollo and the Oceanid Melia. **(Ἀφροδίτη) φέρουσα:** P. transitions seamlessly back to the statue (τὸ ἄγαλμα). **πόλον:** a ceremonial headdress worn by goddesses (v. *LSJ* V). **τῶν χειρῶν:** partitive gen. with the construction τῇ μὲν . . . τῇ δὲ . . . ἑτέρᾳ. **μήκωνα:** Demeter is said to have discovered the poppy plant in Sicyon and to have given the area the name *Mycone* after it (MT 251). Hesiod (*Works and Days* 510–616) describes a fateful meeting between gods and men that took place there. **τῶν . . . ἱερείων:** partitive gen. with τοὺς μηροὺς . . . τἄλλα . . . **πλὴν ὑῶν:** swine were reserved for Demeter (MT 251). **καθαγίζουσι:** "they dedicate as a burnt offering"; P. follows this compound verb with the appropriate double-compound verb συγκαθαγίζουσι. **τοῦ παιδέρωτος:** P. describes this plant in the next subsection.

2.10.6 ὁ παιδέρως . . . πόα: it may be a type of acanthus, but it is unclear which plant is meant here (cf. Frazer 3.68; MT 251). **ἀλλαχόθι οὐδαμοῦ γῆς, οὔτε ἄλλης (γῆς), οὔτε τῆς Σικυωνίας:** "nowhere else on earth, neither in another land nor in Sicyonia." **φηγοῦ . . . πρίνου . . . δρυός:** φηγός is the Valonia oak, with edible acorns; πρῖνος is the holm (or evergreen) oak; and δρῦς is a general term for oak trees. **(τοῖον) σχῆμα δέ σφισιν (i.e., φύλλοις τοῦ παιδέρωτος) οἷον τοῖς (φύλλοις) τῆς δρύος** **τὸ μὲν (μέρος) . . . τὸ δὲ ἕτερον (μέρος)** **ἂν . . . εἰκάζοις:** potential optative (S 1824). **λεύκης:** "white poplar" (v. *LSJ* λεύκη II.1).

2.10.7 ἀνιοῦσιν: directional participle. **Φεραίας . . . Ἀρτέμιδος:** this cult also appears at 2.23.5. **Κλεινίας:** the father of Aratus, mentioned at 2.8.2. **παιδεύουσιν . . . τοὺς ἐφήβους:** "they train ephebes," chiefly in gymnastics and other educational activities. Cf. Roberto Nicolai, *La Storiografia nell'Educazione Antica* (Pisa: Giardini, 1992). **τὰ ἐς ἰξὺν . . . τὰ κάτω:** acc. of respect (S 1601a), "to the waist (i.e., upper half) . . . in the lower half." Cf. the phrase τὰ μετ᾽ ἰξύν (below the waist) at 2.1.8.

2.11.1 πύλην . . . Ἱεράν: the Sacred Gate is connected either with the procession of the children (2.7.8) toward the Sythas River and N or with the archaic acropolis, its temples, and then the area to the SE (MT 252). **ναός . . . Ἀθηνᾶς:** this temple and its complex are on the acropolis of Aegialea, the old city. The cult statue of Athena, long gone in P.'s time, was the work of Scyllis and Dipoenus (MT 252). **Ἐπωπεύς:** Epopeus, a mythical king of Sicyon, is mentioned at 2.1.1, as the bilious father of Marathon; at 2.3.10, regarding the extension of his rule of Asopia to include Ephyra; and at 2.6.1–3, for his abduction of Antiope and death. **τοὺς τότε (ναούς)** **ἔδει δὲ ἄρα:** a Herodotean touch. **ὑπερβεβλημένον:** < ὑπερβάλλω, perf. middle participle. **τοῦδε . . . τὴν μνήμην:** P. remarks on how time diminishes physical things and their memory alike. **οὐ γὰρ τι ἐς αὐτὸν κατέσκηψε:** "for nothing fell upon it"; i.e., it "escaped injury" (Loeb). **οἷον Ἐπωπεὺς ἐποίησε:** this clause refers to the βωμός. **Ἀποτρόπαιοι θεοί:** "Gods Who Avert Evils," i.e., bad dreams, unfavorable omens, diseases, and unnatural occurences. These were unnamed chthonic deities, although the epithet was also borne by individual deities like Apollo. **Ἄδραστον:** at 2.6.6, P. mentions that during Adrastus' exile from Argos, he succeeded his host Polybus as king of Sicyon. **τὸν μὲν Πανὶ ᾠκοδόμησεν, (τὸν ἕτερον) Ἡλίῳ δὲ λίθου λευκοῦ.**

2.11.2 καταβαίνουσι: directional participle; the reader is directed down from the acropolis to the NW (MT 252). **ἱερόν . . . Δήμητρος:** it lies on the slopes of the hill (MT 253). **ἱδρῦσαι . . . ἱδρύσατο . . . ἱδρύσατο:** P. emphasizes the establishment of multiple shrines. **Πλημναῖον:** P. discussed the circumstances of this at 2.5.8. **τοῦ παιδὸς τῆς τροφῆς:** "(thanking the goddess) for the rearing of his son" (v. *LSJ* χάρις A.II.2). **τοῦ . . . ἱεροῦ τῆς Ἥρας:** construe as gen. of separation with ὀλίγον ἀπωτέρω following. **Καρνείου ναός ἐστιν Ἀπόλλωνος:** for the epithet, see 2.10.2. **οὐκέτι οὐδὲ . . . οὔτε . . . οὔτε:** οὐδέ usually has a preceding negative clause (here οὐκέτι, "no longer will you find walls") and can mean, as here, "nor even" (S 2939; D 192–93); the two instances of οὔτε here connect single phrases referencing the two places mentioned, ἔνταυθα and the shrine of Hera Prodromia. Thus P. uses different conjunctions to pair the physical defects of the shrines and their locations. **τῆς Προδρομίας Ἥρας:** "Hera Pioneer" (Loeb) or "Forerunner Hera" (Frazer). Lewis R. Farnell considers her a battle goddess, who ran before the host and showed Phalces the way, as P. states below; see Farnell, *Cults of the Greek States*, vol. 1 (Oxford: Clarendon, 1896), 197. **Φάλκης . . . ὁ Τημένου:** at. 2.6.7, P. reports that Phalces seized Sicyon at night with his Dorian army and shared the rule with the native king Lacestades. MT (253) suggests that P.'s tortuous route here comes from his desire to reproduce, through the ruined monuments, the chronology of the mythical successions from Epopeus and Adrastus, to Plemnaeus, to the Doric invasion and afterward.

2.11.3 τὴν κατ' εὐθὺ ἐς Φλιοῦντα (ὁδόν) δέκα . . . στάδια: P. occasionally notes distances and does so twice in this subsection. **Πυραία:** this area has not yet been identified. **Προστασίας Δήμητρος:** "Protectress Demeter." **Νυμφῶνα:** the noun more commonly means "bride chamber." There is a possible link with *hierogamia*, perhaps between Kore and Dionysus (MT 253). **παρείκασι:** < παρίημι, perf. act. indicative. **τὰ πρόσωπα φαίνοντα:** i.e., only their faces are exposed to view. **ζεύγεσιν ἄβατος διὰ στενότητα:** P. here provides a description of road conditions, in case his readers decide to emulate him.

2.11.4 θεῶν ἃς . . . Σεμνὰς, . . . Εὐμενίδας: i.e., the Furies. P. notes some of this information at 1.28.6. **ἡμέρᾳ μιᾷ:** dat. of time when (S 1540). **μελικράτῳ . . . σπονδῇ:** Oedipus gives the same libation to the Furies at Sophocles *Oedipus Coloneus* 481. Honey was especially offered to the dead and to the gods of the underworld (Frazer 3.69). **ἐοικότα:** "(rites) like (those just mentioned)." **ὁ δέ (βωμός) τοῦ ἄλσους:** gen. of place (S 1448).

Titane

2.11.5 ἥξασιν: < ἥκω, aor. act. participle; a directional participle. Here P. uses three such participles in a row. **Τιτᾶνα:** in Greek mythology, the Titans are the second race of immortal beings, the descendants of the primordial deities and the predecessors of the Olympian gods. **Τιτάνην τὸ χωρίον:** Titane lies on a great spur overlooking the valley of the Asopus River and the route to Nemea. A polygonal wall on the acropolis is well preserved (MT 253). **δοκεῖν δὲ ἐμοὶ:** P. offers a euhemeristic interpretation of the myth, i.e., explaining a god as an ancient human. **δεινὸς:** "clever" (v. *LSJ*

III). **τὰς ὥρας τοῦ ἔτους φυλάξας:** "observing the seasons of the year" (Loeb). See *LSJ* φυλάσσω B.2.b. **Ἀλεξάνωρ ὁ Μαχάονος τοῦ Ἀσκληπιοῦ:** Machaon and his brother Podalirius, sons of Asclepius, served as physicians for the Achaean army at Troy. P. refers back to this passage at 2.23.4. **τὸ Ἀσκληπιεῖον:** this elaborate sanctuary included a temple, porticoes, and a building for the sacred serpents.

2.11.6 περιοικοῦσι μὲν δὴ καὶ ἄλλοι καὶ τὸ πολὺ οἰκέται: "the neighbors are chiefly servants of the god" (Loeb). Frazer (3.70) understands them as suppliants, but Roux (70) considers them servants of the gods (MT 254). **τὸ πολύ:** "for the most part" (v. *LSJ* πολύς III.1.a). **κυπαρίσσων:** construe with δένδρα ἀρχαῖα. **τὸ . . . ἄγαλμα:** prolepsis (S 2182); this is actually the subject of the relative clause (ὁποίου ξύλου γέγονεν ἢ μετάλλου) and the object of the participial phrase (τὸν ποιήσαντα). **πλὴν εἰ μή . . . ἄρα:** "unless perhaps" ("often ironical"; S 2796). P. may be couching his own opinion here. **ἄκραι χεῖρες καὶ πόδες:** "tips of its hands and feet" (v. *LSJ* ἄκρος I.2). **λευκὸς ἐρεοῦς:** asyndeton for the two adjs. modifying χιτών. **ἐρεοῦς:** < ἐρέεος, contract adj., nom. sg. masc., "woolen." Although the uncontracted form is accented on the antepenult in the nom. sg., contracted 2nd-declension adjs. take a circumflex on the last syllable by analogy with the gen. and dat. sg. (S 290c). **κατὰ ταὐτὸν:** literally, "in the same way," i.e., "similar in appearance." **οὐκ ἂν οὐδὲ τοῦτο ἴδοις:** potential optative, "nor would you see even this." **κόμαι τε γυναικῶν . . . καὶ ἐσθῆτος Βαβυλωνίας τελαμῶνες:** double subject of περιέχουσιν. The hair is probably a thank offering for a cure (Frazer 3.70). **ᾧ δ' ἂν . . . θελήσῃ:** present general relative clause. **ᾧ . . . τούτων:** = ὁποτέρῳ, "with whichever (of the two types of the dedications)." **ἀποδέδεικταί οἱ τὸ αὐτὸ σέβεσθαι τοῦτο ὃ δὴ καὶ Ὑγείαν καλοῦσι:** "it has been shown to him that he (the dedicator) worships this same (image) that they clearly call Hygeia"; "the same instructions have been given to him, to worship this image which . . ." (Loeb).

2.11.7 τῷ μὲν (Ἀλεξάνορι) ὡς ἥρωι . . . Εὐαμερίωνι δὲ ὡς θεῷ. . . ἐναγίζουσιν . . . θύουσιν: P. again distinguishes between rites for a hero and rites for a god, as he did at 2.10.1 (cf. commentary ad loc.). **Τελεσφόρον . . . Ἄκεσιν:** a medical deity (perhaps of Celtic origin) who was associated with Asclepius and sometimes depicted as his son. **Κορωνίδος:** Coronis was the mother of Asclepius; she cheated on Apollo, who then had Artemis kill her in revenge. Cf. 2.26.6–7. **οὐδαμοῦ τοῦ ναοῦ:** "in no part of the temple"; her statue is one of the movable ones. **ταύρου καὶ ἀρνὸς καὶ ὑὸς:** for this type of triple sacrifice, see Frazer 3.73. **ἐς Ἀθηνᾶς ἱερὸν:** discussed by P. at 2.12.1. **μετενεγκόντες:** <

μεταφέρω, aor. act. participle. **ὁπόσα . . . καθαγίζουσιν:** direct object of καίουσι below. **οὐδὲ ἀποχρᾷ σφισιν ἐκτέμνειν τοὺς μηρούς:** construe as a parenthetical clause. **ἀποχρᾷ σφισιν:** "they are not content with" (v. *LSJ* A.2.c). P. uses this Herodotean form instead of the usual ἀπόχρη (S 793D). **χαμαὶ δὲ καίουσι:** this is an example of the apodotic use of δέ, i.e., when the particle responds to a dependent clause (D 178). Here δέ responds not to the parenthetical οὐδὲ . . . μηρούς but to the relative clause ὁπόσα . . . καθαγίζουσιν. **τούτους:** this pronoun refers to τοὺς ὄρνιθας, which receive special treatment.

2.11.8 τὰ δὲ (ἀγάλματα) ἐν τοῖς ἀετοῖς Ἡρακλῆς καὶ Νῖκαι πρὸς τοῖς πέρασίν εἰσιν: "the statues at the ends of the gables are . . ." **ἀγάλματα:** construe with Διονύσου καὶ Ἑκάτης. **Ἀσκληπιὸς ἐπίκλησιν Γορτύνιος:** the epithet is derived from Gortyna (or Gortys) in Arcadia, not from Gortyn in Crete. P. describes the temples there at 5.7.1 and 8.28.1. **<οὐκ>έτι πολυπραγμονοῦσι:** "they are no longer concerned (about it)" (v. *LSJ* 1). **Γρανιανὸς Σικυώνιος:** Aelius Granianus won the boys' *stadion* in 133 CE, the regular *diaulos* and *hoplitodromos* in 137, and the pentathlon in 137 and 141. Cf. Mark Golden, *Sport in the Ancient World from A to Z* (London: Routledge, 2004), 3. **νίκας . . . δύο μὲν (νίκας) πεντάθλου καὶ σταδίου τὴν τρίτην (νίκην), διαύλου δὲ ἀμφότερα:** note the lengths that P. goes to in order to provide *variatio*. The use of ἀμφότερος (either [of two]) to mean simply "two" is unusual but may be excused here because Granianus won the *diaulos* twice, once in each version of the race.

2.12.1 Ἀθηνᾶς ἱερόν: this sanctuary lay on the acropolis and may be beneath the modern church of Hagios Tryphon (MT 254). **τὴν Κορωνίδα:** P. mentioned this statue and its occasional journey to the shrine of Athena in 2.11.7. **βωμός . . . ἀνέμων:** this presumably lies at the foot of the acropolis (MT 254). **δρᾷ . . . ἄλλα ἀπόρρητα:** "(the priest) performs other secret rites" (v. *LSJ* δράω II). For worship of the winds among the Greeks, see Frazer 3.74–75. **ἐς βόθρους τέσσαρας:** i.e., other sacrifices and offerings. **Μηδείας . . . ἐπῳδὰς:** Medea was renowned for her magic spells because of her assistance to Jason in acquiring the Golden Fleece.

2.12.2 Προῖτον . . . τὸν Ἄβαντός: Proetus, son of Abas and sometime king of Argos, appeared earlier at 2.4.2, where he was the master of Bellerophon, and at 2.7.8, where he founded a temple to celebrate the cure of his daughters' madness. **τὸν Σικυωνίων . . . λιμένα:** this harbor was separate from the city and had its own fortifications (Frazer 3.75). **Ἑλισσών . . . καλούμενος ποταμός:** this river is a tributary of the Alpheios River and begins at the town of the same name in Arcadia, near Megalopolis. Cf. 8.30.1. **Σύθας:** this river is E of Pallene and serves as the boundary between Achaea and Sicyon. Cf. 2.7.7, 7.27.12. **ἐς θάλασσαν:** i.e., the Gulf of Corinth, N of the Peloponnesus.

Phlius

2.12.3 ἡ δὲ Φλιασία τῆς Σικυωνίων ἐστὶν ὅμορος: i.e., on the S. **τεσσαράκοντα σταδίους . . . μάλιστα:** "nearly 40 stades" (v. *LSJ* μάλα III.4). **ἐκ Σικυῶνος δὲ ἐς αὐτὴν ὁδός ἐστιν εὐθεῖα:** at 2.11.3, P. mentioned a direct route to Phlius too. **ὅτι . . . προσήκουσιν οὐδέν:** this clause is the direct object of δηλοῖ, whose subject is τὰ ἐς τὸν . . . κατάλογον. P. explains why he is treating Phlius here and not in book 8, with the Arcadians (MT 255). **τὰ ἐς τὸν Ἀρκάδων κατάλογον τῆς Ὁμήρου ποιήσεως:** "the sections of Homer's poetry concerned with the catalog of the Arcadians"; cf. *Iliad* 2.603–14. **συγκατειλεγμένοι:** < συγκαταλέγω, perf. passive participle. **ὡς δὲ Ἀργεῖοί . . . Πελοπόννησον:** this whole clause is the subject of φανεῖται. **φανεῖται:** < φαίνομαι, future middle indicative. **προϊόντι ὁμοῦ τῷ λόγῳ:** the preposition ὁμοῦ takes the dat. P. refers here to the fuller narrative of the return of the Heraclidae that he gives at the beginning of book 3, on Sparta. **διάφορα:** < the adj. διάφορος (neut. pl. acc. agreeing with εἰρημένα), not the related noun διαφορά. P. contrasts the many differences in the tales about the Phliasians with τὰ ὡμολογημένα that he provides at 2.12.4ff.—a Herodotean touch. **ἐς τοὺς Φλιασίους τὰ πολλὰ . . . εἰρημένα:** "most of the traditions concerning the Phliasians" (Loeb).

2.12.4 πρῶτον Ἄραντα . . . ἄνδρα αὐτόχθονα: Aras was "sprung from the soil," as the Athenians famously claimed they were. Cf. 2.14.4. **καὶ πόλιν τε ᾤκισε . . . ἐνταῦθά τε δὴ πόλιν ᾤκισε:** P. resumes the thread of the narrative after a series of dependent clauses. Aras' city and the Arantine Hill perhaps lay at the base of Mt. Megalovuni. The historical city of Phlius lies six kilometers away, on the banks of the Asopus River (MT 256). **τῆς Ἥβης . . . τὸ ἱερόν:** cf. 2.13.3. **τὸ ἀρχαῖον:** adv., "in ancient times." **Ἀσωπος Κηλούσης . . . καὶ Ποσειδῶνος:** P. mentioned the river at 2.5.1–2. It runs from the Gulf of Corinth, through Sicyonia, right by Phlius. **τὸ ὕδωρ, ὅντινα . . . Ἀσωπόν:** P. here uses the indefinite relative instead of the normal relative, with little, if any, difference in sense. **τὸ δὲ μνῆμα τοῦ Ἄραντός ἐστιν ἐν χωρίῳ Κελεαῖς:** cf. 2.14.4. **Δυσαύλην:** P. notes at 1.14.3 that, according to the Orphic verses, Dysaules was the father of Triptolemus and Eubuleus, all of whom played a role in the mythology of Eleusis. P. discusses Dysaules' connection to Phlius at 2.14.2ff.

2.12.5 **θήρας:** gen. with ἐμπείρους (S 1419). **τὰ ἐς πόλεμον:** acc. of specification with ἀνδρείους. **ἐς μνήμην:** the Latin equivalent is the familiar *in memoriam*. **Ὅμηρος:** cf. *Iliad* 2.571. **Ὀρνειάς:** P. describes Orneae at 2.25.5–6. **τῆς χώρας:** construe with οὐχ ἑτέρωθι. **καί σφισιν ἐπίθημα στῆλαι περιφανεῖς εἰσι:** i.e., the stelae are on top of the tombs. **πρὸ τῆς τελετῆς ἣν τῇ Δήμητρι ἄγουσιν:** at Celeae; P. describes these at 2.14.

2.12.6 **Φλίαντα:** at 2.6.6, P. says that Phlias, the son of Dionysus, was husband of Cthonophyle and father of Androdamas; in this subsection, he affirms that account and contrasts it with another version. Hyginus (*Fab.* 14) calls him Phliasus, son of Dionysus and Ariadne. **τρίτον . . . ὄνομα:** P. signals three phases of Phlius: Arantia, Araethyrea, and Phlius proper. **Κείσου . . . παῖδα . . . τοῦ Τημένου:** Ceisus and his brothers were disinherited by their father, who preferred his son-in-law Deiphontes (P. covers the related story at 2.26.2 and 2.28.3); this phrase is the object of προσίεμαι. **οὐδὲ ἀρχὴν ἔγωγε προσίεμαι:** "I do not at all even admit" (v. *LSJ* προσίημι II.2). P. rejects the Argive account. **τῶν πλευσάντων ἐπὶ τῆς Ἀργοῦς:** partitive gen. with τοῦτον γενέσθαι λεγόμενον. **τοῦ Ῥοδίου ποιητοῦ τὰ ἔπη:** i.e., Apollonius of Rhodes *Argonautica* 1.115–17. **ἕκητι:** "by the grace of," with gen. **ἑοῦ:** < ἑός, "his own," the Homeric version of the possessive adj. of the 3rd sg. (S 330D1).

2.13.1 **πλὴν Ἀρκάδων:** as MT (256–57) notes, P. here seems to be echoing Thucydides 1.2.3 on the Doric migration. **ὡς πολλὰς μὲν . . . πλείονας δὲ . . . :** double clause of natural result. The particle ὡς is rarely used for ὥστε, but when it does occur, it almost always, as here, takes the infinitive (S 2252). **ἐκ τοῦ Δωρικοῦ (ἔθνους)** **τὰς μεταβολὰς:** "revolutions" (v. *LSJ* II.3). **Ῥηγνίδας . . . ὁ Φάλκου τοῦ Τημένου:** Phalces was guided to Sicyon by Hera (2.11.2) and took over the city by nocturnal incursion (2.6.7). **ἔκ τε Ἄργους:** at 2.18.7ff., P. explains how the Heraclidae took over (or reclaimed) Argos. **τοῖς μὲν . . . Ἵππασος δὲ . . . :** P. divides the Phliasians (partitive gen. τῶν Φλιασίων) into two groups based on their reaction to Rhegnidas' proposal. **ἃ προεκαλεῖτο Ῥηγνίδας:** "what Rhegnidas was proposing" (v. *LSJ* B.II.1) This is the subject of ἐφαίνετο; it is explained by the acc. and infinitive construction following ἀρεστά. **μένοντας:** this acc. subject of δέχεσθαι refers to the same people as τοῖς μέν. **ἐπὶ τοῖς αὑτῶν:** "on their own estates" (Loeb). **ἐπὶ ἀναδασμῷ γῆς:** "redistribution of land"; H. uses similar language at 4.159, to describe the emigration of the Greeks to Cyrene and the allotment of lands there, and at 4.163 (ἐπὶ γῆς ἀναδασμῷ), to describe Arcesilaus' promises to the army that he raises on Samos to reclaim Cyrene.

2.13.2 διεκελεύοντο . . . μηδὲ . . . ἀφίστασθαι: verbs of commanding and willing take objective infinitives (S 1992a) and μή if negative (S 2719). **ἀφίστασθαι:** < ἀφίστημι, present middle participle, "to give up," with gen. (v. *LSJ* B.1). **προσεμένου:** < προσίημι, 2nd aor. middle participle (S 777). Cf. 2.12.6. **προσεμένου . . . τοῦ δημοῦ τὴν ἐναντίαν** ταύτῃ **γνώμην:** "when the people approved the opposite plan" (v. *LSJ* προσίημι II.2.c), i.e., the Dorian proposal. **τέταρτος . . . ἀπόγονος:** fourth counting inclusively with Hippasus as the first. **Πυθαγόρας ὁ λεγόμενος γενέσθαι σοφός:** Pythagoras was not one of the Seven Wise Men of the archaic period but is believed to have lived in the 6th c. BCE. Phlius was an important center of Pythagoreanism and the home of Echecrates, a Pythagorean philosopher from the first half of the 4th c. BCE who appears in Plato's *Phaedo* (MT 257). **τὰ πολλὰ:** adv., "generally."

2.13.3 προσέσται: < πρόσειμι, future middle indicative. **προσέσται . . . ἀξιολογώτατα:** "I will now add an account of the most remarkable of their famous sights" (Loeb). **ἐκ παλαιοῦ:** "from ancient times" (v. *LSJ* παλαιός II.2.a) **Γανυμήδαν:** not to be confused with Ganymede (son of Tros), who succeeded her as cupbearer of the gods. Strabo 8.3.24 calls her Dia. **Ὅμηρος μνήμην ἐποιήσατο ἐν τῇ Μενελάου πρὸς Ἀλέξανδρον μονομαχίᾳ:** cf. *Iliad* 4.2–3, μετὰ δέ σφισι πότνια Ἥβη / νέκταρ ἐοινοχόει. **<ἐν> Ὀδυσσέως ἐς Ἅιδου καθόδῳ:** cf. *Odyssey* 11.603–4, καὶ ἔχει καλλίσφυρον Ἥβην, / παῖδα Διὸς μεγάλοιο καὶ Ἥβης χρυσοπεδίλου. **γυναῖκα Ἡρακλέους . . . εἶναι:** Hebe married Heracles after his death and apotheosis. **Ὠλῆνι:** dat. of agent with ἐστὶν . . . πεποιημένα. The Greeks regularly used the dat. of agent with perf. passive constructions (S 1488). P. occasionally refers to or uses the work of Olen, a legendary Lycian poet, as evidence for assertions (cf. 1.18.5). **Ὡρῶν:** the Horae were the Greek personifications of the seasons.

2.13.4 μέγιστον τὸ ἐς τοὺς ἱκέτας: "the greatest (act of honor) is their behavior toward suppliants." **δεδώκασι . . . ἄδειαν:** "they have given them sanctuary"; cf. H. 2.121ζ, ἀδείην τε διδόντα. **ἱκετεύουσι:** present act. participle. **πρὸς τὰ ἐν τῷ ἄλσει δένδρα ἀνατιθέασιν:** they dedicate the fetters not "to" the trees but "on" them, presumably by affixing them with nails or spikes. **Κισσοτόμους:** "the cutting of the ivy"; this festival was probably connected with the rites of freedom (MT 257–58). **νομίζουσιν:** "they have the custom" (v. *LSJ* I.1); cf. 2.4.6. **ἱερὸς . . . λόγος:** presumably the one that P. is not privy to or cannot share. **ἐπεὶ:** this conjunction is not used here in a temporal or causal way; "though" (Loeb). **τῆς . . . Ἥρας:** gen. of possession with ναός. The cults of Hera and Hebe are also paired at Mycenae (2.17.5–6) and Mantineia (8.9.3). Hebe is similar to Hera Parthenos (MT 258). **ἐξιόντων ἐν ἀριστερᾷ:** directional participial phrase.

2.13.5 **ἄλλος περίβολος . . . ἱερὸς Δήμητρος:** this sanctuary may lie under the church of Panaghia on the acropolis. **ἐφαίνετο ἀρχαῖον εἶναί μοι:** P. references his expertise in the evaluation of artwork. **Ἀσκληπιοῦ ναὸς:** this temple above the theater has been excavated. **οὐκ ἔχον πω γένεια:** i.e., "a beardless youth" (Loeb). At 2.10.3, Asclepius was represented without a beard at Sicyon too. **Δήμητρός ἐστιν ἱερὸν:** this second sanctuary to Demeter is probably connected with a *telesterion* (initiation place) found near the theater on the S slope of the Acropolis (MT 258).

2.13.6 **ἐπὶ τῆς ἀγορᾶς:** the agora is lined with sanctuaries. **αἶξ χαλκῆ:** apart from the explanation P. gives below, goats also have cultic connections to Dionysus and thus to the theater (MT 258–59). **εἴληφε:** < λαμβάνω, perf. act. indicative. **ἐπὶ τῷδε:** "for the following reason." **τὸ ἄστρον ἣν ὀνομάζουσιν αἶγα ἀνατέλλουσα:** P. shifts the gender of the subject for the participle. According to some sources, this goat was Amaltheia, who suckled the infant Zeus. The star is known as Capella ("she-goat" in Latin) and forms the left shoulder of the constellation called Auriga, "Charioteer." **ἵνα δὲ . . . οἱ δὲ:** the first use of δέ here connects a new sentence to the previous, while the second shifts the subject to the Phliasians and can be classified as a duplicate δέ (D 183). **ἄλλοις:** "in other ways." **Ἀριστίου . . . τοῦ Πρατίνου:** in 467 BCE, Aristias won second place in the Athenian City Dionysia with his father's tragedies *Perseus* and *Tantalus* (and one unknown by name) and the satyr play *Wrestlers*, losing out to Aeschylus' Theban tetralogy (*Laius*, *Oedipus*, *Seven against Thebes*, and *Sphinx*). Aristias' father, Pratinas, was considered by some ancient sources to be the first author of satyr plays, and several fragments of his work survive. Cf. Carl Shaw, *Satyric Play: The Evolution of Greek Comedy and Satyr Drama* (Oxford: Oxford University Press, 2014), 43–56, 64–65. **τῶν Αἰσχύλου (σατύρων):** gen. with πλήν.

2.13.7 **οἶκος . . . μαντικός:** "house of divination." **Ἀμφιάραος:** the mantis Amphiaraus participated in the expedition of the Seven against Thebes. After its failure, he and his chariot were swallowed by the earth. Cf. 2.23.2. **μαντεύεσθαι:** construe with ἤρξατο. **τῷ ἐκείνων λόγῳ:** "according to their account" (Loeb). **συγκέκλεισται:** < συγκλείω, perf. passive indicative. **τὸν πάντα ἤδη χρόνον:** "ever since then." **Ὀμφαλός:** this is similar to the one at Delphi, although that one purports to be the center of the world. Cf. 10.16.3. **εἰ δὴ τὰ ὄντα εἰρήκασιν:** P. is rightly skeptical, for Phlius is hardly near the center of the Peloponnese. **ὡσαύτως:** "in the same way," adverbial form of ὁ αὐτός. **μόνον ἔστι:** "it is only permitted."

2.13.8 λέγεται . . . ὧδε . . . λόγος: this expression sets up indirect discourse in the acc. and infinitive construction for the next several lines; P. switches to direct discourse thereafter. **ἀνεσώθη:** "he returned safely" (v. *LSJ* ἀνασῴζω 1). **τὰ μῆλα τὰ Ἑσπερίδων καλούμενα:** the eleventh labor of Heracles was to acquire apples from the Garden of the Hesperides (nymphs) in the far W corner of the Mediterranean. He returned with the apples to Greece, to deliver them to King Eurystheus of Tiryns. **κατὰ δή τι ἴδιον:** "on some private matter" (Loeb). **διαιτωμένου δὲ ἐνταῦθα (Ἡράκλεως):** P. refers to him with the pronoun αὐτόν in the same sentence. **Οἰνέα:** Oineus was the king of Aetolia and fathered Tydeus, who took part in the Seven against Thebes. One of his daughters was Deianira, Heracles' wife, thus making him a κηδεστής, or in-law, of the hero. **ἐγεγόνει:** < γίγνομαι, pluperf. act. indicative. **Κύαθον:** the boy's name varies greatly in the surviving versions of the story, but his name here is quite appropriate, for the common noun κύαθος means "ladle" and refers to one commonly used to draw wine out of a *krater*. This episode is usually located in Calydon in Aetolia. Ps.-Apollod. 2.7.6 calls him Eunomus, the son of Architeles, and says he was pouring water on Heracles' hands. **ἀποθανόντος:** gen. with ἐς μνήμην.

Celeae

2.14.1 αἱ Κελεαί: this sanctuary lies to the S of Phlius, on the left of the Asopus River (MT 259). **πέντε που σταδίους μάλιστα:** not an instance of pleonasm, for που refers to P.'s uncertainty, μάλιστα to the fact that he is giving an approximation. **δι' ἐνιαυτοῦ τετάρτου . . . καὶ οὐ κατὰ ἔτος:** an instance of pleonasm and *variatio*. **ἀποδέδεικται:** "he is appointed" (v. *LSJ* ἀποδείκνυμι A.II.1). **ἄλλοτέ . . . ἄλλος:** "one at one time, another at another time." **αἱρετός:** "chosen" (v. *LSJ* II.2). **ἢν ἐθέλῃ:** = εἰ ἂν ἐθέλῃ, protasis of a present general condition. **τῶν Ἐλευσῖνι:** "the mysteries at Eleusis," later referred to by ἐκείνων, which should be construed with μίμησιν as an objective gen. **τὰ . . . δρώμενα:** a technical term for rituals of mysteries (v. *LSJ* II).

2.14.2 Δυσαύλην . . . ἀδελφὸν Κελεοῦ: P. mentioned the tomb of Dysaules in Phliasia at 2.12.4. Celeus was a legendary king of Eleusis. **Ἴων . . . ὁ Ξούθου:** Xuthus was the son of Hellen and Orseis and fathered Ion, Achaeus, and Diomede. In his description of Attica, P. notes Ion's grave at Potami (1.31.3) and that he was polemarch in the war between Eleusis and Athens. In his tragedy, Euripides depicts Ion as the illegitimate son of Apollo and Creusa, daughter of Erechtheus and wife of Xuthus. **Ἀθηναίοις:** dat. of agent with ᾑρέθη. **ᾑρέθη:** < αἱρέω, aor. passive indicative. **τοῦτο:** this refers to the acc. and infinitive construction after ὁμολογήσω. **τοῦτο . . . Φλιασίοις:** "I will (not) agree with the Phliasians in this"; the verb usually takes acc. of thing agreed on and dat. of person with whom the thing is agreed. **οὐκ ἔστιν ὅπως ὁμολογήσω:** "it is not possible that . . ." (S 2551). **ἀπελαθέντα:** < ἀπελαύνω, aor. passive participle. **τοῦ πολέμου τε ἐπὶ συνθήκαις καταλυθέντος πρὶν ἢ διαπολεμηθῆναι:** at 1.5.2 and 1.27.4, P. says that King Erechtheus of Athens killed Immaradus, son of Eumolpus, in battle; at 1.38.3, he adds that Erechtheus died too and that Eleusis agreed to be subject to the Athenians in all but religious matters. This gen. absolute and the next explain why P. thinks the Phliasian tradition is wrong. **Εὐμόλπου:** Eumolpus was the son of Poseidon and Chione and later became one of the first priests of Demeter at Eleusis and one of the founders of the Eleusinian Mysteries; he even initiated Heracles into the mysteries. P. notes his tomb in his description of Eleusis at 1.38.2.

2.14.3 δύναιτο ἄν: potential optative. **κατὰ ἄλλην τινὰ . . . πρόφασιν:** hyperbaton. **οὐ μὴν οὐδὲ . . . οὐδὲ . . . :** "nor again . . . nor . . ." (S 2768). P. explains why the local tradition about Dysaules being Eleusinian is wrong too. **ἐν τοῖς ἐπιφανέσιν:** "among the famous men (of Eleusis)" (v. *LSJ* II.1). **οὐ . . . ἄν . . . παρῆκεν:** apodosis of a past contrary-to-fact condition. **παρῆκεν:** < παρίημι, aor. act. indicative. **Ὁμήρῳ πεποιημένα ἐς Δήμητραν:** cf. *Homeric Hymn to Demeter* 474–76. **τοὺς διδαχθέντας . . . τὴν τελετὴν:** when a double acc. construction is converted into the passive voice, as here, the second acc. is retained (S 1632). **δεῖξεν:** "(she) revealed"; the subject is the unstated Demeter, and the direct object is δρησμοσύνην ἱερῶν. **Τριπτολέμῳ:** a son of Celeus. **Διοκλεῖ:** another of the first priests of Demeter at Eleusis. **Εὐμόλπου τε βίῃ:** "strong Eumolpus," a poetic use of the gen. (S 1292). **ἐπέφραδεν:** < φράζω, epic aor. act. indicative (v. *LSJ*).

2.14.4 δ' οὖν: "at all events, anyhow" (S 2959). **παραθέμενος:** < παρατίθημι, 2nd aor. middle participle. **Δυσαύλου . . . μνῆμα:** P. mentioned the graves of Aras and Dysaules at 2.12.4 and here argues against the Phliasian tradition about Dysaules, on chronological grounds. **Προμηθεῖ . . . τῷ Ἰαπέτου:** Prometheus, son of the Titan Iapetus, was famous as the god who brought fire to humankind; he was punished for this by being chained to the Caucasian Mountains and suffering the daily consumption of his liver by an eagle until Heracles freed him. **τρισὶν ἀνθρώπων γενεαῖς:** dat. of degree of difference, "(older) by three generations." **Πελασγοῦ . . . τοῦ Ἀρκάδος:** gen. of comparison with πρεσβύτερον. Arcas was the son of Zeus and Callisto; he and his mother were famous for being turned into bears and the constellations Ursa Major and Ursa Minor. **τῶν λεγομένων Ἀθήνῃσιν αὐτοχθόνων:** the Athenians boasted that they were descended from the very soil of Athens and that their kings Cecrops I and Erichthonius were literally born of the earth. **τοῦ δὲ Ἀνακτόρου:** Eleusis had a building by the same name, one thought to be the hall of initiation (Frazer 3.82). **Πέλοπος:** Pelops, the son of Tantalus, was the king of Pisa and the hero after whom the Peloponnesus was named; he was also the father of Atreus and, thus, the grandfather of Menelaus and Agamemnon. He famously defeated Oenomaus in a chariot race to win the hand of Hippodamia.

Cleonae

2.15.1 Φλιασίοις μὲν δὴ τοσαῦτα λόγου μάλιστα ἦν ἄξια: P. signals that he is ending the section on Phliasia. **ἐρχομένῳ:** P.'s directional participles are usually in the plural. **Κλεωναὶ:** Cleonae is about nine miles SW of Corinth and is situated on two hills (the W of which serves as the acropolis) in a valley watered by the Longopotamos River. P. here jumps topographically from one route (Corinth–Sicyon–Phlius–Celeae) to another, as he backtracks to the local hub of Corinth. **παῖδα . . . Πέλοπος Κλεώνην:** the use of παῖς here and θυγάτηρ in the next clause shows that this individual is masc. (i.e., Κλεώνης in the nom.) and that the other is fem. (i.e., Κλεώνη). **ἀπὸ τοῦ ἑτέρου τούτων:** "from one or the other of these (two) people"; ἕτερος is used when two things or people are being referenced. **Σκύλλιδος . . . Διποίνου:** Pliny the Elder (*NH* 36.4) says that they were both born in Crete ca. 580–577 BCE and migrated to Sicyon and that they were the first artists to gain fame for working with marble. He relates an interesting story about how the Sicyonians hired them to make images of the gods but mistreated them in some way, thereby suffering famine and barren soil until they made amends with the sculptors. See Frazer 3.83–85. **Δαιδάλου:** Daedalus is most famous as the father of Icarus and the creator of a fake cow for Pasiphaë, wife of King Minos of Crete, but he was also considered an inventor and artist, and P. occasionally identifies statues as the work of his hand (e.g., 2.4.5). **<ἐκ> Γόρτυνος:** this is probably the city of Gortyn in Crete. **Εὐρύτου καὶ Κτεάτου:** these two were twin sons of Actor and Molione of Elis. They were known as the Actoridae or Moliones. Augeas made them his generals against Heracles, who later ambushed and killed them at Cleonae. Cf. ps.-Apollod. 2.7.2. In the Hesiodic tradition, they are portrayed as Siamese twins (MT 261). **ἐς τὸν ἀγῶνα . . . τῶν Ἰσθμίων:** i.e., the Isthmian Games. **ἔγκλημα ποιούμενος:** = ἐγκαλῶν. **οἱ . . . πολεμοῦντι:** dat., i.e., Heracles.

Nemea

2.15.2 ἀνδράσιν εὐζώνοις: "men dressed for travel" (v. *LSJ* εὔζωνος 2). **ἐπίτομος:** "direct (route)" (v. *LSJ* 2). This route went SE of the valley of Cleonae, over the mountain; the other went SW of the valley, through the mountain pass. **Τρητοῦ:** "pierced." Diodorus Siculus 4.11.3 connects the name to the cave of the Nemean Lion. **τοῦ λέοντος:** i.e., the Nemean Lion, Heracles' first labor. **Νεμείου . . . Διὸς ναός:** the Nemean Games were traditionally founded in 537/536 BCE and celebrated in the second and fourth years of the Olympiad. From the 3rd c. BCE, the games were celebrated at Argos, and the original sanctuary fell into disuse. The temple of Zeus is a peripteral Doric format of 6 × 12 columns without an opisthodomos. It was built in 330–320 BCE, to replace an older one that existed between 600 and 430 BCE (MT 262). **πλὴν ὅσον:** "except that" (v. *LSJ* πλήν B.II.5). **κατερρυήκει:** < καταρρέω, pluperf. act. indicative. **κυπαρίσσων τε ἄλσος:** remains of this grove have been found SE of the temple (MT 262). **Ὀφέλτην:** Opheltes was the son of Lycurgus and Eurydice; an oracle told his parents that he must not touch the ground before he learned to walk. His nurse Hypsipyle set him down, however, so she could direct the Seven against Thebes to the nearest spring. Amphiaraus prophesied that the child's death was a sign that the expedition would fail, but the Argive generals held a funeral for the child and founded the Nemean Games in his honor, as P. relates below. Cf. ps.-Apollod. 3.6.4. **τεθέντα:** < τίθημι, aor. passive participle.

2.15.3 δρόμου προτιθέασιν ἀγῶνα: "they established the running contest" (v. *LSJ* προτίθημι I.3.a). Aratus attempted to reestablish the games at Nemea to spite Argos (Plutarch *Life of Aratus* 28; MT 262). **Νεμείων πανηγύρει τῶν χειμερινῶν:** ca. 134 CE, Hadrian reorganized the cycle of the major games, putting the Nemean Games between November 1 and January 1 (*SEG* LVI.1359 I 65). P. also mentions the winter Nemean Games at 6.16.4. **Ὀφέλτου τάφος:** the tomb and its pentagonal enclosure were discovered in 1979–80 (MT 262). **χῶμα γῆς Λυκούργου μνῆμα:** Lycurgus was the king of Nemea; no trace of his tumulus has been found (MT 263). **τὴν δὲ πηγὴν Ἀδράστειαν ὀνομάζουσιν εἴτε ἐπ' ἄλλῃ τινὶ αἰτίᾳ εἴτε . . . :** P. is often not satisfied with the most well-known explanations of names; MT (263) suggests that this is evidence of his snobbery. **Ἀδράστου:** at 2.6.6, P. mentioned the exile of Adrastus from Sicyon and his later succession to Polybus as king of Sicyon. **ὄρος Ἀπέσας:** i.e., Mt. Phoukas, which dominates the Nemean valley (MT 263). **Περσέα:** Perseus was the son of Zeus and Danaë, the daughter of Acrisius. P. discusses Perseus in the mythical history of Argos at 2.16.2.

Mythical History of the Argolid

2.15.4 ἀνελθοῦσι . . . ἐς τὸν Τρητὸν: i.e., going by the easy route to Argos. **τὴν ἐς Ἄργος (ὁδόν) ἰοῦσιν** **Μυκηναίους . . . ἀνέστησαν:** < ἀνίστημι, 1st aor. act. indicative, "they caused the Mycenaeans to emigrate"; i.e., they destroyed the city. P. explains this event at 2.16.4. **τὰ μὲν ἔτι παλαιότερα οὐ μνημονεύουσιν:** P. notes the limits of human memory. **Ἴναχον:** Inachus was the first king of Argos, as the tradition goes.

2.15.5 λέγεται δὲ καὶ ὧδε λόγος: P. introduces a different tradition. **Φορωνέα:** P. mentions Phoroneus as the father of Car, an ancient king of Megara, several times in book 1 (e.g., 1.39.5–6). An epic poem entitled *Phoronis* (ca. 6th c. BCE) celebrated him and his achievements. At 2.19.5, P. cites a tradition that Phoroneus brought fire to humankind. Hyginus (*Fab.* 143) calls him the first human king. **κρινάντων δὲ (ποταμῶν)** **ὅτι μὴ:** "except" (S 2765). **ὕδωρ:** direct object of παρέχεται. **θέρους:** gen. of time within which (S 1444). **πλὴν τῶν ἐν Λέρνῃ (ῥευμάτων):** preposition with the gen. here, "except" (S 1700). P. discusses Lerna at 2.36.6–2.37.6. **Φορωνεὺς δὲ . . . τοὺς ἀνθρώπους συνήγαγε πρῶτον ἐς κοινόν:** like Athens under Theseus, so Mycenae under Phoroneus underwent synoecism, the concentration of a dispersed rural population into a formal polis. MT (263–64) notes that in this subsection and the previous one, P. introduces the alternative versions of myths in indirect discourse (λέγουσι and λέγεται . . . λόγος) but puts the unified and widespread version in direct discourse. **ἐφ' ἑαυτῶν ἑκάστοτε οἰκοῦντας:** "living as isolated families" (Loeb). **ἠθροίσθησαν:** < ἀθροίζω, aor. passive indicative.

2.16.1 Ἄργος: Argos was the son of Zeus and Niobe, the daughter of Phoroneus. **Πείρασος . . . καὶ Φόρβας:** at 2.17.5, P. names Peirasus as the dedicator of an image of Hera at the Heraeum. Phorbas sired Triopas by Euboea. **Τριόπας:** at 4.1.1–2, P. mentions his daughter Messene; she emigrated from Laconia with her husband, Polycaon, who conquered and renamed Lelegia Messenia after her. **Ἴασος καὶ Ἀγήνωρ:** although Iasus seems to have succeeded Triopas initially, each brother establishes a family line with a claim to the throne of Argos. **Ἰὼ . . . Ἰάσου θυγάτηρ . . . ἐς Αἴγυπτον ἀφικνεῖται:** according to the famous myth, Io was turned into a heifer by Zeus, who sought to hide his lover from the anger of Hera. Growing suspicious, Hera requested that Zeus give her the cow, which Hera had all-seeing Argus (not to be confused with the previously mentioned king Argos) guard. Zeus had Hermes kill Argus, but Hera then sent a gadfly to torment Io and drive her across the world to Egypt, where she regained her human form. Cf. ps.-Apollod. 2.1.3. **εἴτε ὡς Ἡρόδοτος ἔγραψεν εἴτε καθ' ὃ λέγουσιν Ἕλληνες:** P. is referring to the famous introduction to H.'s *Histories* (1.1), where H. explains that Phoenician merchants abducted Io from Argos, thus providing the original cause for the hostilities between Greeks and barbarians. **Κρότωπος:** at 1.43.7, P. relates that Crotopus' daughter Psamathe bore a son, Linus, to Apollo but exposed the infant, which Crotopus' sheepdogs killed, thus incurring Apollo's wrath. The god sent Vengeance herself against Argos. **Δαναὸς:** Danaus, the son of Belus and twin brother of Aegyptus, fled from Egypt to Argos seeking refuge, because he was descended from Io. **πλεύσας ἐπὶ Γελάνορα τὸν Σθενέλα τοὺς ἀπογόνους τοὺς Ἀγήνορος βασιλείας ἔπαυσεν:** at 2.19.3–4, P. relates how this happened. **τὰ . . . ἀπὸ τούτου:** "the events that followed from this." **θυγατέρων τῶν Δαναοῦ:** the Danaides were said to number 50. **τὸ ἐς τοὺς ἀνεψιοὺς τόλημα:** Danaus yielded his daughters to Aegyptus, so that they could marry that man's sons, their cousins, but Danaus bade his daughters to slay their new husbands on their wedding night. In some accounts, they were punished for this with carrying water in sieves in Hades for eternity. Cf. ps.-Apollod. 2.1.5. **Λυγκεὺς:** Lynceus, a son of Aegyptus, was the sole bridegroom to survive his wedding night, thanks to the scruples of his cousin-bride Hypermnestra; he slew Danaus in revenge and then began a new dynasty of Argive kings.

2.16.2 οἱ δὲ Ἄβαντος τοῦ Λυγκέως: Abas sired Acrisius and Proetus by Ocaleia (ps.-Apollod. 2.2.1). At 10.35.1, P. notes that Abas founded Abae in Phocis. The kings of Argos were known as Abantides, after him. **αὐτοῦ:** adv., "here." **Προῖτος:** P. handles the fate of his half of the kingdom in the next subsection. **ὅσα πρὸς θαλάσσῃ τῆς Ἀργείας:** "the parts of Argeia (i.e., the Argolid) that lie along the coast." **σημεῖα:** = "traces" (v. *LSJ* I.1.a). **Ἀκρίσιος:** Acrisius learned from the Delphic oracle that a grandchild would kill him, so he confined his only daughter, Danaë, in a subterranean chamber. When Zeus managed to impregnate her nonetheless, he confined her and her child, Perseus, in a chest and threw it into the sea. Perseus and his mother floated to the island of Seriphos, where they were rescued. **πάντως:** "very much" (v. *LSJ* I). **λόγοις τε χρηστοῖς καὶ ἔργοις:** "with fair words and deeds" (v. *LSJ* I.1). P.'s use of χρηστός here is significant, for he employs the common adj. only rarely—five times in his entire work. These cases usually involve fortune or a fateful event resulting from a noble act: pious people have a τύχη χρηστή (1.17.1); Oenobius' decree to recall Thucydides (ἔργον . . . χρηστόν) leads to the historian's death (1.23.9); τύχη χρηστή does not follow Eubulus' plan to expel the tyrant Lachares (1.29.10); and there is the τύχη χρηστή of Alexander the Great (4.35.4). **οἷα ἡλικίᾳ τε ἀκμάζων καὶ . . . χαίρων:** "inasmuch as he was at the peak of his youth and reveling in . . . ," a circumstantial participle with οἷα showing cause (S 2085). **ἐπεδείκνυτο ἐς ἅπαντας:** "he made displays for everyone" (v. *LSJ* ἐπιδείκνυμι A.I.2.a) **λανθάνει . . . ὑποπεσὼν:** "he escaped notice as he fell under," with dat. **κατὰ δαίμονα:** = τύχῃ, "by chance" (v. *LSJ* δαίμων A.I.1).

2.16.3 τέλος ἔσχεν: "(the prophecy) came to fulfillment." **τὸ χρεὼν:** P.'s use of χρηστός (see commentary on 2.16.2) may be conditioned by his repeated use of τὸ χρεών for "fate," especially "death." Cf. 2.9.4, 2.30.7, 2.34.5. **τὰ ἐς τὴν παῖδα καὶ τὸν θυγατριδοῦν παρευρήματα:** "his precautions . . ." (Loeb); this phrase is the subject of ἀπέστρεψεν. **Μεγαπένθην τὸν Προίτου:** Megapenthes reappears at 2.18.4, where P. relates how the kingdom of Argos was divided into three realms by his grandson's desperation. **τὴν ἐκείνου (ἀρχήν) τοῦ ξίφους:** gen. of separation with ἐξέπεσεν. **ἐς οἰκισμὸν . . . συμβῆναι πόλεως:** "(the sign) corresponded with founding the city" (v. *LSJ* συμβαίνω II.3). **ἤκουσα δὲ καὶ . . . :** P. may be giving a local tradition here. **διψῶντι . . . οἱ:** "it occurred to him being thirsty," dat. with ἐπῆλθεν. **ἀνελέσθαι:** < ἀναιρέω, aor. middle infinitive; here the verb has its original literal meaning of "to take up."

2.16.4 Ὅμηρος . . . ἐν Ὀδυσσείᾳ: cf. *Odyssey* 2.120. **Τυρώ:** Tyro, the daughter of Salmoneus, was the mother of Pelias and Neleus by Poseidon. **Ἀλκμήνη:** Alcmene, the daughter of Electryon, was the wife of Amphitryon and was most famous as the mother of Heracles by Zeus. **Ἀρέστορος:** according to some accounts, Arestor was the father of the many-eyed monster Argus and of the Argus who built the Argo, the ship Jason sailed on with his Argonauts to fetch the Golden Fleece. **Ἠοίας μεγάλας:** the *Great Eoiae* was an epic poem attributed to Hesiod in antiquity and is often cited by P. Cf. 2.2.3, 2.26.2. See Merkelbach-West fr. 246. **ὃν . . . λόγον:** this is the direct object of ἀποδειξαίμην and is explained by the acc. with infinitive following. **Ἀκουσι<λάῳ>:** Acusilaus of Argos (*FGrH* 2) was a famous mythographer of the late 6th c. BCE, and P. often makes use of his genealogies, if only, as here, to criticize them. **διότι μηδὲ αὐτοὶ Λακεδαιμόνιοι:** causal clauses usually take the negative οὐ (S 2240). **Σπάρτης:** Sparte was a naiad of a spring in Sparta; the daughter of the river Eurotas, she was the wife of King Lacedaimon. **καὶ ἀρχὴν ἀκούσαντες:** "even hearing at all" (v. *LSJ* ἀρχή I.1.c).

Mycenae

2.16.5 κατὰ τὴν ἐπιστρατείαν τοῦ Μήδου: i.e., the Second Persian War (480–479 BCE). **Θερμοπύλας:** the famous Battle of Thermopylae in 480 BCE (H. 7.202). Four hundred Mycenaeans also fought at Plataea (H. 9.28). **τοῦτο . . . τὸ φιλοτίμημα:** this phrase is the subject of ἤνεγκεν. Diodorus Siculus 11.65 adds that the Mycenaeans refused to recognize the suzerainty of Argos and claimed direction of the Nemean Games. In 468 BCE, while Sparta, the ally of Mycenae, was occupied with a revolt of the helots, the Argives besieged and captured Mycenae, selling the inhabitants into slavery and razing the city. Diodorus says that the city was uninhabited in his day. There is, however, evidence that the citadel was inhabited in Macedonian times (Frazer 3.97–98). **παροξῦναν:** aor. act. participle. **ἄλλα τοῦ περιβόλου καὶ ἡ πύλη:** see extensive discussion at Frazer 3.98–103. **λέοντες δὲ ἐφεστήκασιν:** these lions can still be seen today at Mycenae. **Κυκλώπων δὲ καὶ ταῦτα ἔργα εἶναι λέγουσιν:** the Cyclopean walls are conventionally dated to 1350 BCE. At 2.25.8, P. notes them also at Tiryns. **Προίτῳ τὸ τεῖχος . . . ἐν Τίρυνθι:** at 2.16.2, P. included Tiryns in the half of the kingdom that Proetus received. P. also stated that Proetus had a period of residence (οἴκησις) at Tiryns.

2.16.6 κρήνη . . . καλουμένη Περσεία: this has been identified as a Hellenistic fountain with two basins on a 5th c. BCE terrace; it is near the W spur of the wall of the acropolis and is fed by a well 300 meters to the E of the acropolis (MT 266). **Ἀτρέως καὶ τῶν παίδων ὑπόγαια οἰκοδομήματα:** excavations at Mycenae have revealed the remains of an extensive palace complex on the acropolis. Atreus was the father of Agamemnon and Menelaus. P. seems to refer to the tholos tombs here (MT 266). **τάφος . . . Ἀτρέως:** two collections of graves, Circles A and B, date back to the Middle Helladic and Late Helladic periods. It is uncertain how much of these were visible to P. (MT 266–67). **εἰσὶ δὲ καὶ (τάφοι τόσων) ὅσους Αἴγισθος:** Aegisthus was the son of Thyestes (brother of Atreus) and Thyestes' daughter Pelopia; he had previously slain Atreus, and after seven years as king of Mycenae, with Clytemnestra as his queen, he was slain, in turn, by Orestes, son of Agamemnon and Clytemnestra, out of revenge for his father's death. **τοῦ . . . Κασσάνδρας μνήματος:** gen. object of ἀμφισβητοῦσι; P. mentions her tomb at Amyclae at 3.19.6. Agamemnon made Cassandra, the prophetic daughter of Priam, his concubine, and she shared his fate. **ἕτερον (μνῆμα) . . . τὸ δὲ (μνῆμα) . . . τὸ αὐτὸ (μνῆμα) Εὐρυμέδοντος:** Eurymedon shared the fate of Agamemnon's companions. **Τελεδάμου . . . καὶ Πέλοπος:** this tradition is not otherwise recorded.

2.16.7 τοῖς γονεῦσιν: dat. with ἐπικατέσφαξε, "he slew (the children) on top of their parents." **<(μνῆμα) Ἠλέκτρας δὲ οὔ>:** Electra was the sister of Orestes and assisted him in the killing of Clytemnestra and Aegisthus. **Πυλάδῃ:** Pylades was the son of King Strophius of Phocis and Anaxibia (the sister of Agamemnon and Menelaus); thus he was the cousin of Orestes, who stayed at Strophius' court during Clytemnestra's affair with Aegisthus. **συνῴκησεν:** "she lived with (Pylades) in marriage" (v. *LSJ* I.2). **Ἑλλάνικος:** Hellanicus of Mitylene (*FGrH* 4) was a 5th c. BCE historiographer and mythographer. **Μέδοντα καὶ Στρόφιον:** these children are mentioned only here. **ἐντὸς δὲ ἀπηξιώθησαν:** "and they were considered unworthy (to be buried) within (the walls)."

Heraion

2.17.1 Μυκηνῶν: gen. of separation with ἀπέχει. **τὸ Ἡραῖον:** the Heraion was the chief sanctuary of Hera outside of Argos. **ὕδωρ Ἐλευθέριον:** this fountain, otherwise known as Cynadra, provided water that slaves drank at the time they received their freedom; it became proverbial for a free life. It is now known as the Rheuma tou Kastrou (MT 267; Frazer 3.179). **αἱ περὶ τὸ ἱερὸν (ἱέρειαι):** statues of these priestesses of Hera stand before the entrance (v. 2.17.3). **τῶν θυσιῶν:** partitive gen. with τὰς ἀπορρήτους. **Ἀστερίωνι:** Asterion was one of the three rivers that awarded Argos to Hera over Poseidon, according to 2.15.5. **Ἀκραίαν:** *Acraeus* and *Acraea* are also epithets for deities who have temples on hills (e.g., Hera at 2.24.1).

2.17.2 τὸ ὄρος . . . τὸ ἀπαντικρὺ: "the hill opposite," with gen. This hill is 300 meters E of the Heraion (MT 267). **ὅσον περὶ τὸ ἱερόν:** "the environs of the sanctuary" (Loeb). **ῥέων:** Poseidon punished Asterion and the other two rivers with dryness, so that they only flow when it rains (2.15.5). This is probably now the Glykas River (MT 267). **ἀστερίωνα . . . τὴν πόαν:** this type of grass has not yet been identified.

2.17.3 ἀρχιτέκτονα . . . Εὐπόλεμον Ἀργεῖον: Eupolemus, who is known only from this passage, built the new Heraeum after the original burned in 423 BCE. P. describes the circumstances of the conflagration at 2.17.7. **ὁπόσα δὲ ὑπὲρ τοὺς κίονάς ἐστιν εἰργασμένα:** P. here refers to both the pediments and the metopes: the birth of Zeus (pediment) and the Gigantomachy (metopes) were depicted on the E, while the capture of Troy (pediment) and the Trojan War (metopes) were shown on the W (MT 268). **πρὸ τῆς ἐσόδου . . . ἐν δὲ τῷ προνάῳ:** P. narrates his entrance into the sanctuary and temple. **τὸν γὰρ ἐπίγραμμα . . . λέγουσιν:** this is an instance of metonomasia, the changing of the inscription on a statue to honor a different person. This practice of inglorious thrift was common in Greek cities of the Roman period but was not approved of by P. or other Greek intellectuals, such as Dio Chrysostom (*Or.* 31). **ὡς εἴη βασιλεὺς Αὔγουστος:** in classical Greek, the optative is used in indirect discourse only when that discourse depends on a verb in the secondary tense. P. is here using implied indirect discourse, which does not depend on a formal verb of saying or thinking (here τὸν γὰρ ἐπίγραμμα) but contains the past thought of a person other than the writer (S 2622). At one point in time, someone applied an inscription stating that the statue was of the emperor Augustus, but the Argives and P. know the score. MT (268) states that the change in the statue's identity may serve a symbolic function, championing Augustus as the avenger of the assassination of his (adoptive) father, Julius Caesar, just as Orestes was the avenger of Agamemnon's murder. **τῇ μὲν (ἀριστερᾷ) . . . ἐν δεξιᾷ δὲ κλίνη τῆς Ἥρας:** probably sacred furniture for a *hierogamia* (sacred marriage) of the goddess (as at Samos) or a *theoxenia* (divine visit) (MT

269). **ἀσπὶς ἣν Μενέλαός ποτε ἀφείλετο Εὔφορβον ἐν Ἰλίῳ:** during the fight over Patroclus' corpse; cf. Homer *Iliad* 17.59–60.

2.17.4 τὸ δὲ ἄγαλμα τῆς Ἥρας: this statue often appears on Argive coins. Cf. *RPC*, vol. 4, nos. 4633 (Lucius Verus), 4630 (Antoninus Pius). **μεγέθει μέγα:** dat. of respect (S 1516). Cf. similar examples at 2.10.2 and 2.34.11. P. occasionally uses acc. of respect too (e.g., 2.1.7). **Πολυκλείτου:** Polycleitus, a native of Argos in the 5th c. BCE, was famous as a sculptor and is credited with the sculptures on the pediments. This statue of Hera was his most famous work (Frazer 3.183–84). **ῥοιᾶς:** the pomegranate is usually associated with Demeter and Kore. A symbol of fertility, it would be appropriate here for a goddess of marriage (Frazer 3.184). **ἀπορρητότερος γάρ ἐστιν ὁ λόγος:** P. expresses scruples about revealing a secret story. **ἀφείσθω:** < ἀφίημι, perf. passive imperative (S 777). **ἤρα:** < ἐράω, imperf. act. indicative, with gen. object. **ἀλλαγῆναι:** < ἀλλάσσω, aor. passive infinitive. **τὴν δὲ ἅτε παίγνιον θηρᾶσαι:** "so that it be her plaything." **τοῦτον τὸν λόγον καὶ ὅσα ἐοικότα εἴρηται περὶ θεῶν οὐκ ἀποδεχόμενος γράφω, γράφω δὲ οὐδὲν ἧσσον:** though P. occasionally expresses incredulity about myths he considers outlandish, he, like H. (7.152), dutifully records them. **γράφω, γράφω δέ:** anastrophe (S 3011). **οὐδέν ἧσσον:** "nonetheless" (v. *LSJ* ἧσσον III).

2.17.5 λέγεται δὲ παρεστηκέναι τῇ Ἥρᾳ τέχνη Ναυκύδους ἄγαλμα Ἥβης: "the statue of Hebe standing next to Hera is said to be . . ." (not "the statue of Hebe is said to stand next to Hera . . ."). This is perhaps an example of enallage (S 3023). Hebe and Hera appear together on an Argive coin of the reign of Antoninus Pius (*RPC*, vol. 4, no. 7769). **Ναυκύδους:** Naucydes of Argos, a sculptor in the 4th c. BCE, was the younger brother of Polycleitus. **Ἥβης:** this goddess was mentioned at 2.13.3; she was the daughter of Zeus and Hera and the wife of the deified Heracles, as P. notes in the next subsection. **Πειράσου τοῦ Ἄργου:** Peirasus was named as one of Argus' two sons at 2.16.1; his brother Phorbas inherited the throne. **Τίρυνθα δὲ ἀνελόντες Ἀργεῖοι:** P. discusses the circumstances of this event at 2.25.8. **ὃ δὴ καὶ αὐτὸς εἶδον:** one of P.'s not infrequent eyewitness statements.

2.17.6 ἀναθήματα δὲ τὰ ἄξια λόγου: P. signals his selection of dedications worthy of comment. **χρυσοῦ . . . καὶ λίθων λαμπόντων:** these describe the ταών following. **Ἀδριανὸς βασιλεὺς:** the emperor Hadrian toured the Peloponnesus in 123/124 CE. **ταὼν:** peacocks were sacred to Hera, and a group of them were kept at her sanctuary on Samos (Frazer 3.185–86). **Νέρωνος:** the emperor Nero (r. 54–68 CE) visited Greece in 66 CE.

2.17.7 τοῦ προτέρου ναοῦ θεμέλιά: the first temple, which was built at the end of the 8th c. BCE or the start of the 7th c. BCE, was destroyed by fire in 423 BCE, in the manner P. describes. Cf. Thucydides 4.133; MT 270. **καὶ εἰ δή τι ἄλλο ὑπελίπετο ἡ φλόξ:** = καὶ ὅσα ὑπελίπετο ἡ φλόξ. **κατεκαύθη . . . τοῦ κατεκαυθέντος:** P. bookends his description of the fire and its aftermath with two forms of the same compound verb. **τὴν ἱέρειαν . . . Χρυσίδα:** direct object of the following phrase ὕπνου καταλαβόντος. Thucydides gives her name as Χρύσις. **καίπερ:** this particle is often used with the gen. absolute (S 2083) and marks it as concessive. **κακοῦ τηλικούτου:** "so great a disaster"; the adj. looks backward (S 333e).

Road to Argos

2.18.1 Περσέως . . . ἡρῷον: there was a priestly college dedicated to the cult of Perseus at Mycenae (MT 270). **μεγίστας (τιμὰς) δὲ ἔν τε Σερίφῳ καὶ παρ' Ἀθηναίοις, οἷς Περσέως τέμενος:** Perseus was especially honored on the island of Seriphus, where he and his mother were shipwrecked, but no source refers to a sanctuary of Perseus in Athens, and P. does not mention one in book 1, although he does note pictures of Perseus in the Athenian Pinakotheke (1.24.7). **Δίκτυος καὶ Κλυμένης:** Dictys was the fisherman who rescued Perseus and his mother, and Clymene was his wife. **Θυέστου:** Thyestes and his brother Atreus were sons of Pelops; Thyestes was the father of Aegisthus. Cf. 2.16.6 and commentary. **τὴν ἄρνα . . . τὴν χρυσῆν:** Atreus had vowed to sacrifice his best sheep to Artemis, but he found a golden lamb in his flock and gave it to his wife for safekeeping. **μοιχεύσας τοῦ ἀδελφοῦ τὴν γυναῖκα:** Thyestes obtained the lamb by seducing Aerope and then used the lamb as leverage to obtain the throne of Mycenae. Cf. ps.-Apollod. epit. 2.10–14. **μετρῆσαι τὴν ἴσην (μοῖραν):** "to give measure for measure" (v. *LSJ* μετρέω III.3), i.e., retribution. **τά ᾀδόμενα δεῖπνα:** "the banquet celebrated in poetry," the infamous Thyestean banquet in which Thyestes was served his own children.

2.18.2 ἀδικίας ἦρξεν Αἴγισθος: Aegisthus seduced Clytemnestra and murdered Agamemnon in revenge for his father's deed against his own father, Thyestes; P. mentioned this event at 2.16.6. **Ταντάλου τοῦ Θυέστου:**

Agamemnon killed both Thyestes' son Tantalus and the son Clytemnestra bore Tantalus. P. notes Tantalus' grave at 2.22.3. **παρὰ Τυνδάρεω λαβόντα:** King Tyndareus of Sparta, the son of Oebalus and Gorgophone, was the husband of Leda and was most famous as the father of Castor, Pollux, Helen, and Clytemnestra. He married his daughters to Menelaus and Agamemnon respectively, when the two Atreidae took refuge in Sparta after Aegisthus killed their father, Atreus. **φύσει σφᾶς γενέσθαι κακούς:** "for being evil by nature," infinitive construction after a verb of condemning (v. *LSJ* καταγιγνώσκω II.3). **ἐπὶ τοσοῦτον:** "to such a degree," i.e., that it led to such dire events. **αὐτοῖς:** dat. with ἠκολούθει. **τὸ μίασμα τὸ Πέλοπος καὶ ὁ Μυρτίλου προστρόπαιος:** Pelops enlisted the help of Myrtilus, the chariot driver of King Oenomaus, in obtaining the hand of Oenomaus' daughter Hippodamia, for Oenomaus forced suitors to compete with him in a chariot race and then decapitated them when he beat them. Myrtilus agreed to sabotage the the king's chariot, in exchange for Hippodamia's favors; Pelops agreed, and Oenomaus died in the competition, but then Pelops reneged on the plan and murdered Myrtilus, who uttered an apparently very effective curse on Pelops and his family. Cf. ps.-Apollod. epit. 2.4–9; P. 8.14.10–11. **προστρόπαιος:** "avenging spirit" (v. *LSJ* II). **Γλαύκῳ τῷ Ἐπικύδους Σπαρτιάτῃ:** P. refers to the famous story about the Spartan Glaucus that H. tells at 6.86. A Milesian man entrusted a large sum of money to Glaucus, but when the man's sons came to claim it, Glaucus balked and decided to consult the Delphic oracle about whether he could somehow keep the money. The priestess explained the consequences and added that asking the god for unjust counsel was as bad as actually carrying it out. See also P. 8.7.8. **ἐπίορκα ὀμόσαι:** = ἐπιορκεῖν. **τοῦδε:** construe with δίκην. **τοῦδε . . . ἐς τοὺς ἀπογόνους κατιέναι τὴν δίκην:** Glaucus returned the money, but his family subsequently died out nonetheless.

2.18.3 **ἀνδρὸς Μυσίου τὸ ὄνομα:** P. mentions Mysius' hospitality again at 2.35.4 and at 7.27.9–10, where he also describes a sanctuary of Mysian Demeter founded by Mysius near Pellene in Achaea. **γενομένου καὶ τούτου . . . ξένου τῇ Δήμητρι:** like Phytalus on the road between Athens and Eleusis (1.37.2). **τούτῳ μὲν οὖν οὐκ ἔπεστιν ὄροφος· ἐν δὲ αὐτῷ ναός ἐστιν ἄλλος:** the sanctuary has no roof, and a temple lies inside it—an interesting variation. **ὀπτῆς πλίνθου:** "of burnt brick," as opposed to the far more common Greek practice of sun-dried brick. **τὸ . . . ἱερόν . . . Εἰλειθυίας:** Eileithyia was the goddess of childbirth. This sanctuary seems to be the same one that P. describes at 2.22.6.

Mythical History of the Argolid (Continued)

2.18.4 Μεγαπένθους: P. mentioned Megapenthes (son of Proetus) at 2.16.3, where the historian reports that Perseus exchanged the city of Argos for his half of the Argolid. **μανία ταῖς γυναιξὶν ἐνέπεσεν:** like H. (9.34) and Diodorus Siculus (4.68.4), P. places this outbreak of feminine madness in the reign of Anaxagoras, but most accounts place it in the reign of Proetus and assign it a divine cause, the anger of either Dionysus or Hera. P. mentions the madness of Proetus' daughters at 2.7.8. Cf. ps.-Apollod. 1.9.12, 2.2.2. **Μελάμπους ὁ Ἀμυθάονος:** Melampus, son of Amythaon, was a legendary soothsayer and seer, who appears as an ancestor of Theoclymenus at *Odyssey* 15.223–42. An epic poem entitled *Melampodia* was ascribed to Hesiod in antiquity and was at least three books long. **ἐφ' ᾧ τε . . . ἕξουσιν:** future indicative in a proviso clause (S 2279). **ὁ ἀδελφὸς Βίας:** according to Homer (*Odyssey* 15.225–38), Melampus helped secure Pero, daughter of Neleus, as a wife for his brother, by rustling the cattle of Phylacus. **Ἀναξαγόρᾳ τὸ ἴσον ἕξουσιν:** Melampus originally asked for a third of the kingdom, but Anaxagoras rebuffed him; Anaxagoras gave in when the disease worsened, by which time Melampus had upped the price to two-thirds of the kingdom (ps.-Apollod. 2.2.2). **πέντε ἄνδρες ἐπὶ γενεὰς τέσσαρας . . . ὄντες Νηλεῖδαι τὰ πρὸς μητρός:** at 2.6.6, P. mentioned Talaüs, the son of Bias. He was the father of Adrastus, who briefly became king of Sicyon during his exile from Argos. **ἐς Κυάνιππον τὸν Αἰγιαλέως:** Aegialeus, the son of Adrastus, was the only one of the Epigoni to die at Thebes (cf. 9.5.13). The tally of the five men may thus be (1) Bias, (2) Talaus, (3) Adrastus, (4) Aegialeus, and (5) Cyanippus. As for the four generations, some sources (e.g., ps.-Apollod. 1.9.13), regarded Aegialeus and Cyanippus as brothers. **γενεαί τε ἕξ καὶ ἄνδρες ἴσοι:** P. mentions Mantius, who was the son of Melampus and fathered Oecles, at 6.17.6; Oecles appears as the father of Amphiaraus at 8.36.6. **Ἀμφιλόχου τοῦ Ἀμφιαράου:** Amphilochus, a gifted seer (like his father), ruled Argos in the absence of his brother Alcmaeon, who had killed their mother, Eriphyle, in retribution for her role in their father's death. The tally of six men may thus be (1) Melampus, (2) Mantius, (3) Oecles, (4) Amphiaraus, (5) Alcmaeon, and (6) Amphilochus. The numbering of six generations may be due to confusion, in the later sources, between the Amphilochus who was the son of Amphiaraus, on the one hand, and the Amphilochus who was the son of Alcmaeon, on the other.

2.18.5 Ἶφις . . . ὁ Ἀλέκτορος: according to ps.-Apollod. 3.6.2, Polynices sought Iphis' advice on how to convince Amphiaraus to go on the expedition against Thebes, and Iphis suggested that he bribe Eriphyle, wife of

Amphiaraus, with the necklace of Harmonia. **Σθενέλῳ τῷ Καπανέως ἀδελφοῦ:** Capaneus was one of the Seven against Thebes and, because of his boasting, was killed by Zeus with lightning. Sthenelus was one of the Epigoni and brought back Priam's unusual image of Zeus from Troy (2.24.3). **Ἀμφιλόχου δὲ μετὰ ἅλωσιν Ἰλίου μετοικήσαντος ἐς τοὺς νῦν Ἀμφιλόχους:** according to Thucydides (2.68), Amphilochus served in the Trojan War and afterward left Argos and founded a new Argos in Amphilochia, on the Ambraciot coast. **μόνος τὴν βασιλείαν ἔσχεν:** thus the kingdom of Argos became whole again. **παροικῶν τε ἐγγὺς:** Orestes was king of Mycenae after his murder of Clytemnestra and Aegisthus. Cf. 2.16.5–7 and commentary. **ἄνευ τῆς πατρῴας ἀρχῆς:** "besides his ancestral dominion" (Loeb; v. *LSJ* ἄνευ III), i.e., Mycenae through his father Agamemnon. **παρειληφὼς:** < παραλαμβάνω, perf. act. participle. **τὴν ἐν Σπάρτῃ βασιλείαν:** Orestes married Hermione, the daughter of Menelaus and Helen; inasmuch as Menelaus lacked legitimate sons, Orestes thus inherited his kingdom, as P. explains below. **συμμαχικοῦ δὲ ἐκ Φωκέων ἀεί ποτε ἐπ' ὠφελείᾳ ἑτοίμου παρόντος:** Orestes was a ward of his uncle Strophius, king of Phocis, and a good friend of Pylades, Strophius' son. **ἀεί ποτε:** "from of old."

2.18.6 **Λακεδαιμονίων:** this word appears twice, once as the gen. object of ἐβασίλευσεν and once as the subject of ἐφέντων in a gen. absolute. **ἐφέντων:** < ἐφίημι, aor. act. participle (S 777). **τοὺς Τυνδάρεω θυγατριδοῦς:** i.e., Clytemnestra's children. **Νικοστράτου καὶ Μεγαπένθους:** P. calls them the sons of Menelaus at 3.18.3 and 3.19.9 and says that they expelled Helen after Menelaus' death. Ps.-Apollod. 3.11.1 says that Nicostratus was the son of Helen and that Megapenthes was the son of the slave Pieris or Tereis. **Πενθίλον:** at 3.2.1, P. states that Penthilus seized the island of Lesbos. **Κιναίθων:** Cinaethon of Lacedaemon, an epic poet in the 6th c. BCE, is credited with several lost epics, including the *Oedipodeia*, *Little Iliad*, and *Telegony*. **Ἠριγόνην τὴν Αἰγίσθου:** Erigone was the daughter of Clytemnestra and Aegisthus.

2.18.7 **ἐπὶ . . . τοῦ Τισαμενοῦ:** "in the reign of Tisamenus" (S 1689.1b). **Τήμενος . . . καὶ Κρεσφόντης Ἀριστομάχου:** Aristomachus was the son of Cleodaeus and grandson of Hyllus, the son of Heracles. The Heracleidae made five failed attempts to invade the Peloponnesus: two under Hyllus, one under Cleodaeus, one under Aristomachus, and one under Aristodemus (son of Aristomachus). **τοῦ τρίτου . . . Ἀριστοδήμου προτεθνεῶτος . . . οἱ παῖδες:** Aristodemus was killed on the fifth attempt, when the Heracleidae tried a naval invasion; his sons Procles and Eurystheus joined his brothers Temenus and Cresphontes. **ὀρθότατα:** "most justly" (v. *LSJ* III.4); construe with ἠμφισβήτουν. **τὸ ἀνέκαθέν:** "by descent." P. uses this phrase occasionally in his *Periegesis*. It appears also at 1.3.2 and 2.37.3. **Τυνδάρεω . . . ἐκπεσόντα . . . ὑπὸ Ἱπποκόωντος:** Hippocoön seized the throne by expelling his brother Tyndareus from the kingdom of Sparta after their father, Oebalus, died. **Ἡρακλέα . . . ἀποκτείναντα Ἱπποκόωντα καὶ τοὺς παῖδας:** because Hippocoön refused to cleanse him of a murder, Heracles killed Hippocoön and his sons and restored Tyndareus to the throne. **παρακαταθέσθαι:** "to give *x* (acc.) in trust to *y* (dat.)." **παρακαταθήκην Νέστορι δοθῆναι καὶ ταύτην ὑπὸ Ἡρακλέους ἑλόντος Πύλον:** Heracles asked Neleus to cleanse him of murder; when Neleus refused, Heracles captured Pylos and killed Neleus and all his sons except Nestor, who was left the throne.

2.18.8 ἐκβάλλουσιν: P. emphasizes the expulsions of the remnants of the old heroic order by placing this verb up front, before the long list utilizing the acc. **Θρασυμήδους:** Thrasymedes was one of the sons of Nestor who went to Troy with him; he survived the war, returned home, and later inherited the kingdom. **Πεισιστράτου:** Peisistratus was a young boy when his brothers and his father left for Troy. He appears in the *Odyssey* as a friend of Telemachus, Odysseus' son. **Ἀντιλόχου:** Antilochus was the younger brother of Thrasymedes and died at Troy while saving his father from Memnon. **σὺν δὲ αὐτοῖς:** P. switches from the descendants of Nestor to the descendants of Periclymenus, Nestor's brother, who famously could change himself into anything due to the gift of Poseidon (ps.-Apollod. 1.9.9). **Τισαμενὸς μὲν οὖν ἦλθε σὺν τῇ στρατιᾷ καὶ οἱ παῖδες ἐς τὴν νῦν Ἀχαΐαν:** ps.-Apollod. 2.8.3 says that Tisamenus died in battle against the Heraclidae.

2.18.9 τοῦτον: prolepsis; this is actually the subject of the indefinite relative clause following but appears as the direct object of οἶδα in the main clause. **Παιονιδῶν:** this was both a clan and one of the classical demes established by Cleisthenes. **Ἀλκμαιωνιδῶν:** this Athenian noble family produced a number of famous Athenians, including Megacles, the eponymous archon who crushed the coup of Cylon in 632 BCE; Cleisthenes, who set the foundations for classical Athenian democracy; the great Athenian statesman Pericles; and the general and adventurer Alcibiades. **Μέλανθος:** P. mentions him at 1.3.3 without a patronymic, as one of the non-Theseid kings. **Θυμοίτης:** Thymoetes was the son of Oxyntes, the grandson of Demophon, and the great-grandson of Theseus; at 1.3.3, P. states that the descendants of Theseus ruled Athens until the fourth generation (by inclusive numbering). Thymoetes refused a challenge to single combat against the Boeotian king Xanthus but offered the throne to whoever would accept the challenge. Melanthus did and won (Frazer 3.189).

2.19.1 τὰ . . . Κρεσφόντου καὶ τῶν Ἀριστοδήμου παίδων: although P. does not mention it here, he narrates the history of Cresphontes and the sons of Aristodemus at 4.3.3–7, for they form a major part of the history of Messenia. **ἤπειγεν:** < ἐπείγω, imperf. act. indicative. **Τήμενος:** P. includes an account of Temenos here because he received Argos as his portion of the Peloponnese. Cresphontes received Messenia, and his nephews, the brothers Procles and Eurysthenes, received Lacedaemon (ps.-Apollod. 2.8.4). **Δηιφόντῃ τῷ Ἀντιμάχου τοῦ Θρασυάνορος τοῦ Κτησίππου τοῦ Ἡρακλέους:** Ctesippus was the son of Heracles by Deianeira. **τῇ Ὑρνηθοῖ:** at 2.28.3–6, P. describes the withdrawal of Deiphontes and Hyrnetho to Epidaurus, as well as Hyrnetho's tragic end. **ὑπωπτεύετο:** "he was suspected of," with infinitive. **αὐτῷ:** a loose dat. of reference (S 1496). **Κεῖσος:** according to ps.-Apollod. 2.8.5, Ceisus killed his father.

2.19.2 ἰσηγορίαν καὶ τὸ αὐτόνομον: "freedom and self-government" (Loeb). ἰσηγορία actually means "equality of speech" and thus equality in political rights, like the expression ἐξ ἴσου πολιτεύεσθαι at 2.8.3. **τὰ τῆς ἐξουσίας τῶν βασιλέων:** "the extent of the authority of their kings." **ἐς ἐλάχιστον προήγαγον:** one would expect the verb κατήγαγον, "reduced," here instead, but the phrasing here emphasizes that the Argives, going forward, limited their kings' power. **ὡς . . . λειφθῆναι:** natural result clause. **Μέλταν . . . τὸν Λακήδου δέκατον ἀπόγονον Μήδωνος:** according to some sources, the Argives condemned Meltas to death for conspiring to restore the power of the monarchy. Argos was ruled by a nominal king as late as the Persian Wars (H. 7.149). **τὸ παράπαν:** "altogether, completely."

Argos

2.19.3 Ἀπόλλωνος ἱερὸν Λυκίου: this was the most important sanctuary in the city, and all public decrees were traditionally displayed here, like Athenian decrees were in the temple of Athena at Athens. It seems to have been located in the N part of the agora, near a large portico and a *dromos* for the celebration of the Nemean Games (MT 274). The cult statue may appear on Argive coins: see *RPC*, vol. 4, no. 5259 (Lucius Verus); vol. 3, no. 342 (Hadrian). **Ἀττάλου . . . Ἀθηναίου:** the date of this sculptor is unknown, but he may belong to the neo-Attic school (MT 274). His name has been found on a statue near the theater (Frazer 3.190). **ξόανα γὰρ δὴ τότε εἶναι πείθομαι πάντα καὶ μάλιστα τὰ Αἰγύπτια:** cf. Alice Donohue, *Xoana and the Origins of Greek Sculpture* (Oxford: Oxford University Press, 1988). **Δαναοῦ:** cf. 2.16.1 and commentary. **Γελάνορα τὸν Σθενέλα:** P. mentioned Danaus' deposition of Gelanor at 2.16.1 and now explains it more fully. **ῥηθέντων . . . πολλῶν τε καὶ ἐπαγωγῶν:** first in a pair of two gen. absolutes. **ἐπὶ τοῦ δήμου:** "before the people (of Argos)." **οὐχ ἧσσον . . . δόξαντος:** the subject of this gen. absolute is Gelanor. **ὑπερέθετο:** < ὑπερτίθημι, "(the people) postponed" (v. *LSJ* II.5). **ἐς τὴν ἐπιοῦσαν (ἡμέραν).**

2.19.4 **ἐσπίπτει . . . προσπεσὼν:** note the use of different compounds of πίπτω. The wolf falls "upon/onto" the flock (as prey) and "at" the bull (as a worthy opponent). **παρίσταται:** "it occurred (to the Argives to)" (v. *LSJ* B.IV). **τῷ μὲν (ταύρῳ) Γελάνορα, Δαναὸν δὲ . . . τῷ λύκῳ:** chiastic order. **ἐς ἐκεῖνο τοῦ χρόνου:** "until that time." **διὰ τοῦτο:** P. resumes the ἐπεί clause.

2.19.5 **Βίτωνος:** this was probably the Biton who achieved fame for helping his brother Cleobis pull their mother in a cart from Argos to the Heraion. P. mentions this story at 2.20.3, and H. relates their story more fully at 1.31. **ὡς δὲ Λυκέας ἐποίησεν:** Lyceas of Argos was a Greek epic poet known only from P. **Ἀργείων ἀγόντων θυσίαν τῷ Διὶ:** gen. absolute. **ἑξῆς . . . τῆς εἰκόνος ταύτης:** "next to this image" **πῦρ . . . Φορωνέως:** Phoroneus was the first inhabitant in Argos, as P. related at 2.15.5. This fire was in the sanctuary of Apollo Lycius and was believed to have fallen from heaven (Frazer 3.191). **οὐ . . . τι:** adv., "not at all." **δοῦναι πῦρ Προμηθέα ἀνθρώποις:** the usual version of the myth. Cf. Hesiod *Works and Days* 50–59. **τοῦ πυρὸς:** construe with τὴν εὕρεσιν.

2.19.6 **Ἐπειοῦ:** Epeius was the famous architect of the Trojan Horse. **Ὑπερμήστρας:** Hypermnestra saved her cousin-husband, Lynceus, who later succeeded Danaus as king of Argos (2.16.1). **τοῦ . . . Λυγκέως:** construe with τὴν σωτηρίαν. **οὐκ ἀκίνδυνον:** litotes. **ἡγούμενος:** P. gives two reasons for Danaus prosecuting Hypermnestra but uses different constructions for them: acc. with the infinitive before the participle, ὅτι with the indicative after it; he cleanly separates them to preserve clarity. **ἀποφεύγει:** "she was acquitted" (v. *LSJ* II).

2.19.7 τοῦ ναοῦ: gen. object of ἐντός. **Λάδας:** Ladas of Argos was winner of the *dolichos* race at the Olympic Games in 460 or 456 BCE. Cf. Mark Golden, *Sport in the Ancient World from A to Z* (London: Routledge, 2004), 95.. **τοὺς ἐφ' αὑτοῦ:** "his contemporaries." **ἐς λύρας ποίησιν:** purpose. **ᾑρηκώς:** < αἱρέω, perf. act. participle. **βάθρον πεποιημένα . . . ἔχον:** the manuscript reads βόθρος, "pit," which editors have emended to βάθρον, "pedestal." πεποιημένα ἐν τύπῳ (figures in relief) would thus be in apposition with ταύρου μάχην . . . καὶ λύκου. Plutarch (*Life of Pyrrhus* 52) describes it as a statue. **ἀφιεῖσαν:** < ἀφίημι, present act. participle (S 777).

2.19.8 Λίνου τοῦ Ἀπόλλωνος καὶ Ψαμάθης τῆς Κροτώπου: Cf. 1.43.7–8 and commentary on 2.16.1. **Λίνου τοῦ ποιήσαντος:** this Linus is usually described as the son of Apollo and the Muse Calliope, and the Greeks considered him the inventor of melody and rhythm. He taught music to Orpheus and Heracles, the latter of whom used Linus' own lyre to kill him when Linus pointed out the hero's errors. Cf. 9.29.6–9; ps.-Apollod. 2.4.9. **οἰκειότερα ὄντα ἑτέρῳ λόγῳ παρίημι:** at 9.29.6, P. describes Linus the musician as the son of Urania and Amphiaraus (son of Poseidon) and reports that Linus was killed by Apollo for rivaling the god in song. **τῷδε:** "here"; do not construe with ἑτέρῳ λόγῳ, which should be construed with οἰκειότερα. **ἡ Μεγαρική μοι συγγραφή:** P. is referring here to 1.43.7–8. **Ἀπόλλων Ἀγυιεὺς:** "Apollo Guardian of the Streets." **οἱ συσπεύδοντες:** "those assisting *x* in *y*," with dat. of person and acc. of thing. **Πολυνείκει:** Polyneices was the son of Oedipus and brother of Eteocles, who drove Polyneices out of Thebes. Polyneices eventually recruited the Seven against Thebes to recover the throne for him. **ἀποθανεῖσθαι:** future infinitive with verb of swearing in indirect discourse (S 2024). **συνώμοσαν:** at *Seven against Thebes* 41ff., Aeschylus describes the unusual ritual that accompanied the oath. **ἢν μὴ . . . γένηταί:** protasis of a future-more-vivid condition.

2.20.1 Κρεύγα . . . ἀνδρὸς πύκτου: Creugas of Epidamnus died in a boxing match at the Nemean Games ca. 400 BCE and was awarded victory posthumously. See 8.40.3–5; Golden 45. **τρόπαιον ἐπὶ Κορινθίοις ἀνασταθέν:** it is unclear to which battle this refers. It is possible that it is connected to the Corinthian-Athenian war begun in 459 BCE (MT 276). **Διὸς Μειλιχίου:** "Mild Zeus" (v. *LSJ* II). A seated Zeus appears on Argive coinage: see *RPC*, vol. 4, no. 9659 (Marcus Aurelius). **Πολυκλείτου . . . ἔργον:** it is unclear which Polycleitus P. is referring to here, but it may be Polycleitus the Younger (MT 276). **πρὶν ἢ:** this clause of definite past action takes an indicative when the main clause has a negative; usually, as here, the subordinate verb is in the aor. tense (S 2441). **Φίλιππος . . . ὁ Ἀμύντου:** Philip II, the father of Alexander III (Alexander the Great). In the autumn of 338 BCE, after his victory at Chaeronea, Philip II made an expedition into Laconia and limited Spartan territory between Mt. Taygetus and Mt. Parnon. Argos obtained Cynuria and the coast of its gulf to Zarax. Cf. 3.26.3 (MT 277). **οἱ Λακεδαιμόνιοι μηδὲν ἔξω . . . περιεργαζόμενοι:** when a participle acts as the protasis of a condition, the negative is μή. **τῷ τοιούτῳ:** demonstratives of quality usually follow the article (S 1180); this resumes the gen. absolute immediately preceding. **ἐνέκειντο:** < ἔγκειμαι, imperf. middle indicative, "they were involved," with dat. σφισιν.

2.20.2 προηγμένου . . . τοῦ μίσους: Cleomenes' impious acts at Sepeia doubtless played a role in the enmity. Cf. 2.20.8–10. **λογάδας . . . χιλίους:** the Argives created this force in 421 BCE, drawing men from the wealthiest classes of the city and exempting the men from all public duties so that they could train constantly for war—much like the Spartans. They took part in the Battle of Mantineia against Sparta in 418 BCE (MT 277). **ἄνδρας . . . τοῦ δήμου:** i.e., the commoners, the general Argive public. **ἀφελόμενος:** < ἀφαιρέω, aor. middle participle; it takes acc. of the thing removed and of the people so deprived. **προεμένων . . . τοῖς χιλίοις (τῶν πολλῶν):** P. has two gen. absolutes here, describing, first, the actions of the people and, second (προαχθέντων . . . ἀμφοτέρων), the battle joined by both sides. **ἀπὸ τούτου:** expressing cause. **κρατοῦσιν . . . κρατήσαντες δὲ . . . :** pseudanaphora. The massacre of the guards occurred in 418 BCE (Thucydides 5.82). **οὐδένα . . . τῶν ἐναντίων:** hyperbaton. **ὑπὸ τοῦ θυμοῦ:** P. sometimes employs this phrase to denote unbridled anger. **ὡς ἐπὶ αἵματι ἐμφυλίῳ:** ὡς with prepositions shows purpose, much as it does with participles (v. *LSJ* C.II.a). The phrase ἐμφύλιον αἷμα means "(spilling of) kindred blood" (v. *LSJ* ἔμφυλος I.1). The same adj. is used for civil wars.

2.20.3 Κλέοβις καὶ Βίτων: see commentary on 2.19.5. **Νεμείου Διός ἐστιν ἱερόν, ἄγαλμα ὀρθὸν χαλκοῦν:** asyndeton. The sanctuary reaffirmed the control of Argos over the Nemean Games (MT 277). The sanctuary of Nemean Zeus was opposite the temple of Apollo Lycius (Frazer 3.194). The cult statue appears on Argive coinage: see *RPC*, vol. 4, nos. 5250 (Antoninus Pius), 3531 (Marcus Aurelius). **Λυσίππου:** cf. 2.9.6, 2.9.8. **Φορωνέως:** see 2.15.5. **Παλαμήδης:** Palamedes, the son of Nauplius and Clymene, was a pupil of the centaur Chiron and was one of the Achaean heroes at Troy. He is credited with a number inventions, including the Greek alphabet and dice, as P. states here. Odysseus blamed Palamedes for Odysseus' enlistment in the Trojan War and conspired to have Palamedes falsely condemned for treason and executed; in anger at his son's unjust demise, Nauplius convinced several wives of the Achaeans to commit adultery and plot against their husbands, and he himself lit beacon fires on the Euboean coastline to lure the returning Achaean ships onto the rocks. Cf. ps.-Apollod. 2.1.5, epit. 3.7–8.

2.20.4 Διονύσῳ . . . καὶ ἄλλας γυναῖκας καὶ ταύτην ἐς Ἄργος συστρατεύσασθαι: there are several myths about Dionysus encountering resistance in Greek cities that he visited to spread his worship; the most famous example was at Thebes in Euripides' *Bacchae*. According to ps.-Apollod. 3.5.2, Dionysus drove the women of Argos mad, as he did at Thebes, and waged war against the city. **λέγοντες:** this participle sets up indirect discourse with an acc. and infinitive construction that extends over two clauses, down to τὰς πολλάς. **ἰδίᾳ:** "on her own, separately"; Choreia received her own grave.

2.20.5 Ὡρῶν: the Horae, or Seasons, were personifications originally of the order of nature and later of justice and cosmic order; they nursed Hera at 2.13.3. P. seems to leave the Argive agora here and move to the slopes of the acropolis Larisa, albeit briefly (MT 278). **ὅσοι . . . τῶν ἐν τέλει . . . μαχόμενοι:** i.e., the Seven against Thebes. **Αἰσχύλος:** P. asserts that Aeschylus reduced the number of heroes to seven in his *Seven against Thebes* to fit the number of gates of Thebes, so that each hero could have a duel. Cf. Frazer 3.194 for the idea that these seven heroes were only the leaders of the final assault on the gates of Thebes. **οἱ τὰς Θήβας ἑλόντες:** i.e., the Epigoni. P. exhibits *variatio* even in this list of names of warriors. **Αἰγιαλεὺς Ἀδράστου:** Aegialeus was a king of Argos; at 2.18.4, P. mentioned his son Cyanippus. Adrastus was the only one of the original Seven against Thebes who survived the expedition. **Πρόμαχος ὁ Παρθενοπαίου τοῦ Ταλαοῦ:** Promachus died in the attack on Thebes, and P. notes his tomb at Teumessus at 9.19.2. **Πολύδωρος Ἱππομέδοντος:** ps.-Apollod. omits Polydorus from his list of the Epigoni at 3.7.2. **Θέρσανδρος:** P. fails to mention that Thersander was the son of Polyneices and became king of Thebes after the Epigoni captured the city. He later went on the Achaean expedition to Troy, but he died at the hands of Telephus when the Achaeans mistakenly invaded Mysia instead of Dardania. Cf. ps.-Apollod. epit. 3.17. **Ἀλκμαίων τε καὶ Ἀμφίλοχος:** P. mentioned Alcmaeon at 2.1.8 and Amphilochus at 2.18.4–5. **Διομήδης:** Diomedes was the son of Tydeus and close comrade of Odysseus in the *Iliad*. **Σθένελος:** Sthenelus, the son of Capaneus, was king of Argos (cf. 2.18.5); in Homer's *Iliad* (4.403–10), he boasts of his parentage and his participation in the capture of Thebes. **Εὐρύαλος Μηκιστέως:** like Diomedes, Euryalus also took part in the Trojan War and was one of the Achaeans inside the Trojan Horse. He lost a boxing match against Epeius at the funeral games of Patroclus (*Iliad* 23.664–99). **Πολυνείκους Ἄδραστος καὶ Τιμέας:** these two sons of Polyneices are not otherwise known.

2.20.6 Δαναοῦ μνῆμα: this tomb was also called Palinthus (Strabo 8.6.9). **οἴκημα· ἐνταῦθα τὸν Ἄδωνιν αἱ γυναῖκες Ἀργείων ὀδύρονται:** Adonis, the lover of Aphrodite, was the son of Myrrha and her father, Cinyras; a boar killed Adonis while he was out hunting. The Adonia festival involved public weeping by women. The sanctuary for the celebration of this festival and the sanctuary of the Cephisus were probably NW of the agora, on the slopes of Larisa (MT 278–79). **ὑπὸ τοῦ Ποσειδῶνος ἀφανισθῆναι:** P. relates the myth at 2.15.5. **συνιᾶσιν:** < συνίημι, present act. indicative (S 777). **(τοῦ Κηφισοῦ) ὑπὸ τὴν γῆν ῥέοντος:** gen. of perception with συνιᾶσιν (S 1361).

2.20.7 Κυκλώπων . . . τοῦτο ἔργον: cf. 2.16.5 and commentary. **Κριτήριον:** this was the ancient Areopagus of Argos and was probably located on a terrace of polygonal work halfway up the slope of Larisa (MT 279). **Ὑπερμήστραν . . . ὑπὸ Δαναοῦ κριθῆναι:** P. described her trial at 2.19.6 and mentions her tomb at 2.21.2. **θέατρον:** the theater is dug into the side of Larisa and consisted of 81 rows of seats. It was completed in the late 4th c. BCE. The statues of Perilaos and Othryadas probably were placed on the stage (MT 279; Frazer 3.195–96). **Ὀθρυάδαν τὸν Σπαρτιάτην:** H. (1.82) tells the story of how Sparta and Argos attempted to settle a land dispute over Thyrea by pitting 300 soldiers from each side against each other in 548 BCE. Two Argives survived and returned home to report the victory; Othryadas was the only surviving Spartan according to H., who says that the Spartan then killed himself out of shame. As one would expect, the battle did not solve the dispute. P. is the only ancient source to report that an Argive killed Othryadas. He recounts the episode at greater length at 2.38.5 (though without mentioning the name of either warrior) and adds that the Spartans won a full-scale battle with the Argives afterward and claimed the land. Cf. Tomlinson 1972, 87–90; Frazer 3.196–97. **Περίλαος Ἀργεῖος ὁ Ἀλκήνορος:** H. names an Alcenor as one of the two Argive survivors. Scholars suspect that P. is giving here an Argive version of the so-called Battle of the Champions. The Perilaos here may also be the Argive tyrant of the 6th c. BCE (Tomlinson 1972, 92). **ὑπῆρχε:** "it befell," with dat. of person and infinitive. **ἀνῃρῆσθαι:** < ἀναιρέω, perf. middle infinitive.

2.20.8 Ἀφροδίτης . . . ἱερόν: this temple already functioned as an open-air sanctuary with altar in the 7th c. BCE; ca. 430–420 BCE, it received a temple that is distyle *in antis* (a temple with side walls extending to the front of the porch and terminating in two antae, with the pediment supported by two pilasters). It is located on a height called Pron, S of the theater, beyond the odeion (MT 279). **ἔμπροσθεν . . . τοῦ ἕδους:** "before the seated statue of the god" (v. *LSJ* ἕδος I.3). P. uses the term ἕδος only here and at 8.46.2. **Τελέσιλλα:** Telesilla was a famous archaic poetess like Sappho, and even less of Telesilla's poetry than of Sappho's remains. The relief was late classical or Hellenistic (MT 280). **βιβλία . . . ἐκεῖνα:** not "those books" but "her books"; the demonstrative may refer to τὰ ᾄσματα just mentioned. **συμβάντος:** impersonal gen. absolute that sets up the acc. and infinitive construction that follows. **λόγου μειζόνως:** gen. of comparison with comparative adv., "unspeakably." **Κλεομένην τὸν Ἀναξανδρίδου:** the Agiad king Cleomenes I (r. 519–490 BCE) was the son of Anaxandrides II (r. 560–525 BCE). He was a very energetic and controversial king who strove to extend Spartan power. Among his other endeavors, he intervened twice in the Athenian civil war between Cleisthenes and Isagoras in 510 BCE. **τῶν μὲν ἐν αὐτῇ πεπτωκότων τῇ μάχῃ:** H. tells the story of the Battle of Sepeia (or, in some manuscripts, Sipeia or Hesipeia) in 494 BCE, at 6.77ff. This is the first of four gen. absolutes that establish the ugly circumstances of Cleomenes' march on Argos. Cf. Tomlinson 1972, 93–97. **ὅσοι . . . κατέφευγον:** this clause explains τούτων, the subject of διαφθαρέντων, in the second gen. absolute. **τοῦ Ἄργου . . . τὸ Ἄργος:** the name of the grove is masc., but the name of the city is neut. Cf. 2.16.1 for King Argos. **τούτων:** P. initially divides the Argive soldiers into two groups, those who died in battle and those who died afterward, and now he divides the second group into two, those who died when they left the grove of Argus under truce (τὰ μὲν πρῶτα ἐξιόντων κατὰ ὁμολογίαν) and those who burned to death in it (συγκατακαυθέντων . . . τῶν λοιπῶν). The Argives were said to have lost 6,000 men; this number is exaggerated, but Argos remained a diminished power for a generation afterward. Cleomenes later was imprisoned at Sparta for madness and committed suicide, a death the Argives attributed to this horrendous act of impiety (H. 6.75).

2.20.9 τούτους: this pronoun looks back to the οἰκέτας and ὅσοι . . . ἦσαν that P. just identified; these are the slaves and males who were normally excused from military duty. **ὥπλιζεν, ὁπλίσασα δὲ:** pseudanaphora. **ὅποσα (ὅπλα) . . . ὑπελείπετο** **τῶν γυναικῶν:** partitive gen. with τὰς ἀκμαζούσας. **κατὰ τοῦτο (τὸ χώριον):** P. immediately explains this with the adverbial relative clause starting with ᾗ. **ὡς . . . ἐνταῦθα:** "when . . . then . . ." **οὔτε . . . τε . . . :** "not only not . . . but . . ." (S 2945). **δεξάμεναί:** "receiving the enemy, waiting for their attack" (v. *LSJ* II.2). **φρονήσαντες ὡς:** this phrase sets up an indirect statement using finite verbs, but P. again varies his approach by first retaining the presumed original future indicative and then employing a future optative, which is only used in indirect discourse to stand in for a future indicative (S 1862–63). **τὰς γυναῖκας:** direct object of διαφθείρασί. **ἐπιφθόνως τὸ κατόρθωμα ἕξει:** "would be an invidious success" (Loeb). **ὑπείκουσι:** agreeing with understood σφισιν, i.e., the Spartans.

2.20.10 τὸ λόγιον εἴτε ἄλλως εἴτε καὶ ὧς συνεὶς ἐδήλωσεν: "whether (H.) explained the oracle understanding it so or otherwise," i.e., wrongly. Note the accentuation of ὥς here: the particle is being used as a demonstrative adv. (= οὕτως, ὧδε; S 2988). H. does not actually explain the oracle: he merely states that the Argives were afraid and tried to mimic the Spartan manuevers. **Ἡρόδοτος:** *Histories* 6.77. H. does not mention Telesilla at all, perhaps giving the reader the Spartan version of the Battle of Sepeia; cf. W. W. How and J. Wells *A Commentary on Herodotus* (Oxford: Oxford University Press, 1989), *ad loc.* **ὅταν . . . ἐξελάσῃ . . . ἄρηται:** future temporal clause with the subjunctive. **ἄρηται:** < ἀείρω, aor. middle subjunctive, "win (glory)" (v. *LSJ* IV.1) **ἀμφιδρυφέας:** "with both (cheeks) torn (in grief)." **θήσει:** H. adds two more lines that P. omits: ὥς ποτέ τις ἐρέει καὶ ἐπεσσομένων ἀνθρώπων / δεινὸς ὄφις τριέλικτος ἀπώλετο δουρὶ δαμασθείς. **ἐς τὸ ἔργον τῶν γυναικῶν:** P. affirms his interpretation of the oracle. According to Plutarch (*De mulierum virtutibus* 4), the Argives memorialized this act of bravery with the festival of Wantonness (τὰ Ὑβριστικά), in which men dressed as women and vice versa. The story of Telesilla's bravery is probably exaggerated and was created to explain the festival and custom. Cf. Tomlinson 1972, 94; Frazer 3.197–98.

2.21.1 κατελθοῦσι δὲ ἐντεῦθεν καὶ τραπεῖσιν αὖθις ἐπὶ τὴν ἀγοράν: P. descends from the Pron toward the agora (MT 281). **ἔστι μὲν . . . ἔστι δὲ . . . :** anaphora. **Κερδοῦς:** Cerdo is the wife of Phoroneus, the first inhabitant of Argos, as P. related at 2.15.5. The proper name is declined like Πειθώ, Πειθοῦς, ἡ, below (S 279N). **Ὑπερμήστρα:** the travails of Hypermestra and her husband, Lynceus, have come up repeatedly in book 2; e.g., P. mentioned how Danaus put his daughter on trial at 2.19.6. **τοῦτο:** this pronoun resumes τὸ . . . ἱερόν just before. **Αἰνείου:** Aeneas, the son of Priam and the founder of the race of the Romans in Italy. **ἐφ' ὅτῳ:** = ἐφ' ᾧ. **οὐ γάρ μοι τὰ λεγόμενα ἤρεσκαν:** P. signals his research but does not communicate its results. We know nothing more about this place called "the Delta" (perhaps so named from its shape).

2.21.2 **Διὸς Φυξίου:** "putting to flight" (v. *LSJ* 2, where this passage is cited). According to ps.-Apollod. 1.9.1, Phrixus sacrificed the ram with the Golden Fleece to Zeus Phyxios when he had reached safety in Colchis. **Ὑπερμήστρας . . . Ἀμφιαράου μητρός:** P. is careful to distinguish between these two homonymous heroines, the former obscure and the latter famous. **Ταλαοῦ τοῦ Βίαντός:** cf. 2.6.6, 2.18.4 with commentary. **τὰ δὲ ἐς Βίαντα καὶ ἀπογόνους τοῦ Βίαντος ἤδη λέλεκταί μοι:** P. covered the tripartite kingdom of Argos in 2.18.4–5.

2.21.3 **Ἀθηνᾶς . . . Σάλπιγγος ἱερόν:** this sanctuary has been identified with the foundations of a temple from the 4th c. BCE (with restorations from the time of Hadrian) that replaced a temple from the 5th c. BCE within a *temenos* active from the archaic period. However, it lies outside P.'s route (MT 282). **Τυρσηνοῦ:** Tyrsenus was often linked to Tyrrhenus, the mythical founder of the Etruscan League in Italy and the man after whom the Tyrrhenian Sea was named. **τὸν δὲ (Τυρσηνὸν) γυναικὸς . . . τῆς Λυδῆς:** this is the Lydian queen Omphale. After Heracles killed Iphitus, he was ordered by the Delphic oracle to serve her as a slave for a year. **Τημένῳ:** one of the leaders of the Heraclidae on their return to the Peloponnesus; cf. 2.18.7. He received Argos as his share of the Peloponnesus. **τοῦ ὀργάνου τὸν ψόφον:** ψόφος usually means "noise," but it can also refer to the sound of musical instruments (v. *LSJ* 1). **Ἐπιμενίδου:** Epimenides was a native of Cnossus and lived in the 7th or 6th c. BCE. He became known as a seer and philosopher, and the Athenians sent for him when they were suffering from a pestilence (Diogenes Laertius 1.109–10). It is unclear when the Spartans captured Epimenides or why they killed him: Diogenes Laertius 1.114 states that the seer foretold to the Spartans their defeat by the Arcadians. At 3.11.11, P. notes Epimenides' tomb in Sparta. **λέγουσιν:** this sets up an indirect statement in acc. with infinitive, which ends with ἀποκτεῖναι. **Λακεδαιμονίους . . . πολεμήσαντας πρὸς Κνωσσίους:** at 3.12.11, P. notes that the Spartans deny that they ever fought with the Cnossians. MT (283) notes that Lyctus, a Cretan city, had a close relationship with Sparta, whereas Cnossus, its enemy, was friendly with Argos. **αὐτοὶ δὲ . . . :** i.e., the Argives here. **ἀνελόμενοι:** < ἀναιρέω, aor. middle participle, "taking up (the body)" (v. *LSJ* B.I.3).

2.21.4 **τὸ . . . οἰκοδόμημα:** this building has not yet been identified, but it may be a circular construction attributed to the age of Hadrian (MT 283). **Πύρρῳ τῷ Ἠπειρώτῃ:** Pyrrhus, king of Epirus, was killed in 272 BCE during an attempt to seize control of Argos from Antigonus II Gonatas. P. describes the event in detail at 1.13.4–9. **ἂν εὕροι τις:** "it can be shown" (Loeb). P. draws a distinction between Pyrrhus' μνῆμα (the site of the pyre) and the actual location of the bones: see τοῦτο μὲν δὴ . . . αὐτὰ δὲ κεῖται . . . τὰ ὀστᾶ below. **οἱ ἐλέφαντές:** at 1.12.3–4, P. gives a brief notice about the use of elephants by Alexander and his successors; in Pyrrhus' rout of the Romans in his first battle with them, he used elephants for "shock and awe." **ἐδήλωσα ἐν τῇ Ἀτθίδι συγγραφῇ:** P. devoted a long excursus of book 1 to a narrative of Pyrrhus' eventful life and exploits (1.11.1–1.13.9). **ἐν τῷ ἱερῷ τῆς Δήμητρος:** Pyrrhus died in street fighting in Argos, and it is said that an old woman threw a roof tile at his head and killed him instantly. At 1.13.8 (but not here), P. notes the Argive belief that the woman was Demeter in disguise. It is unclear whether the shrine of Demeter referred to here is that of Demeter Pelasgis mentioned at 2.22.1. **τοῦ . . . τῆς Δήμητρος ἱεροῦ τούτου:** construe with τὴν ἔσοδον.

2.21.5 Μεδούσης . . . τῆς Γοργόνος: here P. fulfills a pledge he made in the previous book (1.22.7), to handle the events surrounding Medusa later. **ἀπόντος:** < ἄπειμι I, present act. participle. **ἀπόντος δὲ τοῦ μυθοῦ τάδε ἄλλα ἐς αὐτήν ἐστιν εἰρημένα:** i.e., P. aims to give only the historical and factual details about Medusa (as he sees them). **Φόρκου:** Hesiod considered Phorkys a sea god, the offspring of Pontus and Gaea (*Theogony* 238), and regarded Medusa the Gorgon as the spawn of Phorkys and Ceto (274), but P. envisions Phorkys as a Libyan king with a talented daughter. Cf. Diodorus Siculus 3.52–55 for a tradition that places the Amazons in Libya and makes Medusa their queen. **θυγατέρα:** in the indirect discourse set up by ἐστιν εἰρημένα, this is the acc. subject of the five infinitives down to δολοφονηθῆναι (apart from the parenthetical ἕπεσθαι . . . Πελοποννήσου). **τῶν . . . οἰκούντων:** gen. object of βασιλεύειν (S 1370). **τὴν λίμνην τὴν Τριτωνίδα:** at 1.14.6, P. notes the Libyan tradition that Athena was the daughter of Poseidon and Lake Tritonis. **τοῖς Λίβυσι:** dat. object of ἡγεῖσθαι (S 1537). **καὶ δὴ καὶ τότε:** "on one such occasion" (Loeb). The particles introduce a climax attending on her leading the Libyans into battle (S 2847; D 255–57). **στρατῷ:** dat. of military accompaniment (S 1526). **τὸ κάλλος ἔτι καὶ ἐπὶ νεκρῷ:** "beauty still (residing) even on the corpse." **ἐς ἐπίδειξιν:** acc. of purpose.

2.21.6 Καρχηδονίῳ . . . ἀνδρὶ Προκλεῖ τῷ Εὐκράτους: the identity of this man is still debated. Traditionally, scholars have considered him a Hellenistic historian of the 3rd c. or 2nd c. BCE, but it has been proposed recently that he was a contemporary sophist known to P. For an overview and the new theory, see Juan Pablo Sanchez Hernandez, "Procles the Carthaginian: A North African Sophist in Pausanias' *Periegesis*," *GRBS* 50 (2010): 119–32. MT (284) says that the stories in 2.21.5–6 are probably written ones. **θηρία ἀκούσασιν οὐ πιστὰ:** = θηρία ἄπιστα, i.e., incredible beasts. **ἄνδρες . . . ἄγριοι καὶ ἄγριαι . . . γυναῖκες:** chiastic order. **ἐς ὅ:** "until." **συνεπιλαβέσθαι:** double-compound verb, "she assisted him (dat.) with the deed (gen.)." **ὅτι οἱ περὶ τὴν λίμνην τὴν Τριτωνίδα ἄνθρωποι ταύτης εἰσὶν ἱεροί:** see commentary on 2.21.5, for the tradition of the goddess' origin in that area.

2.21.7 Γοργοφόνης . . . τῆς Περσέως: Gorgophone was the daughter of Perseus and Andromeda, whom Perseus famously rescued from a sea beast. See P. 3.1.4, 4.2.4; ps.-Apollod. 1.9.5, 2.4.5, 3.10.3. **δῆλον . . . ἀκούσαντι:** the entire preceding relative clause is modified by δῆλον. **γυναικῶν . . . πρώτην αὐτήν . . . τὴν δὲ . . . :** i.e., she was the first widow to remarry. P. uses the article to resume the pronoun αὐτήν after the parenthetical clause. **Περιήρους τοῦ Αἰόλου:** Perieres, the king of Messene and the son of Aeolus (king of the winds) and Enarete, sired Aphareus and Leucippus by Gorgophone. Cf. 4.2.2, 4.2.4; ps.-Apollod. 1.7.3. **Οἰβάλῳ:** Oebalus, the son of Cynortas, was a Spartan (3.1.3); with Gorgophone, he sired Tyndareus (father of Helen and Clytemnestra), Icarius (father of Penelope, faithful wife of Odysseus), and Hippocoon (cf. 3.1.4–5). **καθεστήκει:** < καθίστημι, perf. act. indicative intransitive, "it was established (practice that)" (v. *LSJ* B.6). **ἐπὶ ἀνδρὶ ἀποθανόντι:** ἐπί with the dat. can give the conditions under which an action takes place (S 1689.2c). There is a similar example at the end of 2.21.9.

2.21.8 τρόπαιον . . . κατὰ ἀνδρὸς: i.e., a victory monument "over" the tyrant (S 1690.1c). **Λαφάους:** it is unclear when Laphaës held a tyranny over the Argives. The Spartans interfered in Athenian politics by driving out the tyrant Hippias in 510 BCE and later assisting the Athenian politician Isagoras (ultimately unsuccessfully) against his colleague Cleisthenes in 508 BCE. MT (284) notes that this interference fueled the traditional hatred between Argos and Sparta. **τοῦτον:** the participles τυραννοῦντα and φυγόντα below agree with this pronoun. **περὶ σφῶν (αὐτῶν):** = περὶ ἑαυτῶν; 3rd-person plural reflexive (S 329). **Λητοῦς:** gen. of Λητώ; see commentary on Κερδοῦς at 2.21.1. Leto was the mother of Apollo and Artemis by Zeus.

2.21.9 εἰκόνα: modified by gen. τῆς παρθένου. **Χλῶριν:** Chloris was the only surviving daughter of Niobe, as P. explains here, giving a reason for her change of name. **Νιόβης:** this Niobe is different from the Niobe who was daughter of Phoroneus and mother of Argus and Pelasgus by Zeus (2.22.5; ps.-Apollod. 2.1.1–2). **τῶν Ἀμφίονος παιδῶν:** Amphion (son of Zeus and Antiope; cf. 2.6.3–4) and Niobe had 14 (or fewer) children, an equal number of boys and girls. Niobe incurred Leto's wrath because she foolishly boasted that she had more children than the goddess. Cf. ps.-Apollod. 3.5.6 for the different traditions about Niobe and her children. **περιγενέσθαι . . . περιγενέσθαι δὲ:** pseudanaphora. **Ἀμύκλαν:** Amyclas was the only surviving son of Niobe and Amphion. **οὕτω δή τι:** "in some way like this" (v. *LSJ* δή I.5). **ἐπὶ τῷ συμβάντι:** "because of the event."

2.21.10 πρόσκειμαι: "I am devoted to," with dat. (v. *LSJ* II.2, where this passage is cited). **πλέον τι:** adverbial phrase, "somewhat more." **μηδένα:** indirect discourse usually takes οὐ for negative, but μή can be used after a verb of assertion or belief (S 2725–26). P. has his own idea about Niobe's children and prefers it, as well as the evidence of Homer, to these Argive tales. **τὸ ἔπος:** i.e., *Iliad* 24.609. **τὼ . . . δοιώ . . . ἐόντ(ε):** these are the nom. dual forms for the article, the adj. δοιοί (two), and the Homeric form of the participle ὤν (S 305). **καὶ . . . περ:** this tmesis occurs regularly in Homer. **οὗτος:** i.e., Homer. **ἐκ βάθρων:** "utterly, completely" (v. *LSJ* βάθρον 3). **ἀποτραπέντα:** < ἀποτρέπω, aor. passive participle.

2.22.1 Ἥρας . . . τῆς Ἀνθείας: "Flowery Hera"; she may be connected to the Peloponnesian festival of the Ἡροσάνθεια, when girls gathered flowers (Frazer 3.201). **πρὸς Ἀργείους:** "against the Argives"; πρός with the acc. denotes friendly or hostile relations (S 1694.3c). **Διονύσῳ συνεστρατευμέναι:** P. describes an attack on Argos by maenads and Dionysus at 2.22.4, where he describes a special grave for the maenad Chorea and refers to a common grave for the other women; the latter may be the grave here. **Δήμητρός . . . Πελασγίδος:** Hera also bore this epithet in Thessaly (Apollonius of Rhodes 1.14 with scholia). **Πελασγοῦ τοῦ Τριόπα:** at 1.14.2, P. mentions a Pelasgus who received Demeter at Argos and helped her spread knowledge of agriculture.

2.22.2 Λυκέας: cf. 2.19.5, 2.23.8. **Μηχανέως . . . Διός:** "Zeus the Contriver"; he was worshipped with that epithet on Cos too (Frazer 3.202). **ὀμόσαι παραμενεῖν:** verbs of swearing often taken a future infinitive in indirect discourse (S 1868e); "they swore that they would remain." **ἔστ' ἂν ἢ τὸ Ἴλιον ἕλωσιν ἢ μαχομένους τελευτὴ σφᾶς ἐπιλάβῃ:** clause identifying a temporal limit as the termination point (S 2426), "until either . . . or . . . stops them (from) fighting." **ἐστιν εἰρημένον:** this phrase sets up indirect discourse with acc. and infinitive.

2.22.3 τὸν μὲν δὴ Θυέστου παῖδα ἢ Βροτέου: Broteas is mentioned at ps.-Apollod. epit. 2.2 as a son of Tantalus (father of Pelops). **τοῦτον μὲν <τὸν> Τάνταλον:** P. mentioned Tantalus as Clytemnestra's first husband at 2.16.2 and 2.18.2. **διοίσομαι:** < διαφέρω, future middle indicative (v. *LSJ* IV). **τοῦ (Ταντάλου) λεγομένου Διός τε . . . καὶ Πλουτοῦς:** this Tantalus was the famous one who butchered and cooked his son Pelops to test the omniscience of the gods. Plouto was a nymph, the daughter of Oceanus and Tethys. **ἰδὼν οἶδα ἐν Σιπύλῳ:** many scholars have interpreted this statement as evidence of Sipylus as P.'s homeland. **Ἴλου τοῦ Φρυγὸς:** Ilus was the son and heir of Tros (son of Dardanus and king of Troy) and the brother of Assaracus and Ganymede; he founded the city of Ilium. Cf. ps.-Apollod. 3.12.2. **οὐδὲ ἀνάγκη συνέπεσεν:** "nor did the necessity come upon (him) that," with acc. and infinitive. **πρὸς δὲ:** the preposition here is used as an adv., "moreover" (v. *LSJ* πρός D). **τάδε μὲν ἐς τοσοῦτον:** both pronouns look backward. **ἐξητάσθω:** < ἐξετάζω, perf. middle imperative 3rd sg., implying completion with permanent result (S 1864c and note). **τὰ . . . δρώμενα:** "sacred rites" (v. *LSJ* (A) II). **Νικόστρατον ἄνδρα ἐπιχώριον:** not otherwise known. **ἀφιᾶσι . . . καιομένας λαμπάδας:** the ritual is attested archaeologically by votive deposits of lamps in connection with the cult of Demeter (MT 285). See Frazer 3.203 for interesting parallels.

2.22.4 Προσκλυστίου . . . ἐπικλύσαι: P. explains an epithet based on a verb (προσκλύζω) by using a related verb (ἐπικλύζω) rather than the base verb. **τῆς . . . χώρας:** partitive gen. with τὴν πολλήν. **Ἴναχος καὶ οἱ συνδικάσαντες:** at 2.15.5, P. told the story of the rivers' arbitration between Hera and Poseidon for possession of the Argolid. **εὕρετο:** < εὑρίσκω, aor. middle indicative, "she procured (from him) that . . ." (v. *LSJ* IV). **ὅθεν:** this refers to an understood ἔνθα *vel sim.*

2.22.5 Ἄργου Διὸς . . . τῆς Φορωνέως Νιόβης: P. mentioned Argos, after whom Argos was named, at 2.16.1. **δοκοῦντος:** "reputed (to be)" (v. *LSJ* II.5). **Διοσκούρων ναός:** the Argives considered the twin heroes as founders of their polis, like the Spartans, and designated a tomb of Castor, since they considered Polydeuces a god. **Ἄναξις καὶ Μνασίνους:** ps.-Apollod. 3.11.2 calls them Mnesileus and Anogon, the sons of Polydeuces and Phoebe and of Castor and Hilaera respectively. **Ἱλάειρα καὶ Φοίβη:** Hilaera and Phoebe, the daughters of Leucippus, were betrothed to Lynceus and Idas, the sons of Aphareus, but Castor and Polydeuces kidnapped them. Hilaera married Castor and bore him Anaxis; Phoebe became the mother of Mnasinous (ps.-Apollod. 3.11.2). **Διποίνου καὶ Σκύλλιδος:** for these two sons of Daedalus, cf. 2.15.1. **τούτοις:** resumptive of τοῖς ἵπποις.

2.22.6 **Ἀνάκτων:** "Kings," a common epithet of the Dioscuri. **σὺν Πειρίθῳ Θησέως ἀπελθόντος ἐς Θεσπρωτοὺς:** Theseus and his friend Peirithoos promised to help each other find wives. Peirithoos helped Theseus abduct the child Helen and bring her to Athens, then Theseus accompanied Peirithoos on his mission to Thesprotia to abduct Persephone, the wife of the king, who imprisoned both men and eventually killed Peirithoos. P. covered these events at 1.17.4–6. **Ἄφιδνά τε ὑπὸ Διοσκούρων ἑάλω:** while Theseus was a prisoner, before Heracles freed him, the Dioscuri attacked Athens, captured the district of Aphidna, set Menestheus on the throne, recovered Helen, and returned home with Theseus' mother as prisoner (1.17.4–6). **ἔχειν . . . ἐν γαστρί:** "to be pregnant" (v. *LSJ* γαστήρ II). **τὴν μὲν παῖδα ἣν ἔτεκε:** according to Antonius Liberalis 27, this child was Iphigeneia, as P. reveals in the next subsection. **αὐτὴν δὲ ὕστερον τούτων Μενελάῳ γήμασθαι:** Tyndareus awarded Helen to Menelaus and forced the suitors to swear to protect her, an oath that played a major role in the Trojan War.

2.22.7 **Εὐφορίων Χαλκιδεὺς:** Euphorion of Chalcis (born ca. 275 BCE) was a famous poet of the 3rd c. BCE, a member of the court of Antiochus III the Great, and the head of the library at Antioch. **Πλευρώνιος Ἀλέξανδρος:** Alexander of Pleuron in Aetolia (fl. ca. 280 BCE) enjoyed the support of Ptolemy II Philadelphus and worked in the Library of Alexandria, cataloging and editing tragedies and satyr plays. **Στησίχορος ὁ Ἱμεραῖος:** Stesichorus of Himera (ca. 630–555 BCE) was one of the members of the canon of nine lyric poets established by Alexandrian scholars; Chamaeleon noted Stesichorus, among them, as mythologically innovative. Stesichorus is said to have been struck blind by Helen for blaspheming her in a poem (Isocrates *Helen* 64; Plato *Phaedrus* 243a). **κατὰ ταὐτά φασιν Ἀργείοις:** "they agree with the Argives that . . ." **Ἰφιγένειαν:** Iphigeneia is generally considered the daughter of Clytemnestra and Agamemnon in Greek mythology. **Σκόπα:** P. named Scopas as the sculptor of a Heracles statue at 2.10.1. **Πολύκλειτος:** not the great 5th c. BCE sculptor but a later namesake. **Ναυκύδης †Μόθωνος†:** the last name here has usually been emended to Μεθωναῖος (Furtwängler) or νεώτερος (Roberts). At 6.6.2, P. says that Polyclitus was the pupil of Naucydes, who must have been his older brother. At 6.1.3, P. calls him Naucydes of Argos, who also appears at 2.17.5. Scholars are divided on the dating of these two artists.

2.22.8 ἐρχομένῳ: P. is now heading to the gate and gymnasium of Cylarabes, SE of the city. **Κυλάραβιν:** Cylarabes was a king of Argos (2.18.5) but died without offspring, which allowed Orestes to seize the kingdom. **Σθενέλου:** Sthenelus was the son of Capaneus (one of the original Seven against Thebes) and helped capture Troy as one of the Epigoni. He inherited the throne of Argos from his uncle Iphis (2.18.5). **Λικύμνιος ὁ Ἠλεκτρύωνος:** Licymnius was a friend of Heracles and the bastard son of Electryon (king of Tiryns and Mycenae) and Mideia (ps.-Apollod. 2.4.5). **Ὅμηρος . . . φησὶ:** MT (287) notes that Homer actually names not Argos but Ephyra and the river Selleis as Tleptolemus' home (*Iliad* 2.662). **Τληπτολέμου . . . τοῦ Ἡρακλέους:** Licymnius was killed in his old age, when he confronted Tleptolemus while the latter was beating a slave (ps.-Apollod. 2.8.2). **ὀλίγον:** adv. with ἀποτραπεῖσι. **τῆς (ὁδοῦ) ἐπὶ Κυλάραβιν** **Σακάδα:** Sacadas was a skilled pipe player who won thrice at the Pythian Games in the early 6th c. BCE. P. describes Sacadas' victories at 6.14.9–10. Cf. Thomas J. Mathiesen, *Apollo's Lyre: Greek Music and Music Theory in Antiquity and the Middle Ages* (Lincoln: University of Nebraska Press, 1999), 59 and n. 62. **τὸ αὔλημα τὸ Πυθικὸν:** the Pythian melody was said to have resembled Apollo's fight with the serpent Python (Pollux 4.84).

2.22.9 ἀπὸ Μαρσύου καὶ τῆς ἁμίλλης τοῦ Σιληνοῦ: = ἀπὸ τῆς Μαρσύου τοῦ Σιληνοῦ ἁμίλλης. Cf. 2.7.9. **Πανία . . . Ἀθηνᾶ:** "Athena Who Causes Panic," in her militant mode. **πολυάνδριον:** "mass grave." Cf. 2.24.7, 2.38.6. **τοῖς μετὰ Ἀθηναίων πλεύσασιν Ἀργείοις ἐπὶ καταδουλώσει Συρακουσῶν τε καὶ Σικελίας:** the ill-starred Athenian expedition to Sicily (415–413 BCE) during the Peloponnesian War. Thucydides 7.44.6 notes that this Argive contingent unsettled the Athenians during battle by singing Doric paeans that made the latter think the former were enemy forces. Cf. Thucydides 7.20.1, 7.26.1. **ἐπὶ καταδουλώσει Συρακουσῶν τε καὶ Σικελίας:** cf. Thucydides 7.66.2, ἐπὶ τῆς Σικελίας καταδουλώσει (the speech of Gylippus to the soldiers before the great naval battle at Syracuse).

2.23.1 ἐντεῦθεν ἐρχομένοις ὁδὸν καλουμένην: Koile was a city quarter, not a road. P. seems to be traveling in the NE part of the city (MT 288). **συμβάσης . . . τῆς . . . ναυαγίας:** gen. absolute. **πρὸς τῷ Καφηρεῖ:** the shipwreck was due to Nauplius' setting up false beacon fires along the Euboean Coast—revenge for the unjust execution of his son

Palamedes by the Achaeans (cf. 2.20.3). **τῶν Ἀργείων:** partitive gen. with τοὺς δυνηθέντας. **εὐξαμένοις . . . γενέσθαι:** verbs of praying or swearing take an aor. infinitive when they do not set up indirect discourse (S 1868). Cf. commentary on 2.22.2. The Argives are seeking immediate relief (e.g., "May a god save us!"). **προῄεσαν:** < πρόειμι (A), imperf. act. indicative 3rd pl. (S 773). **ἦσαν ἠθροισμέναι:** < ἀθροίζω, pluperf. middle/passive indicative 3rd pl. periphrastic (S 599), "they had gathered." **ἐπισκευάσαντες:** "refitting (ships)."

2.23.2 **ὄψει:** < ὄψομαι, future middle indicative 2nd sg. **Ἀδράστου:** the son of King Talaus of Argos and a member of the Seven against Thebes, Adrastus served as a king of Sicyon (2.6.6) and a king of Argos. He alone survived the expedition and arranged for the Epigoni to complete their parents' work: his son Aegialeus took part in it (2.20.5). **Ἀμφιαράου:** famous seer, the brother-in-law of Adrastus, and the husband of Eriphyle. **Ἐριφύλης:** Eriphyle famously took the necklace of Harmonia from Polyneices in exchange for persuading her husband, Amphiaraus, to take part in the Seven against Thebes. Amphiaraus made his son Alcmaeon promise to kill his mother in revenge (ps.-Apollod. 1.9.3). **ἑξῆς δὲ τούτων:** "next to these" (v. *LSJ* II). **Βάτωνος:** cf. ps.-Apollod. 3.6.8. **γένους Ἀμφιαράῳ τοῦ αὐτοῦ τῶν Μελαμποδιδῶν:** cf. 2.18.4–5. **γενομένης δὲ τῆς τροπῆς ἀπὸ τοῦ Θηβαίων τείχους:** i.e., the rout suffered by the Seven against Thebes. **χάσμα γῆς . . . ὑποδεξάμενον:** a prophetic shrine of Amphiaraus was established subsequently in Oropus in Attica (cf. 1.34.2).

2.23.3 **ἐκ τῆς Κοιλης (ὁδοῦ):** cf. 2.23.1. **Ὑρνηθοῦς:** P. mentioned Hyrnetho, daughter of Temenus and wife of Deiphontes, at 2.19.1. **πειθέσθω:** < πείθω, present middle imperative. **πειθέσθω δὲ ὅστις τὰ Ἐπιδαυρίων οὐ πέπυσται:** at 2.28.3–6, P. tells the sad tale of Hyrnetho's death when he reaches Hyrnethium in the territory of Epidaurus, where he believes she is actually buried. Perhaps P. is here encouraging the reader to keep reading his very informative work. **πέπυσται:** < πυνθάνομαι, perf. middle indicative.

2.23.4 **τῶν Ἀσκληπιείων:** partitive gen. with τὸ ἐπιφανέστατον, which is the subject of the sentence. **Ὑγεία:** we have seen this deity often paired with Asclepius; cf. 2.4.5, 2.11.6, 2.27.6. **Ξενόφιλος καὶ Στράτων:** scholars have tentatively dated these two Argive sculptors to the 2nd c. BCE. They are well attested epigraphically at Argos and Epidaurus (MT 289). Cf. Olga Palagia,

"The Functions of Greek Art," in *Oxford Handbook of Greek and Roman Art and Architecture*, ed. Clemente Marconi (Oxford: Oxford University Press, 2015), 302. **Σφῦρος:** both Sphyrus and Alexanor were sons of Machaon and thus grandsons of Asclepius. Cf. 2.11.5–7. **Ἀλεξάνορος τοῦ παρὰ Σικυωνίοις ἐν Τιτάνῃ τιμὰς ἔχοντος:** cf. 2.11.7.

2.23.5 τῆς . . . Ἀρτέμιδος τῆς Φεραίας: construe with τὸ ἄγαλμα after the parenthetical sentence. The city of Pherae is in Thessaly. There was a shrine to Artemis Pheraea in Sicyon (2.10.7). **τάδε δὲ αὐτοῖς οὐχ ὁμολογῶ:** P. disagrees with the Argives regarding three beliefs about the tomb of Deianeira, the tomb of Helenus, and the Palladion. **Δηιανείρας . . . τῆς Οἰνέως:** Deianeira, the daughter of Oeneus and sister of Meleager, was the last wife of Heracles and infamously caused his death by sending him a robe imbued with Nessus' poisonous blood, which she mistakenly thought was a love potion (ps.-Apollod. 1.8.1, 2.7.5–7). **Ἑλένου τοῦ Πριάμου:** one of the few sons of Priam to survive the war, Helenus was captured by the Greeks and revealed to them that Troy could only fall if they obtained the Palladion (ps.-Apollod. 3.12.5). **ἄγαλμα:** construe with Ἀθηνᾶς τὸ ἐκκομισθέν and ποιῆσαν. **ποιῆσαν:** aor. act. participle, neut. acc. sg.; it sets up a factitive clause. **τὸ μὲν δὴ Παλλάδιον:** P. introduces three assertions of the Argives and then refutes them, not in the same order (Deianeira, Helenus, Palladion) or in reverse order but in a mixed order. **(τὸ Παλλάδιον) ἐς Ἰταλίαν κομισθὲν ὑπὸ Αἰνείου:** P. elsewhere notes a painting showing Diomedes taking the Athena statue from Troy (1.22.6) and reports that the Palladion was taken by the Athenians under Demophon from the Argives who landed on the coast of Attica at night on their way back from Troy and mistook the land as hostile (1.28.9). **ὁ τάφος αὐτῇ (Δηιανείρᾳ) πλησίον Ἡρακλείας τῆς ὑπὸ τῇ Οἴτῃ:** Mt. Oeta was the site of Heracles' immolation and death. This city was Heracleia Trachinia.

2.23.6 δεδήλωκεν ὁ λόγος ἤδη μοι: cf. 1.11.1–2. **Πύρρου τοῦ Ἀχιλλέως:** Pyrrhus, or Neoptolemus, was the son of Achilles by Deidameia, the daughter of King Lycomedes of Scyros, who had sheltered Achilles from the Greek forces. Pyrrhus later came to Troy when the Greeks heard that his presence was necessary for the city to fall. He died at the hands of the people of Delphi (1.13.9). **Ἀνδρομάχῃ:** Andromache, the wife of Hector, became the concubine of Pyrrhus after the fall of Troy. **οὐ μὴν οὐδὲ:** "nor again" (S 2768). **λέληθεν:** < λανθάνω, perf. act. indicative. **ὅτι μὴ:** in classical indirect discourse, the negative is οὐ, but this may be an instance of μή in an emphatic declaration (S 2723). **οὐ . . . τι ἕτοιμον:** "(it is) not easy" (v. *LSJ* I.2). **μεταπεῖσαι:** "to persuade (the many: acc.) to change their minds to (the opposite: acc.)." **ὧν:** = ἐκείνων ἅ, the relative pronoun is attracted into the case of its (unseen) antecedent.

2.23.7 κατάγεων οἰκοδόμημα: P. may be referring here to one of the many chambered tombs of the Mycenaean Age in Argos and its environs (MT 289). **τῆς θυγατρὸς:** Acrisius' daughter was Danaë, mother of Perseus. **Περίλαος . . . τυραννήσας:** Perilaos, a tyrant of Argos, probably dates to the age of Peisistratus. We can identify him as the champion of Argos at 2.20.7. **Κροτώπου:** Crotopus was the son of Agenor and father of Psamathe; he became king of Argos after the death of his uncle Iasus (cf. 2.16.1, 2.19.8). **Διονύσου . . . Κρησίου:** more evidence of very ancient ties between Argos and Crete (MT 289). **πολεμήσαντα αὐτὸν (Διόνυσον):** Dionysus' attack on Argos was covered at 2.20.4 and 2.22.1. **λέγουσιν:** although this verb occurs in the middle of the sentence, it establishes the indirect discourse with acc. and infinitive that gives structure to the rest of the sentence.

2.23.8 Ἀριάδνην: Ariadne was the daughter of Minos who famously assisted Theseus in defeating the Minotaur. He later abandoned her on Naxos, where she was found by Dionysus, who married her. **Λυκέας:** cf. 2.19.5, 2.22.2. **δεύτερον:** adv., "a second time," i.e., when the temple was being rebuilt. **κεραμέαν . . . σορόν:** "earthenware coffin" (Loeb). H. appears to use σορός in this sense at 1.68.3 and 2.78. **καὶ αὐτός τε καὶ ἄλλους . . . ἔφη:** "and he said that he himself and others"; the intensive pronoun is nom. because it refers to the subject of the verb that establishes the indirect discourse (i.e., Lyceas). **Ἀφροδίτης . . . Οὐρανίας:** this particular cult appears in Athens too (1.14.6, 1.19.2).

Acropolis of Argos

2.24.1 τὴν . . . ἀκρόπολιν Λάρισαν: although Argos is often said to have two acropoleis, Larisa (the higher one) and Aspis (now Profitis Ilias), the Argives themselves only referred to one acropolis, so both names may refer to the heights as a pair, and the Deiras (Ridge) referred to below may be the ridge between them. For instance, P. speaks only of Larisa, Plutarch only of Aspis. See MT 291–92. **ἀπὸ τῆς Πελασγοῦ θυγατρός:** cf. 2.22.1. **δύο τῶν ἐν Θεσσαλίᾳ πόλεων:** there were a number of other cities with the name *Larissa*. The first Thessalian city P. refers to here is Larissa Kremaste, which lies on the Malian Gulf, in the district of Phthiotis; the other is the most famous Larissa, on the Peneios River. **ἔστι μὲν . . . ἔστι δὲ . . . :** anaphora. **Ἀκραίας Ἥρας:** an appropriate epithet for a deity who guards an acropolis; cf. Τύχη Ἀκραία at 2.7.5. The site of her sanctuary is traditionally identified as the convent of Panaghia Vrachou (MT 290). **ναὸς Ἀπόλλωνος:** this sanctuary, like that of Athena Oxyderkes (2.24.2), has been found under a paleo-Christian church on the SW slopes of Prophitis Ilias. Renovated in the 4th c. BCE, the church is centered on a large altar carved into the rock, with stairs in front of a *naos*. Found to the N are the remains of a stoa and a rectangular building that is probably a *manteion*. The temple of Athena is probably to the SE (MT 290–91). **Πυθαεὺς:** although *Pythaeus* appears as a man's name here, it is most common as an epithet of Apollo. Cf. 2.35.2 and commentary. **Δειραδιώτης:** "Apollo of the Ridge," an epithet found only here. **ἀνδρὸς εὐνῆς εἰργομένη:** "abstaining from intercourse with a man" (v. *LSJ* ἔργω (A) II.2). **ἀρνὸς:** gen. sg. of a noun without a nom. sg. form, "lamb." **κάτοχος:** "inspired by (the god)" (v. *LSJ* II.2).

2.24.2 **Ἀθηνᾶς Ὀξυδερκοῦς:** this shrine may have had a medical and oracular function, like Athena Ophthalmitis at Sparta (3.18.2). Callimachus' fifth hymn describes a rite in which Argive girls bathe the cult statue in the Inachus River while carrying a shield of Diomedes in procession (MT 291). **Διομήδους:** P. is referring to the episode at *Iliad* 5.106ff., where Pandarus wounds Diomedes with an arrow. Athena helps Diomedes recover, so he can kill Pandarus and wound Aeneas and even Aphrodite, Aeneas' mother. **τὴν ἀχλὺν ἀφεῖλεν ἡ θεὸς ἀπὸ τῶν ὀφθαλμῶν:** P. employs hyperbaton to show the goddess keeping the mist from Diomedes' eyes. **τὸ στάδιον:** this stadium lies outside of the walls, between the heights (MT 292). **τῶν Αἰγύπτου παίδων . . . μνῆμα:** Aegyptus was the brother of Danaus, and he and his sons pursued Danaus and his daughters to Argos; P. has already mentioned the deeds of the Danaids and the trial of Hypermestra several times in this narrative (cf. 2.19.6, 20.7, 21.1–2). This tomb could be identified with the Mycenaean chamber tomb on the S side of Profitis Ilias (MT 292). **χωρὶς μὲν . . . χωρὶς δὲ . . . :** anaphora. **ἐν Λέρνῃ σώματα τὰ λοιπά:** P. describes Lerna at 2.36.6–2.37.6. He does not mention a resting place for the bodies, but he does describe a statue of Aphrodite dedicated by the Danaids and a sanctuary of Athena built by Danaus (2.37.2). **ἀποθανόντων δὲ ἀποτέμνουσιν . . . ἀπόδειξιν:** note the repetition of the prepositional prefix ἀπο- here. **ἀπόδειξιν:** appositive for τὰς κεφαλάς, "as proof." **ὧν ἐτόλμησαν:** = (ἐκείνων) ἃ ἐτόλμησαν. Construe with ἀπόδειξιν.

2.24.3 Διὸς . . . Λαρισαίου ναός . . . Ἀθηνᾶς . . . ναός: the remains of one of these temples has been found under the Venetian castle on Larisa. The Palladion probably was kept in this temple of Athena (MT 209–10). **τὸ . . . ἄγαλμα ξύλου:** = ξόανον. **ἑστηκὸς ἦν:** periphrastic form for ἕστηκε, perf. act. indicative. **ᾗ πεφύκαμεν:** comparative clause of manner (S 2463), "in the natural place" (Loeb). **δύο μὲν . . . ὀφθαλμούς, τρίτον δὲ . . . :** P.'s *variatio*. **Πριάμῳ . . . τῷ Λαομέδοντος:** King Priam of Troy was the son of Laomedon and originally had the name *Podarces*; after Laomedon cheated Heracles out of payment for building the walls of Troy, Heracles took the city by storm, and Podarces was ransomed and given the name *Priam* (< πριατός). **ἐπὶ τούτου κατέφυγεν ὁ Πρίαμος τὸν βωμόν:** Priam fled to the altar of Zeus and was cut down there by Neoptolemus. The verb does not take a direct object here: τὸν βωμόν is the object of the preposition ἐπί and is modified by the pronoun τούτου, yielding "to the altar of this (deity)."

2.24.4 ἐπὶ τῷδε: "for the following reason"; cf. with διὰ τοῦτο just above. See Frazer 3.209 for an interesting discussion of the three-eyed Zeus. **ἄν τις τεκμαίροιτο:** potential optative, setting up an acc. and infinitive construction where αὐτόν is the acc. subject. **Δία . . . βασιλεύειν:** acc. with infinitive in indirect discourse, which lies in apposition to the οὗτος λόγος following. **ἔπος τῶν Ὁμήρου:** cf. *Iliad* 9.457. **τοῦτον:** this resumes ὅν . . . ἄρχειν φασὶν ὑπὸ γῆς. **Αἰσχύλος . . . καλεῖ:** the play in which this passage occurred is no longer extant (Frazer 3.209). **ὁρῶντα . . . ἅτε . . . ἄρχοντα:** both participles modify τὸν αὐτὸν τοῦτον θεόν. **λήξεσιν:** < λῆξις, "portions assigned by lot" (v. *LSJ* (A) I.2.a). This is perhaps alluding to the myth of the division of the spheres of power between Zeus, Poseidon, and Hades. **τὸν αὐτὸν τοῦτον θεόν:** an attributive (αὐτὸν here) can be separated from its noun by a pronoun like τοῦτον (S 1181).

Mt. Lycone

2.24.5 ὁδοὶ δὲ ἐξ Ἄργους: P. now moves from Argos to a number of minor sites, before shifting to Epidaurus, the next major site, at 2.26.1. **πρὸς Ἀρκαδίας:** "facing Arcadia" (S 1695.1a). **ὄρος . . . ἡ Λυκώνη:** Lycone lies SW of Argos. **Ἀρτέμιδος Ὀρθίας ἱερόν:** "Athena of the Steep." The sanctuary and its temple have been excavated, and some fragments of the cult statues have been found (MT 293; Frazer 3.210). At 3.16.7–11, P. gives a vivid description of the bloody worship of this goddess at her main sanctuary at the

Limnaeum in Laconia. **Πολυκλείτου:** it is unclear whether these works should be assigned to the elder or younger artist bearing this name. **τῆς λεωφόρου:** "highway."

Mt. Chaon

2.24.6 Χάον . . . ὄρος: Mt. Chaon lies SW of Argos. The Erasinus River, at its base, is known as Kephalari today (MT 293). **ἄνεισι:** < ἀνεῖμι, present act. indicative 3rd sg. The subject of the verb is τὸ ὕδωρ. **τέως:** "up to the point," usually an adv. of time. **Στυμφάλου:** although Stymphalus was grouped with the Argives, the inhabitants of the town were Arcadians by descent, so P. does not discuss them until 8.22.1–9. P. is referring here to Lake Stymphalus. **οἱ Ῥειτοί:** now Lake Koumoundouru; cf. 1.38.1. **πρὸς δὲ τοῦ Ἐρασίνου:** the preposition here takes as its object not the gen. phrase but ταῖς . . . ἐκβολαῖς following.

Cenchreae and Hysiae

2.24.7 ἐπανελθοῦσι δὲ ἐς τὴν ἐπὶ Τεγέας ὁδόν: cf. 2.24.5. P. went SW to Mt. Lycone and Mt. Chaon. Now he backtracks toward Argos. **τοῦ ὀνομαζομένου Τρόχου:** it is unclear what the name "Wheel" meant; Frazer (3.212) theorizes that it was the name given to this part of its road "because of its many windings." **Κεγχρεαί:** not the ancient port of Corinth that P. mentioned as lying at one end of the Isthmus of Corinth at 2.1.5 and whose sights he described at 2.2.3, this site is located S of Argos; its exact location has not been established with certainty (MT 294). **τὸ . . . ὄνομα:** this is an instance of prolepsis (S 2182), for the phrase should be within the ἐφ' ὅτῳ clause. **τὸν Πειρήνης παῖδα Κεγχρίαν:** at 2.2.3, P. mentioned Cenchrias and Leches as children of Poseidon and Peirene (daughter of Achelous). **πολυάνδρια:** on the ancient road to Tegea, about two kilometers beyond Kephalari on the mountain route, is a pyramidal monument traditionally identified as the tomb of the fallen at Hysiae, near the modern village of Helleniko. It is actually the tower of a farmhouse (MT 293–94). **μάχῃ . . . περὶ Ὑσίας:** this is not the more famous Battle of Hysiae in 418/417 BCE, during the Peloponnesian War. Very little is known about this earlier battle, often connected with the Argive tyrant Pheidon. Some scholars deny its existence, calling it an Argive fiction (MT 294). **Ἀθηναίοις ἄρχοντος Πεισιστράτου:** not the famous Athenian tyrant (r. 561–527 BCE) but one of the annual archons. **τετάρτῳ . . . ἔτει τῆς <ἑβδόμης καὶ**

εἰκοστῆς> Ὀλυμπιάδος: the 4th year of the 27th Olympiad, i.e., 669/668 BCE. **Εὐρύβοτος Ἀθηναῖος ἐνίκα στάδιον:** Dionysius of Halicarnassus (3.1) says that his victory occurred in 672/671 BCE. **καταβάντι:** a directional participle in the gen. rather than the usual dat. **ἐρείπια Ὑσιῶν ἐστι πόλεώς ποτε ἐν τῇ Ἀργολίδι:** the Spartan king Agis II invaded the Argolid in 417 BCE, after Alcibiades helped expel a pro-Spartan faction from Argos. He destroyed the walls the Argives were building toward the sea and then stormed Hysiae, executing all the male inhabitants. Cf. Thucydides 5.82–83; Diodorus Siculus 12.81.1.

2.25.1 ἡ δ' ἐς Μαντίνειαν (ὁδὸς) ἄγουσα: Mantineia lies W of Argos. **ἀπὸ τῶν πυλῶν τῶν πρὸς τῇ Δειράδι:** cf. 2.24.1. The route begins at this NW gate of Argos and continues through the valley of Charadros (modern Xerias). P. returns to this route at 8.6.4, in his description of Arcadia (MT 294). **ἱερὸν διπλοῦν:** remains found about one kilometer from the gate of Deiras may belong to this unusual sanctuary (MT 294). **πρὸς ἡλίου δύνοντος . . . πρὸς δὲ ἡλίου δυσμὰς:** *variatio.* **ἔχον:** the subject of the participle is ἱερὸν διπλοῦν. **κατὰ μὲν δὴ τοῦτο:** "at the latter (entrance)." **Ἀργείων, ὅσοι . . . συνεστρατεύοντο:** i.e., the Seven against Thebes. **αὐτῷ:** this dat. can be taken as the object of both τιμωρήσοντες (intending to avenge) and συνεστρατεύοντο (they went on an expedition with).

Oenoe

2.25.2 προελθοῦσι . . . διαβάντων: two different directional participles in two different cases with asyndeton. **Οἰνόη:** *Oenoe* is the name of several places in Greece, most notably in Attica (cf. 1.33.8). The exact location of Argive Oenoe is not known, but it has been traditionally associated with the modern village of Mazi, now Aria (MT 294). Oenoe was the site of an important but now obscure battle in 461/460 BCE that is known only from P. (1.15.1, 10.10.3). See E. Badian, *From Plataea to Potidaea: Studies in the History and Historiography of the Pentecontaetia* (Baltimore: Johns Hopkins University Press, 1993), 97–99. **Οἰνέως:** Oeneus was the king of Pleuron and Calydon in Aetolia and the father of Deianeira (wife of Heracles), Meleager (hero of the Calydonian Boar hunt), and Tydeus (father of Diomedes), among others. **ὑπὸ τῶν Ἀγρίου παίδων:** Agrius was the brother of Oeneus, and Agrius' six sons, including Melanippus and Thersites (the famous Achaean buffoon at Troy), deposed their uncle Oeneus in favor of their father. **Διομήδην:** Diomedes was the son of Tydeus and thus the grandson of Oeneus. He is said to have killed all the sons of Agrius except Thersites. **ἐτιμώρησεν . . . στρατεύσας:** this phrase recalls the similar phrase τιμωρήσαντες . . . συνεστρατεύοντο at 2.25.1, although P. has changed the relationship between the verbs here. **εἰ βούλοιτο:** an optative in a subordinate clause in indirect discourse after the verb ἐκέλευεν in secondary sequence. **πατρὸς . . . πατέρα:** i.e., grandfather. **εἰκὸς ἦν:** "it was fair," with infinitive.

Mt. Artemisius

2.25.3 αἱ πηγαὶ τοῦ Ἰνάχου: at 2.15.2, P. stated that the river Inachus did not have any water except when it rains, the revenge of Poseidon against the rivers that voted for Hera in the contest between Poseidon and Hera for dominion over Argos.

Lyrcea and Orneae

2.25.4 ταύτῃ μὲν δὴ θέας οὐδὲν ἔτι ἦν ἄξιον: P. here signals the end of his account of Oenoe and Mt. Artemisius. **Λύρκειαν:** Lyrcea lies to the NW of Argos, but its exact site has been variously identified as the little hill Paliokastraki near the village of Kato Belesi or as Chelmi near the village of Schinochori (MT 295). **λέγεται:** P. introduces the story in indirect discourse, switches to direct discourse, and then switches back to indirect discourse at the end, with λέγουσι. **Λυγκέα:** P. has covered Lynceus and Hypermnestra several times in this book, most recently at 2.21.1. **τῶν πεντήκοντα ἀδελφῶν:** the sons of Aegyptus, whose heads are buried on the acropolis of Argos, according to P. (2.24.2). **συνέκειτο . . . αὐτῷ πρὸς τὴν Ὑπερμήστραν:** the verb is impersonal here; "an agreement was made by him with Hypermnestra to . . ." **ἢν . . . ἀφίκηταί ποι:** the protasis of a future-more-vivid condition in indirect discourse; it is subjunctive because the original condition, as envisioned by P., is, e.g., "If I reach safety somewhere, I will . . ." Note that ἤν = εἰ ἄν. **ἕτερον (πυρσόν) ἀπὸ τῆς Λαρίσης:** the acropolis of Argos (2.24.1–4). **δῆλα καὶ ταύτην ποιοῦσαν:** "making it clear that she too . . ." **ἐν οὐδενὶ οὐδὲ αὐτὴ καθέστηκεν ἔτι κινδύνῳ:** "that nor was she herself in any danger any longer"; this accumulation of negatives confirms the first one (S 2761).

2.25.5 Λύρκου—παῖς δὲ ἦν Ἄβαντος νόθος: Abas was the son of Lynceus and a king of Argos; his legitimate sons were Acrisius and Proetus

(2.16.2). **ἑξήκοντα μάλιστά που στάδια:** "about 60 stades"; see commentary on 2.14.1. **Ὀρνεάς:** this town has been traditionally located near the modern village of Leondi on the border between the Argolid, Phliasia, and Sicyon (MT 295). **Λυρκείας μὲν δὴ πόλεως:** construe this gen. with μνήμην. **Ὅμηρος ἐν καταλόγῳ:** Homer's *Catalogue of Ships* in book 2 of the *Iliad.* **ὥσπερ τῷ τόπῳ τῆς Ἀργείας ἔκειντο:** "just as (Orneae) was in the territory of the Argolid." **ἐν τοῖς ἔπεσι . . . κατέλεξεν:** Homer mentions Orneae at *Iliad* 2.571; P. actually quoted this verse at 2.12.5. **προτέρας:** construe with Ὀρνεάς.

2.25.6 Ὀρνέως τοῦ Ἐρεχθέως: Orneus was the son of Erechtheus (a king of Athens) and Praxithea. **Πετεώς:** at 10.35.8, P. says that Peteos went to Stiris in Phocia after being expelled from Athens by Aegeus. **Μενεσθεύς:** Menestheus was the son of Peteus and Polyxene or Mnesimache. The Dioscuri placed him on the throne of Athens when they seized Aphidna and recovered Helen (cf. 2.22.6). **Ἀργεῖοι . . . Ὀρνεάτας ἀνέστησαν:** the Argive exiles displaced the citizens of Orneae in 416 BCE, but the town was subsequently razed by the Argives and Athenians (Thucydides 6.7.1–2). **ἀνέστησαν· ἀναστάντες δέ:** pseudanaphora. **ἀνειμένος:** < ἀνίημι, perf. passive participle (S 777). **τὰ ἐπέκεινα:** adverbial, "on the far side." P. marks the W boundary of the Argolid.

Tiryns and Medeia

2.25.7 ἐρχομένοις δὲ ἐξ Ἄργους ἐς τὴν Ἐπιδαυρίαν: i.e., from Argos to the E. **οἰκοδόμημα . . . πυραμίδι μάλιστα εἰκασμένον:** a pyramid of polygonal work lies near the church of Haghia Marina near the village of Ligourio, but this is a farm tower and not a tomb (MT 296). **ἀσπίδας σχῆμα Ἀργολικάς:** acc. of respect (S 1601b). These shields were large and circular. **Προίτῳ περὶ τῆς ἀρχῆς πρὸς Ἀκρίσιον:** at 2.16.2, P. notes the division of the Argolid between Proetus (the Heraeum, Mideia, Tiryns, and the coast) and Acrisius (Argos) but does not explain that it happened after a battle. Ps.-Apollod. 2.2.1 says that Proetus, driven from Argos by Acrisius, went to Lycia and there married the daughter of Iobates, who sent an army of Lycians to restore Proetus to his native country. **τέλος . . . ἴσον:** "a draw." **σφᾶς . . . καὶ αὐτοὺς καὶ τὸ στράτευμα:** "they . . . both themselves and their armies." **ἀσπίσι:** construe with ὡπλισμένους. **πρῶτον:** adverbial acc., "for the first time." **αὐτοὺς καὶ τὸ στράτευμα:** both are modified by ὡπλισμένους.

2.25.8 Τίρυνθός . . . ἐρείπια: Tiryns lies to the SE of Argos. **ἀνέστησαν δὲ καὶ Τιρυνθίους Ἀργεῖοι:** cf. 2.16.5, 8.27.1. Argos reduced Tiryns ca. 479–460 BCE. According to Strabo 8.373, the inhabitants went to Epidaurus and Halieis, and some were transferred into Messenia by the Spartans (MT 297). **Ἄργου τοῦ Διὸς:** Argos was the son of Zeus and Niobe (cf. 2.22.5). **Κυκλώπων . . . ἔργον:** ps.-Apollod. 2.2.1 also says that the Cyclopes fortified it. At 2.16.5, P. notes that the Cyclopes fortified Mycenae as well. **ἀργῶν λίθων:** "unwrought stones" (v. *LSJ* ἀργός (B) II.1). **ὡς ἀπ' αὐτῶν μηδ' ἂν . . . κινηθῆναι:** result clause with ἄν, expressing impossibility and representing a potential optative (S 2270a). **ἀρχὴν:** adverbial acc., "to the slightest degree" (Loeb). **τὸν μικρότατον (λίθον) λιθία:** P. switches to "small stones" here because they play a special role in the construction of the wall. **ἁρμονίαν:** a "joint" in the sense of a way to fasten the bigger stones together (v. *LSJ* I.2).

2.25.9 ὡς ἐπὶ θάλασσαν: the demonstrative adv. ὥς, "in this way to the sea." **οἱ θάλαμοι τῶν Προίτου θυγατέρων:** these women went mad because they offended the gods. Ps.-Apollod. 2.2.2 says that Melampus and Bias cured the women for two-thirds of Proetus' kingdom, but P. placed this division in the reign of Anaxagoras (2.18.4). Tiryns has only one large tholos tomb—which was reused in Roman times—but it lies on the side opposite that indicated by P. The "rooms" placed between Tiryns and the sea could have been Mycenaean tombs (MT 297). **ἐπανελθόντων δὲ ἐς τὴν λεωφόρον:** i.e., back to the road with which P. began at 2.25.7, before the detour to Tiryns to the S. **ἐπὶ Μήδειαν:** Medeia has been identified at the NE edge of the Argolic plain, as a Mycenaean fortress built with Cyclopic work, one kilometer from the modern village of Dendra. It had a palace and a large necropolis of chamber tombs from Late Helladic I–III (16th c. through 13th c. BCE), including a tholos tomb (ca. 1400 BCE). See MT 297. **Ἠλεκτρύωνα . . . τὸν πατέρα Ἀλκμήνης:** at 2.22.8, P. mentioned Electryon as the father of Licymnius. Alcmena was most famous as the wife of Amphitryon and mother of Heracles.

Lessa and Mt. Arachnaeus

2.25.10 κώμη Λῆσσα: this village may lie at Ligourio (MT 297). **τὸ ἐν ἀκροπόλει τῇ Λαρίσῃ:** i.e., the one at the temple of Athena Oxyderces (cf. 2.24.2). **†σάπυς ἐλάτων†:** scholars cannot agree on what name lies behind this textual corruption. Valckenaer suggested Αἶπος ἐλάτων, and Hesychius names a place called Ὑσσέλινον. **βωμοὶ . . . Διός τε καὶ**

Ἥρας: these sanctuaries may be located on the peaks Arna and Prophitis Ilias, where Cyclopean structures have been found (Frazer 3.233–34; MT 297). **δεῆσαν ὄμβρου:** acc. absolute (S 2076A).

Myths of Epidaurus

2.26.1 **ἔχεται τῆς Ἀργείας:** "it borders on the Argolid" (v. *LSJ* ἔχω C.I.3). **ἡ Ἐπιδαυρίων (γῆ):** according to Strabo 8.6.15, Epidaurus was originally called Ἐπίταυρος and was settled by Carians. P. here goes on to describe an original Ionic foundation expelled by the Dorians, but Strabo emphasizes a cohabitation of both Ionians and Carians (MT 288). **πρὶν . . . ἢ . . . γενέσθαι:** P. uses the πρίν and infinitive construction thrice here, twice with ἤ (like H.: cf. S 2460) and once without. **ἀφίξῃ:** < ἀφικνέομαι, future middle indicative 2nd sg. **οὐκ οἶδα . . . οὐ μὴν οὐδὲ . . . ἐδυνάμην:** P. is not shy about his failures in research. **Ἐπίδαυρον:** for the eponymous hero, see the next subsection. **Πιτυρέα Ἴωνος ἀπόγονον τοῦ Ξούθου:** for Ion, son of Xuthus, see commentary on 2.14.2. **Δηιφόντῃ καὶ Ἀργείοις:** Deiphontes was the son of Antimachus and husband of Hyrnetho, daughter of Temenus; he was mentioned at 2.19.1.

2.26.2 **ὁ μὲν:** i.e., Pityreus. His son Procles would lead the emigration of the Greeks from Attica to Ionia (cf. 7.4.2–3). **ὁμοῦ τοῖς πολίταις:** improper preposition with the dat. (S 1701). **Τημένου:** Temenus was the father-in-law of Deiphontes, as P. noted at 2.19.1. **κατ' ἔχθος τῶν Τημένου:** the full account comes at 2.28.36. **πλέον . . . νέμοντες:** "respecting more" (Loeb); there is an assumed τιμῆς after πλέον. **Ἐπίδαυρος . . . ὡς μέν φασιν Ἠλεῖοι . . . κατὰ δὲ Ἀργείων δόξαν καὶ τὰ ἔπη . . . Ἐπιδαύριοι δὲ . . . προσποιοῦσιν:** P. carefully presents three different traditions (naturally, each with different phrasing) about the parentage of Epidaurus, the eponymous hero of the city he is describing in this part of book 2. **τὰς μεγάλας Ἠοίας:** see commentary on 2.2.3 and 2.16.4. **Ἐπιδαύρῳ πατὴρ Ἄργος ὁ Διός:** for Argos, cf. 2.16.1. Ps.-Apollod. 2.1.2 names Evadne as Epidaurus' mother.

2.26.3 **Ἀσκληπιοῦ . . . ἱερὰν μάλιστα εἶναι τὴν γῆν:** this phrase serves as the subject of the main verb συμβέβηκε. **ἐπὶ λόγῳ . . . τοιῷδε:** P. gives three stories about Asclepius' birth, the first here in 2.26.3–5, a second (ἄλλος ἐπ' αὐτῷ λόγος) at 2.26.6, and a third (ὁ δὲ τρίτος τῶν λόγων) at 2.26.7; all presuppose Apollo as Asclepius' father. According to Isyllus of Epidaurus, author of the hymn to Asclepius found inscribed in limestone to the E of the temple of that god in the great sanctuary at Epidaurus, Malus married the Muse Erato, who bore Cleophema, a daughter who married Phlegyas and bore Aegla/Coronis, who bore Asclepius to Apollo (Frazer 3.234; MT 298–99). **Φλεγύαν:** Phlegyas was the son of Ares and Chryse and fathered Coronis, as P. reveals just below. P. discusses the myths of Phlegyas under Orchomenos at 9.36.1–4. **πρόφασιν μὲν . . . ἔργῳ δὲ . . . :** this is akin to the usual classical contrast between λόγος and ἔργον, which P. naturally avoids. The word πρόφασιν is adverbial acc. of manner (S 1608). **ἐπὶ θέᾳ τῆς χώρας:** the noun is θέα (a looking at), not θεά (goddess). **κατάσκοπον:** this noun governs the following objective gen. phrase ("spying on the mass of inhabitants") and a simple indirect question ("aiming to see whether . . ."). In the latter case, it acts like a verb of asking, e.g., κατασκέψαντα. **τῶν ἀνθρώπων:** partitive gen. with τὸ πολὺ μάχιμον. **ἐφ᾽ οὓς τύχοι:** past general relative clause; note the optative. **τοὺς καρποὺς ἔφερε καὶ ἤλαυνε τὴν λείαν:** P. varies the verb of plundering to fit crops and cattle respectively, and the verbs and direct objects are in chiastic order.

2.26.4 **εἵπετο:** < ἕπομαι, imperf. middle indicative. **λεληθυῖα ἔτι τὸν πατέρα ὅτι . . . εἶχεν ἐν γαστρί:** "still concealing from her father that . . ." The verb λανθάνω here takes a personal direct object in the acc., yielding "she escaped her father's notice" (v. *LSJ* A.1), and then a following ὅτι clause that explains in what matter she escaped notice. **ἐκτίθησι:** "she exposed" (v. *LSJ* I). **τὸ ὄρος τοῦτο ὃ δὴ Τίτθιον ὀνομάζουσιν:** this hill may be the site of one of two modern villages, Ligourio or Velonidia (Frazer 3.234). **ἐκκειμένῳ:** this verb serves as the passive of ἐκτίθημι; "the exposed child" (v. *LSJ* A.I.1). The οἱ following is a resumptive pronoun. **τῶν . . . αἰγῶν:** partitive gen. with μία.

2.26.5 **Ἀρεσθάνας:** P. gives the most detailed account of the discovery of Asclepius and is the only author to mention the shepherd Aresthanas. **οὐχ εὕρισκεν ὁμολογοῦντα:** i.e., the number he found did not agree with the number he usually had. **ἀπεστάτει:** this form comes not from ἀφίστημι but from the verb derived from it, i.e., ἀποστατέω. **τὸν Ἀρεσθάναν:** this is the subject of the following infinitives and participles. The scene of discovery appears on some imperial-era coins of Epidaurus: e.g., *RPC*, vol. 4, nos. 5262, 5263 (Antoninus Pius). **ἐς πᾶν . . . ἀφικνεῖσθαι ζητήσεως:** "he engaged in every (measure) of searching"; "he left . . . no stone unturned" (Loeb). **ἀνελέσθαι:** < ἀναιρέω, 2nd aor. middle infinitive, "to take up" (v. *LSJ* B.I.4), not "to kill." **ἀστραπὴν . . . ἐκλάμψασαν:** direct object of ἰδεῖν. **ὁ δὲ . . . :** P. shifts the focus of the story from Aresthanas to

Asclepius. The god, however, is the subject of not the main verb ἠγγέλλετο here but the dependent verbs βούλοιτο and ἀνίστησι. **ὁπόσα βούλοιτο:** past general relative clause; this and the ὅτι clause following are the subjects of the main verb ἠγγέλλετο. **ἐπὶ τοῖς κάμνουσι:** "for the ill" (v. *LSJ* κάμνω II.3). **ὅτι ἀνίστησι τεθνεῶτας:** ps.-Apollod. 3.10.3–4 gives details about how Asclepius did this and about Zeus' harsh reaction to this threat to the cosmic order. Cf. 2.27.4 below. **ἀνίστησι:** < ἀνίστημι (v. *LSJ* A.I.3), present act. indicative transitive.

2.26.6 **Κορωνίδα:** the daughter of Phlegyas mentioned in 2.26.4. **Ἴσχυι τῷ Ἐλάτου:** he is said to have died along with Coronis. Ischys was also the brother of Caeneus, the famous gender-shifting warrior, according to ps.-Apollod. 3.10.3. Elatus was a son of Arcas, the eponymous hero of Arcadia. **ἀμυνομένης:** the verb typically takes acc. of the person avenged and gen. of the reason for the vengeance taken. The participle agrees with Ἀρτέμιδος. **ἐξημμένης:** < ἐξάπτω, perf. passive participle. **Ἑρμῆς:** subject of λέγεται.

2.26.7 **ἥκιστα:** construe this adv. with ἀληθής. **ἐμοὶ δοκεῖν:** parenthetical infinitive. **Ἀρσινόης . . . τῆς Λευκίππου:** Leucippus was a son of Perieres and Gorgophone, whom P. discussed at 2.21.7. He was a prince of Messenia, a detail pertinent for P.'s judgment below in this subsection. **ποιήσας:** modifies ὁ τρίτος (λόγος). **Ἀπολλοφάνει . . . τῷ Ἀρκάδι:** this figure is otherwise unknown. **Φλεγυηὶς:** i.e., the daughter of Phlegyas. For the formation of such patronymics, see S 845.4. **φιλότητι μιγεῖσα:** "engaged in sexual intercourse" (v. *LSJ* φιλότης 4). **ἐνὶ:** poetic form of ἐν. **Ἡσίοδον:** this is probably a reference to Hesiod's *Catalog of Women,* or *Great Eoiae.* **τῶν τινα ἐμπεποιηκότων ἐς τὰ Ἡσιόδου:** "one of Hesiod's interpolators" (Loeb), i.e., one of those who inserted foreign material into his verses (v. *LSJ* ἐμποιέω I.3). **συνθέντα:** < συντίθημι, aor. act. participle (v. *LSJ* A.II.3). This participle agrees with acc. sg. masc. Ἡσίοδον and τινα, not with the τὰ ἔπη right before it.

2.26.8 **τόδε:** this subject of μαρτυρεῖ points ahead. **ἐν Ἐπιδαύρῳ . . . γενέσθαι:** this is the direct object of μαρτυρεῖ. **τοῦτο μὲν γὰρ . . . τοῦτο δὲ . . . :** "first . . . secondly . . ." (S 1256). **Ἀθηναῖοι:** P. notes the Asclepieion at Athens at 1.21.4. **τῆς τελετῆς:** partitive gen. with μεταδοῦναι. **Ἐπιδαύρια:** the Epidauria celebrated Asclepius' arrival in Athens with his daughter Hygeia. It appears to have involved a procession of the initiates to the Eleusinion in Athens, a sacrifice, and an all-night feast. Cf. Kevin Clifton, "The Epidauria and the Arrival of Asclepius in Athens," in *Ancient Greek Cult Practice from the Epigraphical Evidence*, ed. R. Hägg (Stockholm: Svenska Institutet in Athen, 1994), 17–34. **ἀπ' ἐκείνου:** "from that (point)," i.e., when they dedicated part of their Eleusinian Mysteries to Asclepius. **Ἀρχίας ὁ Ἀρισταίχμου:** this figure is not otherwise known. **τὸ συμβὰν σπάσμα:** acc. of respect with ἰαθείς. **θηρεύοντί οἱ:** this pronoun refers to the subject of the sentence, Archias, as does ἰαθείς. **περὶ τὸν Πίνδασον:** a mountain range in W Turkey. **ἐπηγάγετο:** "he introduced (the god)," i.e., his cult (v. *LSJ* II.2). The shrine at Pergamum was founded in the 4th c. BCE and, despite the vicissitudes of fortune, was flourishing in P.'s time as never before. Cf. E. J. Edelstein and L. Edelstein, *Asclepius: Collection and Interpretation of the Testimonies*, vol. 1 (Baltimore: John Hopkins University Press, 1998), 254; A. Petsalis-Diomidis, *Truly beyond Wonders: Aelius Aristides and the Cult of Asklepios* (Oxford: Oxford University Press, 2010).

2.26.9 ἀπὸ δὲ τοῦ Περγαμηνῶν (Ἀσκληπιείου) Σμυρναίοις . . . Ἀσκληπιεῖον τὸ ἐπὶ θαλάσσῃ: the Pergamene cult of Asclepius was established from Epidaurus, then the Smyrnean one came from Pergamum. P. is here giving a "genealogy" of famous Asclepieia in the Greek world. See MT 299–300 for speculation about P.'s sources for the list of Asclepieia here and about reasons for the omission of other major sites (e.g., Cos). **ἐν Βαλάκραις ταῖς Κυρηναίων:** modern Bayda in Libya. **διάφορον . . . Κυρηναίοις τοσόνδε ἐς Ἐπιδαυρίους:** the adj. regularly takes the dat. and a prepositional phrase (usually with πρός) to indicate the two parties at variance. **(τούτου) Ἐπιδαυρίοις οὐ καθεστηκότος:** i.e., the Cyrenaean practice is not established custom among the Epidaurians. The negative is οὐ here because there is no conditional or causal force in the gen. absolute.

2.26.10 θεὸν δὲ . . . φήμην: this long clause is the object of the verb εὑρίσκω. **ἀνὰ χρόνον:** "over time" (v. *LSJ* χρόνος I.4.a). **τεκμαιρίοις καὶ ἄλλοις εὑρίσκω καὶ:** "I infer both from other pieces of evidence and . . ." **Ὁμήρου . . . τὰ περὶ Μαχάονος ὑπὸ Ἀγαμέμνονος εἰρημένα:** P. is citing *Iliad* 4.193–94. Machaon and his brother Podalirius led an army from Thessaly to fight for the Achaeans during the Trojan War. **Ταλθύβι':** Agamemnon's herald Talthybius. The elided letter here is ε, the voc. sg. masc. 2nd-declension ending. **ὅττι τάχιστα:** "as quickly as possible" (S 1086). **ὡς ἂν (λέγοι τις) εἰ λέγοι θεοῦ παῖδα ἄνθρωπον:** "just as (one would say) if one should call a man the son of a god."

Asclepieion of Epidaurus

2.27.1 τὸ δὲ ἱερὸν ἄλσος τοῦ Ἀσκληπιοῦ: the great sanctuary of Epidaurus contains many buildings, but P. omits mention of the gymnasium, *xenon*, and palaestra (MT 300). **οὐδὲ ἀποθνῄσκουσιν <ἄνθρωποι> οὐδὲ τίκτουσιν αἱ γυναῖκές σφισιν ἐντὸς τοῦ περιβόλου:** P. mentions this prohibition here and at the end of his description of the sanctuary (cf. 2.27.6). The boundary markers (ὅροι) mentioned above imply the existence of the περίβολος. **σφισιν:** dat. of relation (S 1495). **ἐπὶ Δήλῳ τῇ νήσῳ:** this island was sacred to Apollo, but births and deaths were prohibited on the island, and all the graves on the island were removed by the Athenians in 426 BCE (Thucydides 3.104; Diodorus Siculus 12.58). **τὸν αὐτὸν νόμον:** "(these activities are prohibited) according to the same law"; this is a rather free use of the acc. of manner. **ἤν τέ τις . . . ἤν τε ξένος ὁ θύων ᾖ:** alternative present general conditions, "whether . . . or . . . ," where ἤν = εἰ ἄν. **καταναλίσκουσιν:** this verb takes τὰ θυόμενα as its direct object; "they consume" (v. *LSJ* 2). **τὸ δὲ αὐτὸ γινόμενον οἶδα καὶ ἐν Τιτάνῃ:** at 2.11.5–7, P. described a sanctuary of Asclepius built by his grandson Alexanor at Titane.

2.27.2 τοῦ δὲ Ἀσκληπιοῦ τὸ ἄγαλμα: this statue appears prominently on the coinage of Epidaurus: e.g., *RPC*, vol. 4, nos. 4638, 7939 (Antoninus Pius). **τοῦ Ἀθήνῃσιν Ὀλυμπίου Διὸς:** gen. with ἀποδεῖ (v. *LSJ* ἀποδέω B). For this statue, see 1.18.6. **ἥμισυ:** acc. of extent; literally, "the statue falls short of . . . by half." **Θρασυμήδην Ἀριγνώτου Πάριον:** the 4th c. BCE sculptor Thrasymedes was famous for this work in particular. His statue was so strongly inspired by Phidias' statue of Zeus at Olympia that Athenagoras attributed Thrasymedes' statue to Phidias too (MT 301). **τὴν δὲ ἑτέραν τῶν χειρῶν:** i.e., the one not holding the staff. **Βελλεροφόντου τὸ ἐς τὴν Χίμαιραν:** this was the Corinthian hero Bellerophontes' greatest deed. The creature is described at *Iliad* 6.179–82 and *Theogony* 319–25 as having a lion front, goat middle, and snake end. **τοῦ ναοῦ:** this is P.'s sole mention of the temple, a peripteral Doric structure with 6 × 11 columns and a cellathat was distyle *in antis* and was decorated with 7 × 4 columns on three sides. It was the work of the architect Theodorus ca. 380–370 BCE. P. does not mention the pediment sculptures designed by Timotheus, depicting the Amazonomachy on the W side and the capture of Troy on the E (MT 301). **(ὁ χῶρος) ἔνθα οἱ ἱκέται τοῦ θεοῦ καθεύδουσιν:** ill worshippers slept in a portico with two aisles N of the temple, in hopes of receiving a vision of Asclepius and instructions from the god about the treatment of their ailment (MT 301–2).

2.27.3 Θόλος: this building was a circular peripteral edifice with 26 Doric columns and had a cella decorated with 14 Corinthian columns. It was built ca. 360–330 BCE, on the plans of Polycleitus. The purpose of the building is unclear: it may have been a heroon (MT 302). The building is SW of the temple of Asclepius (Frazer 3.245). **Παυσίου γράψαντος:** Pausias was a famous Greek painter from Sicyon who lived in the first half of the 4th c. BCE. Pliny the Elder, who says that Pausias was the first to paint ceilings, gives many details of the painter's life and works at *NH* 35.40. According to MT (302), Pausias' paintings were probably small pinakes painted in encaustic, rather than ceiling paintings. **ἀφεικὼς:** < ἀφίημι, perf. act. participle. **Παυσίου καὶ τοῦτο ἔργον (γράψαντος)** **ὑαλίνης φιάλης . . . φιάλην . . . ὑάλου:** *variatio.* **ἴδοις δὲ κἂν . . . πρόσωπον:** note P.'s attention to this small detail of the painting. **στῆλαι:** Strabo 8.6.15 mentions these too. Epigraphical evidence generally agrees with P.'s description (Frazer 3.248–51). **εἱστήκεσαν:** < ἵστημι, pluperf. act. indicative. **τὸ μὲν ἀρχαῖον:** "in ancient times" (v. *LSJ* III). **ἀκεσθέντων:** < ἀκέομαι, aor. passive participle.

2.27.4 ἵππους . . . εἴκοσι: hyperbaton. **Ἀρικιεῖς:** Aricia was an ancient Latin town (now Ariccia just S of Rome); Romans later identified Hippolytus with a local god, Virbius, who was a favorite of Diana (the Roman counterpart of Artemis), and they had a sanctuary of Diana Nemorensis below Aricia on Lake Nemi. **ἀνέστησεν:** "he raised (him) from the dead" (v. *LSJ* ἀνίστημι A.I.3). See commentary on 2.26.5. **ἐβίω:** < βιόω, imperf. act. indicative. **νέμειν . . . συγγνώμην:** "to grant pardon" (v. *LSJ* συγγνώμη 1.a). **ἱερᾶσθαι τῇ θεῷ τὸν νικῶντα:** this acc. and infinitive clause explains what the ἆθλα were. The winner became the *rex Nemorensis* (MT 303). **ἐλευθέρων:** partitive gen. with οὐδένι. **προέκειτο:** "(the contest) is proposed" (v. *LSJ* I.3.b). **ἀποδρᾶσι:** < ἀποδιδράσκω, aor. act. participle.

2.27.5 Ἐπιδαυρίοις δέ ἐστι θέατρον ἐν τῷ ἱερῷ μάλιστα ἐμοὶ δοκεῖν θέας ἄξιον: the theater at Epidaurus is widely regarded as the most beautiful and best-preserved Greek theater from antiquity. It was built around the mid-4th c. BCE, with 21 rows added above the cavea and with rooms added to the scaena ca. 170–160 BCE (MT 303–4; Frazer 3.251–55). **ὑπερῆρκε:** < ὑπεραίρω, perf. act. indicative intransitive; this verb takes a gen. of comparison and a dat. of respect (S 1516). **τὰ μὲν γὰρ Ῥωμαίων (θέατρα) . . . τῶν πανταχοῦ τῷ κοσμῷ (θεάτρων)** **Ἀρκάδων τὸ ἐν Μεγάλῃ πόλει:** cf. 8.32.1. **ἀρχιτέκτων ποῖος . . . γένοιτο ἂν ἀξιοχρέως:** P. indulges here in a rhetorical question. **Πολύκλειτος:** probably Polycleitus the Younger. **οἴκημα τὸ περιφερὲς:** i.e., the Tholos at 2.27.3. **ναός . . . Ἀρτέμιδος:** this was a prostyle hexastyle Doric temple 30 meters SE of the temple of Asclepius. The cella had Corinthian columns on three sides. The temple is dated to the end of the 4th c. BCE (MT 304). **ἄγαλμα Ἠπιόνης:** Epione was the wife of Asclepius, as P. reveals at 2.29.1. Its location has not yet been securely identified (MT 304). **Ἀφροδίτης ἱερὸν:** this probably is the ruined prostyle tetrastyle temple found in the N sector of the sanctuary; it has been dated to the end of the 4th c. BCE (MT 304). **Θέμιδος (ἱερόν):** this has not yet been securely identified (MT 304). **(τοῖον) στάδιον, οἷα Ἕλλησι τὰ πολλὰ γῆς χῶμα:** "(such) a stadium like most Greek stadia (are)—a bank of earth." This stadium is SW of the sanctuary and was probably built in the 4th c. BCE (MT 304). **κρήνη:** a "fountain house." This is probably the great fountain with columns placed at the W end of the great portico N of the *peribolos*. It is of Roman date (MT 304–5). **τῷ τε ὀρόφῳ καὶ κόσμῳ τῷ λοιπῷ:** dat. of cause (S 1517).

2.27.6 ὁπόσα . . . ἐποίησεν: P. lists the donations of Antoninus to Epidaurus. **Ἀντωνῖνος ἀνὴρ τῆς συγκλήτου βουλῆς:** P. is referring here to Sextus Julius Maior Antoninus Pythodorus, a Roman senator from Nysa, on the Meander in Asia Minor (Habicht 1998, 10). MT (305) speculates that the senator was an acquaintance of P. A descendant of King Polemo of Pontus and honored as a benefactor of Epidaurus and Pergamum, Antoninus is recorded as appearing in a dream that Aelius Aristides had about nymphs (Or. 23.281), so he belonged to the same cultural circle as P. in the years 140–60 CE (MT 305). **Ἀσκληπιοῦ λουτρόν:** this building lies just E of the portico of Cotys and near the sanctuary of Apollo Maleates, known from an inscription as also being a gift of Antoninus (MT 305). **θεῶν οὓς Ἐπιδώτας:** Sleep received this epithet at 2.10.2. It is unclear which deities this shrine honored, but MT (305–6) argues that the gods here are Apollo Maleates, Asclepius, and the Asclepiadae and that this temple is a small distyle shrine with a covered court. **Ὑγείᾳ ναὸν καὶ Ἀσκληπιῷ καὶ Ἀπόλλωνι ἐπίκλησιν Αἰγυπτίοις:** the reasons behind these epithets are unknown. This shrine has not yet been identified (MT 306). **στοὰ καλουμένη Κότυος:** Antoninus was related to the royal family of Thrace, several of the kings of which bore the name *Cotys*, and this was the reason for his restoration of the structure (Habicht 1998, 10 n. 53). This is probably the large stoa at the extreme N end of the *temenos* (MT 305). **καταρρυέντος:** < καταρρέω, aor. passive participle. **ὠμῆς τῆς πλίνθου:** "unbaked brick" (v. *LSJ* ὠμός I.5), which is more susceptible to the elements than the baked version. **ἀνῳκοδόμησε:** "he rebuilt" (v. *LSJ* II). **ἐταλαιπώρουν:** "they were distressed that . . ." (S 2247–48). **ὅτι μήτε αἱ γυναῖκες . . . ἔτικτον:** a causal clause with ὅτι usually takes the negative οὐ. The negative here may be due to the emotional character of the verb. **ὁ δὲ . . . :** i.e., the senator Antoninus. **καὶ ἀποθανεῖν ἀνθρώπῳ καὶ τεκεῖν γυναικὶ ὅσιον:** P. stated the prohibitions at 2.27.1. P. highlights the act of a benefactor that respects the religious rules of the place.

2.27.7 τὸ . . . Τίτθιον: P. mentioned this mountain and the reason for its renaming at 2.26.4. It is to the N of the sanctuary. **ἕτερον ὀνομαζόμενον Κυνόρτιον:** this mountain lies E of the sanctuary. **Μαλεάτου . . . Ἀπόλλωνος ἱερὸν:** the meaning of the epithet is unknown but may be connected to Malus from Isyllus' paean to Apollo; see commentary on 2.26.3. This temple is distyle *in antis*, with an adyton and a stoa of the 4th c. BCE. Antoninus added baths, a cistern, and a fountain (MT 306). **ἔλυτρον κρήνης:** "the reservoir (of the fountain)" (v. *LSJ* ἔλυτρον 5). **τὸ ὕδωρ . . . τὸ ἐκ τοῦ θεοῦ:** i.e., rainwater.

2.28.1 δράκοντες δὲ οἱ λοιποὶ καὶ ἕτερον γένος: a variation on the usual ἄλλοι καὶ . . . **ἕτερον γένος . . . τῆς χρόας:** "another kind (of serpent) whose color inclines more yellow." **ῥέπον:** present act. participle modifying ἕτερον γένος. **τρέφει δὲ μόνη σφᾶς ἡ τῶν Ἐπιδαυρίων γῆ:** after asserting that the yellow serpents dear to Asclepius are native to Epidaurus alone, P. cites two other lands that are the sole homes for particular animals, Libya for land crocodiles and India for parrots. P.'s interest in natural history mirrors H.'s and that of imperial writers like Phlegon of Tralles and Aelian. **τὸ . . . αὐτὸ:** "the same (state of affairs)," i.e., that a species is particular to one land. **συμβεβηκός:** perf. act. participle modifying τὸ αὐτό. **μέν γε:** this pair of particles sometimes has the force of "that is to say, for example" (S 2829; D 159–61). **κροκοδείλους . . . χερσαίους διπήχεων οὐκ ἐλάσσονας:** see H. 4.192. **διπήχεων:** gen. of comparison with οὐκ ἐλάσσονας. **οἱ Ἐπιδαύριοι:** this is the subject of φασίν below; the rest of the sentence is acc. with infinitive.

Epidaurus

2.28.2 τὸ ὄρος . . . τὸ Κορυφαῖον: this has been identified as one of the heights that shut in the valley of the sanctuary on the SE and SW (MT 306). **ἐλαίας φυτόν:** i.e., an olive tree. **αἰτίου (ὄντος) τοῦ περιαγαγόντος . . . Ἡρακλέους:** gen. absolute. **Ἀσιναίοις τοῖς ἐν τῇ Ἀργολίδι:** at 2.36.4–5, P. treats Asine and explains the cause behind its deserted state. **ὅρον τοῦτον:** this marks the SE boundary of the Argolid. **εἰδείην:** < οἶδα, 2nd perf. act. optative (S 794). **ἐπεὶ μηδὲ:**

in classical Greek, causal clauses typically take a negative in οὐ. **οἷόν τε (ἐστι) . . . ἐξευρεῖν:** "it is not possible to discover," with acc. τὸ σαφές as the direct object. **τῶν ὅρων:** construe with τὸ σαφές. **Κορυφαίας . . . ἱερὸν Ἀρτέμιδος:** this has not yet been found (MT 306). **οὗ:** gen. with μνήμην. **Τελέσιλλα:** at 2.20.8–10, P. mentioned this famous Argive poetess and her heroic (and possibly fictional) defense of the city against the Spartans. **ἐποιήσατο . . . μνήμην:** = ἐμνήσατο.

2.28.3 τῶν Ἐπιδαυρίων τὴν πόλιν: the city is five miles from the sanctuary (Frazer 3.259). **Κεῖσος καὶ οἱ λοιποὶ Τημένου παῖδες:** P. explained earlier that Temenus favored his son-in-law Deiphontes over his natural sons (2.19.1) and that Deiphontes and Hyrnetho withdrew to Epidaurus after Temenus' death (2.26.2). Now P. vividly tells the dire denouement of this family's dissension. Ps.-Apollod. 2.8.5 gives the sons' names as *Agelaus*, *Eurypylus*, and *Callias*. **ᾔδεσαν:** < οἶδα, pluperf. act. indicative. **Δηιφόντην λυπήσοντες, εἰ διαλῦσαί πως ἀπ' αὐτοῦ τὴν Ὑρνηθὼ δυνηθεῖεν:** this is a future-more-vivid condition in indirect discourse. The original future indicative becomes a future participle, and the original aor. subjunctive with ἄν becomes the aor. optative without ἄν (S 2621). The verb οἶδα takes a participle in indirect discourse (S 2138). **ἐλθεῖν . . . ἐς λόγους:** "to parley" (Loeb; v. *LSJ* ἔρχομαι B.1) **δῆθεν:** this particle is "commonly used of apparent or pretended truth" (S 2850; v. also D 264–66) and is appropriate here because the conference between siblings outside the walls is merely a ruse; "pretending that . . ." (Loeb).

2.28.4 καλοῦσιν: present act. participle, dat. pl. masc. **πολλὰ μὲν . . . πολλὰ δὲ:** anaphora. **δώσειν:** verbs of promising take a future infinitive in indirect discourse (S 1868). **ἀνδρὶ:** modified by τὰ πάντα ἀμείνονι and ἄρχοντι. **Δηιφόντου:** gen. of comparison with ἀμείνονι. **ἀπεδίδου . . . τὴν ἴσην:** "she gave as good as she had received" (Loeb). **Τημένου . . . σφαγεῦσιν:** Temenus was killed by a cabal of his sons and succeeded by Ceisus, which precipitated the withdrawal to Epidaurus by Hyrnetho and Deiphontes; cf. 2.19.1. The noun is dat. because it agrees with ἐκείνοις, which is dat. with προσήκειν.

2.28.5 ἀγγέλλει τις . . . ὡς . . . οἴχοιντο: a historical present counts as a secondary tense and thus takes an optative in indirect statement (S 2627a). **ἄκουσαν:** < ἀέκων (Att. ἄκων), "unwilling." **Ὑρνηθώ:** acc. sg. fem. **ὡς τάχους εἶχεν:** "as quickly as he could" (v. *LSJ* τάχος II). **ἔδεισε, μὴ . . . γένοιτο:** the verb both sets up a clause of fearing (S 2225) and takes the infinitive βαλεῖν (S 2238); the latter explains what he feared to do, the former what he feared would happen if he did it; P. places the pivotal verb in between. **ἔδεισε:** < δείδω (S 703), aor. act. indicative. **συμπλακεὶς:** < συμπλέκω, aor. passive participle, "engaging in close fighting" (v. *LSJ* II.1). **ἀντεχόμενος:** "holding onto" (v. *LSJ* III.1).

2.28.6 (τοῖα) οἷα . . . ἔργα: "what (he had done)." **ἐξειργασμένος . . . ἦν:** periphrastic pluperf. middle indicative. **ἀφειδέστερον:** comparative adv., "more recklessly" (Loeb). **προλαβεῖν τῆς ὁδοῦ:** "to get a start on the way" (v. *LSJ* προλαμβάνω II.3). **συλλεχθῆναι:** < συλλέγω, aor. passive infinitive, "they came together" (v. *LSJ* II). **ἐγεγόνεσαν:** < γίνομαι, pluperf. act. indicative; this initiates a parenthetical sentence explaining who their children were. **Πάμφυλον τὸν Αἰγιμίου:** Aegimius, a Doric king of Thessaly who gave a third of his kingdom to Heracles in return for the latter's help against the Lapiths (ps.-Apollod. 2.7.7), had two sons, Dymas and Pamphylus, the ancestors of two of the branches of the Dorians, the third being Hyllus, Heracles' son (ps.-Apollod. 2.8.3). **Ὑρνήθιον:** P. returns to the place that precipitated the digression (2.28.3). The location is unknown (MT 307). A tribe of non-Dorians called Hyrnathioi was added to the three Dorian tribes of Argos (the Hylleis, Pamphyloi, and Dymanes) in the 7th or 6th c. BCE (Tomlinson 1983, 86).

2.28.7 τοῖς πεφυκόσιν ἐλαίοις: P. called them wild olives at 2.28.3. **καθέστηκε νόμος . . . μηδένα . . . μηδὲ . . . ἐς μηδέν:** μή is used with infinitives in prohibitions (S 2715). The compound negatives reinforce the prohibition: "custom prohibits anyone from . . ." **αὐτοῦ:** adv. **ἱερὰ:** this adj. agrees with τὰ θραυόμενα from above. **εἶναι:** infinitive of purpose, "so that they are (sacred)."

2.28.8 Μελίσσης: H. states that Periander killed his wife, Melissa (3.50–53), and was later visited by her ghost (5.92). The location of her tomb is unknown (MT 307). **Περιάνδρῳ . . . τῷ Κυψέλου:** Periander succeeded his father, Cypselus, in the tyranny of Corinth. See 2.4.4 and commentary. **Προκλέους:** according to H. (3.50–53), Procles caused Lycophron, the younger son of Periander, to be alienated from his father, and Periander attacked and captured Epidaurus and imprisoned Procles in retaliation.

2.29.1 αὐτὴ δὲ τῶν Ἐπιδαυρίων ἡ πόλις: P. now moves to the city of Epidaurus proper. **τέμενος . . . Ἀσκληπιοῦ:** the locations of all of the temples and sanctuaries named here except that of Athena Kissaia are unknown (MT 307). **εἰκάσαις ἂν:** potential optative, "you might liken to." The expression is best attested in the work of P.'s contemporary Galen and is here used differently from P.'s use at 10.29.9. I thank an anonymous reader for this information. **θηρευούσῃ:** "to a huntress," Artemis' usual manifestation. **Κισσαίαν:** "of Ivy," an epithet more appropriate for Dionysus than Athena. The image may have been made from ivy wood (Frazer 3.261). The sanctuary has been identified on the W height of the promontory and acropolis of the ancient city. Dionysus bears this epithet at Acharnae in Attica (1.31.6). See MT 307.

Myths of Aegina

2.29.2 Αἴγιναν τὴν Ἀσωποῦ: Aegina's mother was Metope (daughter of the river Ladon). Cf. ps.-Apollod. 3.12.6. **Οἰνώνης:** the bearer of this name does not appear to be related to Oenone, the lover of Paris. **Αἰακοῦ:** Aeacus was the son of Zeus and Aegina, a fact that P. assumes his readers know. **ηὐξήθη:** < αὐξάνω, aor. passive indicative, "he grew up" (v. *LSJ* II). **οἱ:** not the article but the dat. sg. 3rd-person semireflexive pronoun. **τὸν Δία ἀνεῖναι τοὺς ἀνθρώπους . . . ἐκ τῆς γῆς:** according to another version, Zeus turned the ants on the island into men, the so-called Myrmidons; cf. ps.-Apollod. 3.12.6. **βασιλεύσαντα . . . οὐδένα:** direct object of εἰπεῖν ἔχουσιν. **Πηλεῖ . . . καὶ Τελαμῶνι ἐπὶ φόνῳ . . . τῷ Φώκου:** Phocus was the son of Aeacus and the Nereid Psamathe. Aeacus favored Phocus over his two sons by Endeïs, Peleus and Telamon, who thus conspired to kill Phocus during athletic practice; P. briefly tells the tale at 2.29.10. **συμβὰν:** acc. absolute (S 2076). **τῶν . . . Φώκου παίδων:** this Phocus was the father of Panopeus and Crisus; the latter was the father of Strophius, who was the father of Pylades, Orestes' ally and friend, as P. explains at 2.29.4. This Phocus should be kept distinct from the Phocus P. identifies in the next subsection.

2.29.3 Φώκου τοῦ Ὀρνυτίωνος: P. explained at 2.4.3 that this Phocus was the son of Ornytion and the grandson of Sisyphus and migrated to Tithorea, while his brother Thoas became king of Corinth. P. covers this again at 10.1.1. **γενεᾷ:** "by a generation" or "a generation (earlier)," dat. of degree of difference (S 1513). **<ἡ> περὶ Τιθορέαν τε καὶ Παρνασσὸν (γῆ) πᾶσιν . . . ὅσοι . . . :** "for all the people who . . ." **(τὸ ὄνομα) ἐξενίκησεν:** "the name prevailed." P. treats the land of Phocis at length in book 10. The fact that he does not say he will treat Phocis elsewhere may indicate that he did not yet, at the time of the composition of this book, consider including Phocis (MT 309). **καθήκουσι:** "they reach."

2.29.4 ἀπὸ μὲν Πηλέως οἱ ἐν Ἠπείρῳ βασιλεῖς: the most famous were Peleus' son Achilles and Achilles' son Neoptolemus, or Pyrrhus. **Τελαμῶνος . . . τῶν παίδων:** Ajax and Teucer; the latter was the founder of the line of Teucridae, who rules Cyprus. **Αἴαντος . . . οἷα ἰδιωτεύσαντος ἀνθρώπου:** in fact, P. himself counts Ajax as a king of Megara at 1.42.4. P. uses the verb ἰδιωτεύειν to mean "to be a private person" (i.e., not a king) again at 4.1.2 (where Messene is not content with the status as an ἰδιώτης for her husband, Polycaon, and urges him to go and settle what became Messenia) and at 5.3.4 (neither Amarynceus nor his son Dioris are content to ἰδιωτεύειν, but Amarynceus received part of Augeas' kingdom of Elis). **Μιλτιάδης:** Miltiades led the Athenians against the Persians at Marathon in 490 BCE. **Κίμων ὁ Μιλτιάδου:** Cimon was a major Athenian politician and admiral active ca. 480–450 BCE. **προῆλθον ἐς δόξαν:** "achieved renown" (Loeb). **Εὐαγόραν:** P. is referring to Evagoras II, king of Salamis in Cyprus during 361–351 BCE. **Ἄσιος:** Asius of Samos was a Greek epic poet, probably of the 6th c. BCE. **Ἐπειὸς:** in the *Iliad* (23.664–99), Epeius defeats Euryalus in a boxing match at the funeral games of Patroclus. Homer refers to Epeius as the creator of the Trojan Horse at *Odyssey* 11.523, followed by, e.g., Stesichorus in his *Sack of Troy*. Cf. commentary on 2.19.6. **ἀπόγονος τρίτος:** i.e., grandson, counting inclusively.

2.29.5 χρόνῳ . . . ὕστερον: pleonasm. **μοῖρα . . . διαβᾶσα καὶ γενόμενοι σύνοικοι:** note the change in number for the subject. P. often views Dorization as a fusion of newcomers and old inhabitants, not as a catastrophic event (MT 309). **ὡς . . . πλεῖστα:** natural result clause. **ὡς Ἀθηναίων γενέσθαι ναυσὶν ἐπικρατεστέρους:** the Athenians and Aeginetans fought between the two Persian Wars, and the Athenians suffered a grave defeat in 488/487 BCE (MT 309). **ἐν τῷ Μηδικῷ πολέμῳ παρασχέσθαι πλοῖα μετά γε Ἀθηναίους πλεῖστα:** cf. H. 8.1, 46. **ἐς ἅπαν:** "forever." **γενόμενοι δὲ ὑπὸ Ἀθηναίων ἀνάστατοι:** this occurred in 431 BCE, at the start of the Peloponnesian War; cf. Thucydides 2.27, 4.56. The Athenians had forced the Aeginetans into the Delian League after another war, in 459–456 BCE (MT 309). **Θυρέαν:** P. briefly describes Thyrea at 2.38.5. **ὅτε περὶ Ἑλλήσποντον αἱ Ἀθηναίων τριήρεις:** the people of Aegina returned to their home after the disastrous Battle of Aegospotami in 405 BCE. **ἐξεγένετο:** < ἐκγίγνομαι, "it was not permitted (to them)" (v. *LSJ* III). **ἐς ἴσον:** "to the same degree"; construe with πλούτου and δυνάμεως.

Aegina

2.29.6 **προσπλεῦσαι:** construe with ἀπορωτάτη, an infinitive with adj. (S 2001). **νήσων τῶν Ἑλληνίδων:** partitive gen. **χοιράδες:** "sunken rocks" (v. *LSJ* I.2). **ληστειῶν:** objective gen. with φόβῳ. **φόβῳ:** dat. of cause (S 1517). **καὶ πολεμίοις ἀνδράσι μὴ ἄνευ κινδύνου εἶναι:** μή is not typically used in indirect discourse unless with an idea of hoping or believing (S 2725); "and wished the approach to be perilous to enemies" (Loeb). Note also the litotes. **πλησίον δὲ τοῦ λιμένος:** Aegina had two harbors, a military one on the N end of the island and a commercial one to the SE. P. is referring here to the commercial one (MT 309). **ναός . . . Ἀφροδίτης:** although the sanctuary has not yet been discovered, archaeologists have found a votive anchor for Aphrodite Epilimenia (MT 310). **τὸ Αἰάκειον:** P. now moves to the acropolis (modern Capo Colonna), to the shrine of Aeacus, the center of the Aeacia festival. It has been identified with the remains of a square enclosure on the S side of the temple of Apollo; it dates to ca. 490 BCE (MT 310).

2.29.7 **ἐπειργασμένοι . . . εἰσι:** periphrastic perf. passive indicative. **σταλέντες:** < στέλλω, aor. passive participle. **αὐχμὸς:** see 1.44.9. Ps.-Apollod. 3.12.6 explains the drought as divine anger for Pelops killing King Stymphalus of Arcadia through trickery. **ἐπὶ χρόνον:** "for some time." **ἐς ὅ:** "until." **ἐρησομένους:** < ἐρέω (A), future middle participle, showing purpose. **ὅ τι εἴη (τὸ αἴτιον):** indirect question with indefinite relative (S 2664). **χρῆναι δέ, εἴπερ ὑπακούσει σφίσιν, Αἰακὸν τὸν ἱκετεύσοντα εἶναι:** "and it was necessary that if in fact Zeus would listen to them (at all), Aeacus would be the one to supplicate (for them)."

2.29.8 **δεησομένους:** < δέω (B), future middle participle, again for purpose. **τῶν . . . ἐλθόντων:** construe with εἰκόνας ταύτας. **ὡς αὐτόν:** improper preposition with the acc. (S 1702). **ὡς . . . εἴη Αἰάκου:** indirect statement with λεγόμενόν ἐστιν. **ἐν ἀπορρήτῳ:** "secretly" (v. *LSJ* II.1).

2.29.9 **Φώκου τάφος:** the grave of Aeacus' son. The tomb has been identified in the base of a mound seven meters in diameter dated to the end of the 6th c. BCE. It lies to the NW of the temple of Apollo (MT 310). **κύκλῳ:** "in a circle" (v. *LSJ* I.2). **ἡνίκα Φῶκον Τελαμὼν καὶ Πηλεὺς προηγάγοντο:** P. now describes the murder he mentioned at 2.29.2. **ἀφεῖναι:** < ἀφίημι, 2nd aor. act. infinitive. **Σκίρωνος θυγατρός:** i.e., Endeïs, whom P. only names at 2.29.10. At 1.44.8, P. identifies Sciron as a robber defeated by Theseus on his way to Athens. But several times in his description of the Megarid (1.39.6, 1.44.6), P. also mentions a Megarian warlord with the name *Sciron*, the son of King Pylas. Cf. the Megarian tradition, given by Plutarch (*Life of Theseus* 10), that Endeïs was the daughter of Sciron and Chariclo. **ἀδελφῆς Θέτιδος:** according to one report, both Thetis and Psamathe were Nereids. Thetis became the mother of Achilles by Peleus. **Πυλάδης τέ μοι καὶ διὰ ταῦτα:** Pylades was the great-grandson of Phocus, according to 2.29.4, just as Neoptolemus was the grandson of Peleus. **Νεοπτολέμῳ:** Menelaus' daughter Hermione was betrothed to Orestes and Neoptolemus, the son of Achilles; sources vary over the details of Neoptolemus' death.

2.29.10 τῷ δίσκῳ: this is a slight mistake, since P. just stated in the last subsection that the brothers used a stone instead of a quoit. **φεύγουσιν . . . οἱ Ἐνδηίδος παῖδες:** Telamon fled to Salamis, Peleus went to Phthia, and each became king of their respective new homes. **νεὼς:** < ναῦς, gen. sg. fem. (S 275), the gen. object of ἐπιβάντες. **ὕστερα:** adverbial acc., "later." **ἠρνεῖτο μὴ βουλεῦσαι:** a verb of denial with a redundant μή (S 2740). **εἰ . . . ἐθέλοι:** protasis of a condition in indirect discourse after ἐκέλευσεν. **ἀπολογήσασθαι:** MT (311) notes that this unusual method of adjudication mirrors how P. describes events at Phreattys in Athens (1.28.11). P. explains how Telamon blamed Teucer for the death of Ajax, Teucer's half brother, and refused to allow him to land on Salamis, so Teucer pled his case from a boat; when his return was denied, he sailed to Cyprus and founded the city of Salamis there. **τὸν Κρυπτὸν καλούμενον:** i.e., the military harbor. **καταγνωσθεὶς . . . τελευτῆς:** "condemned as not guiltless in Phocus' death." **τῆς τελευτῆς:** gen. with ἀναίτιος. **τὸ δεύτερον:** "a second time."

2.29.11 θέατρόν: the theater lies in view of this port; parts of the steps were reused in a late Roman wall (MT 311). **κατὰ τὸ Ἐπιδαυρίων (θέατρον):** κατά with the acc. for comparisons (v. *LSJ* B.IV.3). **μέγεθος καὶ ἐργασίαν τὴν λοιπήν:** acc. of respect. **σταδίου:** a trace of the racecourse has been found E of the theater, and blocks from its seats were reused in a late Roman wall (MT 311). **ἀντὶ ἐρείσματος:** "as a support" (v. *LSJ* ἀντί A.III.2). **ἀνάλογον:** adverbial acc., "in return."

2.30.1 ναοὶ: the temple of Apollo, a peripteral Doric building with 6 × 11 columns and a *pronaos* and *opisthodomus* that is distyle *in antis*, lies on the top of Capo Colonna. Built ca. 600 BCE, the temple was rebuilt ca. 520–510 BCE, in Late Archaic Doric with pediment sculptures. Two small temples lie to the W (MT 310–11). **ὁ μὲν Ἀπόλλωνός . . . ὁ δὲ Ἀρτέμιδος, Διονύσῳ**

δὲ αὐτῶν ὁ τρίτος: P.'s typical avoidance of parallelism. **Ἀπόλλωνι . . . ξόανον γυμνόν . . . τέχνης τῆς ἐπιχωρίου:** P.'s artistic judgments are typically laconic. What characteristics possessed by this statue led him to this judgment? **τοῦ . . . Ἀσκληπιοῦ τὸ ἱερὸν:** the cult of Asclepius was imported from Epidaurus and located outside the city, like the cult of Hecate (MT 311).

2.30.2 τελετὴν . . . Ἑκάτης: hyperbaton. **Ὀρφέα . . . τὸν Θρᾷκα:** Orpheus, the mythical Greek bard. **Μύρωνος:** a native of Eleutherae, Myron flourished ca. 460 BCE and was an older contemporary of Phidias and Polyclitus. He generally worked in bronze; the *xoanon* here is an anomaly. Cf. Pliny the Elder *NH* 34.5. MT (312) suggests that P. wrongly attributed the *xoanon* to Myron instead of Micon, the father of Onatas of Aegina. **Ἀλκαμένης:** Alcamenes was a contemporary of Pheidias. P. notes a statue of Ares by him in the Athenian agora (1.8.4) and credits him with a pediment on the temple of Zeus at Olympia (5.10.8). **Ἐπιπυργιδίαν:** "on the Tower" (v. *LSJ* ἐπιπυργιδία, where this passage is cited). **τῆς Ἀπτέρου Νίκης:** P. mentions this temple in his description of the Athenian Acropolis at 1.22.4. **τὸν ναόν:** this is not the direct object of ἕστηκε but the object of παρά.

2.30.3 τὸ ὄρος τοῦ Πανελληνίου Διὸς: at 2.29.8, P. reports that Aeacus sacrificed to Panhellenic Zeus to end a great drought. P. describes the shrine for Zeus Panhellenios in 2.30.4. The mountain is called Oros (MT 311). **Ἀφαίας ἱερόν:** the goddess Aphaia was worshipped at this site since prehistoric times and was connected with Diktynna and Britomartis and later with Athena too. Consequently, the site has a complicated material history. An *oikos* with an *adyton* and double-columned interior was built at the end of the 7th c. BCE. A second building that enclosed the *oikos* is dated to 570 BCE; it was a peripteral Doric temple with 6 × 12 columns, a columned interior, and a *pronaos* and *opisthodomus in antis*. This temple was enclosed in a polygonal *temenos* with a *propylaeum* and altar. A third building was built ca. 500 BCE with similar dimensions to the last, but it had an enlarged *peribolos* with a propylaeum and service annexes, a large altar, and marble pediments and *acroteria*, which were made between 490 and 480 BCE. The W and E pediments show the second and first expeditions against Troy respectively (MT 312–13). **Πίνδαρος ᾆσμα Αἰγινήταις ἐποίησε:** nothing of this hymn survives (fr. 89b Snell). **Καρμάνορος τοῦ καθήραντος Ἀπόλλωνα ἐπὶ φόνῳ τῷ Πύθωνος:** at 2.7.7, P. explained how Apollo and Athena went to Aegialea first but then sought purification from Carmanor in Crete. Construe this gen. phrase with the παῖδα following. **Βριτόμαρτιν:** Diodorus Siculus (5.76.3) gives a similar genealogy for Britomartis but adds that Eubulus was the son of Demeter. **Μίνω:** acc. sg. masc. (S 267). **δίκτυα:** although P. does not make this explicit, this is the etymology for the name that Britomartis bears in Crete, *Dictynna*. **ἀφειμένα:** < ἀφίημι, perf. passive participle. Although P. does not make this explicit, this is the etymology of the name that Britomartis bears in Aegina, *Aphaea*. **ἰχθύων:** objective gen. of θήρᾳ.

2.30.4 τὸ δὲ Πανελλήνιον . . . τὸ ὄρος: Mt. Oros. **ὅτι μή:** "except." **ἄλλο . . . ἀξιόλογον . . . οὐδέν:** hyperbaton. This phrase is interlaced with τὸ . . . Πανελλήνιον . . . τὸ ὄρος, but complete confusion is prevented by the meaning of the sentence and by the placement of the article between ἄλλο and ὄρος, for the former is never separated from its noun by an article. **τὴν Αὐξησίαν καὶ Δαμίαν:** these two deities appear to be related to Demeter. P. gives a different account of them at 2.32.2. **ἐκ μαντείας:** "in obedience to an oracle." **ἐλαίας:** gen. of material with τὰ ξόανα ταῦτα. **ἀπέφερον:** "they were paying tribute" (v. *LSJ* II.2). **ἃ ἐτάξαντο:** "what they had been assigned to pay" (v. *LSJ* III.3). **οἷα Αἰγινητῶν ἐχόντων τὰ ἀγάλματα:** P. omits the fact that the Aeginetans revolted from Epidaurian control and stole the statues, which they set up at Oea on Aegina. οἷα frames "the cause as a fact on the authority of the speaker or writer" (S 2085). **Ἀθηναίων δὲ ἀπώλοντο οἱ διαβάντες διὰ ταῦτα ἐς Αἴγιναν:** in the Athenian version of the story, the Athenians sent a trireme to steal the statues because the Aeginetans refused their request to give them up, but the men sent were unable to move the statues off their bases and were so maddened by a thunderstorm and earthquake that they slew each other. Only one of the men returned to Athens. The Aeginetans, however, say that with the aid of the Argives, they fought off a large invasion by the Athenians. **ταῦτα εἰπόντος Ἡροδότου καθ' ἕκαστον αὐτῶν ἐπ' ἀκριβὲς:** cf. H. 5.82–87 for many details about this incident and its curious connection to Athenian fashion. The incident probably occurred ca. 506 BCE (MT 313). The demonstrative pronoun sums up the three previous ὡς clauses. **οὔ μοι γράφειν κατὰ γνώμην ἦν εὖ προειρημένα:** "it was not my intention to write . . ." (v. *LSJ* γνώμη III.5). **πλὴν τοσοῦτό γε:** "but only this: . . ." **τὰ ἀγάλματα:** the sanctuary of the two goddesses was in Oea, about three kilometers W of the city (MT 314). **Ἐλευσῖνι:** adv., "at Eleusis."

Myths of Troezen

2.30.5 Αἰγίνης . . . μνήμη: hyperbaton; P. formally transitions to Troezen. **Αἰακοῦ . . . καὶ ἔργων:** both are objects of the preposition ἕνεκα. **σεμνύνοντες εἴπερ καὶ ἄλλοι τινὲς τὰ ἐγχώρια:** "the Troezenians boast of their land if ever any people has." **Ὧρον:** an autochthonous figure. He and his son Althepus are otherwise unknown. **ἐμοὶ . . . Αἰγύπτιον φαίνεται καὶ οὐδαμῶς Ἑλληνικὸν ὄνομα:** P. shares H.'s tendency to interpret Greek antiquities in an Egyptian light (MT 314).

2.30.6 ἀμφισβητῆσαι . . . ἀμφισβητήσαντας: pseudanaphora. Poseidon enters another contest for guardianship of a Greek land but with a better outcome. **Πολιάδα καὶ Σθενιάδα:** the Athenians also worshipped Athena Polias (1.27.1–3). At 2.32.7 and 2.34.6, P. notes that Zeus bore the epithet Σθένιος. **νόμισμα . . . τὸ ἀρχαῖον:** these coins still survive. E.g., a coin from the 5th c. BCE shows a helmeted head of Athena on the obverse and the head of a trident on the reverse (*Sylloge Nummorum Graecorum,* vol. 7, no. 1126). Plutarch (*Life of Theseus* 6) also mentions a trident on Aeginetan coins. **ἐπίσημα:** object complement of τρίαιναν καὶ Ἀθηνᾶς πρόσωπον.

2.30.7 ἐπιπολῆς: adv., "on the surface," hence "shallow." **ὥστε καὶ Φοιβαία λίμνη διὰ τοῦτο ἐκαλεῖτο:** it is unclear what the reason for the name here was. It has been identified as the lagoon at the head of the bay of Methana (Frazer 3.272; MT 314–15). **Σάρωνα . . . διώκοντα:** hyperbaton; P. shifts the main actor of the sentence to the front and imposes a parenthetical sentence directly afterward. **ᾕρητο:** < αἱρέω, pluperf. middle indicative, "he preferred" (v. *LSJ* B.2.I.b). "Now he was very fond (of hunting)" (Loeb). **κατέλαβεν:** impersonal verb, "it happened that," with acc. and infinitive construction (v. *LSJ* II.3). **ἐπέλαβε τὸ χρεών:** "fate overtook him," i.e., he died. **Σαρωνίδα . . . τὴν ταύτῃ θάλασσαν:** i.e., the Saronic Gulf.

2.30.8 Ὑπέρητος καὶ Ἄνθα: both are gen. sg. masc. with ἄχρι. **Ἀλκυόνης:** Alcyone was the daughter of Atlas and Pleione (daughter of Oceanus), hence a Pleiad. **τοῦ πατρὸς καὶ τοῦ θείου:** construe with τὴν ἀρχήν. **τὴν ἑτέραν:** direct object of ὀνόμασαι. **Τροίζηνος . . . καὶ Πιτθέως:** Troezen and Pittheus, the sons of Pelops, came from Pisa in Elis. It is unclear why Aëtius shared his rule of the two cities with them. Cf. Strabo 8.6.14. **ἴσχυον . . . μᾶλλον:** "they had more power."

2.30.9 σημεῖον δέ: i.e., evidence of their power. **<ἐς> τὴν νῦν πόλιν συναγαγὼν τοὺς ἀνθρώπους:** i.e., synoecism. **πολλοῖς . . . ἔτεσιν:** dat. of degree of difference with ὕστερον. **ἐς ἀποικίαν . . . ἀπῴκισαν . . . μετοικοῦσιν:** P. uses words with the same base, οἰκ-. **σταλέντες:** construe with οἱ γεγονότες ἀπ' Ἀετίου τοῦ Ἄνθα. **Ἁλικαρνασσὸν:** H. (7.99.3) agrees with P. in this, but other sources report that the Argives colonized Halicarnassus (MT 315). **Ἀνάφλυστος καὶ Σφῆττος . . . οἱ δῆμοι τὰ ὀνόματα ἔχουσιν ἀπὸ τούτων:** The demes Anaphlystus and Sphettus belonged to the tribes Antiochis and Acamantis respectively. **εἰδόσι:** < οἶδα, perf. act. participle. It takes τὰ ἐς αὐτὸν as its object. **τὰ ἐς αὐτὸν οὐ γράφω:** P. naturally covered most of Theseus' life and deeds in book 1. P. does not give an explicit cross-reference here as he does at 2.31.2.

2.30.10 συνοίκους Δωριέων τῶν ἐξ Ἄργους: another instance of the blending of pre-Doric and Doric elements in a city (MT 315). **Ὅμηρος ἐν καταλόγῳ φησὶν:** i.e., at *Iliad* 2.559–68. **Διομήδης . . . καὶ Εὐρύαλος:** both were among the Epigoni who captured Thebes. **Κυάνιππον τὸν Αἰγιαλέως:** P. mentioned Cyanippus at 2.18.4–5. **Σθένελος δέ, ὡς ἐδήλωσα ἐν τοῖς πρότερον:** Sthenelus was the son of Capaneus and succeeded Iphis as king of Argos (2.18.5); his son Cylarabes became king too. **οἰκίας . . . ἐπιφανεστέρας:** gen. of origin (S 1298); i.e., the family of Anaxagoridae. **προσήκουσα:** "belonging to," with dat. (v. *LSJ* III.1). **τοσαῦτα Τροιζηνίοις ἐχόμενα ἱστορίας:** P. transitions from the historical précis on Troezen to the monuments on the ground. **παρὲξ ἤ:** "except for" (v. *LSJ* παρέκ B.4). **ὅσα ἄλλα ἐς ἐπίδειξιν:** another way of saying θέας ἄξια or ἀξιόλογα. **τὸ ἐντεῦθεν:** superfluous article.

Troezen

2.31.1 ἐν τῇ ἀγορᾷ Τροιζηνίων: this is generally located just N of the Hellenistic wall (MT 315). **ναὸς καὶ ἀγάλματα Ἀρτέμιδός . . . Σωτείρας:** this probably lies on the E side of the agora (MT 316). **Ἀστερίωνα τὸν Μίνω:** in archaic lyric, it is the name of Europa's spouse, a king of Crete who predates Minos. Lycophron 1301 and ps.-Apollod. 3.1.4 make Asterion the Minotaur (MT 316). **τῶν κατειργασμένων:** = τῶν ἔργων. **ἀνδρείᾳ:** dat. of respect, "in strength." **τό . . . τοῦ λαβυρίνθου δυσέξοδον:** "the difficulty he faced in exiting the Labyrinth." **<τὸ> λαθόντα ἀποδρᾶναι μετὰ τὸ ἔργον:** articular infinitive with an acc. subject. **ὡς προνοίᾳ θείᾳ καὶ αὐτὸς ἀνασωθείη Θησεὺς καὶ οἱ σὺν αὐτῷ:** indirect statement explaining what the εἰκὼς ὁ λόγος was. **οἱ σὺν αὐτῷ:** i.e., Ariadne (Minos' daughter who assisted Theseus in escaping) and the Athenian tributes, seven young men and seven maidens.

2.31.2 θεῶν τῶν λεγομένων ὑπὸ γῆν ἄρχειν: it is unclear which deities P. includes here besides Hades. **ἐξ Ἅιδου Σεμέλην τε ὑπὸ Διονύσου**

κομισθῆναι: Semele died in a blast of fire when Zeus revealed his divine form to her, but their child, Dionysus, fetched her from Hades later, and she was deified as Thyone. Cf. 2.37.5; ps.-Apollod. 3.4.3, 3.5.3. **τὸν κύνα τοῦ Ἅιδου:** i.e., Cerberus, one of Heracles' Twelve Labors. **οὐδὲ . . . ἀρχὴν:** "absolutely not." **τὰ δὲ ἐς τὸν ὀνομαζόμενον Ἅιδου κύνα ἑτέρωθι ἔσται μοι δῆλα ὁποῖα εἶναί μοι δοκεῖ:** P. is referring to 3.25.5–6.

2.31.3 **δικάζειν:** "(they) sat in judgment." **ἄνδρας δύο:** his brother Troezen and the native ruler Aëtius, who P. said shared power (2.30.8). **λέγουσιν . . . ἔλεγον . . . νομίζουσι . . . φασί . . . φασιν . . . λέγοντες:** P. repeatedly emphasizes the local sources of his information in this subsection. **ἱερὸν Μουσῶν:** this sanctuary lies on the S side of the agora (MT 316). **Ἄρδαλον παῖδα Ἡφαίστου:** Ardalus is named by Plutarch (149f–150a) as one of the Seven Wise Men (MT 316). **τι βιβλίον Πιτθέως δὴ σύγγραμμα:** this could be a use of the ironical δή (S 2842). **ἐκδοθὲν:** "published" (v. *LSJ* ἐκδίδωμι I.7). MT (316–17) takes this as an instance of the limits of P.'s critical spirit and as evidence of P.'s overly favorable view of the Troezenians because of their long ties with Athens. **ἐπελεξάμην:** "I read over" (v. *LSJ* III.2). P. occasionally mentions his reading of monographs written by his subjects (at 1.12.2, he says that he read the *Memoirs* of King Pyrrhus of Epirus). It is curious that P. says nothing about the quality of the book here ascribed to Pittheus. **Ὕπνῳ θύουσι:** at 2.10.2, P. noted a statue of Sleep Epidotes near the sanctuary of Asclepius at Sicyon. Sleep is usually described as the brother of Death (Hesiod *Theogony* 211).

2.31.4 **τοῦ θεάτρου:** the theater lies on the slope of the acropolis, next to the sanctuary of the Muses (MT 316). **Λυκείας ναὸν Ἀρτέμιδος:** Apollo bears the epithet Λύκιος, perhaps related, at 2.9.7 and 2.19.3–4. This temple lies on the W side of the agora (MT 316). **Ἱππόλυτος:** at 1.22.2, P. mentions a grave of Hippolytus at Troezen and explains that Theseus sent his son there to be raised by Pittheus to be king of that city. **παρὰ τῶν ἐξηγητῶν:** "from the local guides." P. is left to his own deductions. **ἐξελεῖν:** < ἐξαιρέω, 2nd aor. act. infinitive. **παρ' ὧν τὰ πρὸς μητρὸς ἦν:** "from whom he was descended through his mother" (Loeb), πρός with gen. for descent (S 1695.1b). Hippolytus' mother was the Amazon Antiope, according to 1.2.1. **εἴη δ' ἂν ἔτι καὶ ἄλλο οὐ γινωσκόμενον ὑπὸ ἐμοῦ:** P. modestly admits there may be other explanations. **ποτε ἄνδρες Τροιζηνίων ἐννέα Ὀρέστην ἐκάθηραν ἐπὶ τῷ φόνῳ τῆς μητρός:** several spots in Greece and beyond claimed to be the site of Orestes' purification for the murder of Clytemnestra: e.g., Delphi, Thrace, Cilicia, Comana in Cappadocia, and Athens. The Troezenians, however, have the "booth of Orestes"; cf. 2.31.8 (MT 319; Frazer 3.276–79). **ἐκάθηραν:** < καθαίρω, aor. act. indicative.

2.31.5 Σαώτου: poetic for Σωτήρ. **Θεμίδων:** a plural manifestation of Themis, the goddess of order, law, and custom. **Ἡλίου . . . Ἐλευθερίου:** this cult is well attested in the Peloponnese, from Corinth to Hermione and especially at Rhodes (MT 317). **εἰκότι λόγῳ:** "for a plausible reason." **δουλείαν ἀπὸ Ξέρξου τε καὶ Περσῶν:** "slavery at the hands of Xerxes and the Persians" (S 1684.1c.2); i.e., during the Second Persian War, in 480–79 BCE. At 2.31.7, P. comments more on Troezen's important role in this conflict.

2.31.6 τὸ . . . ἱερὸν τοῦ Ἀπόλλωνος τοῦ Θεαρίου: this shrine was probably also on the W side of the agora (MT 316). **ἀρχαῖος μὲν . . . ἀρχαῖος δὲ:** anaphora. **Ἅρπαγός . . . ὁ Μῆδος:** Harpagus and the Persians seized Phocaea, but only after the inhabitants of the city sailed off to avoid subjection to the Persians. See H. 1.164ff. for the travails and travels of the Phocaeans. **πλὴν:** simple conjunction, "but." **Αὐλίσκου:** nothing else is known of this Auliscus. **Ἕρμωνος Τροιζηνίου:** this artist is probably archaic, because of the *xoana*. These figures of the Dioscuri appear on coinage of Troezen in the age of Commodus (MT 318; Frazer 3.276).

2.31.7 ἐν στοᾷ τῆς ἀγορᾶς: this stoa forms the N side of the agora (MT 316). **ἃς Ἀθηναῖοι Τροιζηνίοις γυναῖκας καὶ τέκνα ἔδωκαν σῴζειν:** when the Persians advanced in the fall of 480 BCE and razed Thespiae and Plataea, the Athenians were forced to abandon Athens. H. 7.141ff. says it was an emergency action, but the so-called Decree of Themistocles states that the evacuation was planned in advance. A copy of this decree from the 4th or 3rd c. BCE (*SEG* XVIII 153, XXIX 376) was found in the NW corner of the agora. This decree may represent a rapprochement between Athens and Troezen, which were estranged for most of the 5th c. BCE after the Persian Wars (MT 318–19). **ἀρέσαν:** < ἀρέσκω, aor. act. participle, acc. sg. neut.; P. employs this form here as an acc. absolute: "when they resolved to . . ." (Loeb; v. *LSJ* IV). **μηδὲ:** the use of μή here is appropriate due to the presence of ἀρέσκω, a verb of will. **στρατῷ πεζῷ:** the use of the adj. here is not superfluous (v. *LSJ* στρατός 1), especially since the Athenians would soon meet the Persians on the sea with their στρατὸς ναυτικός. **οὐ γὰρ δὴ πολλαί τινες ἐκεῖναι:** the indefinite adj./pronoun τις can be used with other pronouns; "for those (statues) are not numerous." **τούτων:** this pronoun refers to ὁπόσαι δὲ ἀξιώματι προεῖχον—i.e., the noble women—and is modified by the μόνων at the end.

2.31.8 τοῦ . . . ἱεροῦ τοῦ Ἀπόλλωνος . . . ἔμπροσθεν: hyperbaton. **ἐπὶ τῷ αἵματι . . . τῆς μητρός:** variation for ἐπὶ τῷ φόνῳ τῆς μητρός at 2.31.4. **πρότερον:** this adv. serves as a forerunner of the πρίν clause (S 2440), although P. places it afterward. **ἀφήγνισαν:** "they had finished purification" (Loeb). Cf. 2.31.4 for the purification of Orestes at Troezen. **αὐτῶν:** this pronoun resumes τῶν καθαρσίων from the gen. absolute at the start of the sentence.

2.31.9 καθαρσίοις καὶ ἄλλοις καὶ ὕδατι: sacrificial victims and water for purification. Such rites could involve sprinkling the blood of a victim on someone. **Ἵππου κρήνης:** at 2.3.5, P. noted a fountain in Corinth where water flows through a hoof of a statue of Pegasus. Hesiod refers to another such fountain at *Theogony* 6. **Πηγάσῳ . . . τῇ ὁπλῇ:** this sentence is very intricate. καὶ οὗτοι λέγουσι sets up an indirect statement, the core of which is τὸ ὕδωρ ἀνεῖναι τὴν γῆν; the rest is a dat. phrase showing attendant circumstance. **τοῦ ἐδάφους:** gen. object of θιγόντι. **Αἴθραν:** Aethra, the daughter of Pittheus, was the wife of Aegeus (king of Athens), by whom she bore Theseus, although some report that Poseidon was Theseus' real father. **πρὶν δὲ γῆμαι:** only this infinitive belongs in the πρίν clause; the other two are in the main clause, in indirect discourse, with φυγεῖν complementing συμβῆναι. **φυγεῖν ἐκ Κορίνθου:** Bellerophon fled from Corinth because he killed his brother (ps.-Apollod. 2.3.1). P. has mentioned him several times in this book, including as a king at 2.4.2.

2.31.10 Ἑρμῆς . . . Πολύγιος: the significance of the epithet is obscure. **τοῦτο:** this pronoun refers to τὸ ῥόπαλον. **ὅτῳ πιστὰ (ἐστιν):** "to whomever (the story) is trustworthy"; alternatively, "if anyone cares to believe the story" (Loeb). P. signals his discernment: the reader can believe it if they want, but he does not. He uses the same phrase at 9.10.1 and a similar phrase (εἴ τῳ πιστά) at 1.43.2. **ἐνέφυ:** < ἐμφύω, 2nd aor. act. indicative (S 687), "it took root in (the earth)." **Ἀέτιον τὸν Ἄνθα:** P. mentioned him at 2.30.8 as one of the kings of Troezen. **Χρυσορόαν:** this has been identified with the Gephyraion river that runs along the W side of the city (MT 320). **ἐπὶ ἔτη . . . ἐννέα:** hyperbaton.

2.32.1 Ἱππολύτῳ . . . τέμενός . . . ναὸς: this extraurban *temenos* lies to the NW of the city (MT 315). The quadrangular precinct has a monumental *propylaeum* on the E side and a terrace with a polygonal *peribolos* closed on the W by a tiny shrine *in antis*; the *peribolos* may have been Hippolytus' "secret tomb." The shrine, fronted by a large altar oriented to the W, has been interpreted as the *naos* of Hippolytus. (MT 320) **ἱερώμενος:** < ἱεράομαι, "serving as priest." **ἀποκείρεταί . . . κειραμένη δὲ:** P. repeats a verb but uses the simple, uncompounded form. Corinthian children dedicated locks of hair to Medea's sons, according to 2.3.7. **συρέντα ὑπὸ τῶν ἵππων:** when Phaedra told Theseus that Hippolytus had raped her, Theseus called on Poseidon and cursed Hippolytus, who subsequently died in a chariot accident. For an unusual coda to the story, cf. 2.27.4. **συρέντα:** < σύρω, aor. passive participle, acc. sg. masc. **οὐδὲ τὸν τάφον ἀποφαίνουσιν εἰδότες:** at 1.22.2, P. stated that Hippolytus' grave was in Troezen. **τὸν . . . ἐν οὐρανῷ καλούμενον ἡνίοχον:** i.e., the constellation Auriga. **τιμὴν παρὰ θεῶν ταύτην:** i.e., καταστερισμός, "placing among the stars." Ps.-Eratosthenes' *Katasterismoi* collects a number of similar tales.

2.32.2 ναός . . . Ἀπόλλωνος Ἐπιβατηρίου: "Apollo the Seafarer" (Loeb; this passage is cited at *LSJ* II). This temple is probably the small (6 × 9 m) temple, perhaps tetrastyle *in antis* and oriented to the E, that stood SW of the *temenos* of Hippolytus (MT 320). **τὸν χειμῶνα ὃς τοῖς Ἕλλησιν ἐπεγένετο ἀπὸ Ἰλίου κομιζομένοις:** the storm was unleashed on the Achaean fleet in response to the impieties committed by the army when they stormed Troy, chiefly the rape of Cassandra by Locrian Ajax in the temple of Apollo. P. already told the story of the Argives shipwrecked at Caphareus during this storm (2.23.1). **τὸν ἀγῶνα τῶν Πυθίων Διομήδην πρῶτον θεῖναι . . . τῷ Ἀπόλλωνι:** the usual myth about the founding of the quadrennial games involves Apollo making amends for his killing of the serpent Python at Delphi. For a survey of ancient accounts, see John Davies, "The Origins of the Festivals, Especially Delphi and the Pythia," in *Pindar's Poetry, Patrons, and Festivals: From Archaic Greece to the Roman Empire*, ed. Simon Hornblower and Catherine Morgan (Oxford: Oxford University Press, 2007), 47–70, especially 49–52. **τὴν Δαμίαν καὶ Αὐξησίαν:** a small complex of rooms around a *megaron* in the SW corner of the *temenos* of Hippolytus has been associated with these goddesses (MT 321). **ὃν Ἐπιδαύριοι καὶ Αἰγινῆται λόγον (λέγουσιν):** cf. 2.30.4. **Λιθοβόλια:** see Frazer 3.266.

2.32.3 στάδιόν . . . Ἱππολύτου: near this racecourse is the so-called gymnasium of Hippolytus (MT 321). **ναὸς . . . Ἀφροδίτης Κατασκοπίας:** "Aphrodite the Spy" (v. *LSJ* κατασκοπία, where this passage is cited). This temple lies in the N end of the *temenos* (MT 321). **ὁπότε γυμνάζοιτο ὁ Ἱππόλυτος:** past general temporal clause (S 2414). **τὰ φύλλα ως καὶ πρότερον ἔγραψα ἔχουσα τετρυπημένα:** P. is referring to 1.22.2, where he described the same leaves in nearly the same way: τὰ φύλλα διὰ πάσης (τῆς μυρσίνης) τετρυπημένα. In that passage, he explains that Phaedra used her hairpin to pierce the leaves because of τῆς ἐς τὸν ἔρωτα ἄσης. **ἐς ταύτης**

τὰ φύλλα . . . τῆς μυρσίνης: unusual position of a gen. phrase around the acc. object of a preposition. **ἐσιναμώρει:** "she wantonly destroyed," a very strong verb choice (v. *LSJ*).

2.32.4 τάφος Φαίδρας: this tomb probably lies halfway between the *temenos* of Hippolytus and the temple of Aphrodite Kataskopia (MT 321). **τοῦ Ἱππολύτου μνήματος:** at 1.32.1, P. stated that the Troezenians do not reveal the μνῆμα of Hippolytus, although they know where it is. Perhaps not all of them were tight-lipped. **τοῦ . . . Ἀσκληπιοῦ τὸ ἄγαλμα:** there is evidence for a sanctuary of Asclepius on Troezen where the ill slept in hopes of a cure, much like they did at the Asclepieion at Epidaurus, but P. does not mention it. It has been identified with a vast peristyle complex of the 4th c. BCE with a banquet hall. A Doric peripteral temple of the 4th c. BCE with 6 × 11 columns and a cella with *pronaos* and *opsithodomos* probably belongs to Asclepius too (MT 321). **Τιμόθεος:** the sculptor Timotheus was born in Epidaurus and is dated to the 4th c. BCE. He was a rival of Scopas of Paros and one of the sculptors involved in a massive project at Halicarnassus, the tomb of Mausolus, in 353–350 BCE. **τὸ ὕδωρ:** direct object of ἀνευρόντος. **Ἡρακλέους:** P. already mentioned Heracles' presence in Troezen at 2.31.2 and 2.31.10.

2.32.5 τῆς Σθενιάδος καλουμένης ναός . . . Ἀθηνᾶς: P. mentioned the worship of this deity at Troezen at 2.30.6. This temple lies on the peak of the acropolis, under a medieval castle (MT 322). **Κάλλων Αἰγινήτης:** a sculptor of the archaic age. **Τεκταίου καὶ Ἀγγελίωνος:** at 9.35.3, P. mentions these artists for their work on Delos. **Διποίνῳ καὶ Σκύλλιδι:** at 2.15.1, P. mentioned this pair as the creators of the statue of Athena at Cleonae. He also said that they were the pupils, or sons, of Daedalus. At 2.22.5, he credited them with crafting wooden statues of the Dioscouri, their wives, and their sons. The present passage shows P.'s concern for artistic pedigrees.

2.32.6 Λυτηρίου Πανός . . . ἱερόν: "Pan the Deliverer." This sanctuary may lie on the SE edge of the hill (MT 323). **λοιμοῦ πιέσαντος τὴν Τροιζηνίαν:** this plague occurred in 429 BCE (MT 323). **ναὸν . . . Ἴσιδος:** this temple has not been found (MT 323). **Ἀφροδίτης Ἀκραίας:** at 1.1.3, P. mentions several sanctuaries to Aphrodite at Cnidus in Caria, one of which had the famous cult statue of Aphrodite Acraea. This sanctuary has been identified with a structure positioned on a terrace—a temple, probably Doric, with a cella, *pronaos*, and base for a cult statue; it dates to the 6th c. BCE (MT 323). **ἅτε ἐν μητροπόλει (οὔσῃ) τῇ Τροιζῆνι:** P. stated at 2.30.9

how the descendants of Aetius, son of Anthas, founded Halicarnassus, whose inhabitants called themselves Antheadae. Cf. Strabo 14.2.16.

2.32.7 ἰοῦσι δὲ τὴν διὰ τῶν ὀρέων ἐς Ἑρμιόνην (ὁδόν): this is S of the city (MT 323). **τοῦ Ὑλλικοῦ ποταμοῦ, Ταυρίου δὲ τὸ ἀρχῆς καλουμένου:** Sophocles mentions this river in his play *Aegeus* (Athenaeus 3.122f). The name *Hyllicus* seems to be connected with the Doric Hylleis tribe. (MT 323) **πέτρα Θησέως:** this is popularly identified with a large rock near the modern village (MT 323). **ἀνελομένου Θησέως ὑπ' αὐτῇ κρηπῖδας τὰς Αἰγέως καὶ ξίφος:** after giving instructions for Theseus to recover these items when he came of age, Aegeus left Aethra at Troezen and went back to his home and throne in Athens. Cf. ps.-Apollod. 3.16.1. **ἀνελομένου Θησέως . . . ποιήσαντος Θησέως:** P. introduces two explanations of geographical markers in a similar way. **βωμὸς ἐκαλεῖτο Σθενίου Διός:** P. mentions this rock/altar again at 2.34.6. **Ἀφροδίτης . . . ἱερὸν Νυμφίας:** "Bridal Aphrodite"; Theseus kidnapped young Helen from Sparta, prompting a retaliatory invasion of Attica by the Dioscuri. **ποιήσαντος Θησέως ἡνίκα ἔσχε γυναῖκα Ἑλένην:** cf. commentary on 2.22.6.

2.32.8 Ποσειδῶνος ἱερὸν Φυταλμίου: "Poseidon the Nurturer," an epithet he shares with Zeus (v. *LSJ*). But P. seems to have a different etymology in mind. Cf. Loeb, ad loc. This shrine lies at the base of the heights SE of the city (MT 323). **εἴξας:** < εἴκω, aor. act. participle. **ἀνῆκεν:** < ἀνίημι, aor. act. indicative. **Δημήτηρ Θεσμοφόρος:** ceramics and lamps of the 7th c. through the 2nd c. BCE have been found (MT 324). **Ἀλθήπου:** this early ruler of Troezen was the son of Posideon and Leis; cf. 2.30.5.

2.32.9 καταβαίνουσι: P. is moving NE toward the harbor closer to the city (MT 324; Frazer 3.283). **Γενέθλιον:** "Birthplace" (cf. Loeb). This site may be connected with the archaic cult of Poseidon Genethlios known at Sparta (cf. 3.15.10) but also recognized in the Argolid with the epithet *Genesios* (at Lerna; cf. 2.28.4). See MT 324. **Θησέως καὶ ἐνταῦθα Ἀμαζόνας μάχῃ κρατήσαντος:** as P. implies below, Theseus was said to have defeated the Amazons in several places throughout Attica; cf., e.g., 1.2.1, 1.15.2, 1.17.2, and 1.25.2. **αὗται δ' ἂν εἴησαν:** "These must have belonged . . ." (Loeb). This is an example of a potential optative, which "ranges from possibility to fixed resolve" (S 1824a). **τῶν . . . ἀγωνισαμένων:** partitive gen. with αὗται.

2.32.10 ἐπὶ θάλασσαν . . . τὴν Ψιφαίαν: the Psiphaean Sea has been identified with a lagoon to the SW of the peninsula of Methana (MT 324). **ῥάχους . . . καλοῦσι Τροιζήνιοι πᾶν ὅσον ἄκαρπον ἐλαίας:**

P. sometimes notes dialectical oddities he encounters. ῥάχος generally means "thorn hedge." **κότινον καὶ φυλλίαν καὶ ἔλαιον:** a κότινος is a wild olive tree, and P. considers it distinct from φυλίας, which Homer names as one of the two bushes under which the shipwrecked Odysseus slept (*Odyssey* 5.476ff.)—the other being ἐλαία and from ἔλαιον. It is unclear what differentiates these three (Frazer 3.284). **ἐνσχεθεισῶν αὐτῷ τῶν ἡνιῶν ἀνετράπη τοῦ Ἱππολύτου τὸ ἅρμα:** see commentary on 2.32.1. **ἐνσχεθεισῶν:** < ἐνέχω, aor. passive participle. **τούτου:** construe gen. of separation with οὐ πολὺ . . . ἀφέστηκε. **τῆς Σαρωνίας Ἀρτέμιδος:** construe with τὸ ἱερόν. This has been securely identified with a stone foundation near the village of Psiphti; the cult also existed at Epidaurus (MT 324). **τὰ ἐς αὐτὸ ἐμήνυσεν ὁ λόγος ἤδη μοι:** cf. 2.30.7. **τοσόνδε δὲ ἔτι δηλώσω:** P. adds one more detail and signals a transition away from Troezen proper.

Sphaeria and Calaureia

2.33.1 νῆσοι δέ εἰσι Τροιζηνίοις: P. now heads E toward the other port of Troezen, toward Sphaeria (MT 324). **διαβῆναι ποσὶν ἐς αὐτήν ἔστιν:** "it is possible for one to cross on foot . . ." **Σφαιρία:** this island has been identified as the W of the two little islands between the modern port of Galatas and the island of Calaureia (modern Poros). See MT 324–25. **τὸν Σφαῖρον:** there is an unclear relationship between Sphaerus and Pelops' more famous charioteer Myrtilus, who cursed his boss and his stock; cf. 2.18.2. **τούτῳ:** construe with κομίζουσα . . . χοάς, "for this man." **κατὰ δή τι . . . ὄνειρον:** "in accordance with some dream." **διέβαινεν . . . διαβάσῃ δὲ:** pseudanaphora. Note the use of διαβῆναι earlier: the traveler can wade to Hiera/Sphaera just like Aethra did—but hopefully with a better outcome. **Αἴθρα:** Aethra was the daughter of Pittheus (son of Pelops) and mother of Theseus; P. here cites the legend of Poseidon as father of Theseus. **ναὸν . . . Ἀθηνᾶς Ἀπατουρίας:** "Deceitful Athena" (v. *LSJ*). MT (325) connects this epithet to ἀπάτορες (fatherless young men) and to a rite of passage that was well known at Athens. The matrimonial rite below seems connected.

2.33.2 λέγεται δὲ καὶ τοῦτο, ἀντιδοῦναι τὰ χωρία σφᾶς ἀλλήλους: Strabo 8.6.14 says that Poseidon gave Leto Delos in exchange for Calauria and gave Apollo Delphi for Taenarum. **ἶσόν τοι . . . νέμεσθαι:** "it is all the same to you to inhabit . . ." (v. *LSJ* νέμω A.III.1). The epic form of ἴσος has a properispomenon accentuation. τοι is the epic form of σοι (S 325D1). **δ'**

οὖν: "at any rate" (Loeb). This collocation of particles often indicates a return to the main topic (here, the prominence of Poseidon on the island), "which has temporarily been lost sight of" (D 463–64). **Ποσειδῶνος ἱερὸν:** this sanctuary lies on a plateau in the center of the island of Calaureia and is composed of a *propylaeum* and a series of 5th or 4th c. BCE stoas (three to the N, two to the S), which give access to the *temenos* proper. This *temenos* has two *propylaea* (one to the S, one to the E) and contains the temple of Poseidon Kalaureios, only the foundations of which remain; it was a peripteral Doric temple of 6 × 12 columns and a cella with *pronaos* and *opisthodomos*, as well as an internal colonnade. It is datable to 520–510 BCE. Votive deposits began in the 8th c. BCE (MT 325). **ἔστ' ἂν . . . προέλθῃ:** "until she reaches . . ."; for future action, Greek uses a subjunctive with ἄν (S 2426). **ὥραν . . . γάμου:** "the time for marriage" (v. *LSJ* ὥρα B.I.2).

2.33.3 **Δημοσθένους μνῆμά ἐστι:** P. gave an account of Demosthenes' death at 1.8.2–3 and here supplements it with details. The tomb of Demosthenes has been identified with a quadrangular building to the SW of the temple, but MT (325–26) argues that this building is most probably the urban Asclepieion. The tomb may instead be a circle foundation to the W of the temple. **Ὁμήρου:** construe with τούτου as objects of ἐπί. **ὡς εἴη βάσκανον:** "malicious" (v. *LSJ* II.1), indirect statement in secondary sequence after δεῖξαι. P. reflects on the cruelty of fate. **Ὅμηρον . . . προδιεφθαρμένον . . . πτωχεύοντα:** direct objects of ἦγε and πιέζουσα. P. parrots the ancient tradition of Homer as a blind, poor, peripatetic bard. **τοὺς ὀφθαλμοὺς:** acc. of respect with προδιεφθαρμένον. **κακὸν δεύτερον:** in apposition with πενία. **φυγῆς:** construe gen. with λαβεῖν πεῖραν, which is periphrastic for πειραθῆναι. **ὁ θάνατος . . . βίαιος:** in 322 BCE, the Greeks lost the Lamian War, and Demosthenes, along with other anti-Macedonian politicians, was being hunted down by Archias, an agent of Antipater. Cornered in this sanctuary of Poseidon, Demosthenes took poison to avoid capture. **καὶ ἄλλοις καὶ αὐτῷ Δημοσθένει:** dat. of agent with εἴρηται. **πλεῖστα:** "again and again" (Loeb; v. *LSJ* πλεῖστος III.1.a). **ἦ μὴν τῶν χρημάτων . . . μὴ μεταλαβεῖν αὐτόν:** this entire clause is indirect discourse after εἴρηται, but P. heightens it with μή (used in emphatic declarations in indirect discourse: S 2723) and especially with ἦ μήν (used in strong asseverations: S 2865): "that he did *not* in fact take any of the money . . ." **τῶν χρημάτων:** gen. with μεταλαβεῖν. **ἃ ἐκ τῆς Ἀσίας ἤγαγεν Ἅρπαλος:** in 324 BCE, Harpalus, a friend and treasurer of Alexander the Great, stole 5,000 talents from Babylon and escaped to Greece. He took refuge in Athens and was kept under guard there. The assembly voted to approve a proposal of Demosthenes to entrust the 700 talents Harpalus had brought to a committee headed by the orator; later accusations of mishandling of the funds arose when there was no account for half of the money. Cf. A. B. Bosworth, *Conquest and Empire: The Reign of Alexander the Great* (Cambridge: Cambridge University Press, 2001), 215–20.

2.33.4 τὸ δὲ ὕστερον λεχθὲν: < λέγω, aor. passive participle, "the statement made subsequently" (Loeb), i.e., the report of Philoxenus below. **Ἅρπαλος μὲν ὡς ἐξ Ἀθηνῶν ἀπέδρα διαβὰς ναυσὶν ἐς Κρήτην:** eventually Harpalus left Athens and attempted to start a campaign as a mercenary general in Crete, in the fall of 324 BCE (Bosworth 217). **οὐ πολὺ ὕστερον ὑπὸ τῶν θεραπευόντων ἀπέθανεν οἰκετῶν:** Harpalus was dead by October of 324 BCE (Bosworth 217; see note on previous section for full citation). **οἱ δὲ ὑπὸ ἀνδρὸς Μακεδόνος Παυσανίου δολοφονηθῆναί φασιν αὐτόν:** according to some sources, he was murdered by his lieutenant Thibron. Harpalus' band of mercenaries then found work in Cyrenaica (Bosworth 217). **Φιλόξενος Μακεδὼν:** Philoxenus, the satrap of Caria, had sent agents to Athens to demand that the Athenians surrender Harpalus, but Demosthenes insisted that they hold out until Alexander's agents arrived. Harpalus was allowed to withdraw from the city in the meantime (Bosworth 217). **τὸν δὲ παῖδα τοῦτον ἔχων ἤλεγχεν:** "having (custody of) this slave, he examined him (under torture)" (v. *LSJ* ἐλέγχω II.1). **τῶν Ἁρπάλου (χρημάτων) τι:** Demosthenes was alleged to have received 20 talents as a bribe (Bosworth 216).

2.33.5 αὐτῶν: partitive gen. with ἕκαστος. **οὐδὲ . . . ἀρχὴν:** "not at all." **Ἀλεξάνδρῳ τε ἐς τὰ μάλιστα ἀπεχθανομένου:** Demosthenes was a longtime opponent of both Alexander and Alexander's father, Philip. **αὐτὸς ἰδίᾳ προσκρούσας:** i.e., Philoxenus. P. cites Demosthenes' absence even from Philoxenus' letters as evidence that he was not guilty; it is unclear what "private quarrel" (Loeb) Philoxenus had with Demosthenes (v. *LSJ* προσκρούω III.2). **τιμαὶ . . . παρὰ τῶν Καλαυρείας εἰσὶν οἰκητόρων:** Demosthenes eventually was fined and imprisoned, but he was allowed to escape to Troezen and later to Aegina. He returned after Alexander the Great's death in 323 BCE.

Methana

2.34.1 τῆς . . . Τροιζηνίας γῆς: gen. of separation. P. is now turning back to the W (MT 327). **ἰσθμὸς:** the town lies on the W coast of the peninsula. The Athenians fortified this isthmus in 425 BCE during the Peloponnesian War (Thucydides 4.45; Diodorus Siculus 12.85). See MT

327; Frazer 3.286–87. **Μέθανα:** Methana became an important naval base for the Ptolemies ca. 245 BCE, under Ptolemy II Philadelphus (MT 328). **Ἴσιδος . . . ἱερόν . . . καὶ ἄγαλμα:** these are perhaps in the lower city, near the chapel of Panaghia (MT 327). **τοῦ . . . πολίσματος:** gen. of separation with ἀπέχει. **θερμὰ λουτρά:** the hot springs lie below the modern village of Kato Mouska, at Vromolimni on the E coast and at Vroma in the middle of the N coast (Frazer 3.288). P. here seems to refer to the latter location. **Ἀντιγόνου τοῦ Δημητρίου Μακεδόνων βασιλεύοντος:** it is unclear whether this refers to Antigonus II Gonatas, the son of Demetrius I Poliorcetes and ruler of Macedonia (272–239 BCE), or to Antigonus III Doson, the son of Demetrius the Fair and ruler of the same land (229–221 BCE). **φανῆναι, φανῆναι δὲ . . .** : anastrophe. **ἐγγὺς:** an adv. here. **οὔτε (ἐστὶν) ἐκπεσόντα . . . ἀκινδύνως νήχεσθαι:** "nor is it possible for one who falls into the sea to swim safely." **κύνας:** "sharks."

2.34.2 **ὃ δὲ ἐθαύμασα . . . μάλιστα, γράψω καὶ τοῦτο:** P. describes a strange, somewhat gruesome ritual that he learned about at Methana. This description is a reminder that P.'s θαύματα include more than places and monuments. **ὁ Λὶψ:** the Greek name for a SW wind. **ἀλεκτρυόνα . . . λευκὰ:** "a rooster bearing white feathers throughout," direct object of διελόντες. **διελόντες:** < διαιρέω, aor. act. participle, "cutting in half" (v. *LSJ* I). **ἐναντίοι περιθέουσι:** "they run in opposite directions" (v. *LSJ* ἐναντίος I.1.b). **ἐς τὸ αὐτὸ:** "to the same (place)."

2.34.3 **πρὸς τὸν Λίβα:** i.e., as a remedy for the wind's deleterious effects. **νησῖδας . . . Πέλοπος:** these islands lie in the Gulf of Epidaurus, between Aegina and Methana. The Athenians won a victory over the Peloponnesians off of Cecryphala (modern Anghistri) in ca. 459 BCE (Thucydides 4.105; Frazer 3.289). **ἀριθμὸν:** acc. of respect. **τοῦτο δὲ εἰ τοιοῦτόν ἐστιν:** "if this be the case" (Loeb). **οἱ περὶ τὰ Μέθανα:** i.e., the neighbors around Methana. **ἐπεὶ:** not "since" but "and yet," for the conjunction has an adversative force here (G 719.2); P. is responding to the first clause of the sentence and essentially saying, "I don't know if *this* is true, . . . and yet I saw men keep *hail at least* away." **χάλαζάν γε:** direct object of ἀποτρέποντας.

Hermione

2.34.4 **Ἑρμίονα Εὔροπος:** nothing more is known of Hermion or Europs than what P. gives us here. **ἦν γὰρ δὴ Φορωνέως:** P. mentioned

Phoroneus as the first man in Mycenae at 2.15.5 and mentioned his grave at 2.20.3. **Ἡροφάνης ὁ Τροιζήνιος:** not otherwise known, but doubtless a local historian of the area, given his provenance. **Ἄργον τὸν Νιόβης θυγατριδοῦν ὄντα Φορωνέως:** P. mentioned Argos as the successor of Phoroneus at 2.16.1 and mentioned Niobe as Phoroneus' daughter at 2.22.5. **τὴν ἐν Ἄργει περιελθεῖν ἂν ἀρχὴν:** this is the apodosis of a contrary-to-fact condition in indirect discourse; the aor. indicative becomes an infinitive, but the ἄν is retained. **παρόντος Φορωνεῖ γνησίου παιδός:** this gen. absolute acts as the protasis for the past contrary-to-fact statement: "if there had been . . ."

2.34.5 ἔμελλεν . . . οἴσεσθαι: μέλλω often takes a future infinitive (S 1959). **ὁ παῖς (Εὔροπος):** i.e., Hermion. **παιδὶ . . . Διός γε εἶναι δοκοῦντι:** "child reputed to be (the son) of Zeus" (v. *LSJ* δοκέω II.5). **ἴσα οἴσεσθαι:** "would win an equal share (as)," with dat. (v. *LSJ* φέρω A.VI.3). **Ἑρμιόνα:** the city founded by Hermion is known both as Hermione and as Hermion. Hermionis, mentioned in 2.34.6, is the territory of the city. **Δωριεῖς οἱ ἐξ Ἄργους:** P. described the return of the Heracleidae to Argos at 2.18.7–8. **ἐλέγετο γὰρ ἄν ὑπὸ Ἀργείων (εἰ πόλεμος ἐγένετο):** past contrary-to-fact with omitted protasis.

2.34.6 ἔστι . . . ὁδὸς ἐς Ἑρμιόνα ἐκ Τροιζῆνος: P. returns to Troezen to illustrate a mountain route to Hermion, the same route that he ended at 2.32.9 (Frazer 3.290). **Σθενίου Διὸς βωμός, μετὰ δὲ Θησέα ἀνελόμενον τὰ γνωρίσματα . . . :** P. explained this change of name at 2.32.7. **Ἀπόλλωνος . . . Πλατανιστίου:** "Apollo of the Plane-Tree Grove" (Loeb). Curiously, P. does not mention any plane trees in the vicinity. The sanctuaries of Apollo and Demeter have not been found but were probably near the internal plateau of Ilia, which P. calls Eileoi (MT 328). **ἱερὸν Δήμητρός . . . Θερμασίας:** this sanctuary was probably near the lagoon now called Thermisi. The epithet was probably connected with the goddess' ability to make grain ripen with heat (MT 328).

2.34.7 ἄκρα Σκυλλαῖον: Cape Scyllaeum is modern Cape Skyli, which forms the S end of the Saronic Gulf, between Troezen and Hermion (Frazer 3.290). **ἀπὸ τῆς Νίσου καλουμένη θυγατρός:** P. explains Scylla's treachery at 1.19.4: she precipitated the capture of the city by cutting a colorful and magical lock of hair off her father's head. This Scylla is not to be confused with the terrible sea monster encountered by Odysseus during his journey home. **Νίσαιαν:** Nisaea was the port of Megara. **οὔτε . . . καί . . . :** "not only not . . . but also . . ." (S 2945). **τὸν νεκρόν . . . διαφορηθέντα:** i.e., torn apart.

2.34.8 πλέοντι ὡς ἐπὶ τὴν πόλιν: ὡς is used before prepositions to show direction in geographical expressions (v. *LSJ* C.II.b). P. here describes sailing from Cape Bucephala (modern Cape Korakas), at the other end of Hermionea, to the SW of the territory, which he rejoins at Cape Scyllaeum (MT 328). **νῆσοι, πρώτη μὲν Ἁλιοῦσσα . . . μετὰ δὲ Πιτυοῦσσα . . . τρίτη δὲ ἣν Ἀριστερὰς ὀνομάζουσι:** *variatio*. Halioussa is to the E of Porto Cheli. Pityussa is modern Spetses. Aristeras is modern Spetsopoula or Rasteri (MT 329). **ἄκρα Κωλυεργία:** this is modern Cape Milianos (MT 329). **νῆσος Τρίκανα:** this island is now known as Trikeri (MT 329). **ὄρος . . . Βούπορθμος:** this is modern Cape Mouzaki (MT 329). **πεποίηται μὲν . . . πεποίηται δὲ . . . :** anaphora. **Προμαχόρμα:** "Champion of the Anchorage" (Loeb).

2.34.9 νῆσος Ἀπεροπία: modern Dokos (MT 329). **νῆσος Ὑδρέα:** modern Idra (MT 329). **αἰγιαλός . . . μηνοειδὴς:** the port of Kapari. **τῆς ἠπείρου:** the use of the gen. with παρήκω is not found in *LSJ*. **ἀκτὴ:** here a synonym for ἄκρα. This is a long neck of land called Bisti that runs out into the sea from the village of Kastri (Frazer 3.293). **Ποσείδιον:** the remains of this shrine have been found on the summit of the promontory (Frazer 3.293). **ᾗ πλατυτάτη (ἐστιν):** "where (the headland) is widest."

2.34.10 ἡ προτέρα πόλις: as contrasted with the "modern" city that P. describes in the next subsection. The earlier city here may have been abandoned after the sack of the city by pirates in the first half of the 1st c. BCE, according to Plutarch *Life of Pompey* 24 (MT 329). **ἱερὰ . . . Ποσειδῶνος μὲν (ἱερὸν) . . . δὲ . . . ναὸς Ἀθηνᾶς:** the temple of Poseidon is a peripteral Doric structure of 6 × 13 columns and a cella with *pronaos* and *opisthodomos*; it can be dated to the 4th c. BCE (MT 330). **τῇ ἀρχῇ:** object of ἐπί. **ἐς τὰ μετέωρα (γῆς):** i.e., father inland. **τοὺς Τυνδάρεω παῖδας:** i.e., Agamemnon and Menelaus. The circumstances of their competition there is unknown, and the racecourse has not been found. **ἱερὰ . . . ἀπόρρητα Δήμητρι:** dedications to Demeter have been found. The locations of these *periboloi* and the other shrines mentioned here are unknown.

2.34.11 τοσαῦτα μὲν Ἑρμιονεῦσίν ἐστιν ἐνταῦθα: P. transitions from the coastal sites and islands to the modern city of Hermione. **ἡ . . . ἐφ' ἡμῶν πόλις:** the Roman city lies less than one kilometer to the E on the slopes of the height called Pron (the name appears at Argos too; cf. 2.20.8) on the E portion of the ancient center (MT 329). **τὰ πρῶτα:** adverbial acc.; construe with ἐν ὁμαλῷ. **ἠρέμα ἐς πρόσαντες ἄνεισι:** "gently rising up a slope"

(Loeb). **τὸ δὲ (πρόσαντές) ἐστιν ἤδη (μέρος) τοῦ Πρωνός** **τὰ δὲ ἐς συγγραφὴν καὶ ἄλλα παρείχετο καὶ ὧν αὐτὸς ποιήσασθαι μάλιστα ἠξίωσα μνήμην:** P. signals his discretion in making a selection of items worthy of inclusion. **Ἀφροδίτης ναός . . . ναὸς ἕτερός . . . Ἀφροδίτης:** MT (330) speculates that the two temples may indicate two harbors.

2.34.12 ἤν (= ἐὰν) . . . μέλλῃ φοιτᾶν: the protasis of a present general condition. **παρὰ ἄνδρα . . . φοιτᾶν:** "to remarry" (Loeb). **ἁπάσαις . . . καθέστηκεν:** "it is the custom for all (these women) to . . ." **ὡς ἐστὶν εἰρημένον ἤδη μοι:** cf. 2.34.6.

2.35.1 Διονύσου . . . Μελαναίγιδος: "Dionysus of the Black Goatskin" (v. *LSJ* μελάναιγις I). **ἁμίλλης κολύμβου καὶ πλοίων:** construe with ἆθλα. These games may be connected with Dionysus' adventure with the pirates (*Homeric Hymn to Dionysus* 7; Frazer 3.294). **(προ)τιθέασιν ἆθλα:** "they offer prizes" (v. *LSJ* ἆθλον I). **Ἀρτέμιδος . . . Ἰφιγενείας:** Iphigeneia was a daughter of Agamemnon, who sacrificed her to Artemis to curb the goddess' anger and allow the Achaeans to proceed to Troy. According to some versions, an animal was substituted for Iphigeneia, whom Artemis transported to the land of the Taurians to serve at her temple. Cf. ps.-Apollod. epit. 3.21–22. **τὸ τῆς Ἑστίας (ἱερόν):** this and the sanctuary of Artemis Iphigeneia were probably in the agora of the city, which P. does not mention (MT 330–31).

2.35.2 Ἀπόλλωνος . . . ναοὶ τρεῖς: these three temples and that of Tyche are probably not far from the city center. MT (331) says that the three temples of Apollo may recall the oldest phase of Argive domination. **τὸν . . . Πυθαέα:** cf. 2.24.1 (and commentary), where P. says that Pythaeus built a temple to Apollo on the acropolis of Argos when he came from Delphi. That report fits the below information that P. acquired from Telesilla. **Ὅριον:** "(Apollo) Guardian of Boundaries" (v. *LSJ*). **Τελέσιλλά:** cf. 2.20.8–10. **τὸν . . . Ὅριον:** construe with ἐφ' ὅτῳ καλοῦσιν. **σαφῶς μὲν οὐκ ἂν ἔχοιμι εἰπεῖν, τεκμαίρομαι δὲ . . . :** without other evidence, P. falls back on his native reason.

2.35.3 κολοσσὸς: this was a colossal statue. Such statues are of particular interest to P. Cf. 1.18.6. **κρήνας δὲ τὴν μὲν σφόδρα . . . ἀρχαίαν (κρήνην) . . . τὴν δὲ ἐφ' ἡμῶν (κρήνην)** **ἐπιλείποι δὲ οὐκ ἄν ποτε, οὐδ' εἰ . . . ὑδρεύοιντο ἐξ αὐτῆς:** a future-less-vivid condition.

2.35.4 ἱερὸν . . . Δήμητρός . . . ἐπὶ τοῦ Πρωνός: this was the principal sanctuary of the Pron, at the W gates of the new city but outside the walls of the old city; its site is now occupied by the church of Haghios Taxiarchis. This sanctuary includes the temple of Demeter, the temple of Clymenus (2.35.9), the temple of Ares (2.35.10), the stoa of Echo (2.35.10), three enclosures with a *chasma* (2.35.10), and the sanctuary of Eileithyia (2.35.11). See MT 331. For this long passage, see the helpful analysis of L. Prauscello, "Demeter and Dionysos in the Sixth-Century Argolid: Lasos of Hermione, the Cult of Demeter, and the Origins of Dithyramb," in *Dithyramb in Context, ed. Barbara Kowalzig and Peter Wilson* (Oxford: Oxford University Press, 2013), 76–92. **τοῦτο τὸ ἱερὸν:** direct object of τοὺς ἱδρυσαμένους. **Κλύμενον Φορωνέως παῖδα:** P. gives three accounts of this figure and Chthonia: the Troezenian tradition, the Argive, and his own belief. **Ἀθέραν . . . καὶ Μύσιον:** at 2.18.3, P. mentioned the Argive Mysius as giving hospitality to the visiting goddess. **λέγουσι:** this verb sets up two constructions of indirect discourse: first ὡς with the optative, then infinitives. **Κολόνταν:** refusing hospitality to a god and suffering the consequences is a recurrent motif in Greco-Roman myth. **ταῦτα:** direct object of ποιεῖν (αὐτόν is the subject); ἀντὶ τούτων just below refers to the same inhospitable acts. **οὐ κατὰ γνώμην Χθονίᾳ τῇ θυγατρὶ:** "(it was) not his daughter Chthonia's wish (that he . . .)." **συγκαταπρησθῆναι τῇ οἰκίᾳ:** "he was incinerated along with his house."

2.35.5 **δ' οὖν:** see commentary on 2.33.2. **Χθόνια ἑορτὴν:** this description of the Chthonia festival resembles that of the Bouphonia at Athens (cf. 1.24.3, 1.28.10; Aelian *De natura animalium* 9.4). See MT 331; Frazer 3.295–96. **ἄγουσιν . . . ἄγουσι δὲ . . . :** pseudanaphora. **ἡγοῦνται:** the subjects of this verb are οἵ τε ἱερεῖς τῶν θεῶν καὶ ὅσοι . . . ἔχουσιν. **τῆς πομπῆς:** gen. object of ἡγέομαι. **οἱ ταύτῃ:** article with adv., "the natives" (Loeb). **ἔπεστι δέ οἱ καὶ τὰ ἐπὶ τῷ θρήνῳ γράμματα:** the hyacinth is said to bear the Greek letters AI (< αἴ) because the flower grew from the blood of the accidentally killed Hyacinthus. Frazer (3.296) notes that hyacinths were among the flowers that Kore was picking when she was abducted.

2.35.6 **τοῖς . . . τὴν πομπὴν πέμπουσιν:** "those who form the procession" (Loeb); see *LSJ* πομπή II.1.a. Cf. H. 5.56.2. **διειλημμένην:** < διαλαμβάνω, perf. passive participle. **οἱ μὲν . . . , ἕτεροι δὲ . . . :** a variation on the most common οἱ μὲν . . . , οἱ δὲ . . . **ἔσω φέρεσθαι:** "to rush into" (v. *LSJ* φέρω B.I.1). **ἀναπεπταμένας:** < ἀναπετάννυμι, perf. passive participle. **προσέθεσαν:** < προστίθημι, aor. act. indicative 3rd pl.

2.35.7 **γρᾶες:** < γραῦς, nom. pl. fem. **δρεπάνῳ:** construe with ὑπέτεμε. **ἥτις ἂν τύχῃ:** "whichever (of the old women) happens upon the cow," a present general relative clause, just like ἐφ' ἥντινα . . . ἂν πέσῃ below. **προσελαύνουσιν (οὗτοι) οἷς ἐπιτέτακται** **τῶν πλευρῶν:** partitive gen. with ἥντινα. **ἀνάγκη πεσεῖν καὶ πάσας (βοῦς ἐπὶ ταύτην τὴν πλευράν).**

2.35.8 **τὸν εἰρημένον τρόπον:** acc. of respect. **ἀναμένουσιν:** this verb governs the acc. and infinitive construction following. **ἐσελαθῆναι:** < εἰσελαύνω, aor. passive infinitive. **ἐσελαθῆναι καθ' ἑκάστην τῶν βοῶν:** = ἑκάστην τῶν βοῶν ἐσελαθῆναι. **ἐγὼ μὲν οὐκ εἶδον, οὐ μὴν οὐδὲ ἀνὴρ ἄλλος οὔτε ξένος οὔτε Ἑρμιονέων αὐτῶν:** P. admits that his research failed him. **αὐτὸ:** "the thing itself" (Loeb). **ὁποῖόν τί ἐστιν:** direct object of ἴστωσαν. The enclitic indefinite pronoun τι here gives an oxytone accent to ὁποῖον and takes from ἐστιν. **ἴστωσαν:** 3rd pl. imperative of οἶδα (= ἴστω); cf. S 794, 466.3.

2.35.9 **περὶ πάντα . . . αὐτόν:** "all around it." **Κλυμένου:** Lasos of Hermione (a poet and musicologist who visited the court of Hipparchus at Athens at the end of the 6th c. BCE) says that Persephone was the consort of Clymenus (Athenaeus 14.624e; MT 332). **ἔγωγε . . . ἡγοῦμαι:** P. contrasts his opinion with what he implies is the common wisdom. **τοῦ θεοῦ δέ ἐστιν ἐπίκλησις:** Κλύμενος means "famous/infamous" and is not infrequently used as an epithet for Hades, as P. states here. **λόγος:** "legend" (Loeb); see *LSJ* V.2.

2.35.10 **τοῦ . . . ἱεροῦ:** construe with κατὰ τὴν δεξιάν. **στοὰ . . . Ἠχοῦς:** this stoa has the same name as the famous stoa at Olympia (5.21.17). It may lie a little to the NW of the church of Haghios Taxiarchis (MT 332). **τὰ ὀλίγιστα:** "at least" (v. *LSJ* ὀλίγος VI.2). **ἐς τρὶς:** the preposition is superfluous. **πέφυκεν:** "it happens naturally" (v. *LSJ* φύω B.II.5). **χωρία:** three minor precincts. **λίμνην Ἀχερουσίαν:** several swamps and rivers in ancient Greece bore this name. **τοῦ Ἅιδου τὸν κύνα:** at 2.31.2, P. noted a place in Troezen where Heracles dragged up Cerberus from Hades. There were many such places in Greece: Taenarum (3.25.5) and Coronea in Boeotia (9.34.5) also boasted such a sacred hole in the earth.

2.35.11 **Μάσητα:** the seaport of Hermione; cf. 2.36.2. **Εἰλειθυίας . . . ἱερόν:** this sanctuary is attested epigraphically; some remains of the gate have been found (MT 332). **ἄλλως μὲν δή:** an unusual collocation of particles. The μὲν sets up a contrast with the δὲ below (P. compares the magnificent and frequent rites with a hidden image), and the δὴ here may be both transitional from the previous sentence and emphatic of this member of the new contrast (cf. D 258–59, 391–93). The ἄλλως here is difficult and essentially ignored in the Loeb translation. We may connect it with the following καὶ θυσίαις καὶ θυμιάμασι by analogy with ἄλλως τε καί: "They propitiate the goddess in other ways but especially with both sacrifices and offerings of incense." **μεγάλως:** "magnificently" (Loeb). **οὐδενὶ πλὴν εἰ μὴ ἄρα ταῖς ἱερείαις:** "(it is not possible for) anyone (to see) except perhaps the priestesses" (Loeb; v. S 2966a); P. reasons that if anyone were to see it, it would logically be the priestesses.

Helice and Mases

2.36.1 κατὰ δὲ τὴν ἐπὶ Μάσητα εὐθεῖαν (ὁδόν): P. is moving to the NW but takes a detour to Helice, modern Port Cheli (MT 333). **τὰ μὲν ἐφ' ἡμῶν:** "in my time." **ἔρημος:** the city was abandoned, perhaps after an earthquake of 250 BCE devastated the E Argolid (MT 333). **Ἁλικῶν λόγος:** "mention made of citizens of Helice" (v. *LSJ* VI.2.c). **ἐν στήλαις ἐστὶ ταῖς Ἐπιδαυρίων αἳ τοῦ Ἀσκληπιοῦ τὰ ἰάματα ἐγγεγραμμένα ἔχουσιν:** P. lets the reader know that he made a thorough investigation of the dedications at Epidaurus. Cf. 2.27.3. These stelae have actually been found (Frazer 3.298). **ἐγγεγραμμένα:** < ἐγγράφω, perf. passive participle. **σύγγραμμα οὐδὲν . . . ἀξιόχρεων:** "no document worthy (of belief)." **τοῦ τε Πρωνὸς μέση καὶ ὄρους ἑτέρου:** "midway between Pron and another mountain" (v. *LSJ* μέσος I.1.c). **ἀπὸ δὲ τῆς Διὸς ἐς κόκκυγα τὸν ὄρνιθα ἀλλαγῆς λεγομένης ἐνταῦθα γενέσθαι:** at 2.17.4, P. explains the presence of the cuckoo on the scepter of a statue of Hera at the Heraeum.

2.36.2 ἐς τόδε: "to the present day" (Loeb). **τοῦ γε Κοκκυγίου πρὸς τοῖς πέρασι:** "at the edges (i.e., foot) of Mt. Cuckoo." **οἵ:** not the article but the pronoun. **Μάσητα:** Mases is a little NW of the modern village of Kampo (MT 333). **Μάσητι δὲ οὔσῃ πόλει τὸ ἀρχαῖον . . . ἐπινείῳ:** dat. object of ἐχρῶντο. **καθὰ καὶ Ὅμηρος ἐν Ἀργείων καταλόγῳ πεποίηκεν:** *Iliad* 2.562.

Near Mases

2.36.3 ἄκραν καλουμένην Στρουθοῦντα: this is probably modern Vourlia; it lies at the W end of Hermionis (MT 333). **†πεντήκοντά . . . διακόσιοι (στάδιοι)†:** a clear error (Frazer 3.298; MT 334). **Φιλανόριόν . . . Βολεούς:** these places have not yet been found (MT 334). **Διδύμους:**

this place, modern Didima, lies in the middle of Hermionis. **ἔστι μὲν . . . ἔστι δὲ . . .** : anaphora. **ἐπὶ . . . αὐτοῖς:** "in addition to them" (v. *LSJ* ἐπί B.I.1.e). **ὀρθὰ:** not "straight" but "upright," i.e., not seated (v. *LSJ* I.1.a).

Asine

2.36.4 τὸ δὲ ἐντεῦθέν (χωρίον) Ἀσίνης . . . <ἐρείπια>: the remains of Asine can be seen near modern Tolo, SE of Nauplia. It was inhabited in prehistoric times and has polygonal walls from the 3rd c. BCE (MT 334). **Νικάνδρου:** tracing the descent of Nicander, a Eurypontid king of Sparta (r. ca. 750–725 BCE), P. here follows the list of Eurypontid kings that H. gives at 8.131, with the one modification mentioned below. P. retells this historical episode at 3.7.4. **τοῦ Χαρίλλου:** in *Politics*, Aristotle uses two forms of his name, Χάριλλος and Χαρίλαος. P. notes at 3.7.3 that Charillus invaded the Argolid and launched the Spartan campaign against Tegea. **τοῦ Πολυδέκτου:** P. here reverses the order of H.'s king list by giving the name of Charillus' father as *Polydectes* and not *Eunomus*; P. gives the same order of kings at 3.7.3 and 4.4.4. **τοῦ Εὐνόμου:** little is known of Eunomus, whose name literally means "under good laws." At. 3.7.2, P. states that Sparta was at peace during Eunomus' reign and the reign of Polydectes, Eunomus' son. **τοῦ Πρυτάνιδος:** P. states at 3.7.2 that the conflict between Sparta and Argos started in the reign of this king. **τοῦ Εὐρυπῶντος:** Eurypon was the son of Soos, the grandson of Procles, and a descendant of Heracles through Aristodemus (cf. 2.18.7); he became the namesake of the Eurypontid dynasty of Sparta. **συνεσέβαλόν:** "they made an inroad (into the Argolid) with them (i.e., the Spartans)." σφισιν is the dat. of accompaniment here, whereas στρατιᾷ is dat. of military accompaniment. This verb complements the ἐσβαλόντων in the gen. absolute that dominates the first half of the sentence. **Ἔρατος:** nothing else is known about this king of Argos.

2.36.5 Λυσίστρατον ἐν τοῖς δοκιμωτάτοις ὄντα Ἀργείων: this man is not otherwise known. **τὴν αὐτῶν (πόλιν) ἐς ἔδαφος καταβαλόντες:** "razing (Asine) to the ground." This site does not seem to have been wholly abandoned (MT 334). **τὴν γῆν προσορισάμενοι τῇ σφετέρᾳ (γῇ):** "adding the land to their dominion." **Πυθαέως . . . Ἀπόλλωνος . . . <τὸ> ἱερὸν:** the remains of a small sanctuary on Mt. Barbuna NW of the city have been identified—though not securely—with this sanctuary (MT 334).

Lerna

2.36.6 τεσσαράκοντα καὶ οὐ πλείω στάδια: P. appears here to give a more precise distance than usual. Frazer (3.300) notes that P. jumps from the E side of the Argolic Gulf to resume his description of the W side: "It would have seemed more natural if he had continued his route from Asine to Nauplia, and so round the head of the Argolic Gulf to Lerna. Instead of which he crosses over from Asine to Lerna and then works his way back to Nauplia." **ὁ Ἐρασῖνος:** at 2.24.6, P. mentions the river Erasinus passing the foot of Mt. Chaon. Erasinus is the modern Kephalari (MT 335). **τὸν Φρίξον:** this river has not yet been identified with certainty (MT 335); the same situation obtains for the Cheimarrus River mentioned in 2.36.7. **Διοσκούρων . . . Ἀνάκτων:** P. gives the Dioscuri the same title at 2.22.6.

2.36.7 ἀναστρέψας . . . διαβήσῃ καὶ . . . ἀφίξῃ: rather than his usual directional participles in the gen. or dat., P. here shifts to the 2nd-person sg., for *variatio.* **τὸν Πλούτωνα ἁρπάσαντα ὡς λέγεται Κόρην τὴν Δήμητρος:** this was the central myth of the cult of Demeter and Kore. **ἐς τὴν ὑπόγεων νομιζομένην ἀρχήν:** i.e., Hades. **ἡ . . . Λέρνα:** Lerna lies near the modern village of Myli, 10 kilometers SW of Argos (MT 335). **ὡς καὶ τὰ πρότερα ἔχει μοι τοῦ λόγου:** P. appears to refer here to 2.36.6.

2.36.8 ὄρους ὃ καλοῦσι Ποντῖνον: modern Tziveri (MT 335). **τὸ ὕδωρ . . . τὸ ἐκ τοῦθεοῦ:** i.e., rainwater. **αὑτὸ:** = ἑαυτό, the reflexive pronoun. **Ἀθηνᾶς Σαΐτιδος:** H. states at 2.175 that the Egyptian king Amasis established a temple of Athena at Sais. The epithet may, however, be linked to σάος and σαότης (cf. 2.31.5). See MT 335–36. **Ἱππομέδοντος:** Hippomedon was the son of Talaus and brother of Adrastus. He was one of the Seven against Thebes and father of Polydorus, one of the Epigoni, as P. stated at 2.20.5.

2.37.1 τὸ πολὺ: construe with πλατάνων, "chiefly of plane trees" (Loeb). **τῇ μὲν ποταμὸς ὁ Ποντῖνος . . . τῇ δὲ ἕτερος ποταμός:** "on one side . . . on the other." **Ἀμυμώνη:** according to ps.-Apollod. 2.1.4, Danaus sent his daughters out to find water because Poseidon had dried up all sources of water after Inachus sided with Hera in the dispute over the ownership of Argos (cf. P. 2.15.4). While Amymone was hunting for deer, she hit a satyr by mistake and had to summon Poseidon to rescue her. She became pregnant from Poseidon's attentions and bore Nauplius (not the father of Palamedes). At 2.37.4, P. again mentions the river named after her, which has been identified with a stream that issues under the rocks at the foot of Mt. Pontinus, about a half a mile to the S of the river Pontinus (Frazer 3.300). **Δήμητρος Προσύμνης:** at 2.17.1, P. named Prosymna as one of the river Asterion's daughters who nursed the goddess, and he stated that the land under the Heraion was named after her. Thus Prosymna's name became a cult title for the goddess. An inscription containing a dedication to Demeter Prosymne and Dionysus has been found NW of Lake Alcyonia (v. 2.37.5); as a result, scholars think it was the site of the temple (Frazer 3.301).

2.37.2 καθήμενον ξόανον: in apposition to Διόνυσος Σαώτης. P. immediately uses a different construction. **τὸν ἱερὸν . . . τῆς Ἀθηνᾶς:** hyperbaton. **Φιλάμμωνά:** Philammon was a mythical pre-Homeric poet said to have been the son of Apollo and a nymph. At 4.33.3, P. names Philammon as the father of the bard Thamyris by the nymph Agriope. Ps.-Apollod. 1.3.3 agrees. **ἐπὶ τοῖς δρωμένοις:** "to accompany the rituals" (Loeb).

2.37.3 τῇ καρδίᾳ . . . τῇ πεποιημένῃ τοῦ ὀρειχάλκου: "the heart made of orichalcum," an ancient variety of bronze or brass. It seems to be some sort of cult object kept at Lerna for the mysteries there. **Ἀρριφῶν . . . τὸ μὲν ἀνέκαθεν Τριχωνιεὺς τῶν ἐν Αἰτωλίᾳ:** this scholar is not otherwise known but excites P.'s admiration for his discovery. **τὰ δὲ ἐφ' ἡμῶν Λυκίων τοῖς μάλιστα (δοκίμοις) ὁμοίως δόκιμος:** "and he is as famous a Lycian as any today" (v. *LSJ* μάλα III.2.a for a parallel in Demosthenes). **δεινὸς δὲ ἐξευρεῖν:** P. uses this adj. only twelve times in his entire *Periegesis*. At 2.11.5, he used it to describe the astronomical abilities of Titan. **ἃ μή τις πρότερον εἶδε:** relative clauses with an indefinite antecedent take a negative in μή (S 2505b). **ὅσα οὐ μετὰ μέτρου μεμιγμένα ἦν τοῖς ἔπεσι:** i.e., prose passages. **τὴν αὐτὴν . . . φωνήν:** "the same (Greek) dialect (as) . . ." (Loeb). Perhaps this was a Mycenaean dialect (MT 336). **ἠφίεσαν:** < ἀφίημι, imperf. act. indicative with double augment. **ἐς ἅπαντας ἠκούετο Ἕλληνας:** "(the name of the Dorians) was familiar to all Greeks" (Loeb). The phrasing with the preposition ἐς is nonclassical but gives the reader the impression of geographical diffusion. P. argues that since the words are in Doric, they must postdate the return of the Heracleidae and thus cannot be the genuine words of the primordial Philammon.

2.37.4 ταῦτα μὲν δὴ (Ἀρριφῶν) ἀπέφαινεν οὕτως ἔχοντα **τῆς δὲ Ἀμυμώνης . . . ἐπὶ τῇ πηγῇ:** not "fountain" here (which is a κρήνη) but "source." **ταύτῃ:** construe with τῇ πλατάνῳ. **μεγέθει διενεγκεῖν ὑδρῶν ἄλλων:** "differed in size from other snakes." **τὸν ἰὸν οὕτω δή τι . . . ἀνίατον ὡς . . . :** clause of natural result. **τὸν Ἡρακλέα ἀπὸ τῆς**

χολῆς αὐτοῦ τὰς ἀκίδας φαρμακεῦσαι τῶν ὀϊστῶν: Heracles defeated the Lernaean Hydra as his second labor. Cf. ps.-Apollod. 2.5.2 for details of this fight. **Πείσανδρος . . . ὁ Καμιρεύς:** Pisander was a native of Camirus on the island of Rhodes and composed an epic poem in two books, entitled *Heracleia,* that established the canonical labors for the hero. He is dated approximately to the mid-7th c. BCE. **ἵνα . . . δοκοίη . . . γίνηται:** the secondary sequence of the verb ἐποίησε mandates an optative but allows a subjunctive in the purpose clause; here P. uses the subjunctive to show the purpose as still continuing (S 2197c).

2.37.5 πηγὴν Ἀμφιαράου καλουμένην: this has not been found and may have been subsumed in Lake Alcyonia (Frazer 3.301–2). **τὴν Ἀλκυονίαν λίμνην:** Lake Alcyonia has been identified with the water between the national highway and the rail line near the modern village of Mili. The diameter is about 60 meters, with abundant vegetation around it (MT 337). **δι' ἧς φασιν Ἀργεῖοι Διόνυσον ἐς τὸν Ἅιδην ἐλθεῖν Σεμέλην ἀνάξοντα:** after Semele was immolated by Zeus' divine form, Dionysus traveled to Hades to retrieve his mother, who became the goddess Thyone. At 2.31.2, P. notes the spot where the god is said to have returned with her. **Πόλυμνον:** this figure is also known as Πρόσυμνος. He guided Dionysus to the middle of the lake to show him the entrance (Frazer 3.302; MT 337). **πέρας τοῦ βάθους . . . ἐς τὸ τέρμα αὐτῆς (λίμνης) . . . ὅρον τοῦ βάθους . . . βυθὸν:** this use of four ways of saying "the bottom/depth" in the same passage shows well how devoted P. is to *variatio.* **οὐκ . . . οὐδέ τινα . . . οὐδεμιᾷ . . . οὐδὲ . . . οὐδένα:** the accumulation of negatives emphasizes P.'s assertion that no one can discover the depth of the lake. **ὅπου:** "since" (v. *LSJ* A.II.2). **Νέρων:** P. referred to Nero's attempt to cut through the Isthmus of Corinth at 2.1.5, though without mentioning the emperor by name. **εἰ δή τι χρήσιμον ἄλλο ἐς τὴν πεῖραν:** = (ποιήσας) ὅ τι χρήσιμον ἄλλο ἐστίν.

2.37.6 ὡς ἰδόντα εἰκάσαι: "as one looking at it would think"; absolute infinitive (S 2012). **παρεχόμενον . . . ὑπολαβὸν:** these participles are governed by τὸ ὕδωρ, which is also the subject of the verbs πέφυκε and ἀπήνεγκε. **καθέλκειν πέφυκε:** "naturally drags down" (v. *LSJ* φύω B.II.2). **ὅσον τε σταδίου τρίτον:** "about a third of a stade" (v. *LSJ* ὅσος IV.3). **ἐπὶ . . . τοῖς χείλεσιν αὐτῆς:** "on the banks of it" (v. *LSJ* χεῖλος II). Cf. H. 2.70, 94. **τὰ δὲ ἐς αὐτὴν Διονύσῳ δρώμενα:** "the sacred rites performed in it (the lake) in honor of Dionysus." **οὐχ ὅσιον ἐς ἅπαντας ἦν μοι γράψαι:** P. refuses to divulge sacred secrets. The use of the imperf. here is a little unusual, but it may be explained by the idea that P. himself witnessed these rites during his journey in the area and thus is using this past tense to state what was and continues to be an impious act to contemplate doing (S 1901). Plutarch may describe these rites at *Isis and Osiris* 35.

Temenium and Nauplia

2.38.1 ἐς Τημένιον . . . ἐς τοῦτο οὖν τὸ Τημένιον: P. resumes the main topic after a lengthy parenthetical sentence, much like the one he used to introduce the Acrocorinth at 2.4.6. He repeats the directional participle ἰοῦσιν too. **Τημένιον:** Temenium was the main port of Argos, to which it was connected by a wall (Thucydides 5.82). It lies between the rivers Inachus and Erasinus, near the modern village of Nea Kio (MT 338). **Τημένου τοῦ Ἀριστομάχου:** Temenus was a son of Aristodemus and a descendant of Heracles, as P. stated at 2.18.7. Temenus' preference for his son-in-law Deiphontes over his sons also led to the tragedy of Hyrnetho that P. movingly related at 2.28.3–7. **ἐπολέμει . . . τὸν . . . πόλεμον:** cognate acc. **Τισαμενὸν καὶ Ἀχαιοὺς:** Temenus, Cresphontes, and the sons of Aristodemus expelled Tisamenus (son of Orestes) from Argos at 2.18.7–8. **Ποσειδῶνος ἱερὸν . . . καὶ Ἀφροδίτης ἕτερον:** neither sanctuary has been located (MT 338).

2.38.2 Ναυπλία: P. continues N up the coast, to Nauplia, an old Mycenaean foundation. He here recounts how Nauplius, the father of Palamedes, founded it, but at 4.35.2, he says that the Nauplians originally came with Danaus from Egypt. **πεντήκοντα ἐμοὶ δοκεῖν σταδίους:** P. uses an absolute infinitive to give an approximate distance. **Ναύπλιος Ποσειδῶνος λεγόμενος καὶ Ἀμυμώνης:** for Amymone, cf. 2.37.1 and commentary. **τειχῶν ἔτι ἐρείπια:** the city possesses a polygonal wall from the 4th c. BCE (MT 338). **Ποσειδῶνος ἱερὸν:** remains found in modern Nauplia could belong to this temple (MT 338). **πηγὴ Κάναθος:** this spring has been identified as the spring of the convent of Haghia Moni SE of the small village of Pronia (MT 338).

2.38.3 οὗτος . . . λόγος τῶν ἀπορρήτων ἐστίν: here P. reveals a holy secret; contrast with his fastidiousness at 2.37.6. **τὰ δὲ ὑπὸ τῶν ἐν Ναυπλίᾳ λεγόμενα:** P. contrasts this story with the sacred myth just before it. Below, he then dismisses such talk as "unworthy of mention." **ἐπιφαγὼν:** < ἐπεσθίω, aor. act. participle, "nibbling down" (Loeb). **ἀφθονώτερον:** construe with τὸν καρπόν as the direct object of ἀπέφηνε. **διὰ τοῦτο . . . ἅτε ἀμπέλων διδάξας τομήν:** "for this reason—that (the donkey) taught (men) the pruning of vines." **παρίημι οὐκ ἀξιόλογα ἡγούμενος:** a rhetorical flourish worthy of Cicero, This is an example of praeteritio or paraleipsis (S 3036), the pretended omission of a topic or fact for rhetorical effect. Here P. even gives all the details about the donkey before dismissing the whole matter as unworthy of inclusion in his treatise.

Genesion and the Thyreatis

2.38.4 ἔστι δὲ ἐκ Λέρνης καὶ ἑτέρα . . . ὁδὸς: from Lerna, P. is now going S along the coast, to reach the S end of the Argolid (MT 339). **Γενέσιον:** both Genesion and the Apobathmoi lie in a coastal plain N of Mt. Zavitsa (MT 339). **γῆς . . . τῆς Ἀργολίδος:** gen. with ἐνταῦθα, "at this point in the Argolid." **Ἀνιγραῖα καλούμενα:** direct object of διελθοῦσιν. This mountain route goes W of Mt. Zavitsa, to the border between the Argolid and the Thyreatis (MT 339). **ὁδὸν καὶ στενὴν καὶ ἄλλως δύσβατον:** also a direct object of διελθοῦσιν. **καθήκουσα . . . ἀγαθὴ:** construe with γῆ. **δένδρα:** direct object of τρέφειν. **ἐλαίας μάλιστα:** P. does not mention the city of Ἐλαιοῦς, which lies S of the village of Kiveri and W of Kalamaki; cf. ps.-Apollod. 2.5.2 (MT 339).

2.38.5 χωρίον: P. has moved to the plain of Thyrea, which, along with Cynuria to the S, was long contested by Sparta and Argos. **λογάδες Ἀργείων τριακόσιοι . . . :** the Battle of the Champions; cf. 2.20.7 and commentary. **ἀριθμόν:** acc. of respect with ἴσους. **ἐχώσθησαν:** < χόω, aor. passive indicative. **γενομένου πανδημεί σφισιν ἀγῶνος πρὸς Ἀργείους:** the battle over the Thyreatis occurred during the reign of the Eurypontid king Theopompus, the son of Nicander (mentioned at 2.36.4); cf. 3.7.5. **ἐκαρποῦντο:** "they enjoyed the free use of" (v. *LSJ* II.3); the direct object is τὴν χώραν. **ὕστερον Αἰγινήταις ἔδοσαν ἐκπεσοῦσιν ὑπὸ Ἀθηναίων ἐκ τῆς νήσου:** cf. 2.29.5 and commentary. **τὰ . . . ἐπ' ἐμοῦ:** adverbial phrase, "in my time." **Θυρεᾶτιν:** P. notably defers stating the name of the place until the end of the subsection. **φασὶ δὲ ἀνασώσασθαι δίκῃ νικήσαντες:** "they say that they recovered it by winning a legal case." After his victory over the Greek alliance at Chaeronea in 338 BCE, Philip II of Macedonia restored to the Argives all the lands of which the Lacedaemonians had deprived them (Polybius 18.14). The Argives probably argued that they had won the Battle of the Champions 2:1.

Anthene, Neris, Eua, and Mt. Parnon

2.38.6 τῶν πολυανδρίων: this monument may be located on the peak of Mt. Zavitsa (MT 339). **Ἀνθήνη:** Thucydides (5.41) and Lysias call this place Ἀνθήνη, and Stephanus of Byzantium calls it Ἀνθάνα. It may be located on the S slopes of Mt. Zavitsa, where a polygonal enclosure has been found. The more S fortification walls near Haghios Andreas at the S end of the Thyreatis could be walls that Thucydides 4.57 reports the Aeginetans to be building. (MT 339–40). **Νηρίς:** this village has not yet been located with certainty; it may be near Kato Dolina (MT 340). **Εὔα:** Eua is located near Helleniko, S of the monastery Moni tis Loukous, a little to the NW of the modern village of Astros. The ancient city was a fortified site one kilometer in perimeter (MT 340). **ἱερὸν τοῦ Πολεμοκράτους:** Polemocrates was a grandson of Ascelpius. The monastery probably sits on the site of this sanctuary. This is epigraphical evidence of a relationship between the great benefactor Herodes Atticus, on one hand, and Eua and its main sanctuary, on the other (MT 340). **Μαχάονος:** the mortal son of Asclepius, as P. affirmed at 2.26.10 with a quote from Homer. **Ἀλεξάνορος:** at 2.11.5–6, P. notes that Alexanor built a sanctuary to Asclepius at Titane and received worship there as well. **τοὺς ταύτῃ:** "the people here," i.e., "the people of the district" (Loeb).

2.38.7 Λακεδαιμονίων ἐπ' αὐτοῦ πρὸς Ἀργείους ὅροι καὶ Τεγεάτας: P. quietly ends his second book and tour through the Argolid. **ἑστήκασι δὲ ἐπὶ τοῖς ὅροις Ἑρμαῖ λίθου:** P. begins the next book, on Laconia, from this very spot (cf. 3.1.1). Three cairns of stones there may have no connection with the Herms (Frazer 3.310). **διὰ τῆς Ἀργείας:** in the very last line of the book, P. repeats the same term for the Argolid that appears in the very first line of the book (MT 341).

Selected Bibliography

General Introductions to Pausanias

Habicht, Christian. 1998. *Pausanias' "Guide to Ancient Greece."* Berkeley and Los Angeles: University of California Press.

Hutton, William. 2005. *Describing Greece: Landscape and Literature in the Periegesis of Pausanias.* Cambridge: Cambridge University Press.

Pretzler, Maria. 2007. *Pausanias: Travel Writing in Ancient Greece.* London: Duckworth. Chapters 9–10 are a concise description of the nachleben of Pausanias' work and its continuing importance in classics.

Commentaries on Book 2

Frazer, George. 1897–1913. *Pausanias' "Description of Greece."* 6 vols. London: Macmillan. Vol. 1 consists of a translation of the entire *Periegesis*, and vol. 2 includes a commentary on books 2–5. Still useful for mythical, cultural, and historical issues, Frazer's text includes elaborate maps and extensive archaeological material but, due to its age, must be supplemented by more modern sources.

Hitzig, Hermann, and Hugo Blümner, eds. 1896–1910. *Pausaniae Graeciae Descriptio.* 2 vols. in 6 parts. Leipzig: O. R. Reisland. Vol. 1, pt. 2 comprises the text of book 2 and the authors' commentary on it, useful for textual and grammatical issues.

Imhoof-Blumer, F., and Percy Gardner. 1885–87. *A Numismatic Commentary on Pausanias.* London: Richard Clay and Sons. Despite their age, this source's extensive lists of passages in Pausanias and of the coins that are thought to depict the mythological figures, works of art, and buildings described by Pausanias are still very useful. Pictures of the coins are included. A PDF can be found at http://archive.org/details/numismaticcommenooimhoiala.

Musti, Domenico, ed., trans., and comm., and Mario Torelli, comm. 1986. *Pausania, Guida della Grecia, libro II: La Corinzia e l'Argolide.* Rome: Fondazione Lorenzo Valla.

Roux, Georges, ed., trans., and comm. 1958. *Pausanias en Corinthie (livre II, 1 à 5): Texte, traduction, commentaire archéologie et topographique*. Paris: Les Belles Lettres.

Specialized Monographs

Akujärvi, Johanna. 2005. *Researcher, Traveler, Narrator: Studies in Pausanias'* Periegesis. Studia Graeca et Latina Lundensia 12. Stockholm: Almqvist and Wiksell International.

Alcock, Susan E., John F. Cherry, and Jás Elsner, eds. 2001. *Pausanias: Travel and Memory in Ancient Greece*. Oxford: Oxford University Press.

Arafat, Karim W. 1996. *Pausanias' Greece: Ancient Artists and Roman Rulers*. New York: Cambridge University Press.

Knoepfler, Denis, and Marcel Piérart, eds. 2001. *Éditeur, traduire, commenter Pausanias en l'année 2000: Actes du colloque de Neuchâtel et de Fribourg (18–22 septembre 1998) autour des duex édítions en cours de la Périégèse*. Geneva: Université de Neuchâtel and Librairie Droz.

Lolos, Yannis A. 2011. *Land of Sikyon: Archaeology and History of a Greek City-state. Hesperia supplements*, 39. Princeton: American School of Classical Studies at Athens.

Pirenne-Delforge, Vinciane. 2008. *Retour à la source: Pausanias et la religion grecque. Kernos* Supplement 20. Liège: Centre International d'Étude de la Religion Grecque Antique.

Pritchett, William Kendrick. 1998–99. *Pausanias Periegetes*. 2 vols. Amsterdam: J. C. Gieben. Of particular relevance among this source's long examinations of special topics are "Pausanias and the Demosion Sema" and "Pausanias on Greek Religion" in vol. 1 and "Alleged Topographical Errors," "Wooden Statues," "Ruins in Pausanias," and "Festivals" in vol. 2.

Salmon, J. B. 1984. *Wealthy Corinth: A History of the City to 338 B.C.* Oxford: Oxford University Press.

Sanders, Guy D. R., et al. Forthcoming. *Ancient Corinth: A Guide to the Site and Museum*. 7th ed. Athens: American School of Classical Studies at Athens. This highly anticipated update to the official guide has been delayed several times and was still unavailable at the time of the present book's writing.

Strid, Ove. 1976. *Über Sprache und Stil des Periegeten Pausanias*. Uppsala.

Tomlinson, R. A. 1972. *Argos and the Argolid: From the End of the Bronze Age to the Roman Occupation*. Ithaca, NY: Cornell University Press.

Tomlinson, R. A. 1983. *Epidauros*. Austin: University of Texas Press.

Greek Grammars and Grammatical Works

Denniston, J. D. 1954. *The Greek Particles*. 2nd ed. Oxford: Clarendon.

Goodwin, W. W. 1890. *Syntax of Moods and Tenses of the Greek Verb*. Boston: Ginn.

Smyth, Herbert Weir. 1956. *Greek Grammar*. Revised by Gordon Messing. Cambridge, MA: Harvard University Press.

Greek Lexica

Liddell, H. G., and Robert Scott, eds. 1968. *A Greek–English Lexicon*. Revised by Sir Henry Stuart Jones with the assistance of Roderick McKenzie, with a supplement. Oxford: Clarendon.

Editions of the Text

Dindorf, Ludwig August, ed. 1882. *Pausaniae Descriptio Graeciae*. Paris: Firmin-Didot.

Hitzig, Hermann, and Hugo Blümner, eds. 1896–1910. *Pausaniae Graeciae Descriptio*. 2 vols. in 6 parts. Leipzig: O. R. Reisland.

Rocha-Pereira, Maria Helena, ed. 1989–90. *Pausaniae Graeciae Descriptio*. 2nd ed. 3 vols. Leipzig: Teubner.

Spiro, Friedrich, ed. 1903. *Pausaniae Graeciae Descriptio*. 3 vols. Leipzig: Teubner.

English Translations

Jones, W. H. S., trans. 1959–61. *Pausanias, "Description of Greece."* 6 vols. Loeb Classical Library edition. Cambridge, MA: Harvard University Press. Vol. 1 covers books 1 and 2 of the *Periegesis*.

Levi, Peter, trans. 1979. *Pausanias, "Guide to Greece."* 2 vols. New York: Penguin Books.

Nachleben

Georgopoulou, Maria, et al., eds. 2007. *Following Pausanias: The Quest for Greek Antiquity*. New Castle, Delaware: Oak Knoll Press. This source features an excellent short introduction to Pausanias and a well-illustrated series of essays that explain the history of the *Periegesis* from antiquity to the nineteenth century and especially the growing importance of Pausanias to antiquarians of the West in the fifteenth through eighteenth centuries.

Indcx